CHOOSING GOD-

CONVERSATIONS WITH JEAN

CHOOSING GOD—CHOSEN BY GOD

Conversations with
Jean-Marie Cardinal Lustiger

Translated by
Rebecca Howell Balinski

IGNATIUS PRESS SAN FRANCISCO

Title of the French original:
Le Choix de Dieu: Entretiens avec
Jean-Louis Missika et Dominique Wolton

Cover by Riz Boncan Marsella

ISBN 0-89870-230-5
Library of Congress catalogue number 90–85063
Printed in the United States of America

CONTENTS

PART TWO:
BELIEVING AND KNOWING

PART THREE:
THE CHURCH AND SOCIETY

PART FIVE:

THE UNIVERSAL CHURCH

ACKNOWLEDGMENT

The translator would like to express her gratitude to Jean Duchesne, friend and aide to Cardinal Lustiger, who generously gave of his time to read the final draft of the English text—answering various questions, clarifying complex subjects and providing much valuable information for footnotes along the way.

INTRODUCTION

What makes us want to know more about a man?

A trenchant phrase from a television interview ("it was as though all of a sudden crucifixes were wearing the yellow star"); the unusual journey of the son of Polish-Jewish immigrants who became Cardinal-Archbishop of Paris; the depth of a facial expression caught by a photograph; the need to go beyond clichés; reflections on the place religions hold in contemporary societies; the haunting question of good and evil after Auschwitz—all of these reasons, no doubt, and many more, conscious or unconscious.

Since there are two of us, our respective motivations ought to be distinguished. We are Jew and Catholic, skeptic and agnostic. One of us is trying to understand conversion, that taboo word in his family; the other is trying to understand the Church and Catholicism. One does not believe; the other cannot be certain. In short, two approaches have converged in this single undertaking.

It was with these motivations and a great deal of innocence that we embarked on our three-year adventure—an adventure that has been strewn with pitfalls. We first proposed this book to Jean-Marie Lustiger in June of 1984. Our idea was simple, inspired by *Spectateur engagé,* a book we published with Raymond Aron. We were not looking for an autobiographical narrative or for theological or moral declarations. Instead, we wanted to show how this one person's itinerary condenses the major spiritual and intellectual questions of twentieth-century Europe.

Our intention was to provoke a confrontation between a man of faith and two "honest men" representing secularized society and modern rationalism. After a period of discussion and deliberation, Jean-Marie Lustiger accepted the risks of such a confrontation. His decision is admirable: prominent persons who voluntarily expose themselves to debate are more and more rare. Although our age is supposedly one of communication, it is most often characterized by either violent or accommodating monologues that fall on virtually deaf ears. Therefore, this book is also an attempt to return to dialogue and critical examination, essential elements for the evolution of ideas.

In preparing for our conversations, we read works of philosophy, theology and Church and religious history, all the while keeping in mind that the dialogue should not become too specialized. We also met with several lay and religious personalities in Rome and in Paris, among whom towers the eminent French theologian Henri de Lubac. In general, we have given little space to the problems of the Church as an institution and of its divisions in France—first of all, because, since we do not belong to the "shop", we know nothing about many of its mysteries, and especially because our plan called for something different: we wanted to try to understand the entanglements and occasional conflicts between spiritual and intellectual life, using the tragic history of the last fifty years as a backdrop.

Given our education and interests, questions on society, politics and history predominate. Persons with literary, theological or spiritual orientations would have produced very different dialogues. However, as the twentieth century comes to an end, the Church is expected to respond to questions raised by society, as well as to nourish faith. The intellectual background of Jean-Marie Lustiger and, in particular, the decade he spent at the Sorbonne as chaplain at the Centre Richelieu have certainly made our desired confrontation much easier. At least a part of his experience and thought falls within the contemporary context of the human sciences. We have also taken up theological subjects, in which our competence is more limited, when they were necessary for the understanding of spiritual themes.

We are entirely responsible for the book's structure. It has been divided into five main parts, with each part devoted to a particular theme that is introduced by biographical questions so that the reader can situate the epoch and the man in that epoch:

- The first section concerns relations between Judaism and Christianity, and the origin of anti-Semitism.
- The second deals with the human sciences and their relationship to belief.
- The third discusses politics and society.
- The fourth treats the pastorate and certain aspects of theology.
- The fifth explores the Church's opening to the world and to both the profane and sacred future.

Cardinal Lustiger had no objections to our thematic and chronological divisions of the book. There were, of course, no previous arrangements as to questions. But, as had been agreed, Jean-Marie Lustiger did recast some of his responses after he saw them in print.

Most of the conversations took place between August and December 1985. They represent sixty-five hours of recording, or an original manuscript of 1,800 pages. Hence, preparing the text's final version was a long and delicate process. Although the Church as an institution was never the focus of our work, during the editing process we had the occasion to discover her constraints and mechanisms. Nevertheless, the mere fact that the book exists, in spite of all the difficulties encountered, proves that freedom of thought and the desire for a respectful dialogue eventually prevailed.

This book suggests that we may be nearing the end of a cycle. For the past two generations, following a long period of clashes with rationalism and modernism, the Church has sought to come closer to society and to adapt her message to the secular values that, in Europe at least, had triumphed. Her political commitment, with the resulting excesses at both extremes, was an illustration of this tendency. The new openness was frequently synonymous with an adjustment to prevalent social ideologies. "Modernization"—of the Church as well as society—was the key word. Salvation was going to come from involvement in the major issues of the century. Today, the world's disenchantment[1] touches secular values as well as those of religion, and the nature of the problem has changed. It now centers on what must be done to achieve spiritual renewal in secular societies that are not about to abandon reason, in spite of its immoderation, for mysticism.

Although he belongs to the Catholic tradition, Jean-Marie Lustiger is neither by origin nor education a prisoner of all the contentions that French Catholicism has experienced: that is why his analyses often vary from classical interpretations. He is trying to think through his faith without either opposing or submitting it to reason. He rejects the temptation of acceding to the social and political values of our times, but he also rejects the retreat of religion into private life. He is neither traditionalist nor modernist, because he simply does not think of religion in those terms. Thus, his responses stimulate a debate that, extending beyond the circle of Christians and believers, is interesting to all who are attentive to intellectual life.

This book—with its dissensions and divergences—represents, in the end, an approach to religion at the close of the twentieth century. Our hope is that it will be welcomed as a written expression of those unspoken, often contradictory questions that many of us raise about God, religion and the meaning of life.

Jean-Louis Missika
Dominique Wolton

[1] This is an indirect allusion to Marcel Gauchet's provocative book, *Le désenchantement du monde* (Paris: Gallimard, 1985), which claims that Christianity is actually responsible for secularization because it refuses any sacralization of the profane and thus leaves the world "disenchanted" once the secular ideologies (as substitutes for faith) have proved to be failures.—TRANS.

PART ONE

ROOTS

I

CHILDHOOD (1926–1939)

A Dry Goods Store

JEAN-LOUIS MISSIKA: *Let us begin, as usual, with childhood. You were born in 1926, in Paris. . . .*

JEAN-MARIE LUSTIGER: Yes, in the twelfth *arrondissement,* at the Rothschild Hospital. I spent my early years on the Boulevard de Strasbourg and then in Montmartre. My parents' store was at the bottom of the Rue Simart, the apartment was on the Rue Marcadet.

MISSIKA: *What kind of store was it?*

LUSTIGER: A dry goods store. I remember vividly my first years in the neighborhood school on the Rue Ferdinand-Flocon. It was a red brick building, higher up as you go toward the *butte. . . .* It still stands, unchanged. And I remember the moment when, at home two years before I started to school, I *knew* how to read.

DOMINIQUE WOLTON: *Did you have brothers and sisters?*

LUSTIGER: I have a sister, four years younger.

WOLTON: *When did your parents come to Paris?*

LUSTIGER: My father arrived in France around 1918. He had left his native region in western Poland, near the border with Silesia, which had been under Russian rule before the war. . . . He was a part of the Jewish youth who had become Westernized and were eager to escape an economic misery made worse by the constant threat of persecution. My paternal and maternal grandparents were related; they had the same name. It was a very large family.

MISSIKA: *Then both your father and mother were called Lustiger?*

LUSTIGER: Yes. The two families were socially well established. My paternal grandfather owned a bakery. My father began his working life as a baker. I often heard him describe recipes—for example, how to make challah, the braided bread for the Sabbath, how a glaze of egg white would make it golden brown. . . .

WOLTON: *What was his village called?*

LUSTIGER: Bendzin . . . It was not a village but a town.

MISSIKA: *Were your grandparents old-fashioned Jews?*

LUSTIGER: They were traditional, according to what my parents told us about their childhood.

MISSIKA: *To what extent did your father's immigration represent an emancipation from his parents or from a religiously strict, ghettolike environment?*

LUSTIGER: Bendzin is located in an industrial region where some villages were then entirely Jewish. It is not very far from Czestochowa, by the way. One part of the family lived in Sosnowitz, the other in Bendzin. . . . Those strange-sounding names, heard so often in my childhood, belonged to a faraway land that I only pictured in my imagination until I discovered, not so long ago, that they are both near Auschwitz. Recently, distant cousins, originally from Warsaw, made themselves known. So the large family became dispersed and, in general, emancipated. By the time my father left, some of them were already in distant places, some had gone to university and had professions. For my father, leaving was certainly a liberation from family traditions. He first worked in Germany, in various factories, and after a time, came to Lorraine and then on to Paris where my mother had been living with her father since the beginning of the century.

WOLTON: *But why did he leave?*

LUSTIGER: Why? I do not know the precise reason. . . . A whole generation was leaving at the time, from Russia, from Poland, from all of Eastern Europe. They settled in Western Europe or went to the United States. They were escaping material hardships, a traditional way of life that seemed unbearable and, especially, they were escaping persecution.

MISSIKA: *Was your father also escaping Polish anti-Semitism? Did he ever speak about that?*

LUSTIGER: Certainly, he spoke about it. One of the stories I heard in my childhood was about a Christian holiday—in retrospect, I think it must have been Corpus Christi—when Jews had to hide themselves because gangs of young Christians would roam about their neighborhoods breaking windows, pulling beards, picking fights. As a very small child, I heard stories where the word *pogrom* alone was enough to make me understand the kind of relations that Jews had with "others"! *Pogrom,* as you know, is a Russian word that designates the systematic massacre of Jews by those whom the Jews of Eastern Europe could only label as "Christians". As far back as I can remember, I heard my parents and all Jews speak about pogroms. From the moment that I was conscious of existing, I learned about the threat of pogroms and persecutions. When I read the Bible, a short time later, it struck me that this kind of threat obviously belonged to the Jewish condition: the oppression by Pharaoh, the deportation to Babylon, the complaints and warnings of the prophets—in Isaiah, Jeremiah and the book of Esther. For me, these biblical accounts and the destroyed Temple were simply superimposed on the sufferings and dispersion of the Jewish people in modern times. The Bible described what I had already heard from my parents about Jewish existence. It was one of the accepted facts of our identity.

MISSIKA: *And how did your mother come to Paris?*

LUSTIGER: My maternal grandfather lost his wife in Poland, and he came to Paris with his four children before the war of 1914. My mother, the eldest, brought up the family. My grandfather had been a rabbi in Poland.

WOLTON: *What picture have you kept of him?*

LUSTIGER: He was a traditional Jew, with the beard, the sidelocks, the hat. He did not speak French, only Yiddish and Polish.

At the beginning of their marriage, my parents sold their goods at open-air markets. I have always remembered what they told me about their life at that time. Later, they bought a store in Paris. When I became a bishop, a number of people came to tell me about that period in my parents' life. Some of the things they recounted moved me deeply. A lady who lived just above the store in Montmartre told how *Maman* would always leave the awning down at night—you know, those cloth awnings that protect from sun and rain—so that the *clochards* could sleep in front of the doorway. My parents left vivid impressions with their neighbors and acquaintances. After the war, when my father was living alone, he spent his days at the store in Montparnasse. He had a silent and kindly presence and became something of a confidant for the people in the *quartier.* My sister came upon him one day quizzing a little boy who lived on the street on his catechism.

MISSIKA: *And your mother?*

LUSTIGER: She was extremely active, vivacious and passionate.

MISSIKA: *Did your parents have French nationality?*

LUSTIGER: They acquired it. My father was naturalized—I do not know the exact year—and my mother must have had French nationality from her father.

WOLTON: *And the family milieu?*

LUSTIGER: What kind of memories do you want?

MISSIKA: *What kind of upbringing did you have?*

LUSTIGER: We lived austerely. Austerely, with a rigorous thriftiness and discipline. I do not know how to say it differently. . . . I remember a happy childhood, but it was strict.

WOLTON: *Did your parents often speak to you about your Jewish and Polish roots?*

LUSTIGER: Yes and no. We were French Jews, and that took precedence over everything else. I do know that my parents' values marked me deeply: there was a very great respect for knowledge, a very great love of wisdom. We were taught to esteem science, not in the positivist sense, but for learning's sake, as something to be understood. For my parents, knowledge and wisdom were of paramount importance and an inseparable part of Jewish tradition. The same was true for books. And there was also an emphasis on very strict moral standards: good and evil existed. We had a proud consciousness of being Jewish, and we were to act justly—not like pagans, the goyim—because Jews are called by God to be just. That is why pagans had set us apart, had persecuted us. We were never to forget our vocation.

MISSIKA: *Your parents did not go to the synagogue?*

LUSTIGER: Probably not. I suppose my father went from time to time, for Yom Kippur. For a while, he was the secretary of an association of compatriots who came from Bendzin, but that implies nothing about his religious practices.

MISSIKA: *Did they celebrate Jewish holidays?*

LUSTIGER: I have no specific memories. There is only one scene that comes to mind. It is of my mother having my sister and me recite a prayer for the first fruits, and my asking her to explain the meaning of the mysterious words. My parents did, however, pass on many details of Jewish customs. But, above all, they insisted that my sister and I should speak only French.

MISSIKA: *What language did they speak to each other?*

LUSTIGER: Yiddish, when they wanted to keep a secret.

MISSIKA: *Since it was a forbidden language, you must have wanted to learn it?*

LUSTIGER: Exactly. But even without it, I always had a keen consciousness of being Jewish—if only because of my name, Aaron—associated with the experience of being set apart.

WOLTON: *Did your parents start very early to push you in your studies?*

LUSTIGER: They were very ambitious for us.

MISSIKA: *Was it a specific ambition?*

LUSTIGER: No, but I knew right away what I wanted to be: a doctor. It is easy to understand why. If you combine the desire for justice and concern for man's happiness, you have the goal of medicine. The doctor is the one who helps; he is the lay pastor. My parents arranged for my sister and me to have piano lessons when we were very young. At one point, it was not ruled out that I might become a pianist. My teacher urged my parents to push me, saying that I could enter the conservatory, etc. And then, things turned out differently. . . .

MISSIKA: *Did your parents discuss politics?*

LUSTIGER: I do recall hearing some discussions around 1936. I was just ten, and I can picture myself at the well-known intersection in Montparnasse scanning the newspapers. I can still see the headlines in *Paris soir.* My parents' lives revolved around two themes: love of justice and love of freedom. They were very skeptical about the disinterestedness of politicians.

Jewish and French

MISSIKA: *From time to time, one sees in a newspaper biography, "Lustiger, son of a Bundist"....* [1]

LUSTIGER: That is true. My father was a member of the Bund when he was young. I know because I could not have invented such a word! It comes from my earliest memories. I cannot recall how he spoke about it. After the war, I found an old photograph of him, taken in Czestochowa. He must have been about seventeen or eighteen and was dressed in a gymnast's uniform. He had also been a scout. He belonged to that segment of young Jews who were going out into the world. They met each other in sports, cultural and political organizations.

MISSIKA: *Did he quit the Bund when he came to Paris?*

LUSTIGER: I think so, but I am not certain. My parents had close ties with Parisian Jews. They had all sorts of friends. The Judaism of my childhood was a sensibility, a way of living, an environment, folklore—and Jewish recipes. There was borscht, the ways of preparing matzos [unleavened bread], the Hebrew word that the Ashkenazi Jews pronounced *matzes*.... We did not keep a kosher kitchen, but we knew many of the laws.

MISSIKA: *How were French Jews regarded in your family?*

LUSTIGER: French Jews of "old stock" were not much appreciated because they often seemed to be ashamed of being Jews. Their problem was that they had been assimilated. The word *assimilated* was pejorative: an assimilated Jew was one who had lost his pride in being Jewish, who was hiding who he was.

WOLTON: *Did you hear that said in your family?*

LUSTIGER: Yes, of course. But, at the same time, my parents were proudly proclaiming their French nationality. They were French; that is what they wanted to be. They loved France and taught me to love France. Nevertheless, they did not like "the assimilated", those who had changed their names, those who hid. They were very hard on French Jews who disdained the "Polacks", the newcomers, and who showed no solidarity with them. And the idea of a

[1] The Bund (General Union of Jewish Workers of Lithuania, Poland and Russia) was a Jewish revolutionary organization very active in Eastern Europe at the beginning of the century.

"conversion" was an abomination. The converted Jew was a renegade, one who had ceased to be what he was, what he had the honor to be.

MISSIKA: *During your childhood, before you went to* lycée, *did you ever meet any believers, either Jews or Christians?*

LUSTIGER: I have often asked myself that question. Only confused and sometimes strange memories have emerged. I owe to my mother a sense of God. My father was less talkative on the subject, except that he felt that both rabbis and priests "spouted foolishness".... I often heard him say that. I remember that my first visit to a church occurred when my parents and I were out for a walk and we wandered into the basilica of the Sacré-Coeur. I remember that we entered by the left-hand door. In the semidarkness, the figure of a priest stood out. I can now identify the components of this distinct image. He had a beard, and he must have been wearing a stole and surplice. He was seated next to a confessional, looking at the passersby. Amazed, I stepped up close to him, wanting to get a better look at such a queer fellow.... He motioned to me in a friendly way, muttering something—I do not know what. I was about five or six years old.... And that utterly terrorized me! I bolted back to my parents.

Later, when I already knew how to read, there was an attempt at religious instruction—my parents had discussed the subject of the bar mitzvah. That attempt lasted only a few months. My mother began to grumble: the rabbi's apprentice they had found to instruct me was dirty, she said.... He could not speak French and prattled all kinds of nonsense, my father complained. So my mother chucked him.

WOLTON: *Who had asked him to come?*

LUSTIGER: I do not know if it was my father or my mother.... I must have been about seven.

MISSIKA: *But the bar mitzvah comes much later.*

LUSTIGER: Yes, but it was just the beginning of instruction, learning the Hebrew alphabet.

MISSIKA: *Could your parents be called atheists?*

LUSTIGER: Certainly not. I never fully probed the thickness of the skepticism that masked my father's faith. My mother spoke about God and prayed to him. That fact is profoundly etched in my memory.

Another memory, going further back, illustrates the strange relationship of a Jewish child to Christianity. The incident, in retrospect, seems bizarre because I am incapable of recalling the sequence of events that could explain it. We were on vacation, in the summer, at the seaside in Brittany. My mother left my sister and me to play in a shallow inlet where there were few people. The sand was very fine, and I amused myself—honestly, I do not know why—by shaping a crucifix. At the top I drew a rectangle in which I wrote the letters INRI,[2] but I cannot imagine why! I was totally unaware, I assure you, of what I was doing. A lady was passing by with a small child who approached, stared for an instant and then asked his mother, "What did he write? Why did he write that?" And she replied with a strange witlessness, "He wrote INRI because his name is Henri." And you know, I believed that for a long time.

I think that it was the following year, when we were again on vacation by the sea, that I was overcome by the metaphysical intuition of contingency. I am not joking. I believe that at seven, children have already entered the metaphysical age, the age when the most fundamental questions are asked. In any case, I know that when I was seven, I faced evil and death, illness and the denial of justice. This reflection was linked with the striking impression, for a child whose home base was the asphalt of Paris, made by the ocean's waves: repetition and music, crashing and thundering. Those waves and the tides that wash away masterpieces in sand led me to discover the fragility and vanity of everything. Let me say in passing that for an adult to talk down to a seven-year-old is a great mistake. It is an age when a person asks the most serious of questions. Adults ought to respond to these questions, even if they have to admit their ignorance. And never say to a child, "You are still too young, you will understand later. . . . "

MISSIKA: *And at school—primary school—do you have any memories of anti-Semitism?*

LUSTIGER: Yes, but they are very confused. I can see myself at the school in Montmartre, in the courtyard where we played, sad and crying because someone had hit me. Whether I had been pushed out of a group I had wanted to play with or whether I had been hit simply because I was a Jew, I do not know anymore. But I always went to school with great enthusiasm. I was never really bored. Avid for knowledge, I had the impression that I was always learning something. Before entering *sixième,*[3] in *lycée,* I spent a year

[2] *Jesus of Nazareth, King of the Jews,* according to the text dictated by Pilate and written in Hebrew, Greek and Latin on Christ's Cross. Many old crucifixes have these initials.

[3] *Sixième* is the equivalent of the sixth grade in the United States and of the upper third form in Great Britain.—TRANS.

at the primary school on the Rue Huyghens in Montparnasse. *"Le Maître",* as we always called him, was an admirable lay teacher to whom I owe a great deal. An example will show you something about the social and intellectual world of France during 1935–36. *"Mes enfants,"* he would announce, "what I am going to teach you now is known by the *président de la République* himself. So you are going to know something that he knows!" The social pyramid of knowledge had the president of the republic at its summit. He was the gauge of the good and the true, of justice and science, etc. It seems to me that the system of values that our teachers passed on to us was meant to help us integrate "a certain idea of *la France*" . . . and we integrated it.

WOLTON: *Was there a gap between your French republican schooling and life at home?*

LUSTIGER: As for classmates and friends, I have a vague memory of a strongly felt difference marked by feelings of both inferiority and superiority. The inferiority came from the threat—in the eyes of a Jewish child of Polish immigrants—of persecution. The superiority came from the consciousness of a heritage, a history, a responsibility: Remember, you are Jewish. I knew the significance of circumcision, the sign of the Covenant: Thou shalt not lie, thou shalt not lapse, thou shalt behave fairly, not like the "pagans". My difference became an obligation; racial memory established a duty. From a very young age, I knew that since I was not "like the others", then the opinion of "the others" was not sufficient for approving or legitimating my conduct. I learned early what faithfulness means, even if it has to be paid for by the bitter price of solitude and exclusion.

And then there was the Jewish tradition, which was no small thing. For example, I knew that the Name of God must not be pronounced, because his Name is transcendent. I knew that it was blasphemous, disrespectful, to pronounce the Name of God.

I also knew that normally Jewish men cover their heads out of respect for God. In the end, my religious sensibility was probably richer than might be supposed given my parents' indecisive position and their detachment from a Judaism that was "superstitious, archaic and prevented the liberation of the Jews"—these are the words I heard at home.

Another thing that was very "structuring" for my childhood: my father told me stories about the twelve tribes of Israel. He explained that they had all merged, except for Aaron's sons, the Cohens and the Levis—that is, the priests and the Levites, their assistants—whose traditions passed from father to son. Only the *Cohanim* and *Levyim* were allowed to give the benediction at worship services after the Temple had been destroyed. He told me that I was, like him and my ancestors, a Levite. And I have never forgotten it. From other stories, I learned many popular customs of Judaism. I also received, along with my love for the Jewish people and my pride in being one of them, many traits of Jewish piety and sensibility.

Reading the Bible in Secret

MISSIKA: *It was in 1936 that there occurred a very important event in your life, the discovery of the Bible....*

LUSTIGER: Yes, I see the setting clearly: the living room of the apartment on the Rue Jules-Chapelain in Montparnasse. It was the year I entered the Lycée Montaigne, or maybe the year before. The Bible was inside a locked bookcase standing next to the piano. I slept in the living room, and above my bed, which was between two windows looking out on a quiet courtyard, there was a large nineteenth-century engraving of Moses carrying the tablets with the Ten Commandments. The building was very old, rather cockeyed and strange. My parents had arranged for my sister and me to have piano lessons from a White Russian lady whose husband was a taxi driver—an ex-general, no doubt! In principle, I was supposed to practice three hours a day—all alone because my parents were at the store during that time. Doing scales was tremendously boring, and I had a passion for reading. Since I was fairly resourceful as far as the piano was concerned, I spent more and more time reading. My teacher was not fooled, but she and I had a kind of understanding, *à la Russe.*

I had discovered the hiding place of the bookcase's key. During the time that I should have been doing scales, I read lots of books, all kinds of books from Abel Hermant[4] to Émile Zola, whose *Germinal*[5] impressed me greatly. I remember that, a year or so later, our French teacher asked us to write a composition describing the life of people living on a barge. I wrote a description that was an imitation of Zola! The bargeman came home drunk, the crockery was chipped—in short, everything was rather seedy! There was a discussion in class when the assignment was corrected. The teacher did not agree with me and tried to find out what had been going on in my head: "Why do you want the bargeman to be drunk?" "Why? Because that's the way it is!" I would not budge: "That's what reality is like!" He was very puzzled as to how I could be so certain.... I must have read one or two meters' worth of Fayard's *Collection jaune* by that time!

[4] Abel Hermant (1862–1950) wrote satirical but realistic descriptions of various classes of Frenchmen in the Third Republic. Like Zola's, his work had a tone of social polemic.—TRANS.

[5] Written in 1885, *Germinal* is a novel describing a French miners' strike at the end of the Second Empire.—TRANS.

WOLTON: *Did your parents read a great deal?*

LUSTIGER: My father, especially, was a great reader. I was absolutely forbidden to read any comics whatsoever: my parents said that they were "stupid". So instead I developed a taste for serious reading. I could read as much as I liked, as long as I read books and not comic strips. But on my way home from school, I always stopped at the same newspaper store on the Rue Notre-Dame-des-Champs and read *Tintin et Milou,* which lay open in the window. Sometimes, I would go inside and stand for half an hour or so leafing through the comic books until the owner would chase me away. My parents always gave me very handsome bound books, bought secondhand. Most of the time they were seventeenth-century French classics, to which Shakespeare—translated in alexandrines[6]—was eventually added. . . .

Among the books I read, there was one that seemed very strange to me. I recall even its smallest details—I must have been about ten. It was the account of the martyrdom of some English Catholics at the time of the Reformation. They were imprisoned and persecuted for their faith. In one way, it was totally incomprehensible, since I had not yet studied history and had no idea about England or the Reformation, or the difference between a Catholic and a Protestant or even who Henry VIII was. I might have been reading a story about Indians or Papuans. But I did recognize the meaning of martyrdom and the absolute of God. For God's sake, to be faithful to what he asks, one must give everything. The martyr makes the offering of his life out of faithfulness and for the salvation of men. He is somewhat similar to the suffering Messiah of Isaiah.

I read this book just after the Bible. It must have been the year I entered *sixième.*

MISSIKA: *Did you find the Bible shocking?*

LUSTIGER: No, not shocking. I really had the impression that I had known about it already. Because I did know. I knew about Abraham, I knew about Moses. Aaron is my name—*Maman* had told me, "He is Moses' brother." My mother's name was Giselle-Léa. I had heard the story of Leah and Rachel. Thus, it was not like reading the Upanishad. I was much more surprised by Greek mythology. With the Bible, I was exploring a world whose existence I had heard about: I was entering a familiar world, one to which I belonged but of which I had only fragmentary knowledge. I remember that it was a Segond edition with a green cover.

[6] The alexandrine is the commonest form of French verse, consisting of a line of twelve syllables with a caesura usually falling after the sixth syllable.—TRANS.

MISSIKA: *Then it was a Protestant Bible? What was a Protestant Bible doing in your home?*

LUSTIGER: I have no idea. What particularly impressed me was that there was a continuity between what is called the Old Testament and the New one. I read them straight through. From that time on, the reading of the New Testament took a place in my Jewish consciousness. For me, it dealt with the same spiritual subject, the same benediction, the same stakes: the salvation of men, the love of God, the knowledge of God. I am persuaded that the identification between the suffering Messiah and persecuted Israel was something intuitive and immediate for me. It is true that I had absorbed the paternal and maternal accounts of persecutions perpetrated by Christians, but I felt that their stories concerned anti-Semites and not the Christians spoken about in the New Testament: Jesus and his Disciples.

MISSIKA: *What did your parents say about Christianity?*

LUSTIGER: They warned us against it—not against Christianity as such (on that subject there was total silence except for the Jewish legends about Jesus), but against certain "Christians". "Christians" were to be treated in a friendly way, but there were the good ones and the bad. And you had to be careful with all of them because the good ones could become bad, and then, they killed.

WOLTON: *Did your parents speak to you about Christian anti-Semitism?*

LUSTIGER: Christian or not, the question was not raised. I simply knew that anti-Semitism was a permanent fact of life. I did not tell my parents, but I read *La France juive* by Drumont.[7]

WOLTON: *But why on earth had they bought such a book?*

LUSTIGER: I really cannot say! But I read it some time before I was twelve. Therefore, I knew perfectly well what anti-Semitism was like. That reading gave substance to the remarks I had heard my parents make. My father was a foreigner, naturalized as an adult, and consequently without any real French culture. He had had all of his schooling in Poland, and there was a cultural gap between him and me. He did not speak French very well; he had a characteristic accent. My mother had no accent because she had been in France since

[7] Edouard Drumont (1844–1917) was a French politician and journalist who was an outspoken anti-Semite, violently nationalistic and anti-Dreyfus.—TRANS.

early childhood. My father's culture was altogether different. It had other references. He read Yiddish novels, and he loved Yiddish poetry and history. I had no access to that world. The cultural gap was inevitable since our parents pushed us to enter into French culture, which was, in their eyes, not only their adopted culture but the culture of freedom.

MISSIKA: *You hid the fact that you were reading the Bible from your parents?*

LUSTIGER: Well, yes, since I was reading it instead of doing my scales!

MISSIKA: *Did you ever suddenly feel that you wanted to talk about it with them?*

LUSTIGER: No.

WOLTON: *But you spoke about it with friends?*

LUSTIGER: It was not until later, at the *lycée,* that I had friends with whom I could discuss such things. Before, in primary school, I had good playmates. The father of one of them owned a bistro flanked by the Coupole and the Rotonde, the celebrated cafés of Montparnasse. We must have been a pretty mischievous pair. I had another friend whose father was an engineer. We spent our time together making crystal sets.

At the Lycée Montaigne, I had close friendships and intellectual exchanges with my classmates. I have special memories of my best friend. His family was Protestant, and he lived in a magnificent apartment on the Montagne Sainte-Geneviève where I spent many hours. He loved music and the piano and did some composing. I was more attracted by literature. We had very lively discussions and during vacations carried on an extraordinary correspondence, long letters with proposals for musical themes, ideas for operas. The great challenge was to surpass Debussy. That was just before the war.

The Professors' Role

MISSIKA: *Did religion have an important place in your conversations?*

LUSTIGER: I do not recall. I suspect not.

MISSIKA: *I have the impression that it was a secret domain.*

LUSTIGER: Among classmates, with friends, it remained secret. But not with my teachers, who played a capital role in my evolution. I remember every one of them by name. You cannot imagine what an influence they had, each one in his own way.

For example, in *sixième,* my first year at the *lycée,* there was our French teacher. I learned later that he was Jewish. He was one of those men who treat boys of ten like gentlemen, and he truly taught us how to think. The curriculum for the year dealt with all the ancient civilizations and thus included the Hebrew civilization. I remember being scandalized by the derisory place given to it in "Malet-Isaac"[8]—so little about the Hebrews and so badly said.

Then, there was the first German lesson. The professor ushered us into his class. And these were his first words: "*Messieurs,* here we do not lie." I find that first contact with a group of ten-year-olds fantastic! The love of truth, respect for the other person and oneself without which there is no genuine access to works of the mind... Those were the principal conditions for learning a living language!

The teacher of natural science was a fabulous person. A tall man with Asiatic features that gave him a Mongolian air, he had lost a leg in the war of 1914 and wore a prosthesis. He had taught for a long time in Indochina. For his doctorate, he had written a thesis on termites. And he continued to study his termites at the Museum of Natural History! His approach to the science curriculum was highly original, and we found it fascinating, gripping. Basically, we had a three-year course—from *sixième* to *quatrième*[9]—in anthropology, which I fully understood only much later. He was a passionate Augustinian. He was well acquainted with all the Church Fathers, but he knew Saint Augustine particularly well. A man of faith and prayer, he could also be as stubborn as a mule. He called himself a clerical anarchist and was a fierce advocate of freedom. "We stormed the Bastille!" was one of his favorite expressions.

One day I witnessed a scene that is at the origin of the unlimited respect I have had ever since for the university. An inspector had come to observe the class, and, at the end of half an hour, he began to criticize—in front of the pupils—the way the course was being taught. The program specified that we were to study the fly, the beetle, the May bug and the frog in that order. But our teacher was giving us an overall view of evolution, a general understanding of things. So the inspector began to reprimand him. Our teacher retorted indignantly, "*Monsieur,* you have nothing to teach me about my profession. I am a doctor of science, I am an *agrégé*[10] of the university, and I have tenure. Get out of this room!" Hearing and seeing all this, we were terrorized and hardly

[8] The official history text used in French *lycées* at the time. It reflected the ideology of the Third Republic, although Jules Isaac was Jewish.... —Trans.

[9] *Quatrième* is the equivalent of the eighth grade in the United States.—Trans.

[10] A person who has passed the highest competitive examination for teachers in France.—Trans.

dared to breathe. Then our teacher turned to us and explained, "I am an academic! The administration does not tell me what to do!"

For him, "the administration" was the bureaucrats whom it was necessary to abolish; it was they who got in the way of learning—they knew nothing about education or research or intellectual freedom. At the age of ten, I learned about the prestige of the university. That was, after all, a pretty important lesson.

I still remember what he told us about the metamorphism of rock masses and my vertiginous discovery of the prehistoric ages. And when we came to the origin of the human species, he explained that man is an animal, but a different animal because he is a being "capable" of communicating with God, he is a "mystical animal". I think that it was from him that I first heard that expression. And he talked about the Bible! About the Old Testament! He referred to it in ways that, in comparison with what I was hearing about the Hebrews in history class, made my heart swell with pride.

We all had a great respect for him. But he could spread terror in his classes. From time to time, he would fly into a dreadful rage and even go so far as to detach his wooden leg and hurl it across the room! He was also passionate about the prehistoric ages and archaeology and was delighted to discuss these subjects with students who interested him. There was always a small group who stayed after class. He told us about his experiences in the Great War and in the Far East and answered our questions. He was both brusque and patient. A good pedagogue, but never a demagogue. He treated us like adults. He also spoke about Orléans and its environs, because he had an intense love for his native region. He told us about Saint Aignan,[11] about his crypt, a pre-Roman gem that he had begun to explore—it has since been unearthed. He spoke spontaneously and responded to our eager curiosity. In our eyes, he was a great man of science. We respected him deeply because he was an honest man.

WOLTON: *Did you speak about religious matters with him?*

LUSTIGER: Yes, with the same group of students. I knew that he was Catholic, but I would not have been able to define what he believed. Moreover, I now think that he treated me with such particular consideration not so much for my personal talents—this is only an interpretation, of course—as for the great respect he had for a boy who had the name of Aaron, the High Priest.

A Fight at School

MISSIKA: *What were your religious feelings during this period?*

[11] A bishop of Orléans who defended the city against Attila in 451 A.D.—TRANS.

LUSTIGER: As I said, everything was rather confused. I have the impression that I had childishly mixed up all the metaphysical and philosophical questions. Having them fall into place came later, when I read Pascal.

MISSIKA: *And when was that?*

LUSTIGER: I think it was in 1940. The war had already begun; it was at some point between Paris and Orléans. I was in *troisième.*[12] I probably discovered Pascal simply because he was on the reading list. I read a great deal between *sixième* and *troisième.* For example, I read Molière, Corneille (all of his plays), La Fontaine . . . except for the fables! I had no access to them! I also read Marivaux and Beaumarchais, whom I liked very much. But the religious plays of Corneille and Racine were my favorites.

WOLTON: *Were you already attracted by Christianity at that time?*

LUSTIGER: I do not know! Really, I cannot say. I thought of myself as Jewish. It was during that period (I mean the period before the war) that I spent two summers in Germany, and they were decisive.

WOLTON: *Before speaking about Germany . . . Do you have any memory of anti-Semitism at the* lycée?

LUSTIGER: In looking back, I would say that the Lycée Montaigne was quite bourgeois. I stood out because of my clothing; my mother made my trousers. Compared to the other students, I was not very well dressed, or rather, I was dressed differently. I recall two precise events. Once in the courtyard, during a break, a group of boys who were getting ready to go to catechism were huddled in discussion. I walked up to them, out of curiosity, without a second thought. And was I ever kicked out, but literally kicked out! "You're a Jew, it's none of your business! Scram. . . . " I was really quite upset. And then, another time, there was a fight that was blatantly anti-Semitic. I was beaten up as I had never been beaten up, just in front of the school on the Rue Auguste Comte, at the small gate leading to the orchard in the Luxembourg Garden. I can still picture the exact spot. I remember that I fought with all my strength to defend myself. There were several boys, and they had attacked me because I was Jewish.

WOLTON: *You had no Jewish classmates?*

[12] *Troisième* is the equivalent of the ninth grade in the United States and of the lower fifth form in Great Britain.—TRANS.

LUSTIGER: No. I have no memory of having met another Jew at the Lycée Montaigne.

The Summer of '36 in Germany

MISSIKA: *Your parents sent you to Germany in 1936 to learn German, but Hitler was already in power!*

LUSTIGER: Yes, they sent me to Ziegelhausen, near Heidelberg, for a month. They had chosen a couple who were "safe" in their eyes. He was a doctor and seemed to me to be very aged. His wife, a former primary school teacher, was a charming old lady. They had no children. I quickly understood that they were anti-Nazi. I do not know why my father had such an idea. I had begun to study German at the *lycée,* and he wanted me to speak correctly. Hitler did not frighten him: he was Germany's problem. My parents thought that France was strong, that it would defend freedom. They had an indestructible confidence in France.

MISSIKA: *And so you arrive in Germany...*

LUSTIGER: I arrive in Germany at that juncture. I had never before lived with Christians. I do not know whether they were Catholic or Protestant, or whether they were practicing. I do remember that the church at Ziegelhausen was divided in half, one part for Catholics, the other for Protestants. That was typical of the villages that had lived through the Reformation.

There were several lodgers that summer, including a Swiss girl who must have been about eighteen. I remember them all the better since I recently found a snapshot of four of us who were of different ages: I was the youngest. For the first time, I was plunged into another world. In it there prevailed a calm good-naturedness, steeped in morality and the Gospel, that is perhaps the best of the Germanic way of life. It was such a peaceful world, in marked contrast to the Nazi violence. It was there that I learned to respect "the others"—I mean the ones whom I might have seen as the enemy. Do not forget that I am talking about the feelings of a French child growing up between the two wars, for whom the Germans were the hereditary enemy.

One scene comes back vividly: one day when we went walking in the mountains, we were shown the wildflowers that it was forbidden to pick because they were a protected species. Fascinated, I picked one all the same! And I was caught! However, I was reprimanded with words of such a tranquil gravity that I was much more impressed than if I had received a few slaps. That reprimand contained not only the law but also nature, culture.... The spiritual values of that world, albeit so different from the one I inhabited in Paris, were not alien to me. Our hosts knew who I was because of my name, but I still ask myself how it could have happened that I came to be there. In 1950, I spent the last six months of my military service in Berlin. Once discharged, I wanted to recapture my memories of that peaceful Germany I had known, and I went back to Heidelberg and Ziegelhausen. And I found that couple with whom I had stayed.

WOLTON: *What did they do when they saw you?*

LUSTIGER: They had been elderly already before the war, but they had survived everything! My childhood memories were confirmed. I was almost twenty-five, and my impressions were the same as when I had been ten. That couple was really what I had sensed them to be, and they had survived. There was Nazism in those memories, of course, but there was also the courage of this couple. In 1936, I had seen Nazism through their sibylline remarks. They were cautious about what they said because they felt threatened. He was the archetypical doctor, an old-style graduate of the University of Heidelberg with the traditionally "gashed" cheeks and an independent mind:[13] the best of what respectable Germany offered. But when I left their house, I read the anti-Semitic newspapers posted everywhere in the streets, in the stores. I asked no questions because my father had warned me, "Above all, keep quiet!"

WOLTON: *So he had, after all, given you some warning before you left?*

LUSTIGER: Oh, yes. He had warned me, "You must never say that you are Jewish. It is dangerous. Be careful, hold your tongue and keep your eyes open." He had me invert two letters of my name, making it "Arno" instead of "Aron" [the French spelling of Aaron].

WOLTON: *What an idea to send a ten-year-old Jewish boy to Nazi Germany!*

LUSTIGER: Yes, that makes you realize just how much confidence my father had in his French nationality and in France. But what struck me most in Germany was the discovery of a Christian family.

MISSIKA: *Did you go to church?*

LUSTIGER: No. My father had been asked specifically if he wanted me to go, and his reply was no; that was all. I never stepped inside a church with my

[13] German students used to have duels using swords or sabers. These students were proud of their scars.—TRANS.

hosts. Once I went inside to visit the war memorial. As I recall, it was the Swiss girl who took me.

It was only during my second summer in Germany that I saw Nazism directly. That was in 1937. My parents, pleased with my school results in German, sent me to another town for a month. There I stayed with a couple who were schoolteachers. They had several children close to my age, and there were several foreign lodgers. I remember particularly an English-speaking boy from Mauritius. We fought like cats and dogs. He claimed that the French were incapable of conquering anything other than desert empires—the Sahara, for example—whereas England knew how to take the choice spots in the world. . . . I was fiercely nationalistic and very anti-English, which went along with my passion in those days for Napoléon. Like all German youth of their age, the children of the family belonged to the *Hitlerjugend* if they were boys or to the BDM[14] if they were girls. One of the sons was just a bit older than I—he must have been about thirteen—and was supposed to be my companion. We often took walks together, and he told me about what happened at the meetings of the *Hitlerjugend,* what he was being taught. I have the impression that he did not know that I was Jewish, even though his parents certainly did.

MISSIKA: *And what did the boy tell you?*

LUSTIGER: Oh, about everything that went on: Saint John's day, the summer solstice, the Aryan traditions of the Germans. . . . He would show me his *Hitlerjugend* knife and boast, "We are going to kill all the Jews." It was a brutal, crude Nazism as experienced by a thirteen-year-old, unconscious of what he was repeating. But it was clear to me that Nazism represented a mortal danger and that it was the resurgence of the "pagan" and "goyim" idolatries.

WOLTON: *That must have caused you to feel terribly anxious.*

LUSTIGER: I do not think so. I can assure you that I have no memories of such moods. I was hardened.

MISSIKA: *And did you speak about all this with your parents when you went back home?*

LUSTIGER: I spoke about it, of course, but I have no memories of prolonged conversations on the subject, because we all knew what was going on with Hitler and Nazism.

14 The BDM was the Bund Deutscher Mädel.—TRANS.

MISSIKA: *You had understood?*

LUSTIGER: Yes, it was clear. But for me, one thing was at least as important: that was that, even in Germany, not all Christians identified themselves with the anti-Semites. Christians could be divided into two different categories. The Germans I met at that time had unwittingly given me the striking proof that one can make a distinction between Christians and anti-Semites.

MISSIKA: *But were your hosts for the second summer practicing Christians?*

LUSTIGER: I suppose they must have been believing Protestants, but they were discreet with me. I do recall that the parents were anti-Nazi. Hence, believing Christians were not all Nazis, just as the Christians I had spotted among my *lycée* professors were not anti-Semitic.

WOLTON: *Historically, that may be glossing things over just a bit.*

LUSTIGER: It was the case with the practicing Christians that I knew then. I felt that no confusion was possible. Nevertheless, I can assure you that I had a critical eye and a thin skin. I was well acquainted with anti-Semitic themes, but they did not correspond with what I had read in the Bible or the New Testament or with the attitudes of the people I had met. I never heard a remark—from any of the adults I have mentioned—either on Christ or the contents of the Christian faith, that had the slightest anti-Semitic connotation. In any case, I was never subjected to a direct discourse on Christianity. I had, I would say, only the cultural discourse, or rather the ordinary witness of people whom I had spotted as Christians. And I saw very well that you had to distinguish between Christians and Christians. My parents, like all Jews, lumped them all together. It seemed to me that the word could have several possible meanings, even though they were all "goyim", "pagans". . . .

WOLTON: *Were you not afraid when you went back to Germany that anti-Semitism might have taken on more dramatic proportions?*

LUSTIGER: I do not know today if I was capable of reasoning in those terms. I have no idea of how I pictured the political situation. But I did have the feeling of a mortal danger, a permanent danger for Jews. I knew that we had to bear our "difference" with courage. That lesson came from my parents.

So that you understand fully: the hidden side of this attitude is the pride in being Jewish. Almost nothing of what was approaching seemed surprising or new: it had already been like that in Pharaoh's time. It had been that way for a very long time; it had always been like that. In other words, I had no *political* and *short-range* perception that would have allowed me to identify the political conflict between the dictatorships—"fascism", "Hitlerism"—and the democracies, the *"république"*. My reference was the Bible—that is, it was *historical* and *long range.* I knew that I belonged to a people "chosen" by God and that the Nazi claim was an outrageous usurpation.

II

THE WAR AND CONVERSION (1939–1945)

Flight to Orléans

JEAN-LOUIS MISSIKA: *Shall we talk about the war?*

JEAN-MARIE LUSTIGER: As I said, in the summer of '37 I went to Germany for a second time. I was to have gone to England during the summer of '38—my parents wanted me to learn English—but they had been frightened by the threat of war. So once again we spent our vacation, a very boring one, at the seaside. Oh, those horrible beaches with their games in the sand! We were at Berck where paralyzed and crippled children were sent for treatment. That month was spent in involuntary meditation on the injustice of suffering.

Before the war broke out in 1939, Paris was in a state of panic. All French children had been brought up with tales about the First World War, and here was a new war starting up with Germany! My father was mobilized; Paris was being emptied of her children. What to do? Where to go? Where could we retreat? At the time of the first "exodus", just after war was declared, I said to my parents, "We can go to Orléans."

MISSIKA: *Why Orléans?*

LUSTIGER: Because of my professor of natural science who had told us so much about Orléans.

DOMINIQUE WOLTON: *Then all the family went to Orléans?*

LUSTIGER: Yes. Why not Orléans rather than somewhere else? It was south of Paris. My father had been called up. I can still see him in uniform; he had a leave when we went there.

MISSIKA: *That means that the store was closed?*

LUSTIGER: Temporarily, yes. We quickly packed our suitcases and left Paris. We found the town crowded with refugees.

MISSIKA: *But did you know anyone in Orléans?*

LUSTIGER: Once we arrived, it was impossible to find that professor! My parents got their bearings; we slept in a hotel. And then they decided to leave my sister and me there, while my mother returned to Paris to look after the store. It was the only reasonable solution. The children have to be in a safe place, they said. At the city hall, there was a reception center for refugee children. It presented the usual scenes associated with the outbreak of war. My parents entrusted my sister and me to one of the persons who came forward to offer help. And I entered the Lycée Pothier in *troisième.*

WOLTON: *In September 1939?*

LUSTIGER: In October. That stay in Orléans was of paramount importance. But now I am coming to events that are more difficult to talk about. They fall within the strictly autobiographical category, which is not the object of our exchange. Therefore, I shall not say everything that might answer your questions.

Conversion

LUSTIGER: I am truly not certain about the chronology. I did ask a close witness to corroborate my memories. He replied that he was already too old, that his memory played tricks on him. I have kept no material reminders of what happened. I would like to be able to verify what are only fleeting impressions or uncertainties, memories or blanks as to what I could have been doing and thinking at the time. What escapes me is the sequence of events, but I have kept the precise and vivid memory of the interior experience.

First the facts: during the *drôle de guerre,*[1] when the threat of invasion seemed to have waned, my parents brought us back to Paris. That return did not last very long—there was to be another exodus in the late spring of 1940—but while it did I found myself back with my best friend at the Lycée Montaigne. Our separation had provoked an exchange of fascinating letters, which I kept for a very long time. Was this return to Paris due to the fact that I had announced to my parents that I wanted to become a Christian? I am no longer sure. Both my father and mother were present when I told them about my desire to be baptized. But at the time of the second exodus, my father was

[1] The "phony war", literally, the "funny war"—a war with little action—between September 3, 1939, when France and Great Britain declared war on Germany and May 12, 1940, when the Germans invaded France.—TRANS.

absent since he had been caught in the *débâcle.* At what point in that year of 1940 did I tell my parents about my intention to ask for baptism and my wish that they would give their permission? I no longer know.

I do have a definite chronological marker of the moment when I decided that I wanted to be baptized. It happened in the Orléans cathedral during Holy Week, just before Easter in 1940. The *débâcle* came in June, thus the return to Paris must have taken place between April and June.

MISSIKA: *But what had led up to this decision?*

LUSTIGER: I shared the daily life of devoted Christians. They knew very well that my sister and I were Jewish, and they always showed an exemplary discretion.

MISSIKA: *When you say "exemplary discretion", does that mean that there was no proselytizing?*

LUSTIGER: Yes, there was none, absolutely none. In Orléans I rediscovered the Christian world from the interior. This time it was French, not German. I encountered its culture, its thought, its way of living and behaving. Simultaneously, there was a drastic change for me: I was a *petit Parisien* who had never known the country, except during summer vacations. And Orléans was a garden. It was also a picture of provincial France. Since I was curious and observant, I asked all sorts of questions as I went about discovering extraordinary places: Germigny-des-Prés, a Carolingian church; Cléry, a Gothic church with Louis XI's tomb; the banks of the Loire; all the many monuments and churches in Orléans. In a word, I wanted to know about everything that was a part of the landscape. And in learning about it, a certain content of Christianity became accessible to me, from the interior, by means of culture and everyday life.

This was not the most important or decisive thing, but I am trying to explain what the filters were. My classmates formed another filter, although we never discussed religion.

WOLTON: *Did the students at Orléans know that you were Jewish?*

LUSTIGER: Of course. My name was Aaron.

MISSIKA: *Were there other Jews in the lycée?*

LUSTIGER: Oh, certainly, but I have no memories of them. I was the only one in my class.

MISSIKA: *Did your mother come to see you regularly?*

LUSTIGER: Yes, every week. As I was saying, the contact with my classmates furnished another ground for exchange with Christianity. But it seems that mixing socially with young Christians came after baptism. However, I do remember having asked the person with whom we were living to lend me a New Testament. I was given a small edition of the Crampon translation of the Bible, in four separate parts, each containing a Gospel. I started with the Gospel according to Saint Matthew, which comes first. I was also reading Pascal at that time. I read Saint Matthew's words assiduously and began to copy them by hand, underlining certain passages that struck me. I did not complete the project; I never went beyond a few chapters. That must have been around Christmas. In any case, it was wintertime, I remember.

And then I was always questioning whoever was available about Christianity—certainly I questioned the person who had taken us in.

WOLTON: *Your sister was with you?*

LUSTIGER: Yes. She was attending a Catholic school.

MISSIKA: *And did you discuss all this with her?*

LUSTIGER: I do not think so. And then, a few months later, I entered the cathedral. I passed by it every day on my way to and from school. It stands at the center of a large windswept square, not built up then. It is an enormous edifice with an austere beauty, always in a state of reparation. I wandered in on what I now know was Holy Thursday. At the south transept, I stopped before a brilliant profusion of flowers and candles. I stood there quite a while, transfixed, not knowing why I was there or why I was reacting as I was. I was ignorant of the significance of what I saw. I did not know what holiday was being celebrated or what the people were doing there in silence. I went home to my room and said nothing about this to anyone.

The next day, I returned to the cathedral. I wanted to see it again. But the church was empty, spiritually empty also. I experienced the ordeal of that emptiness. I did not know that it was Good Friday—I am only describing the materiality of things—and at that moment I thought: I want to be baptized. Right away, I went to the person with whom I was staying. It was the simplest thing to do. I knew that she was Catholic, that she went to Mass. I had observed her and knew what kind of person she was.

She told me, "You must ask your parents." But she did send me to the Bishop of Orléans, Monsignor Courcoux. He was a very cultivated Oratorian and gave me private instruction in Christianity. From our first meeting, he, too, urged me to obtain my parents' permission. The chronology escapes me, but I remember very well the day that I informed my parents. It was an extremely painful scene, completely unbearable. They ended up by accepting, but that is another story.

WOLTON: *Both of them refused initially?*

LUSTIGER: Of course. My father must have been on leave again. I explained that baptism would not make me abandon my Jewish condition—quite the contrary, it would lead me to find it, to receive the plenitude of its meaning. I did not have the feeling that I was betraying my heritage, or camouflaging myself or abandoning anything whatsoever. Just the opposite: I felt that I was going to find the import, the meaning of what I had received at birth. For my parents, this reasoning was thoroughly incomprehensible, insane and insufferable, the worst of things, the worst of misfortunes that could befall them. I was acutely aware that I was causing them unendurable pain. I was torn apart by their suffering, and I truly took the step only because of an interior necessity. Another solution would have been to bury all this in myself, to say nothing and wait. But I did not want to envisage that solution.

Monsignor Courcoux was very respectful of others. I do not know whether he was aware of what my request represented for my parents. Even today, I have no idea of how much he knew about Jews from our background. He was very cultured and intelligent. The Jews he knew were the liberal Jews of the French intelligentsia of whom Bergson was a representative. . . .

Finally, my parents consented—for both my sister and me.

MISSIKA: *Your sister, too, wanted to convert?*

LUSTIGER: She followed me, but by conviction. However, we have never spoken about it.

MISSIKA: *Both of you followed the same evolution during that period in Orléans?*

LUSTIGER: In any case, the same instruction, the one given by the bishop. I regret having thrown away the fascicules of the course of study he had had printed for use in secondary school. Since he was an Oratorian, perhaps he had taught at Juilly or Saint-Martin de Pontoise before becoming curé at Saint-Eustache in Paris. Be that as it may, the intellectual level of his course was remarkable. From the start, I was introduced to the study of Christian origins and the earliest texts with a great historical rigor; in a word, I received a Christian initiation of an intellectual and spiritual quality rarely proposed to an adolescent. It confirmed my keen intuition that Christianity is the continuation of Judaism. Monsignor Courcoux talked about a among many names he brought up was that of Fathe for example. And he also broached the relationship be This is all to say that I was not badly treated.

WOLTON: *You were lucky.*

LUSTIGER: In this domain, I met only people who inspi respect.

WOLTON: *Why did it appear obvious to you to go from Judaism to Christianity rather than turning toward the Jewish religion?*

LUSTIGER: But Christianity is the fruit of Judaism! To be specific: I believed in Christ, the Messiah of Israel. Something that I had carried within me for years, without having spoken about it to anyone, crystallized. I knew that Judaism held the hope of the Messiah. I knew that the response to the scandal of suffering was the hope of man's redemption and the fulfillment of God's promises to his people. And I *knew* that Jesus is the Messiah, the Christ of God.

WOLTON: *Could you not have been simply a rebellious teenager?*

LUSTIGER: The discovery of the Messiah of Israel, the Son of God, also confirmed God's existence. I was still in the metaphysical age, but concurrently I had entered the age of doubt: "Does God exist?" It is a question of critical rationality, a haunting or subliminal intellectual question, and it took me fifteen to twenty years to emerge from it, given the culture to which I belonged and my personal evolution.

MISSIKA: *You mean you had this doubt at the time of your conversion or discovery?*

LUSTIGER: I had both the absolute certainty that God exists and its radical negation that says: God does not exist. The two thoughts dwelt in me successively and sometimes simultaneously. But I knew, deep down, even when I was no longer certain of believing, that God existed, because I was Jewish.

WOLTON: *How was that?*

LUSTIGER: Because I knew that God had chosen Jews to show that he exists!

MISSIKA: *You have made a big point, and I understand why, of the fact that there was no proselytism by the people with whom you were living.*

LUSTIGER: I insist on it, because proselytism is the first idea that comes to mind in this kind of situation. That is also the accusation that my parents made immediately.

MISSIKA: *I am going to say the same thing: Isn't the successful proselytism the one that is discreet?*

LUSTIGER: I do not know. All I can say is that I was an impossible adolescent, very proud with a strong personality. It was better not to step on my toes. I suppose that I can be manipulated—everybody can be to a degree—but the people involved were men and women of an obvious honesty. Moreover, they did me the favor of criticizing me, to put me in my place.

WOLTON: *Did your parents not propose an alternative solution: deepening the Jewish faith?*

LUSTIGER: Yes, of course. We had a meeting with a well-known figure in Judaism, a discussion at his house that went on for two hours. I "demonstrated" to him that Jesus is the Messiah. As we were leaving, he said to my parents, "There is nothing you can do, let him go ahead."

WOLTON: *The family conflict must have been very intense. Did you eventually find comfort in either of your parents?*

LUSTIGER: It is very complicated. My mother died too early. She was deported and died at Auschwitz. With my father, there was an evolution that could not take place with her; thus, it is impossible to answer. My father was rather sparing of words. When he spoke, the effect was tremendous. My mother, on the contrary, was expansive, more nervous, more expressive.

MISSIKA: *Given the historical context, could your parents also have concluded that perhaps this conversion was not such a bad thing?*

LUSTIGER: They made that calculation. They did see it as a protection from the Germans. I think that it was for that reason that they finally conceded. But I protested, "That will not change a thing."

MISSIKA: *And what about you? Did these historical circumstances not bother you? What I am trying to say is, was it not hard to leave Judaism just at the moment when Jews were being persecuted?*

LUSTIGER: I was not thinking in political terms. There was never for one instant a question of disowning my Jewish identity. Quite the contrary, I perceived Christ as Israel's Messiah, and I was surrounded by Christians who had deep esteem for Judaism.

MISSIKA: *Have you never met Christians who were lacking in that esteem?*

LUSTIGER: I felt that anti-Semites were unfaithful to Christianity.

MISSIKA: *That does not leave very many Christians in France!*

LUSTIGER: The anti-Semites were goyim, pagans; they were not Christians.

MISSIKA: *But even though for you things were happening on a spiritual level, wasn't the historical reality present?*

LUSTIGER: But, of course, the historical reality was extremely powerful, but it did not take the form of a political expediency in my case. A few years later, I read the underground issues of *Témoignage chrétien* and rediscovered my convictions clearly articulated. De Lubac, Fessard and Journet, who were writing clandestinely about the resistance to Nazi paganism and about Judaism, said what had to be said.

WOLTON: *Do you remember the date of your first Communion?*

LUSTIGER: Baptism and Communion were on August 25, 1940, and confirmation, by the Bishop of Orléans, took place on September 15, 1940, in the chapel at the bishop's palace where almost forty years later I was to celebrate Mass as Bishop of Orléans.

MISSIKA: *Did you change your name at that time?*

LUSTIGER: No, I kept the name on my birth certificate, Aaron, which was my paternal grandfather's name. Tradition had it that when the grandfather died, one of the grandsons took his name. I kept it at baptism because it was my name and because Aaron, the High Priest, appears in the Christian calendar. I added Jean and Marie. Jean was the name of my godfather.

The National Humiliation

WOLTON: *Were the Germans already in Orléans at the time of your first Communion?*

LUSTIGER: Yes. I remember very well the sudden break represented by their appearance. For me, it had seemed impossible that France would collapse. It was an unheard of blow, a wound, a humiliation. And when I saw the Germans moving in, I knew that Jews were going to be killed. I knew it better than my parents. It was clear that that would happen. I can still picture the uniforms of the German Army. . . . I could understand what they said, because I spoke German well. I can still see that first soldier in a sidecar stopping in the Rue Saint-Marc at the intersection where we lived. And at that moment, I had to face the unthinkable. I remember vividly the Senegalese infantryman who was killed on the little bridge leading to the Faubourg de Bourgogne. The last soldier to defend the bridge, he fell beside the bronze bust of Péguy. He had been billeted in the house where I was living. He only barely spoke French and laughed like an overgrown child. To our amazement, he could catch mice with his hands! He defended France's honor to the very end. Yes, I experienced that defeat as an inconceivable humiliation.

I can see the German tanks rolling across the Place du Martroi, which was in ruins after the recent bombardments. My memory restored that scene intact when, as Bishop of Orléans, I led the Fêtes de Jeanne d'Arc in 1980. I had wanted to attend the military parade, but when I saw the French tanks approaching in the same way, I had to struggle to hold back my tears because all of a sudden the two images were superimposed. It was the second time in my life that I had seen tanks crossing the Place du Martroi, but this time they were French. I understood that, up until that day, the humiliating picture of that destroyed square filled with German tanks had never been erased. Maybe it seems strange to say so today, but that is the way I felt.

MISSIKA: *Did the Germans' entry into Orléans cause you to become more aware of the political stakes?*

LUSTIGER: The political problem as I saw it then was not the one that, even today, people continue to analyze. Like all French children, I had heard talk about the war in Spain, the conflicts with the extreme right, the demonstrations and political violence in France. In a word, I was aware of everything that adults were discussing and that filled the newspapers. But, beyond that, it seems to me that I saw certain fundamental stakes: the right to justice, man's destiny and, inescapably, given what I had heard talked about, the Jewish problem. That problem was at the heart of the political situation, because in

Germany there were Nazism and anti-Semitism; in France, there was anti-Semitism that was taking Léon Blum as a target. Thus, the Jewish issue was mixed with the political one. And as far as I was concerned, the Jewish issue was primarily concerned with man's relationship to faith, to God and the problem of salvation.

I do not think that I am reinterpreting when I say that it was on that level that I understood events. As for everything else, I was like all the French: Who could understand what was happening? A world was crashing in upon us. My parents had taught me to respect knowledge, teachers, doctors, judges, public officials—in short, all those people responsible for the humane values that had made France. The education I had received repeatedly appealed to the mind, freedom and reason as well as to confidence in men, institutions, law and truth. The rout and defeat of the French were a complete denial of all this. A world was destroyed, and its values held up to ridicule. After that, it was necessary to try to comprehend and to establish one's own fidelity. How could you be faithful to France against the French? Where were the traitors? I think that, because of being Jewish, I was prepared for this ordeal in a certain sense. We already knew that the law is often mocked by power, and justice is often betrayed by those who have received the mission to serve it. That is simply the way things happen. The duty to serve the truth always demands a certain sacrifice. And you must not be surprised if it relegates you to solitude. It is the experience (in a sense, "Messianic") of all Jewish children of my generation who had already learned the word *persecution,* the word *pogrom.* They had become familiar words that armed us in advance for the struggle.

Christian Initiation, Anti-Jewish Persecution

MISSIKA: *How long did you stay in Orléans?*

LUSTIGER: From the end of *troisième* until *première,*[2] from 1940 to 1942. Hence, two years. Two very important years. It was during this period that I received a Christian initiation, that I made my entry into Christianity. All that went smoothly. I never noticed the slightest indiscretion on the part of the people around me. I immediately turned toward my Catholic classmates at the *lycée* and joined the JEC.[3] When I was in *seconde,* I was placed in charge of some younger members. That proves that the leaders did not lack audacity,

[2] *Première* is the equivalent of the eleventh grade in the United States and of the lower sixth form in Great Britain.—TRANS.

[3] JEC stood for *Jeunesse étudiante chrétienne,* a branch of the "Catholic Action" (*l'Action catholique*) movement in France, which organized lay militants according to socioprofessional divisions.—TRANS.

because laws against Jews had been promulgated and applied. In fact, I was known as a Jew. I was called Aron at school. At the JEC meetings, I was called Aron-Jean-Marie.

Even in retrospect, I find that the milieu was unusually diverse, thanks to which I came to know many interesting personalities among the Catholic youth groups, the JEC, the students at the Collège Sainte-Croix and the chaplains and priests who were associated with them. I never encountered any expression of hate or contempt for Jews or foreigners. Perhaps I was blind—since then I have asked myself that question. Heaven knows, however, that I am hypersensitive. But I never heard any wounding remarks or anything that would have incited me to defiance. I was never made to feel that I was some sort of oddity, never asked to relate how I had come to be where I was. Anyway, I would have refused to talk about it. I have never liked exhibitionism, whether voluntary or involuntary.

MISSIKA: *Were you in groups where you had to sing "Maréchal nous voilà!"*[4]

LUSTIGER: Sure! Everybody sang it, the whole *lycée.* And that was not the only song I sang to the *maréchal*'s glory.

MISSIKA: *Did you ever meet anybody who said to you, "What is happening to the Jews is a good thing"?*

LUSTIGER: Some people at the *lycée* thought it. But they never dared to say it to my face. Furthermore, the very closely knit Catholic circle with whom I kept company had been alerted to this kind of danger. Several professors, known as Catholics, were also known for their outspoken anti-Nazism.

MISSIKA: *The anti-Jewish laws date from October 1940. How did you ensure your safety?*

LUSTIGER: My parents had hesitated to declare themselves. All French Jews were asking themselves whether they should register or not. Monsignor Courcoux got in touch with the *commissaire* for Jewish affairs. In fact, after the war, an Israeli historian found his letter in archives stored in Jerusalem. He gave me a copy of that letter and the response to it. Monsignor Courcoux had pleaded the cause of my parents by writing: "Must they declare themselves? They are French citizens and are honorable people whom I know." And the

[4] During the German occupation, this song expressing support for Marshal Pétain replaced the "Marseillaise" as the song habitually sung at the beginning of the school day.—TRANS.

commissioner had replied, "As French citizens, they have nothing to fear. Tell them to go ahead and declare themselves. There is no need to worry." (I am quoting approximately, from memory.) If you look at the dates on the letters and what was already taking place at that time, you know that his reassurance was an outright lie. My parents ended up by registering as Jews. They wore the yellow star. I never did. I should have been registered in Paris, since my parents were. To avoid arrest, my mother used to hide the yellow star when she made trips between Paris and Orléans.

In 1941, when things began to grow worse, my father left Paris clandestinely to go to the *zone libre.* He was to make preparations for resettling the whole family. After being helped by successive channels—you know, it was really a strange period—he finally arrived in Decazeville.[5] He found a job in a priority factory—that is, one exempted from police controls. It produced bitumen, a much-needed substance, from schist. It was a small experimental concern belonging to an iron- and steel-making company from northern France that had relocated in Decazeville. The company still exists. They only recently suppressed the rolling mill and extinguished the fire in the smelting furnace. Two years ago, I had a reunion with the engineer who had run the factory. It was he who had hired my father, who was relatively protected there. Among the workers there were former Spanish republicans, anarchists of all shapes and sizes, a motley collection of men, each of whom had something to hide. It was an extraordinary world. Decazeville is in the heart of a coal-mining region, and it was even more sinister during the war. Fortunately, the countryside provided food supplies! My mother dragged her heels about leaving Paris because she wanted to keep her eye on the store, in spite of the fact that an "Aryan" administrator had been named. It was becoming increasingly urgent that she leave. The plan was that my father, the first to go, would find a place to live and some means of supporting the family; then my mother would join him while my sister and I were to follow at the end of the school year. But, in the meantime, my mother was arrested and sent to Drancy.[6]

WOLTON: *Was she caught in a major raid?*

LUSTIGER: No. A neighbor denounced her. She was arrested at home. The apartment was completely emptied, looted, and the doors were sealed. My parents had left a few objects with neighbors; everything else was stolen.

[5] Decazeville is a small industrial town located south of the Massif Central and four hundred miles south of Paris.—TRANS.

[6] Drancy is a suburb northeast of Paris. In 1941, a transit camp for French and foreign civilians bound for concentration camps in Germany and Poland was set up there.—TRANS.

One day, after the war, a little old lady came to see my father and said, "Here, when they took everything away from your apartment, I picked up these from the street. . . . " They were photographs. That is how we recuperated a part of the family album.

WOLTON: *Why didn't your mother go to live in Orléans?*

LUSTIGER: But there was nothing for her to do in Orléans! It was not any more protected than Paris. And the store was in Paris. We children were in a more or less shadowy zone there.

MISSIKA: *But were you ever denounced?*

LUSTIGER: There were collaborators in the *lycée* and its *entourage* who played cat and mouse with me. At a certain point, it became clear that it was better that I should move on.

MISSIKA: *How did you learn about your mother's arrest?*

LUSTIGER: I do not recall exactly who let us know or how—neighbors in Paris, no doubt. A certificate of civil status delivered after the war informed us that she was arrested on September 10, 1942. Very soon we heard that she was at Drancy. There was a horrible period of official postcards and clandestine letters, until her deportation. Then I had to clear out, too. My sister stayed in Orléans; she seemed easier to protect.

MISSIKA: *So your sister never wore the yellow star either?*

LUSTIGER: No, she did not. When my father reached the free zone, we corresponded by means of *interzones* cards. Our messages were very cryptic, very prudent and were carried by a third party. It was decided that I should be sent, so as to hide, to do my final year in *lycée,* in philosophy, at the *petit séminaire de Paris*[7] at Conflans. Meanwhile, I had declared my intention of becoming a priest to Monsignor Courcoux. He had replied, "You have plenty of time! You will see later." But I went to the *petit séminaire* because it was a safe place.

MISSIKA: *Were there other Jews like you in this school?*

[7] A *petit séminaire* is a French preseminary—a secondary school for early vocations as well as for other Catholic boys.—TRANS.

LUSTIGER: Perhaps, but the rule was to say nothing. Ostensibly, there were only baptized and Catholic students. A certain number of them were considering the priesthood or had already decided on it.

WOLTON: *Apropos of the persecution of Jews, what kinds of discussions did you have with the Catholics you saw in Orléans?*

LUSTIGER: I have an overall memory of my conversations with Monsignor Courcoux. His theological and spiritual perception placed a great emphasis on Jewish-Christian relations, but the Judaism he knew was that described in the Bible; he had no concrete acquaintance with Jewish milieus. His position in regard to Germany and Nazism was explicitly negative, and he was wary of Marshal Pétain.

But we have to speak more generally about what the French were thinking then. It has to be said that France, by and large, was Pétainist. At the same time, among the people I saw, all—or almost all—were hostile to the Germans. Some of them, including comrades from the *lycée,* were already in the *Résistance.* Those who had been in philosophy or *math-élem* (in *terminale,* as we would say today), those whom I had known the previous year, were heaven knows where doing heaven knows what. Underground activities? The *Résistance?* In the STO?[8] There was a lot of talk about the STO.

In contrast, I remember a boy a year older than I, a perfectly upright and idealistic person, whose father was a public school teacher. To our general stupefaction, he joined the LVF.[9] He did it by conviction, to defend the Christian West against communism. One day he came back to the *lycée*—in a German uniform—to see his friends. We had never been close friends, but we knew each other. When I saw him appear in the hall, I really bawled him out: "Get the hell out of here, hide yourself! What are you doing? Do you want to get yourself killed?" I closed him in a classroom to avoid incidents. I do not know what became of him. Perhaps he died on the Russian front. His father was overwhelmed with grief by his son's choice.

I am just giving you a few images. It was a strange situation, a heartbreaking situation. However, all the people with whom I was closely associated were against the Germans and Nazism.

MISSIKA: *But, for the most part, they were Pétainists?*

[8] STO stood for *Service du Travail Obligatoire,* or mandatory labor service. Many young Frenchmen were forced to work in German factories and farms, as substitutes for men drafted into military service.—TRANS.

[9] LVF stood for the *Légion de Volontaires Français pour le Front de l'Est,* the "legion" of French volunteers who served with the Germans on the Russian front.

Lustiger: Yes, for the most part. But do not delude yourself. It was only in 1944—thanks to de Gaulle—that France discovered that it had "resisted". I do not know when we French will be able to write the history of this period, will be able to look it straight in the face without having it tear us apart again. Must we wait another fifty years?

France was Pétainist, which is not to say that it was Nazi. It foundered and passed through a dreadful ordeal. The war was an anguish for my generation, which witnessed the collapse of all values: truth, justice, confidence. The credibility of institutions and of those who were responsible for them was devastated. But I think that it is important to be able to explain such a collapse. It is not enough to have a few trials and sacrifice a handful of scapegoats as was done at the liberation. Is there not elsewhere, somewhere in our country's history, a flaw, a profound flaw? I have always believed that when a house caves in, it does not do so all at once, without reason. Our house caved in. We have to know why. But what a question!

A Spiritual Crisis

Wolton: *Then you would say that the collapse was due to a spiritual crisis?*

Lustiger: Yes: 1940 cannot be explained by 1940. The succession of political errors does not suffice to explain this knuckling under. Of course, there was a series of factual causes—troops were not sent to the Rhine in time, Hitler was not resisted when that was still possible, we re-armed too late—in a word, we took none of the tactical steps that good political leaders could have taken if they had had the courage or the possibility of doing so. But I am thinking of a much deeper phenomenon: the acquiescence of the people.

France did not resist. Poland has been resisting for more than forty years now! Why was France so powerless? Because there was a spiritual crisis that began well before 1940, a crisis of modern society of which the 1914–18 massacre is a part. I remember a cartoon from 1940—it must have been in *Le Figaro.* You saw a peasant turning the earth with his spade, and beside him, a country squire, with leather gaiters and a Basque beret, carrying the battle-ax of the Franks,[10] was saying to him, "All you have lost is Gide and those maleficent authors whose works you were reading too much. . . . " That was typical of the contemporary explanations whose absurdities were being shown up by the cartoonist. From that time on, the political misadventures

[10] The battle-ax of the Franks had been adopted by the Pétainist Vichy regime as the symbol of the national "renewal", based on historic values and virtues. André Gide (1869–1951) had criticized traditional bourgeois values in his novels and had become an admirer of the Soviet Union.—Trans.

of the Vichy regime and collaboration discredited the values that are a part of a nation's essential patrimony, and, therefore, they no longer seemed defensible.

The Vichy government replaced the republican motto *Liberté-Égalité-Fraternité* with the slogan *Travail-Famille-Patrie.* After the liberation and for almost half a century now, these three values, which are, after all, fundamental social values, have been halfway erased from the French vocabulary, from the national consciousness, because they were contaminated. The word *work* came to be accepted again only because of the ideological hold of Marxism on the French elite. We do not yet know how to speak about the "family". New words were needed, and they have been used only timidly and with reservations. The "homeland" has been nobly spoken about, but only by repressing shameful memories. And even though the theme of patriotism was quickly restored, it took root in a wounded national conscience. In my opinion, all this is the fruit of the bad conscience of a conquered nation, betrayed by its elite.

There are certain facts that people would prefer to forget. This one, for example: the family name of one of my friends (I met him after the war) is Israel. A Jew, born in Alexandria, a French citizen, a very brilliant engineer, he was an officer during the war of 1939–40. In 1940, he was degraded in the Army of the Armistice because Jews no longer had the right to be officers. Subsequently, he refused to put another name on false papers. "When your name is Israel, you do not change it", he said. I understood this very well. Somehow he succeeded in not being caught in a raid.

MISSIKA: *When you speak of a spiritual crisis, are you thinking of moral values?*

LUSTIGER: Of culture in general.

MISSIKA: *Do you think that it is a crisis of the elite or of the people as a whole?*

LUSTIGER: It can only be a crisis of the people as a whole, and it is a spiritual crisis. The word *crisis* can be used in two different domains. First, it can apply to what preoccupies intellectuals, to the evolution of ideas, to the latest theories, to what it is that makes, every ten years or so and sometimes in even less time, an idea become dominant, what makes such and such a concept obsess the best minds and constitute the standard to which one must conform. When sooner or later a certain prior evidence is challenged by the fluctuations of intellectual fashion, people say that there is a crisis of this or that.

I am not talking about this completely normal play of ideas. Admittedly, it has some influence on culture, but there is a time lag between this activity of the intelligentsia and the appropriation of ideas by a people, a nation. The latter requires more time because ordinary people do not evolve at such a rapid pace. And even intellectuals, in fact, imperturbably hold on to what they take for granted longer than one might think. They have the capacity to toy with ideas, to reflect abstractly. That is their job, perhaps their mission, but sometimes they risk disguising quick-wittedness as a deepening of thought. The impregnation of a population with images, ideas, judgments and values is much slower and much more involved with life's concrete choices. Only intellectuals can permit themselves to be schizophrenic—that is, to laud evil and do good or vice versa, to live in a completely ordinary fashion—like a plumber or a blacksmith of former times—while speculating on the man of the future. This gap between the intellectual and speculative field and the practical life with wives, children, work and money is common in the lives of great men.

But, above all, I apply the notion of crisis to the ordinary fabric of social relations and behaviors, the value judgments that sustain a nation. These values are ordinary virtues transmitted by an ordinary education. The legacy of family and moral virtues is an invaluable resource for a society. This treasure, accumulated by the efforts of generations—the spiritual continuity of education, if you prefer—was the most precious of patrimonies. Well before 1940, however, too often it had seemed meager, too meager, and had lost its moral vigor. There was already a profound crisis within the French people. You have to go back to the eighteenth century, or perhaps further, to find its origin.

People like Léon Bloy, Péguy and Bernanos had already spotted it. How else can you explain that France, whose citizens knew how to distinguish good from evil—as our teacher in the public school on the Rue Huyghens used to explain to us—could suddenly sink into cowardliness and denouncement?

MISSIKA: *Don't you believe that, in such tragic circumstances, it is only a minority who are ever capable of resisting and refusing the lie and lawlessness?*

LUSTIGER: You can say that, but you can also say that the social fabric was simply not very resistant. And why is it that this minority did not have more influence?

MISSIKA: *Perhaps it is the role of the elite that is decisive. In France, the majority of the government and political leaders deemed it advantageous to accept the unacceptable.*

LUSTIGER: That played a role, but the explanation seems insufficient. In occupied France there were many people who no longer knew the difference between what was good and what was bad, between what you should or should not do. And such a confusion of values does not establish itself as a social norm in just two years. Of course, vast numbers of men and women remained faithful to the moral law and truth. They were the ones who, without realizing it, "saved" France. But in 1940, there was no longer any social objectivity concerning truth and morality. Remember the *Résistance* slogan: "Radio-Paris lies. Radio-Paris lies. Radio-Paris is German."

Drancy-Auschwitz

MISSIKA: *Was your mother held for a long time at Drancy? Or was she deported soon after her arrival?*

LUSTIGER: She stayed in Drancy for quite a long time, since she was deported only in February of 1943. She succeeded in surviving there by dint of tenacity. We have kept the correspondence that she managed to send out by bribing—at great cost—a *gendarme.* I have not had the heart to reread those clandestine letters. There is only one point that I wish to underline: she knew. And if she knew, the others knew. And if we knew, then everybody knew. At Drancy, they knew that they were heading toward death. I still see those precise words that my mother wrote: "*Mes enfants,* it is a fatal illness; above all, protect yourself against it." It must not be said that people were unaware of what was going on.

MISSIKA: *Did you try to see her at Drancy?*

LUSTIGER: But come now, what do you think? It was impossible! We were in hiding, constantly threatened. We had not had the foresight to change our name. If we remained shielded, and heaven knows how we did, it was thanks to the wall of silence around us. A little gust of wind would have sufficed to expose us, and the game would have been up! I still cannot understand how both my parents and I could have been so imprudent. But, of course, the fundamental reason was my parents' confidence in France. They continued to hope that France would not abandon the Jews, that it would not give in to the Nazis. That is why they did not protect themselves in time. What eventually happened had been inconceivable to them, and they resigned themselves to the idea only when forced to do so by circumstances.

WOLTON: *How did you pass your* bac?[11]

LUSTIGER: I took my *bac* at Conflans, at the *petit séminaire.* Although I

[11] The *bac,* an abbreviation for *baccalauréat,* is a national examination taken at the end of secondary school; only those who pass it can enter university.—TRANS.

was in hiding, I was able to pass it just before leaving for Decazeville. Moreover, I took it under my own name. That was in June 1943 when the oral part of the exam had been suppressed, so the risk was minimal.

During the year at Conflans, I came to know three priests who were in charge. Monsignor Lallier, the superior, welcomed me with great kindness and warmth. He was later made a bishop and is now retired and lives in Paris. Not so long ago, he asked me, "But how were you able to survive in that atmosphere of the *petit séminaire?*" When I told him that nothing had been painful for me, that I had seen only the good, he was amazed.

Monsignor Delarue was *préfet de division.*[12] Dead now, he was the first bishop of Nanterre. The young abbé Pierre Veuillot was our philosophy professor, and he was appointed my *directeur spirituel*—a guide for personal religious life and prayer. Until his death in 1968, when he was Cardinal-Archbishop of Paris, we maintained a very friendly relationship, based on trust and respect. His philosophy course was very carefully prepared, and I realized only later just how rich it was: a history of philosophy that included both Freud and phenomenology . . . subjects that were not yet well known, even in the university.

MISSIKA: *Were you shocked by your discovery of philosophy?*

LUSTIGER: What was especially striking was the change in the level of reflection after the historical type of literary culture that had been taught by my professors at Orléans. The history of philosophy leads to reflections about history itself! At least it allows one to locate the intellectual tools! Little was known about Hegel in those days. . . . Jean Hyppolite translated Hegel's *Phénoménologie* only after the war.

WOLTON: *Did you know what you wanted to do after your* bac?

LUSTIGER: Yes, I knew that I wanted to be a priest, and I felt that philosophy was the academic discipline that would best prepare me, because philosophy attempts to answer the fundamental questions of existence, those concerning the meaning of life, and because it tries to understand what makes something true or false. I considered philosophy as a doorway, as part of the edifice in which the reality of faith and religion is inscribed.

During that year at Conflans, I discovered what it was like to live in a boarding school: I shared the everyday life of people with whom I had little in common. I suppose that I must have seemed quite strange to them because I

[12] The *préfet de division* coordinates studies and activities and deals with individual problems for a particular grade in French Catholic schools.—TRANS.

was really not very disciplined and I was decidedly independent. They must have spotted me right away as being one of the good students and at the same time as something of a rowdy. I seemed strange, too, because I knew neither the habits nor the rules of the place. Consequently, I did all sorts of things that the others did not think possible—and vice versa. Most of the students had entered the school at the same age, several years previously, while I was something that had been inserted from the outside. But I never noticed any rejection—which would not have been surprising in such a world—or jealousy or curiosity or anything like that.

Above all, I discovered a Christian life of rigor and beauty. Before leaving Orléans, I had been going to Mass almost every day, or as often as seemed possible for someone for whom such a practice meant getting up early in the morning. . . . It had been particularly painful because I always spent half the night reading on the sly. At Conflans, that became more difficult because I slept in a dormitory. Thus, I discovered a regularly organized Christian life. Every day there were the Mass and prayer services and also time for personal meditation. Each week some elements for enriching our religious life were proposed to us. What for some of my fellow students had become a routine, of which they were possibly weary, struck me as an extraordinary novelty.

WOLTON: *Then you enjoyed being a boarder in a religious school?*

LUSTIGER: Yes, wholeheartedly.

MISSIKA: *How did the other students who had come there in a more orthodox way strike you? Did you have the impression that there was a wide gulf between them and you?*

LUSTIGER: Yes, but I was not yet capable of appreciating just how great the distances were. There was a diversity of social backgrounds. Some, like me, were sons of immigrants but had been brought up in a working-class Catholic environment that was certainly different from the one I had known. I was always an attentive listener, while never letting anything about my personal or family situation escape my lips. I cannot say how I struck the others. I do not want to imply that I felt like the odd man out, but it is true that I was brought into contact with ways of life and types of Frenchmen that I had not known before. Neither at the Lycée Montaigne nor the one in Orléans would I have been able to meet young people like them, several of whom have remained my friends.

MISSIKA: *Was the word* Jew *on your identity card?*

LUSTIGER: No, I was just sixteen, still too young to be required to have one. Toward the end of the school year, the mayor of a small village in the Loiret[13] produced my first official *carte d'identité,* a "false" one on which Jean-Marie was substituted for Aaron.

WOLTON: *Did you know then that your mother had been deported?*

LUSTIGER: One day we deduced that she was no longer at Drancy, because there had been no acknowledgment of a succession of packages we had sent—although not surprisingly: other packages had sometimes been stolen before reaching her. We had no idea where she had been sent.

At the liberation, we questioned the Red Cross for a long time, but no one knew anything. We pretended to hope that she would be coming back. On the basis of some vague information, I was convinced that she had been sent to Ravensbrück. We searched in vain to find some leads. Finally, the French government gave us a certificate of deportation. It took Robert Badinter[14] to modify the law—in 1985—so that death certificates for *déportées* were obtainable. But those initial certificates acknowledged only disappearances, since people were alive when they left France and their deaths had never been declared. It was from Serge Klarsfeld's book, *Le mémorial des Juifs de France,*[15] which came out only in 1978, that I learned the exact day on which my mother left Drancy and where she was taken. It is true that since then I have found an *acte de disparition* sent to my father on March 3, 1952, and it mentions that the destination was Auschwitz.

MISSIKA: *So you found your mother's name in* Le mémorial des Juifs de France?

LUSTIGER: Yes, she was on the list for convoy number 48, which left for Auschwitz on February 13, 1943.

[13] The Loiret is one of the ninety-five main administrative divisions of France that are called *départements.* Orléans is its capital.—TRANS.

[14] Robert Badinter (1928–), professor of law, was appointed *Garde des Sceaux, Ministre de la Justice* by François Mitterand in 1981.—TRANS.

[15] Serge Klarsfeld is a French lawyer who, with his German wife Beate, has relentlessly hunted down Nazi war criminals and worked to establish records of arrests, deportations, executions and disappearances so that such atrocities will not be erased from history.—TRANS.

Decazeville-Toulouse

WOLTON: *What did you do after your* bac?

LUSTIGER: I went to join my father in Decazeville. My sister was still in Orléans. I was all alone when I secretly crossed over the boundary into the *zone libre.* The only thing I remember is that I was terribly afraid of being caught. Once I was in the free zone, thanks to my false ID card, I spent the night in the train station at Brive-la-Gaillarde. Nevertheless, I took the precaution of sleeping in a freight car on a siding. And the next day, I took the connecting train to Decazeville.

Once there, I was immediately hired by the factory for which my father was working. Since I had my *bachot,*[16] the manager entrusted me with the "responsibility" of the control laboratory, which meant that there were people much more experienced than I who were working under me. At Decazeville, I entered adult life; I was a worker with a pay slip and a ration card for tobacco. . . . I started to smoke, because it was a way of asserting my rights before Marshal Pétain: I was not about to let my portion go on the black market! But it was especially the worker's life and the discovery of his world that fascinated me. Religiously, that was a very difficult period. My father forbade any kind of practice. Thus, I was obliged to bury myself completely and go to Mass only when I could do so without his knowing it. But Decazeville is a very small town. . . . Everything is seen, everything is known. It was a period of extreme tension, a very hard time.

Decazeville is also a tough town; life there was harsh. Our living conditions were very different from what we had been used to in Paris. A few months ago, I returned to Decazeville to preach, and I recognized everything—the factory is still there. . . . I had a reunion with some of my fellow workers and that was a great joy. It was a straitened life, not just for the refugees, but for all the workers. We did profit from a relative prosperity: milk, butter, meat and potatoes were obtainable. All we had to do was take a bicycle and go in search of them. Of course, we had to pay dearly, but we found what we needed. There was also the advantage that we had as much coal as we could wish for.

By listening to the conversations of the Spanish republicans, anarchists and people of all sorts, I encountered a cosmopolitan world that until then I had known only in the abstract. There were some very colorful characters. Nobody in the workplace said who he was, but I took part in all kinds of fantastic discussions that greatly marked and instructed me. Inevitably, everybody wound up by letting you glimpse something of his previous life. And those people adopted me: I was still a little boy, really a boy. They were especially

[16] *Bachot* is slang for *baccalauréat.* —TRANS.

considerate of me because I did not have calloused hands. And since I had my *bachot,* I was an intellectual. None of them had a *bachot!*

At Decazeville, I met with still more human diversity, including that of the worker-peasants, the Rouergats. Before I left, I had begun to learn a bit of their patois, the *langue d'oc.* Today I can remember only the swear words. You know, I was at the age when one is avid to understand. A kind of brutal fraternity reigned among us. It was not always generous, it is true, because the reflexes of flight and self-preservation are very powerful: absolute altruism that goes as far as giving one's life is a rare virtue. But even so, there was something very healthy in that world of rather rough and secretive people. I was different in that marginal world, but it was a place where everyone had his differences.

WOLTON: *In what way did you feel different?*

LUSTIGER: Well, for one thing, I was a Jew in hiding. I cannot very well say how the Spanish anarchist felt.

MISSIKA: *Why did you leave Decazeville?*

LUSTIGER: We were threatened again. I was called in by the police: "Show us your papers. Come on, tell the truth, we know very well who you are. . . . " Then they stamped "Jew" on my official false ID card. At that point I knew that the noose was being tightened, and I said to my father, "It's time we left."

On the advice of the engineer who headed the factory, I had been to Toulouse two or three times during that year to see about enrolling in some chemistry courses at the Faculté des Sciences. I had used those occasions to make some contacts. In those days the train trip was long. We left abruptly, without saying a word to anyone. My father was completely lost; it was as though our roles had been reversed. I took charge and arranged to have him hidden in an agricultural school run by Jesuits. With false papers, he was hired as an agricultural worker.

MISSIKA: *What year was that?*

LUSTIGER: In the spring of 1944. After making arrangements for my father, I had to find something for myself. I also had to hide, of course, and to get false papers. At first, I was taken in by a group of young resisters associated with *Témoignage chrétien.* I slept on bundles of that clandestine journal that were yet to be distributed. The network protecting me was directly connected with a Jesuit, Father Ponchet, a student chaplain at Toulouse, and I went to see him.

I got past the next stage, thanks to Abbé Bezombes, vicar at Saint-Michel, since then a military chaplain, who was an important figure in the *Résistance*. He proposed that I take a job as a counselor at a summer camp he had organized for underprivileged children from Toulouse. Therefore, I spent the final weeks of the occupation—until the liberation of Toulouse—at Saint-Sulpice-sur-Lèze, a picturesque village in Haute-Garonne.

MISSIKA: *You have said that you knew that death was involved in deportation, but when did you discover the extent of the genocide?*

LUSTIGER: Oh, only afterward! We had had no idea of what was happening. However, my father did have quite a strange premonition in 1938. Even though he had never set foot in Poland since he left in 1918, that year he decided to go and see his family. I remember very well the account he gave of that trip. It was a final visit to a world about to be obliterated.

III

JUDAISM AND CHRISTIANITY

The Pagan Temptation of Christianity

DOMINIQUE WOLTON: *Can we go back to your discovery of Christianity?*

JEAN-MARIE LUSTIGER: It was as though I knew about it already. Not its customs, rites, practices, but its content. I seemed to have understood it beforehand. I was even surprised when other people did not understand what I understood. I continue to be, by the way. Those affirmations touching on the mystery of God, the meaning of the revelation through Christ, God's call to humanity—to his people—are all evident to me. They are a part of the logic of faith, and I am stupefied to discover that there are believers, steeped in Christianity since childhood, who do not understand this.

WOLTON: *Do you have an example?*

LUSTIGER: Oh, many! The Eucharist, the Mass. Even though I had not had a Jewish education, I knew enough to recognize the ritual of the Passover in the Eucharist. It is the sacrifice of the Lamb, of the suffering Messiah; it is deliverance and salvation, the grace of God. When I discover Christians who have lost this reference and no longer understand the Eucharist, I say to myself: they are pagans. They do not know what they are saying or doing or how much they are in contradiction with what they are supposed to believe.

Another example: my memory of the first Holy Week in which I took part in 1941 is still fresh. I went with a group of classmates to an Oratorian seminary in Montsoult. For three afternoons, we joined the community in singing the office of Tenebrae, a service made up of Psalms and biblical readings. Chanting the Psalms, listening to the Lamentations of Jeremiah, I felt it was obvious that Catholics were sharing the inheritance that God had initially destined for Israel, the elder son, the firstborn.

WOLTON: *You saw a definite continuity between the two?*

LUSTIGER: I saw more than continuity. At last, I was able to grasp the solution to what had been insoluble problems. I mean, the key to the enigma was given to me, in a new mystery: the mystery of Christ, the crucified Messiah.

The continuity is marked in the texts of the revelation and in Christianity's use of the Bible. In the chapel at Montsoult, there were stained-glass windows depicting the relationship between the two Testaments. Also, at the cathedral in Chartres, I was able to greet holy King David. At Germigny-des-Prés, a Carolingian church, I joined the angels who, in the mosaic in the apse, are worshipping the Ark of the Covenant.

I was not in alien country. I was one of the older sons. I did nothing more than begin to enjoy the heritage that had been promised to me. Only much later was I able to express more precisely what I had immediately understood intuitively: the problem of God's relationship to pagans and Jews is at the heart of all Scripture, of both the Old and New Testaments.

WOLTON: *To pagans and Jews, admittedly. But to Jews and Christians?*

LUSTIGER: But they have the same history. The problem raised by Saint Paul and practically all of the New Testament writers concerned "Christians", "Messianics", who, both Jews and pagans, had entered into the new Covenant of the Spirit. One of the proofs that the Messiah has come is that pagans also have access to the Covenant because the Spirit has been given to them. Through faith, they too can unite themselves to the King of Israel. "In Christ" (that is, in the Messiah), according to Saint Paul's expression, all fulfill the precepts of the law and share in the New Covenant where they obey God, thanks to the gift of the Holy Spirit. In other words, the promises regarding the universality of God's reign are on the way to being carried out.

WOLTON: *You mean fulfilled. . . .*

LUSTIGER: "Fulfilled"? The word is too ambiguous and has stirred up too many arguments. It is acceptable only if it conveys a sense of plenitude, of obtaining the full measure of what has been promised. But this realization evidently implies an internal mutation and choices. The question of Israel's historic destiny and its election, the question of the destiny of the Jewish people was at one time an obsession for me, and it still is in some ways. It is completely different from the question about the Basques' or Bretons' relationship to the French nation. It is a question that involves the salvation of humanity. Some people will diagnose my obsession as Jewish paranoia. I wish to emphasize that I am purely and simply a believer.

WOLTON: *Do you really believe that most Christians share your point of view?*

LUSTIGER: Pagans, even when they become Christians, are constantly tempted to refuse the particularity of history and divine election. They are tempted to make Jesus the projection of the ideal man that each culture and civilization creates within itself. That is the most instinctive way of bringing God down to man's scale—in other words, of falling into idolatry by worshipping oneself. Each pagan civilization that becomes Christian is likely to be enticed into making Jesus its Apollo and projecting on him its own image of man, an image that it finds pleasing.

Christ himself, the figure of Christ in its reality, can assume every face of humanity, but that can happen only because he is first of all the individual who was born in Bethlehem of Judea. A phrase from Saint Matthew can enlighten us: the Magi who arrive are pagans and they ask, "Where is the King of the Jews?" He has to be searched for, and in the end, after scrutinizing the Scriptures, they find him "in Bethlehem of Judea", and not somewhere else. And it is Jesus they find, not "an" infant, but "this" infant. Thus, the contingency of the Absolute is the very form of Revelation.

Fundamentally, the mystery of God's becoming human flesh remains an almost insurmountable contradiction.... A rational mind can dismiss it as a myth, something that will not stand up to logic. After all, what does God-man mean? The mystery is of the same nature when God speaks with Moses "as a man speaks to a friend" (Ex 33:11), and it deepens when the Word of God makes itself human word and inscription on the two tablets of the law. It is very difficult for our minds to conceive that the Transcendent communicates himself. Is it possible that he who is beyond all representation, who cannot be imagined, can become accessible? Certainly man can conceive that there is another side to the frontier that his thought has established. He can say to himself that although he has determined that frontier, every limit has a beyond that is greater than all thought, too great to be imagined. But Transcendence, as it has historically revealed itself in person to the Jewish people, is the Almighty whose initiative literally stuns the human mind: it places it vis-à-vis God. God is not simply the "no-man's-land" beyond the limit that man himself has discovered and will have to cross sooner or later.

God's revelation manifests the Presence of the One who presents himself in person as Absolute Subject, in the face of whom man himself materializes as subject. It is the revelation of the One who is both Creator and Redeemer. The Inconceivable declares himself, he says who he is, and makes himself accessible to man. That act drastically changes the human condition and in a sense even annihilates it: "Then I will take away my hand, and you shall see my back; but my face shall not be seen", God says to Moses. "You cannot see my face; for man shall not see me and live" (Ex 33:23, 20). And, simultaneously, this Presence gives substance to man by saying to him who *man* is, thus allowing him to live accordingly.

The fact that God presents himself and speaks to Moses "as a friend" is already the mystery of the Incarnation of God's Word who makes himself our flesh, makes himself known to us and gives of himself. And the fact that the Messiah is the eternal Son of God made flesh is *also* a metonymy: he is Israel, not by substitution, but by inclusion. He is the one in whom the filial condition of the holy nation is realized. Jesus observed and fulfilled the commandments given by God to Moses for his people, Israel. He faultlessly fulfilled what had been required of the Jew for living in holiness—a holiness required for the salvation of all nations, for the redemption of the sons of Adam, for bringing together and uniting all that divine generosity has spread and lavished on the world. Through him comes deliverance from sin and access to life.

WOLTON: *Is what you have been saying obvious to Christians?*

LUSTIGER: It is difficult for Christians to recognize Jesus' Jewish roots. Some of them would reason that Christ chose a country, a civilization, a culture, a language, and that as Christians, we must love what Christ chose. But there is something absurd about such reasoning if it implies that Christ in his condition and human will was able, unlike other men, to choose the time and place of his birth. The eternal Word of God became flesh in Mary, daughter of Israel, because God his Father had previously chosen Mary's people and had confided his Name and his Word to them. Christ was sent in the fullness of time. He was expected by God's people and was to be recognized by them. In plain language, Jesus could not simply pick a place and date for his birth. It was not by preference or chance that he was born in Bethlehem rather than Lutetia or Rome. If he was going to be recognized as the "King of the Jews" and the envoy of the unique God, he could be born only in Bethlehem. That this title is often ignored or refused, not by the Church, but by a certain number of Christians or Christian generations, is a sign of forgetfulness, of a grave deficiency in thinking; indeed, it is a sign of sin.

WOLTON: *Yes, but this forgetfulness has lasted a very long time and has had considerable effects....*

LUSTIGER: Forgetfulness is always blended with memory to make up the moving forces of human history. Each Christian generation is characterized as much by its blindnesses as by its intuitions. That explains why entire peoples can drift along over long periods in situations that have no exit. For example, there were those barbarians who were both Christians and Arians,[1] meaning that they did not believe in the Son's divinity. Other examples can be found in Christianity's internal divisions, the separation of the churches of the East and the West, or what happened in the sixteenth century at the time of the Protestant Reformation. Thus, today there exist various and sundry ways of being Christian. Over time, these differences have been transformed into cultural elements and are transmitted by education. That this can be so remains an enigma. Either these blindnesses, these omissions are normal divergences in mankind's history, or else they are departures from faith, departures from fidelity to the Faith. I happen to believe that they are the latter.

Continuity and Newness

WOLTON: *Do you think of Christianity as being a fulfillment of Judaism?*

LUSTIGER: There you go with that word again. "Fulfillment" has many meanings. Of course, human history is not finished. According to the Bible, we are in a time of the Covenant and a time of passage. For Christians, the coming of Christ and his paschal mystery renew the divine Covenant and give man full access to God. In his Messiah, God fulfilled the promises made to Israel. And the Scripture again uses the expression "the fullness of time" for announcing the return of Christ and his glorious manifestation. Fulfillment connotes all that.

WOLTON: *But in religious history, the word is often used by Christians to define the relationship between the two religions.*

LUSTIGER: We cannot speak in terms of chronological stages that would determine ruptures or continuity. For the Christian faith, the coming of the Messiah is a divine intervention. It was previously announced, promised and prepared. The novelty of this visit by God does not annul the preceding divine interventions: it attests to them and reveals their universal, divine significance. God did not go back on his promise when he revealed in his own Son what had been hidden in his chosen people and what, in the Resurrection of his Christ, became the eternal *nouveauté* promised to Israel and hoped for by all the sons of Adam. It is in this way that the New Covenant realizes the divine Testament whose promises it makes "old" as well as fulfilled. There is a traditional adage: "The New Testament is hidden in the Old; the Old comes

[1] Arianism, a Christian heresy initiated by Arius of Alexandria, was condemned at the Council of Nicaea in 325.

to light in the New." The question remains throughout time: Are these divine revelations to be recognized and welcomed, or are they to be refused?

WOLTON: *Fine. I am going to word my question differently. Why is it that most Christians find it so difficult to accept what you see as the natural link between Judaism and Christianity?*

LUSTIGER: Throughout the Christian tradition there are witnesses to and precedents for a belief that you seem tempted to attribute to me alone, or to the Church after Vatican II or else to regard as something entirely recent. The link between Judaism and Christianity has never been broken, and the understanding of the relationship between the two Testaments has never disappeared.

I suggest that you look at Father de Lubac's work on the meaning of Scripture.[2] In excavating the treasures left to us from the patristic age, he shows us ways of understanding Scripture and its present relevance. He brings together a wealth of citations from early and medieval authors, and, in particular, he demonstrates that the opposition *carnal-spiritual* is not the equivalent of the distinction between the Old and New Testaments. There can be a "carnal" understanding of the New Testament, just as there is a "spiritual" understanding of the Old. The Messiah, Christ, frees us from the "carnal" understanding and initiates us into a spiritual one because in his Person he is the new and eternal Truth of the Covenant and of all its structure and development. The theological tradition that teaches this has solid support, but its opposite can also be found, because theories on the "deicidal people" and their rejection of Christ have been formulated and expounded.

JEAN-LOUIS MISSIKA: *It is the theories on the deicidal people that have dominated for quite a long time.*

LUSTIGER: Yes, but it is essential to verify the context in which they were nurtured. I do not have the historical competence to do it. However, it does seem clear that the state of theology, of the evolution of Christian thought, can be assessed by its positions on the subject of Israel. I believe, for example, that Luther's anti-Semitism is not innocent and has something to do with his nominalism.

WOLTON: *Are you saying that, at any given moment in history, support for the theory of a discontinuity between the Old and New Testaments reflects a weakness of theology?*

[2] Henri de Lubac (1896–) is a French Jesuit theologian and historian who was made a cardinal by John Paul II in 1983. The work referred to is *L'Exégèse médiévale.* —TRANS.

LUSTIGER: Yes. It is a sign of perversions and divergences. Theology is not a neutral science. It is the means by which men try to articulate the contents and implications of the revelation with the aid of the Church's Magisterium. At the same time, it is a source of progress for human thought since, in confronting the mystery, it fertilizes the fields of philosophy and anthropology. But the theologian's understanding of the revelation is commensurate with his capacity for thought. By that very fact, his own fidelity is subjected to a terrible ordeal.

There is always discontinuity where sin and death reign. But the continuity of sacred history attests that God's faithfulness is ever greater. To sum it up, the Christian Tradition witnesses to the continuity of God's plan and his fidelity to the election of Israel. But, in spite of significant examples, this witness has often been overshadowed. Saint Augustine's works are sometimes tinged with an anti-Semitism that is considered aggressive today because we read his texts with an awareness of Luther's rereading of them. Simultaneously, in the *City of God,* Augustine shows a remarkable understanding of the continuity of the history of salvation. What he says may seem new to you. He declares that all that has been said and given to the Jews is a part of the history of salvation and remains offered to them irrevocably. What is offered to the Jews, he says, is a grace that spills over to Christians of pagan origin, allowing them to enter into the Covenant and to come to know God through the deeds of the Messiah, his Son, and through the gift of the Holy Spirit. Everything that Augustine says there has belonged to Christian thought from its origins.

MISSIKA: *That may be so, but it was the Church Fathers who theorized Christian anti-Semitism.*

LUSTIGER: To some extent, I agree. But you cannot read Saint John Chrysostom in the light of *Mein Kampf.* No! That would be grossly anachronistic, and it will not hold up historically. Let me go into more detail. In the tradition of the Church Fathers, there were certain ones, like Saint John Chrysostom, who spread intolerably hostile notions about Jews. But in the same tradition, there exist texts that have such a strong theological and spiritual continuity with the Old Testament that today it is impossible to know whether they are Jewish or Christian. And do not forget that the early Church adopted the Psalms as its prayers.

There is anti-Judaism in that tradition. But the traditional polemic with the Synagogue was a dispute between inheritors. It was not a refusal of the heritage—which makes it completely different from modern anti-Semitism. It is just not the same thing! Christians reproached Jews for an infidelity to the faith and tradition of Israel that they recognized as being of divine origin. But the Nazis loathed the Jews, their faith and their traditions with an equal intensity.

On the religious plane, the overshadowing of the relationship between the Testaments and the contempt for Jews are always signs of a grave deficiency among Christians. In the second century, a heresy led by Marcion wanted to suppress all references to the Old Testament, to purge from the Scriptures all mention of it. No one would dare to call himself a Marcionite today, but Marcionism remains latent and sometimes explicit in Africa and Asia. Cardinal Ratzinger has recently reminded us of this. He was referring to people who, under the pretext of affirming their cultural roots, say, "What do we have to do with the Jews? Our Old Testament is our traditional culture." But, in that case, Jesus risks becoming a black Apollo or an Asiatic Hercules.

WOLTON: *But in the Church's history, it is rather the tendency that has insisted on the rupture and difference between the Old and New Testaments that has dominated.*

LUSTIGER: I beg your pardon! History and sociology may support your opinion, but it is not true from the point of view of faith and theology. I am not forgetting the persecution of Jewish communities in medieval Christianity. But the points of view must be distinguished.

The Church Fathers remind us incessantly that Moses was speaking to Israel in the name of God. If they criticized Jews, it was for being unfaithful to their vocation and their own Scriptures. The Church Fathers knew the Bible by heart. There has never been a Christian Bible without the Old Testament.

I am not saying that Christian thought has always been perfectly unequivocal on the matter or that it has not also undergone temptation. Every man is tempted. Where did Hegel come from? Where has all that thought—often rationalist, often gnostic and, thus, anti-Jewish—come from, if not from the temptations of the West? But these thoughts are found just as often among Jewish thinkers. Spinoza is a rather well-known Jew, and there is a celebrated Hegelian called Marx. In fact, the history of religious thought and the history of humanity merge, and men are forever tempted and tried in their freedom. History is not static. It is freedom and the adventure of the human mind that test our faith.

WOLTON: *Precisely. Why is it that there has never been a general council on this fundamental question of the relationship between the two Testaments?*

LUSTIGER: Because the relationship has never been contested. Many important beliefs have never been defined by a council because they were never questioned. They are truths so confidently possessed that an authenticated definition has been unnecessary.

WOLTON: *Looking back on my religious education, I recall that the Old Testament was never forgotten, but its position was inferior to the New.*

LUSTIGER: Were you taught that the liturgy refers to "Saint Abraham"?

WOLTON: *No, "Saint Abraham" was never mentioned!*

LUSTIGER: Of course, you were not taught to say "Saint" Abraham. But in the thirteenth century, he was invoked. I asked the question because I knew what your answer would be. In fact, since the seventeenth century there has been an overshadowing of a certain number of similar elements that were previously a part of the Church's everyday teaching. Take iconography. The representation of the Synagogue in Church architecture is not limited to the blindfolded figure on the cathedral in Strasbourg. And even there, the Synagogue is shown as the sister of the Church. There are also figures representing the holy patriarchs, the tree of Jesse, and all the honored prophets who are venerated along with the evangelists as spokesmen for God. What I am telling you reflects the concrete position of the Church. The people who built the cathedrals were not on the fringes of society! The images we see there were not conceived by a few eccentric or clandestine Church members. This iconography represented "official" thought. It is significant, too, that Saint Thomas raised the question as to whether circumcision could be considered a sacrament. And he also reflected on how the doctrine of the sacraments could be applied to the faith of the Old Testament. I am reminding you of all this so that you understand that it would have been completely inexplicable if the Ecumenical Council of Vatican II had suddenly published a text that changed Church doctrine and thus contradicted all that Christianity had taught up to that time! Such an occurrence is impossible, by definition.

But what, from the nineteenth century I think, was called anti-Semitism remains to be explained.

Christian Anti-Judaism and Atheistic Anti-Semitism

MISSIKA: *Yes, it began to be called anti-Semitism in the nineteenth century. For the preceding period, it is more accurate to speak of anti-Judaism. But the change of words does not preclude their association. Besides, the word* anti-Semitism *makes no sense.*

LUSTIGER: None at all. It is a great pity that Pius XI chose to say, "We are spiritual Semites." Although he meant well, he conceded too much to anti-Semites by acknowledging their category. But he was using the language of the times in his protest against Nazism.

It seems to me that we have to go back to the eighteenth century to understand the problem. It was then that, in Western Europe, the emancipation of Jews and the rise of modern anti-Semitism began simultaneously. What was the prevalent attitude of the philosophers and preachers toward Jews? In both philosophy and religion there was a theology of the Enlightenment that was extremely summary, and there were also the first signs of an anti-Semitism of the Voltairean type. Why was Voltaire such an anti-Semite?

WOLTON: *What would you answer?*

LUSTIGER: My answer is that Voltaire, although a product of Christian civilization, is not Christian. And I believe that Hitler's anti-Semitism had its roots in the anti-Semitism of the Enlightenment and not in a Christian anti-Semitism. I do not know if historians have pushed their analyses that far.

WOLTON: *You really believe that there cannot be Christian anti-Semitism....*

LUSTIGER: I believe that profoundly. There can be antagonisms, there are heartbreaking conflicts. The Church can disagree with Judaism as far as the Messiah's person and the salvation of nations are concerned, but there is no anti-Semitism of the Voltairean sort—that is, an intolerance toward the Jewish existence in its substance, toward the Jew's power of revelation.

MISSIKA: *Meaning?*

LUSTIGER: A refusal of the Jews' divine election, a hate for their religious singularity, which is considered irrational and hence unacceptable. In looking at this question, the anti-Semitism of Voltaire and Diderot must not be discounted. It was their current of thought that created feelings of shame in German Jews during the eighteenth and nineteenth centuries.

WOLTON: *Then Christians are absolved?*

LUSTIGER: I did not say that. But one fact must not hide another. It is essential to observe the spiritual histories of societies and to understand how they are modified by the values pursued.

Until the eighteenth century, the spiritual history of the West merges with the history of Christianity. Throughout this history, Christianity's relationship to Judaism is a test of its faithfulness to its source. Thus, Christianity's annals record both the faithfulness and unfaithfulness of Christian nations to this source. It is a record of sins and of God's mercy toward peoples to whom he gave the grace to receive the revelation. Even ideal societies—I mean by that particular communities founded on an ideal of holiness: religious orders, for example—have histories that are made up of sin and reform, of periods of decadence and rebirth.

My thesis is that, yes, spiritual history is marked by anti-Semitism. By its very nature, Christianity cannot be anti-Judaic, but the anti-Semitism of Christian nations has to be explained. By the way, I count Voltaire—as well as Hegel and Marx—among Christian thinkers. They were all inheritors of Christian culture. Christianity was a part of their backgrounds whether they liked it or not. They are lost children, rebellious children, but they spoke the language of the Christian West. And Nazism was born among a people who had been baptized. But Nazism was a refusal of Christianity, a pagan resurgence. Official Soviet anti-Semitism is also of this nature. They are both fruits of the same rationalism . . . and too many Christians have succumbed to it.

WOLTON: *You are saying that anti-Semitism has deeper roots in atheism than in Christianity?*

LUSTIGER: They cannot be separated like that. The explanation has to be all-encompassing. The West has been marked by the Jewish as well as the Christian tradition. Then why has it treated Jews the way it has? This maltreatment is a sign of its crisis. And in citing certain influential Western authors who are rarely included in the history of anti-Semitism, I am making the point that modern, rational, atheistic thought is anti-Semitic. More so than Christian thought. Modern anti-Semitism is bound to be radical because it is an antitheism. The Church, on the contrary, in being strictly faithful to her message, can resist and condemn the anti-Semitic practices of Christian peoples, the social injustices, the persecutions and exclusions of minorities that are born of jealousy, self-rightousness, envy or ambition.

WOLTON: *And why can atheism not do this?*

LUSTIGER: Because atheism cannot accept that the Jew is the figure of the Absolute present in a contingent revelation, in the specificity of history. Whereas Christianity speaks of the humiliated Messiah, Maurras,[3] who is no longer Christian, speaks of "Jewish venom" that the Church spread in spite of the Roman Empire. That is also what Hitler said, and the Stalinists: One must

[3] Charles Maurras (1869–1952), a French writer and political activist of the extreme right, was a cofounder of *l'Action française* and attacked what he thought to be the causes of disorder in art and political life.—TRANS.

be wary of Jews. Just as one must be wary of Christians. Atheism cannot tolerate the particular presence of the Absolute in history. The only absolute it can admit is in men's hands. For the atheist, the Jew will never be reliable, unless he, in turn, declares himself to be an atheist. Otherwise, he is a potential traitor.

MISSIKA: *But why should atheistic thought be more anti-Semitic than anti-Christian?*

LUSTIGER: Because it can always attempt to harness Christianity by proposing that it become a national religion. It can try to secularize Christianity and hence reduce its influence. But the Jews are on the margins of society, they are "foreigners". As Jews, they remain "unsecularizable", unassimilable. Admittedly, with the Enlightenment a certain secularization of Jews began. But almost three hundred years later, Jewish "foreignness" continues to set them apart. It may be possible for Christians to think temporarily that they are sheltered from such threats, but they should make no mistake about it, as Maritain said, "when Jews are persecuted, Christianity is menaced in its flesh." As proof, it suffices to evoke the nihilist invectives, so common in modern literature, against Christ as a figure of cowardliness and resentment, the figure for the religion of the weak.

MISSIKA: *I wish to make an objection. A little while ago, you made a comparison between early Christian anti-Semitism and pagan or atheistic anti-Semitism dating from the Enlightenment. It should be noted that the former has had a much longer time to do its harm. All the anti-Semitic themes, all that has been said about Jews for the past twenty centuries, was articulated between the first and fifth centuries, especially by the Church Fathers. The carnal Jew, the worshipper of the golden calf, the thief, the fiendish Jew, the trafficker—not to mention the Jews who spilled the blood of Christ. If Voltaire is anti-Semitic, it is because his writings echo a theme that was perfected in the polemic of the early Christians against the Synagogue.*

LUSTIGER: No, a pagan anti-Semitism, predating Christianity, did exist.

MISSIKA: *I disagree completely with what you say. Jules Isaac's*[4] *work on the genesis of anti-Semitism clearly shows that there was no real anti-Semitism before Christ.*

[4] Jules Isaac (1877–1963) was one of the prominent secularized French Jewish thinkers at the turn of the century and an author of the Third Republic's "official" history.—TRANS.

LUSTIGER: Well, then, we disagree. Pagan anti-Semitism has to be explained. Why were the Romans so fierce in pursuing the Jews?

MISSIKA: *Because the Jews resisted.*

LUSTIGER: Yes, they were the only ones to resist ancient paganism when it clothed itself in political authority.

MISSIKA: *They were simply a people who fought back.*

LUSTIGER: It was more than that. Take another look at such authors as Theodore Reinach and Marcel Simon.

MISSIKA: *Extracting what Roman authors said about Jews does not make sense unless the citations are compared with what was said about other peoples, the Gauls or the Greeks, for example. If all non-Romans are scorned, it is impossible to speak of a specific anti-Judaism in antiquity.*

LUSTIGER: But your examples do not date from the same period. The ancient pagan anti-Semitism penetrated the Church after Constantine. Some of its themes were purely and simply taken over by the Church at that time. Such themes are completely absent from the New Testament. There are traces of the ongoing religious conflict in the Scriptures and in the first writings of the Fathers, but the nature of the conflict was different. As far as I can see, the institutional opposition to Jews began with Constantine. It was then that things began to take on another face. It is important to situate the precise date—and it is not to exonerate Christianity that I say this—when the political conflict between the Synagogue and the Church began. It happened coincidentally with the union of the empire and the Church, and the disappearance of the Jewish church in Jerusalem.

MISSIKA: *There was also the problem of competition between the religions.*

LUSTIGER: Yes. Throughout the first century, Christianity was a Jewish affair. The religious competition between Jews and Christians was very keen. Then came the conflict with Rome and the problem of Israel's permanence as a people. Although Jewish proselytism existed throughout the Roman Empire, the physical existence of Jews as a people was being threatened. During the first Christian century and again at the beginning of the second, those who were called "the Jews" were Jews of the Synagogue and their proselytes, while the others, who were called Christians, were Jews who believed in Christ and were united in the churches with the pagans who had been converted to the

Gospel. We must not project onto the religious argument of this period, which was indeed sometimes harsh, the one that came into existence later, at the beginning of the fifth century.

MISSIKA: *You have cited Saint John Chrysostom. What he says is interesting because he invalidates the often-advanced thesis that there existed a popular anti-Semitism that the Church Fathers—or, in any case, the priests of the epoch—were forced to go along with. Saint John's polemic against the Synagogue was intended to dissuade Christians from going there, to dissuade them from consulting rabbis for answers to moral questions. He was struggling against a fusion, against the building of any bridges between the Synagogue and the Church.*

LUSTIGER: Yes, but there is also Saint Jerome who consulted the rabbis because he wanted to learn Hebrew in order to translate the Bible into Latin.

WOLTON: *Nevertheless, was it not at that time that all the main themes of anti-Semitism took shape?*

LUSTIGER: That is partly true. What I challenge is a completely uniform vision of history that would maintain that for twenty centuries Christian anti-Judaism and atheistic anti-Semitism have been one and the same. The Jewish minority was always physically menaced, and it is a fact that an ideology of conflict was elaborated. But it is false to say that this ideology has remained unchanged from 30 A.D. to the end of the twentieth century.

MISSIKA: *But it did crystallize during the first millennium.*

LUSTIGER: There were exceptions. Some believers said and did the contrary. How do you explain Córdoba? How do you explain the first Poland?

MISSIKA: *I admit that there were exceptions. But even so, the system generating the decline in Jewish-Christian relations was set up during the first thousand years. What happened afterward was simply the continuation of that policy of contempt and degradation.*

LUSTIGER: I repeat, I am not convinced of that. The periods must be delineated more clearly. I would almost be ready to concede that what you are saying applies to the period that extends from the eighteenth to the twentieth century. Within these years there appeared an ideological anti-Semitism that has engendered great turbulence and unspeakable crimes. I am not saying that there were no disgraceful injustices in previous periods—

the accusations of ritual murder, the *rouelle,*[5] the segregation, the Marranos.[6] But, during the first thousand years, all of Christian Europe claimed the heritage of Israel; it was even proud of it to the point of jealousy. Christian generations reproached the Jews for not being faithful to their fathers and their prophets, but they never doubted the sacred history of Israel. Projecting the modern ideological radicalization of atheistic and political anti-Semitism onto a religious past when Christians and Jews venerated the same heritage would reflect a serious misunderstanding of Western history. The old anti-Jewish polemics are certainly not sufficient for explaining the concentration camps.

MISSIKA: *And you do not believe that there is a link between the two?*

LUSTIGER: There is more to it than that. The Nazis wanted to exterminate homosexuals, the physically and mentally handicapped and the Gypsies as well. They also wanted to annihilate the Poles in concentration camps. Their contempt for man was directed at all sorts of men. But the Jews, as figures of election, caused jealousy and catalyzed on themselves the Nazis' negation of man and God.

WOLTON: *Would you go so far as to say that, in the ideas that led up to the concentration camps, atheistic thought had more responsibility than Christian thought?*

LUSTIGER: Atheistic thought is a temptation born of Christian thought. Only someone who has been confronted with the question of God can be an atheist. Only a Jew or a Christian can become an atheist. A Buddhist cannot become an atheist like us. Moreover, the source of this atheism must be specified. Does it come from Christians in general? From theologians? From clerical political parties? And what are the responsibilities we are talking about? Do you mean to say that Churchmen should have been more lucid? In their particularity, the Jewish people carry the heart of the revelation. And in a certain way, they also bear the image of the Messiah, of Christ. The way nations or generations treat Jews is an indication—this is my personal conviction—of how they treat Christ, of what they really think of God. What they do to Jews confirms what they do to Christ. What is said against Jews condemns those who say it. All this goes well beyond the economic, social or political aspects of the matter. If Jews are singled out for persecution, it is not only because Christians have elaborated specific arguments against them. It is

[5] The red and white "little wheel" that Jews were forced to wear as a mark of identification in fourteenth-century France.—TRANS.

[6] Spanish Jews who were forced to convert in the fifteenth century, among whom certain ones remained secretly faithful to the Jewish religion.

because Jews carry within themselves that which is most sacred and, hence, least tolerable to others: the sign of divine election. That is why anti-Semitism cannot be completely assimilated with racism and xenophobia. Anti-Semitism is one of the most serious spiritual questions in all of history.

Judaism Today

WOLTON: *How do you view Judaism and its relations with Christianity?*

LUSTIGER: I have no authorization to express Judaism's opinion of Christianity.

MISSIKA: *I propose a solution. Suppose we take a dispute from the Middle Ages between the Church and the Synagogue. Very often these disputes between priests and rabbis focused on the following question: "Has the Messiah come?" One of the rabbis' arguments was: "Is it possible to affirm the Messiah's presence in a world where Jews are suffering so much?" How would you answer that argument today?*

LUSTIGER: The rabbis' question is pertinent. I would like to say a few words about both the question and the response.

The Messiah is a suffering Messiah. For Christians, his coming is an enigma, something incomprehensible, paradoxical, because the Messiah in whom we believe is humiliated and crucified. His work of redemption is still hidden, and history is not finished. As for the rabbis, when they speak of Messianic hope, they are evoking the completion of history. The Hassidic movement with its great diversity foresaw something else; it more or less identified the Messiah with Israel. To the question of how one can say that the Messiah has come if Israel is still suffering, Hassidim's response—at the most extreme point of Israel's suffering in the eighteenth century, just as the Enlightenment is bursting forth at the dawn of modern times, which are going to bring the most violent wave of anti-Semitism ever and the Jews' most cruel ordeal since the destruction of the temple—is completely astonishing: the Messianic subject as they describe it is Israel identified with the suffering Messiah. At least, that is the way I interpret their point of view.

The Christians' Messiah is a humiliated Messiah; he is presently hidden, his glory is concealed, in his disciples and his Body. His glory is with God, because the end of history has not yet come. The Messianic hope is given in this continuing history, and Israel still has its role to play in it. The Messiah's hidden role in which his disciples, the "Messianics"—that is, Christians—believe and the role or the mission of Israel have something mysterious in common. That is why I said that the rabbis' response was partly right: the Messiah will come again in glory. But why did he have to suffer before entering into his glory? It is a formidable question that the Apostles, the first disciples, themselves came up against. And it was then that their spiritual "healing" took place because their act of faith, a gift from the Spirit, restored their sight, healed what the Gospel calls a blindness or a hardening of the heart. Christ's disciples eventually understand that it was necessary that the Messiah suffer before entering into his glory—and even now, in the members of his Body, his suffering continues. History had to go on, and it had to be a history, not of errancy and despair, but of compassion and redemption.

MISSIKA: *Then Israel (and hence Judaism) has its raison d'être as long as the Messiah has not come in glory?*

LUSTIGER: Yes, Israel has its raison d'être until the coming of the heavenly Kingdom.

MISSIKA: *In spite of Christianity?*

LUSTIGER: The "Christian" category does not erase the categories of Jew and pagan; the Church does not deny the differences, she relativizes them by referring them to Christ.

MISSIKA: *But what about the Jew who is completely disinterested in Jesus? Is he in error or in truth?*

LUSTIGER: In error or truth? It is not man but God who can answer that question.

WOLTON: *Let me word it differently. What meaning does the Christian give to Judaism's presence today?*

LUSTIGER: Well, Saint Paul articulates the answer for us. The Jews, the Jewish people, exist because God has chosen them. They have no other reason for existing, not even national sentiment. Otherwise, we would be able to give a sociohistorical explanation by saying that the Jewish people's survival is of the same order as that of the Basques or Hungarians. Not for one second do I accept this kind of explanation. The existence of the chosen people concerns God's plan for humanity: if Israel exists, it is because God has chosen this people for the purpose of saving all mankind. But election is not so much a privilege as a mission.

I mention in passing that Nazism perverted the notion of a chosen people in order to create a diabolical messianism of their own. It was not subjected to

God, but on the contrary looked to the coming of the Superman and thus to the annihilation of the rest of humanity. Nazism identified "election" with domination and unconscionable privilege.

To come back to your question, it is God who has favored Israel. God brought it into existence for the salvation of all humanity, for the coming of the reign, and, according to the promise, it is in Israel that the Messiah, suffering, has already appeared. Until the Messiah's coming in glory, the Jew remains, and he remains a Jew, whether he is Christian or not.

WOLTON: *But the Jew who is Christian accepts the Messiah, while the one who is not refuses him.*

LUSTIGER: It cannot be said that Israel did not recognize the Messiah. The original Church, after all, was a Jewish Church.

MISSIKA: *But that was never in doubt.*

LUSTIGER: But it was! It is a historical truth that was obscured for a long time! The research of the past fifty years, in various domains, has brought this back to light. The Jewish Church was first leveled by the Byzantines and then by Islam; hence, it was twice destroyed. The Chaldean Christians, whose liturgical language is Aramaic, say that they are the direct descendants of the Jewish communities that bordered the Euphrates. Some people claim that the present Melkite Christians represent the Semite Church in the East. They were twice assimilated, but they survived. They adopted the Byzantine rite while the other churches kept the Syriac liturgy—whether Chaldean, Syrian-Occidental, or Antiochene (more or less influenced by the surrounding culture with its Byzantine and Latin elements). Moreover, they also adopted Arabic, whereas the other groups kept their own languages in the liturgy. These Christians are perhaps the remnants of that first Church.

Why did the totality of the Jews not recognize Jesus as the Messiah? It is a tough and troubling question. Saint Paul reminds us of God's patience, men's sin and their redemption. I ask a corresponding question: "Why did the totality of the pagans not recognize the Messiah that Israel was awaiting?" Because neither have all pagans entered into the Covenant—far from it.

MISSIKA: *But if you reason in quantitative terms, Christ's message has nevertheless had more success with pagans than with Jews.*

LUSTIGER: That does not make much sense. Beyond a certain period, no comparison is possible. In the third century, the Jewish Church ceased to be identified as such; it no longer had a legitimate place. There are both a sin and a tragedy in that fact. The term that Saint Paul uses to characterize the relationship between Jews and pagans is "mutual jealousy": the pagans deny the existence of Israel, and Israel is afraid of losing its specific identity and special relationship to God. The fear of merging with others and disappearing is a legitimate fear, and Israel's survival by God's fidelity remains a testimony inscribed in the history of God's irrevocable gifts and calls. But the fear of acknowledging that pagans also can receive the grace of the Covenant is something else, because that promise had already been made by the prophets—Amos, Hosea, Isaiah and Jeremiah. The promise that pagans will come from Egypt, Assyria and elsewhere to worship the living God is found in all of them.

MISSIKA: *And the Crucifixion?*

LUSTIGER: I refer to Saint Paul. People are always saying that it was the Jews and not the pagans who crucified the Messiah. But that is simply not true. According to Saint Paul, he was crucified by all men. At the time the evangelists were writing, the argument with the Synagogue was intense; nevertheless, the accounts of Christ's Passion in the Gospels and the Acts of the Apostles place the responsibility for the Messiah's death on all men, Jews and pagans.

Saint John gives a prodigious presentation of the dialogue with Pilate, a dialogue that most of the time we tend to forget. We think of Pilate as a colonial governor who was dealing with the natives while understanding nothing of their affairs. That is simply untrue. The Roman law represented the highest ambition of rationality and justice, and yet Pilate is going to commit, from the legal point of view, an absolute denial of justice. It is he who carries the juridical responsibility, and it was Roman soldiers who crucified Jesus. The pagans showed themselves to be sinners in a situation where they were pretending to observe the law, just as the Jews did not recognize the One whom it was their mission to recognize. Human history is that way; it is filled with injustices and infidelities.

But the measure of the grace of forgiveness and mercy that the Messiah brings is infinite. The revelation of every man's sin that takes place through him is not made for condemnation but for liberation as long as this light available to man—namely, the recognition of his sin—is accepted. If he refuses it, he closes himself into his blindness. But the Messiah's light is a gift of mercy. It is constantly being offered. Through the human condition of his own Son, of Jesus, the unique One, God "has redeemed all sin". Israel was already a much-beloved son and remains so.

WOLTON: *On that point, I would like to know how you feel about the thesis (defended in particular by René Girard) that says that Jesus divested the sacrificial mechanism by consciously offering himself but that afterward the Church, by a sacrificial interpretation of the Cross, fell back into mythology by accusing the Jews of having killed Christ and thus restoring the mechanism of the scapegoat.*

LUSTIGER: From the point of view of Catholic theology, that argument does not hold up. Imagine a child who has never seen a Jew in his life; he does not even know if such people exist anywhere in the world and has heard about them only through the Gospels. What will his reaction be if people say to him, "You see, those wicked Jews killed Jesus"? That argument is based on a crude interpretation, too summary as to facts. Any Christian who reads the Gospel is going to have the same reaction as Pascal. He is going to hear the Crucified One say to him, "I shed this drop of blood *for you.*" And, like Saint Paul, he will say, "He loved me and gave himself up *for me*", for *my* sins. The believer recognizes in the Crucified the One in whom everyone's refusal to turn to God is represented and *also* the One who delivers us from our refusal. In other words, whoever pretends that he is innocent of that death, that it is the "others" who killed him, cannot believe in Christ. His attitude is even a proof that he does not believe, because to believe in Christ is to have a "broken heart". It is to conform to the image of the fifty-first Psalm and to Jeremiah: the hardened heart becomes "a broken and contrite heart" through the greatness of God's love, which wants to forgive, so that the heart of stone becomes a heart of flesh.

In Christ's death there echoes another question whose full depth is perceived only by someone nourished and instructed by the Bible: Why do the just suffer? This lamentation is heard already in the book of Job. Israel never ceases to raise the question, obstinately, all the while maintaining, against all obstacles, the idea that if man obeys God, he attains his happiness. That idea is profoundly true, but it is paradoxical and sometimes almost unbearable—because the just do suffer. "What have I done, Lord? Surely you know! Then why do you hide yourself? Why do you not speak? Why do you remain silent?" The Just One suffers, the Messiah suffers and we are all responsible for his suffering. Every Christian recognizes himself as culpable for Christ's death. If he does not, then he is not Christian. Saying that "it was not I who did it, it was somebody else", is placing yourself outside of Christianity. That is why anti-Semitism, in its pseudotheological version—"It is the Jews, not us, who killed him"—is blasphemous. It denies the universality of redemption. It refuses to see in the face of the Crucified—the Son of Israel unjustly persecuted— God's power, which reveals everyone's sin so as to be merciful to everyone.

WOLTON: *What would have happened if all Jews had recognized Jesus as the Messiah?*

LUSTIGER: I cannot envisage something that does not precisely belong to us—that is, a picture of eschatological times.

WOLTON: *But as far as the history of salvation is concerned, is the fact that Israel still exists the proof that the Parousia[7] has not been realized?*

LUSTIGER: Yes, and Israel is a guarantee of the Parousia's coming.

WOLTON: *Then Judaism bears witness to an unfinished history?*

LUSTIGER: Yes, but not like some archaeological fragment.

WOLTON: *Would it not have been possible, except for accomplished eschatology, for all Jews to convert to Christianity? What would happen if, by a kind of miracle, Judaism recognized the Messiah?*

LUSTIGER: Who can speak in the name of all Jews? Your supposition resembles a little what the Hassidim say: for the Messiah to come, all Jews in the world must, at a given moment, be perfect saints.

WOLTON: *That gives us a little time!*

LUSTIGER: Your irony has such a nice smell of skepticism. You understand that my point of view is different. For me, it is a matter of the work of redemption. Besides, the Hassidim say that Jews must be either perfect saints or complete sinners. The question remains. It does not belong to us. Saint Paul says, in his letter to the Romans (I am quoting from memory): If the Jews' refusal took place for the reconciliation of the world, what will their reintegration be like? It will be like a resurrection of the dead. In other words, the Jews are not a people called to experience something that would be alien to them, something unprecedented. They are a structural part of the history of salvation; if all Israel recognized the Messiah, that would mean that all other nations would also have recognized him.

Christ is the Messianic subject: Christ and his brothers. His brothers are those who are born in him through baptism. The rite of acceptance is baptism. Those who enter the New Covenant do it not by circumcision but by baptism. John the Baptist's baptism became the baptism in Christ's name. It is given to all, Jews and pagans, and henceforth signifies this: we have all been at fault; we have all broken the Covenant. None of us, Jew or pagan, is worthy of the gift made to him. To enter into the New Covenant in the Holy Spirit,

[7] The Parousia is the Second Coming of Christ in glory.

the one announced by the prophets, we must receive this baptism, the baptism of repentance preached by John the Baptist for the remission of sins. It is the baptism that the Messiah performs in the Spirit. And this rite of acceptance and renewal is also a rabbinical rite. Look at what happened in the state of Israel when the rabbis insisted that the Falashas[8] be formally recognized as Jews.

WOLTON: *The Falashas were opposed to it.*

LUSTIGER: Rightly or wrongly.

As Messianic subject, Christ is composed of all those who belong to him through baptism and by faith. And in a certain way—I repeat, in a certain way—the Jewish people are a part of him: "According to the flesh", as Saint Paul says. "According to the flesh" does not mean solely according to biology or the continuity of carnal generations; it also connotes an always promising and always too short moment in the history of salvation.

Not so long ago, I heard a charming but exceedingly naïve song, a Christmas carol from Normandy. The words went something like this: "Had he been born in Bricquebec, we would have loved him very much. With the Virgin Mary", etc. I find those words amazing!

WOLTON: *Why?*

LUSTIGER: Well, because they show an incredible lack of comprehension of the Christian mystery! In the first place, he was not born in Bricquebec....

WOLTON: *Do you have something against Bricquebec?...*

LUSTIGER: No, but I find the hypothesis reflects a profound misunderstanding. It seems to be saying that "we" in Bricquebec would have behaved better than the people in Bethlehem, because we are "good"... and not "bad" like them.

The Doctrine of the Witnessing People

MISSIKA: *I would like to come back to a point that seems important: you have developed a variant, or an updating, of a theological point of view going back to Saint Augustine, the doctrine of the witnessing people. Most of the time, however, Jews*

[8] Falashas are Ethiopian Jews who lived for centuries isolated from the rest of the Jewish community. Some of them recently immigrated to Israel.

challenge this doctrine; they do not like it very much and some say that it is anti-Semitic.

LUSTIGER: I was not speaking of a "witnessing people" in that sense but rather of a people who are actors in the history of salvation. Judaism is not an archaeological site, not an Indian reservation that is preserved so that one can say: That is the way they used to live. . . .

WOLTON: *But you do acknowledge that this doctrine was widespread in the Church for a long time.*

LUSTIGER: Yes, but it also had a positive meaning.

MISSIKA: *Even for Saint Augustine? "They have become our book bearers", is a very well known phrase. "They have become our book bearers in the same way that slaves march behind their master carrying his books."*

LUSTIGER: Yes, but many of Saint Augustine's other remarks convey a better understanding of both the dignity of the people to whom the Bible was entrusted and its mission in bearing witness to the truth.

MISSIKA: *I also have a similar quotation from Pascal: "It is necessary for the proof of Jesus Christ both that the Jewish people survive and that they be miserable because they crucified him." This sentence leads me to conclude that very often the doctrine of the witnessing people is accompanied by the idea that their decline is essential for proving the truth of Christianity. The Jews have to be here, but in a wretched state. . . .*

LUSTIGER: What you have just said belongs to the arsenal of fantasies that as far as I am concerned, is completely unworthy of Christianity. Such affirmations, not to speak of such condemnations, "forget about" the universality of sin and redemption. What does remain true is the enigma of Israel's separation. But a setting apart is a holding in reserve. The one who is set apart is hidden in God's hand, in view of his plan.

In spite of its infidelities, Israel remains beloved until finally, the time of tears that is man's history having ended, all of Israel, "Khol Israel", discovers the totality of the redemption. All of Israel means both the living and the dead. To understand this forgotten dimension of history, you have to be open to a religious vision that escapes cultural and rational consideration. I do not see what the universality of salvation could mean if it did not include the dead—those whom we call dead—as well as the living. "All men" refers to all who are held, somewhere, in the divine consciousness, in the heart of the one who is the Creator and Redeemer of all. Otherwise, we are nothing more than a swarm of midges swallowed up by evolution and time. If the dead do not count, if they have no right to human dignity, to human existence, religion loses its meaning. The human condition cannot be reduced to the biological condition that is perishable, precarious and perpetually challenged, a condition in which individual existence is less stable than the existence of the species. Such a vision, basically materialistic, takes no account of the human spirit or the hope that is in man. Every Jew hopes for Israel's conversion, and Israel's conversion means the turning back to God of the whole of Israel.

WOLTON: *Could you clarify that point?*

LUSTIGER: When Jesus says that the suffering, whether directly imposed or brought about by indifference, of any of his brothers will have been inflicted on him, he is speaking of those who will have become his brothers in baptism, but perhaps also of all those who, in the coming generations, will be sharing "according to the flesh" his Messianic mission. There is a connection. Nevertheless, Israel is not, through itself or itself alone, a substitute Messianic subject.

MISSIKA: *There is something I still cannot understand.... Do you consider Christ's message universal? In that case, are those who ignore it not in error? On the one hand, you say that they are not, that their way can be legitimate, and on the other, you maintain the universality of the message.*

LUSTIGER: You are forgetting history, or rather, time's duration. Mankind's history is unfinished. The Church is the sign and sacrament of salvation for all humanity. By the Church I mean the assembly of the Messiah, the Body of the Messiah, the spiritual Body formed by all the Church's members. At present, the Church of God is at work in human history, like yeast in dough.

You say to me: If you are Christian, you think that Christianity is the truth for everybody. I reply: Yes, of course. You conclude: Then those who are not Christian are in error? Here you are confusing the true and the false. The adhesion to the truth about which the Church speaks is not identical to the recognition of a mathematical principle. Her truth is a revelation, and it redeems sinful human freedoms so that they can participate in divine life. The revelation spreads itself like life. Not every partial revelation or partial truth is mistaken. In the first place, divine truth is God who calls and commands. It is accessible only to the extent that man lets himself be seized by God and receive what God ordains, to the extent that man is delivered from his blindness and sin. Divine truth is the mystery of God's Word speaking first in

Israel's history and then becoming flesh in the Messiah and giving of itself through the Messiah's brothers.

While on this subject, I remind you of one of the great scandals for the Christian mind; it tormented believers for centuries: What is the place in the history of salvation of those people who have not been evangelized? This scandal burst forth in the West when it was discovered that it did not cover all of mankind's history. How do you inscribe in the history of salvation those who, in good faith, died without knowing about Christ, without baptism, without hearing the Gospel?

WOLTON: *That is something like the question about children who die without having been baptized.*

LUSTIGER: Exactly. It is the same question.

WOLTON: *And what is the response?*

LUSTIGER: In the first place, it is the secret of God and his mercy! We are not to substitute ourselves for God's justice. God alone is judge. Who are we to judge?

This kind of debate allows us to understand a great deal. To say that the last days, eschatological times, have begun is not to deny history but to confirm its unwaning gravity. The Messiah's glory remains hidden in God, and man's history goes on. Hence, the births and deaths, the uses of knowledge and speech, the multiplicity of languages—everything that makes up the human, corporeal, historical, ethnic and national condition remains in God. Nobody can claim to give the divine and authorized vision of these historical developments. Saint Augustine attempted this meditation in the *City of God* at the time of the Roman Empire's collapse. From century to century, thinkers have been fascinated by the question of how to give a spiritual interpretation to universal history. This is just as true of Jewish thinkers as of Christian ones. The coming of the Messiah awesomely deepened the question rather than suppressed it. It confirmed and demonstrated the universality of the biblical message that affirms that we are all made by the same Creator and Father and that, hence, all men are brothers. It is a fantastic affirmation that breaks with so many primitive mythologies according to which "we" are men and "the others" are not. In the unique human history, it is not just those who recognize Christ as the Messiah who work with him for the world's redemption.

MISSIKA: *You consider that Judaism also works toward that redemption although it does not recognize the Messiah?*

LUSTIGER: The Jewish people were and *are* still the inheritors and witnesses to God's promises and Abraham's faith. Those promises are irrevocable. Believing in the promises associates them with the plan for salvation.

WOLTON: *But did the New Covenant not invalidate the preceding one?*

LUSTIGER: Neither of the Covenants ever expires.

MISSIKA: *Then why would Christianity be useful to Jews? If I follow you, it is necessary only for the pagan nations.*

LUSTIGER: Is it not important for a Jew to know who the Messiah is and to hear the Word of God? Is it not important for everyone to know what we are still hoping for?

Why and how does anybody recognize the Messiah? That is the mystery of God. An act of faith is a grace from God who offers himself to each person's freedom. Faith is born in men's hearts by the gift of the Spirit.

WOLTON: *We would like to present you with a quotation from Rosenzweig, who wrote* L'étoile de la rédemption *and holds some positions quite close to yours on relations between Judaism and Christianity. On the brink of conversion, Rosenzweig stops; he does not step across the threshold. On the contrary, he affirms his Judaism and, after a dramatic night, he writes, "It is impossible; it is no longer necessary." And a little further on he explains that Christianity is a Judaism . . .*

LUSTIGER: . . . for pagans.

WOLTON: *Yes, for pagans. What do you think of that observation?*

LUSTIGER: It is equivocal, because it can be interpreted in at least two different ways. It is true that Christianity is Judaism for the pagans, *in the sense* that, for the Christian, it is in Christ that Judaism receives its plenitude and recompense by making God accessible to pagans. And pagans can believe in Israel's Messiah only if a part of Israel has, by faith, recognized its Messiah, God's Messiah.

But there is *another meaning* that is unacceptable. It amounts to saying that Christianity is a product for exportation, something of reduced value, intended for the nations who have rejected idolatry, so that they can receive a certain justice and have a share in an elementary Covenant—a "Noachian" Covenant made by the Creator with his creatures of flesh and blood. I do not need to go into the reasons for which this latter interpretation seems to me to be erroneous and dangerous. It suffices to say that the essential is passed over in silence: the Messiah and the Holy Spirit are given to all the sons of Adam.

IV

GENOCIDE

The French Church under the Occupation

Jean-Louis Missika: *The major reproach made against Rome as well as against the French Church is that they did not oppose the Jewish persecutions either resolutely or publicly.*

Jean-Marie Lustiger: I do not feel qualified to comment on that; it is for history to judge. Serge Klarsfeld, in his book *Vichy-Auschwitz,* says that if the Catholic clergy had not intervened as forcefully as they did and if all the Catholic networks had not functioned, the persecution of Jews would have been much more deadly. There is no doubt that Catholics played a determining role in saving a certain number of Jews in France. I do not think that the French Church deserves the reproach of having remained indifferent to the fate of Jews during the war. As a direct witness, that is not what I saw. I distinguish that accusation, however, from Pétainism.

Missika: *Which means?*

Lustiger: The collusion of the French Church with Pétainism is another story. In this country, marked as it was by *l'Action française*[1] and an anti-Semitism whose roots could be found in Drumont and that, in a part of the French right, was confused with Catholicism, the general reaction of believing Catholics, the clergy and bishops was praiseworthy and quite positive. In my opinion, there is hardly a Jew who survived who did not, in one way or another, one day or another, receive help from a Catholic or a priest, or from a network connected with Catholicism or Protestantism.

Dominique Wolton: *You are citing clandestine action. But what about the Church's public statements? I am thinking of the anti-Jewish laws that dated from* 1940. *After such a shocking political act, there very well might have been a declaration from the French episcopate.*

[1] *L'Action française* was a daily newspaper published from 1908 to 1944 by Charles Maurras and his associates in a political movement of the extreme right. The Vatican condemned the movement in 1932, but the ban was lifted by Pius XII in 1939.—Trans.

LUSTIGER: There were a number of protestations sent to Marshal Pétain. But it would be impossible for me to do the historian's job. I have no documented response to your question. I can give you my overall feeling, an account of what I saw. I myself was conveyed at random by various networks. I met only commendable reactions in the Catholic circles that I knew. I realize very well that one cannot generalize from a particular experience. That is why I refer you to Serge Klarsfeld. It seems to me that he has been very fair. He is a highly respected authority on the history of the deportation of French Jews. And the picture that emerges from his book is rather positive for the clergy and the bishops.

As for the Church's relations with the Vichy government, that is another matter. It seems to me that her attitude in regard to Vichy, the *Résistance* and the Germans reflects that of the French population in general. The history of that epoch remains obscure and painful. I am struck by the fact that it is almost impossible to bring up the subject, even today.

WOLTON: *But would you not have expected the episcopate's attitude to differ from that of a cross section of Frenchmen? The bishops' official position was "loyalty without allegiance". What did that mean? Was it sufficient?*

LUSTIGER: I repeat: my personal experience does not permit me to say very much on this subject. I have a more distinct idea of what French society was like during that period.

I can relate a few contradictory testimonies on a significant event: the liberation of Paris. I find it really astonishing that there has never been an annual Mass celebrated at Nôtre-Dame for the anniversary of the occasion. Traditionally, a Mass is requested every year by the *Association des Anciens de la Deuxième Division Blindée,* whose inspirer and soul was Leclerc.[2] But it is a Mass for war veterans and does not officially commemorate the liberation of Paris. On the fortieth anniversary of the liberation, as Archbishop of Paris, I wanted to celebrate a special Mass at Notre-Dame. I invited all the leaders of national and city government, thinking that such a celebration was an act of historical significance for which I could take the responsibility. Only a few people sensed the significance that I saw in it—namely, a step toward national reconciliation and the affirmation of a common memory of that time of war. On that day, I had the grace to have Cardinal de Lubac beside me, and I was able to quote some of his articles that in wartime had appeared in the underground journal *Témoignage chrétien* and that do great honor to the Church. These spiritual and theological texts were also political, in the

[2] Leclerc was the pseudonym of Philippe de Hautcloque, *maŕechal de France* (1902–47). He was the head of the Second Armored Division of the Free French forces that helped to liberate Paris.—TRANS.

strongest sense of the word; they spoke of respect for man and its idolatrous negation. The very fact that, forty years later, Cardinal de Lubac and I were concelebrating that Mass in the cathedral of Notre-Dame de Paris in the presence of government officials meant that a judgment was being passed on that period—and to me that seemed very important.

In these circumstances, I had the occasion to meet some of the people who were witnesses to what had happened on August 25, 1944, in the cathedral. I do not know if a historian will eventually manage to trace the sequence of events. Why was Cardinal Suhard[3] not there? It has been said that Monsignor Chevrot, curé of Saint-François-Xavier, had prevented his coming by blocking the street. Monsignor Badré, the present Bishop of Bayeux-Lisieux, who was one of the principal agents of the *Résistance* at the Interior Ministry and served as secretary-general under Parodi,[4] gave another version.

WOLTON: *But did you ever find out why Cardinal Suhard did not show up?*

LUSTIGER: He was prevented....

WOLTON: *By whom?*

LUSTIGER: Nobody really knows. Some say it was Chevrot and Bruckberger,[5] others say the *Résistance*—but who in "the *Résistance*"? Nobody knows for sure. It was certainly not de Gaulle. And then there was what happened at the cathedral and the chapter's reaction, all of which are highly revealing details. According to the canons' oral tradition, the debate at Notre-Dame centered on whether or not to sing a *Te Deum* when de Gaulle arrived. Only the legitimate head of state can request the cathedral's chapter to sing a *Te Deum.* But could de Gaulle be considered the legitimate head of state? They sang the Magnificat instead. Again, some people say that de Gaulle himself started singing it. But a priest who was there assured me that he was the one who began the hymn. Another priest is said to have remarked to de Gaulle, "What a pity the Cardinal is not here." And de Gaulle, standing, allegedly replied as he surveyed the congregation stretched out on the floor under gunfire, "I cannot very well imagine what the Cardinal would do in these circumstances and in this place."

[3] Emmanuel Cardinal Suhard (1874–1949) was Archbishop of Paris from 1940 until 1949. —TRANS.

[4] Alexandre Parodi (1916–) rebuilt the French Interior Ministry after the liberation of Paris.—TRANS.

[5] Raymond Leopold Bruckberger (1907–), Dominican priest, writer and filmmaker, was the chaplain for the *Résistance.* He welcomed de Gaulle at Notre-Dame on August 26, 1944.—TRANS.

But whatever happened, even if you allow for the wartime situation and the requisite secrecy that results in an extreme compartmentalization of experiences and vantage points, you still find intact today all the stereotypes of forty years ago, each person maintaining, even in his slips of tongue, his wartime character. France is a country that is ill from its own history. And that is also true of the Church's responsibility in the face of the German occupation. The French bishops certainly did not collaborate. Some like Cardinal Saliège and Cardinal Gerlier[6] spoke out forcefully. But the majority had feelings that reflected quite accurately the French nation in general. There are facts that one can discuss at length: de Gaulle and Bidault[7]—it seems that it was Bidault more than de Gaulle—wanted the heads of I do not know how many French bishops.

WOLTON: *Georges Bidault, minister of* Affaires étrangères *and a Catholic, asked Pius XII to persuade twenty-four bishops, including three cardinals, to resign.*

LUSTIGER: Monsignor Roncalli, the future John XXIII, who was appointed nuncio in Paris after the war, succeeded in limiting the resignations to two or three.

WOLTON: *That is a telling indication of the Church's situation: twenty-four bishops, one-third of the total, is a considerable number. Did you know then that Bidault, the head of the MRP, had asked for these resignations?*

LUSTIGER: I knew nothing at all about that. It was not at that level that I was following events.

WOLTON: *Were you politically involved?*

LUSTIGER: I was *"engagé"*, as we used to say. I could identify quite easily with the Christian-Democrat party. I belonged to the MRP, if you insist on labeling me. I was a part of the generation that was saying: Never again must things be allowed to happen as they did before; nuts to the Troisième République and to the Pétain regime! We could never have imagined that the old politicians would be able to resurface. My generation believed the two masterstrokes passed on by the press just after the war ended. The first was de Gaulle's saying that France had resisted. That seemed true to us because we

[6] Cardinals Saliège and Gerlier were archbishops of Toulouse and Lyon, respectively, during the war.—TRANS.

[7] Georges Bidault (1899–1983) succeeded Jean Moulin as president of the *Conseil nationale de la Résistance* in 1943 and was one of the founders of the *Mouvement républicain populaire* (MRP). Between 1944 and 1954, he served several times as minister of foreign affairs.—TRANS.

were among those who had chosen the *Résistance.* We recognized ourselves in his speech.

MISSIKA: *But you knew very well that most of France was Pétainist.*

LUSTIGER: Yes, but de Gaulle threw a veil over that. This was easy for us to accept because it represented our own conviction.

The second masterstroke was that the MRP, the Christian-Democrat party, showed to the public a Catholic face that abruptly sent the Pétainist attractions into oblivion.

WOLTON: *Precisely. You could not know about Bidault's demand that certain bishops had to go, but you were participating in a movement that was saying "never again"; as a Christian, you must surely have had a feeling about the French episcopate's conduct during the war.*

LUSTIGER: We had no idea what this question involved. We knew about the message of the Archbishop of Toulouse; otherwise, we had only snatches of information. Things were so shadowy, even for the immediate actors. Perhaps Bidault had an overall vision.

WOLTON: *But when information was progressively made public, you must have formed an opinion. . . .*

LUSTIGER: That information was never publicly aired! When the first election for the *Assemblée* took place, the Christian-Democrat party promptly rallied the whole of the Catholic vote throughout the country. There were only three parties left.[8]

WOLTON: *Do you honestly have no memories of how you felt?*

LUSTIGER: Excuse me, but not from that period. What I referred to as the two masterstrokes were like veils of pardon, like amnesia or amnesty—I do not know how to say it—that restored our honor. And we had an enormous thirst for honor. I mean, an enormous thirst to restore France's honor. I had doubts when we were told that we had defeated Germany. It was unbelievable, but we wanted to believe. . . .

WOLTON: *I understand. But with time, things have become clear. Take another example: there was only one encyclical issued by Pius XII during the war. That was in*

[8] Socialist, Communist and MRP.—TRANS.

1943, and it concerned the Mystical Body. Do you find it normal that this was the sole encyclical from that period?

LUSTIGER: But there were radio messages at Christmas. They had the same weight. I remember that their texts were circulated and had considerable repercussions. The one for Christmas 1942 condemned the arrests and deportations of innocent persons "for reasons of race". Everybody knew what that meant and should have drawn the appropriate conclusions. Making a comprehensive historical judgment of those years is something else. You are asking me about what I thought at the time. I am answering you.

Memory and Forgetfulness

MISSIKA: *Then let us take a step backward. When discussing the attitude of the French vis-à-vis their own history during the occupation, you have recalled that there was a forgetfulness, a veil, a concealment—indeed, a lie. Do you think that this is a serious problem? Were the reconstruction and economic boom possible only under these conditions—that is, in a state of oblivion? Is it necessary to re-examine that period today, or would you say that the illness has passed, that time has done its work?*

LUSTIGER: I think that there can be true healing only if there is remembrance, only if the illness is named and there is an acknowledgment of faults, or, shall we say, at least of facts. I am convinced that it is only at that price that there can be national concord and hence that a people can be spiritually healthy.

What happened at the liberation—that is, what de Gaulle did—I called a masterstroke. I did not use the word *lie.* It was not at all the same thing! Perhaps it was simply a bandage, but it was a necessary bandage because the shame was unbearable, because it was essential to restore the people's honor—the characteristic of the Vichy regime having been to play on shame and to have consented to the unacceptable. If one wanted France to regain a certain face, it was crucial, at least for a time, to put a bandage over that shame; otherwise, the nation was going to tear itself apart again.

De Gaulle was keenly conscious of his historical role. Perhaps you have noticed just how limited the ethical content was in what he was saying in those days about France. His expressions were virtually tautological. He did not go so far as to say, *"La France, c'est la France,",* but he came close. I am convinced that he expressed himself that way because he could not afford to say more. Nothing more would have been tolerable or even audible to the French. Anything more would have made it impossible to create a consensus and restore the nation's integrity. That the people in London had restored the value of the words *honneur* and *patrie*—words from Saint-Cyr's motto[9]—that honor could mean something again and that the word *patrie* could even be respected after *Travail-Famille-Patrie,* was after all a very important achievement. I wonder what future judgment the French will make regarding what happened in those days just after the liberation, what will they think about the *"épuration"*[10] that took place?

But what is utterly astonishing is that there was such a taboo concerning the fate of the Jews, that nobody talked about it, that nobody wanted to talk about it. In this matter, the suffering was too great, too horrible. Nobody managed to talk about it.

WOLTON: *But weren't you outraged by this silence?*

LUSTIGER: But I could not talk about it either. I had no desire to bring up the subject! It was inexpressible, an inconceivable distress—you cannot imagine! I can see myself at the village square in Saint-Sulpice-sur-Lèze, where I was working as a camp counselor, in that month before the liberation. It was evening, the sun was setting and I touched the corners of my lips and asked myself, "Will you ever be able to smile again?" And I thought, "Never again." I tell you this so that you understand the absolute depths of the tragedy my life had become when I was seventeen. I did not think of suicide. I had decided to try to make the most of my life—there was no question of "destroying" myself. The question was to know if I could ever find within myself, somewhere, any joy in living.

We were unable to speak about these depths, this abyss. It was years before I could discuss what happened to the Jews; I could not even broach the subject of the deportations. Even among ourselves we spoke about it with reticence. How would you want us to talk about it? I cannot believe that there was a single Jewish father of that generation who spoke about it with his children, who would have been able to or would have wanted to speak about it! You do not transmit horror. You prefer to spare those who have survived. Nobody had anything to say about what had happened during the occupation. Silence was the rule in Germany, but it was also the rule in France. Germany's case was different, since it had been destroyed and banished from the nations. There it was understood that it was the Nazis who had done all the evil and not the Germans. But for France, it was another story.

WOLTON: *When did it become possible for you to speak about it?*

[9] Saint-Cyr is the small town near Versailles where in 1808 Napoléon founded the French Military Academy, which came to be called by the town's name. De Gaulle graduated from the school in 1911.—TRANS.

[10] *Épuration* literally means "purification, purge, weeding out".—TRANS.

LUSTIGER: Oh! Much later. Certainly, there was the official discourse on the occupation and the *Résistance.* A "black-and-white" discourse, placing the members of the *Résistance* on one side and the Nazis on the other. It became a stereotype.

MISSIKA: *But nothing about the role played by the French themselves in the deportation?*

LUSTIGER: That is correct. That subject was avoided completely.

WOLTON: *When did you regain your voice?*

LUSTIGER: Much later. Much later. I am not able to give dates. When I went to Israel and saw the Memorial to the Deportation, Yad Vachem, for the first time, it was literally unbearable for me! I could get through that visit only in silence and tears, tears that I could not show. And still today I have that same psychic and physical sensation. Since that time, I can speak about it. But even so, although time has passed . . .

I read Elie Wiesel late in life. I am very fond of Wiesel because in his short book, *Night,* he succeeded in speaking about the unspeakable. It contains barely a hundred small pages, but they had to be written, and he managed to do it.

But to come back to the national experience: I think that we have to dare to acknowledge and heal the wounds and sins so that there can be a reconciliation.

WOLTON: *And now?*

LUSTIGER: When I was appointed Archbishop of Paris, I thought of this reconciliation as a duty and a mission. That is one of the motives that led me to say a certain number of things on the subject in both France and Germany. It was a very painful step. Even today there are discourses that I cannot give or hear. When I see television programs on the deportation, I switch channels.

MISSIKA: *You have no desire to see even Lanzmann's film,* Shoah?

LUSTIGER: I cannot see it! Lanzmann spoke to me about his film after he had finished it. He invited me to the premiere. . . . I shied away from it. It is impossible. No, I cannot. And yet I promised to see it someday.

MISSIKA: *Do you feel that his work was necessary?*

LUSTIGER: He did it. It is a good thing that somebody did it. Yes, it had to be done. I cannot say whether he did it well, if it is fair, if it is partisan; I know nothing about that. Also, what Serge Klarsfeld has been doing is necessary. That work I know better.

MISSIKA: *Do you consider that "hunting down the Nazis" is legitimate?*

LUSTIGER: I think that the Klarsfelds are right. They are not doing it in a spirit of vengeance but in a search for truth. They are not out to get revenge but to remind men of what men are capable of doing, of what some men have suffered. The persecution of Jews as well as other people can start all over. If men are not able to name their sins, they will repeat them.

The nature of sin is to label as good something that is bad, or to conceal what is bad, which amounts to the same thing. But the cause of such suffering, the source of such horror must be identified. If humanity is to regain its self-respect, it has to be done! We have to know why men committed such deeds, how they could have been able to perpetrate such wickedness. We have to know.

MISSIKA: *Were you not struck, precisely, by the Nazis' incapacity to realize what they had done? That impression emerges from all the trials we have observed: Eichmann's or even the Nuremberg trials. And the same was true with Barbie.*

LUSTIGER: No, I am not surprised. These men are only weak creatures, puppets, immersed in an absolute evil that surpasses them. They are victims of their own ignominy. You may demonstrate that a particular person is a sadist, but you will have given only a limited explanation. You may show that this sadist controlled the levers of an immensely powerful machine that brought about an appalling death for his victims, but you are still faced with someone insignificant, who does not suffice to explain what happened. That "pathetic man" is only a contemptible man, and it is normal that he should seem insignificant because the face hidden behind his is Satan's. It is the face of evil in our world, of evil's power, which is so vast as to be unimaginable for the human mind. Those men we see are only the servile actors. But they are not anonymous. They must be named. Yes, they are individuals who should unquestionably be held responsible for crimes committed, but the evil that surged up in them infinitely surpassed them. And this is true of every sinner and every crime. But here it is not just a question of individual crimes; we are talking about a historical problem—I dislike the word *collective* because it has a dangerous connotation—and this historical crime touches governments, nations, people, consciences and cultures.

How can you explain that a civilization that espouses reason and justice could swing in the opposite direction? How can you explain such an undertaking of annihilation and absolute absurdity! When I was twenty, I imagined that Nazism was a unique historical occurrence. It was the face of the devil! For years, I could not see photographs of Hitler without wincing. I had instinctive reactions of retreat and fear when I saw German uniforms or photographs of the Nazi emblem. It took me a long time to overcome this impulse to run away. Then I had equated absolute evil with Nazism. However, since that time, the disclosures concerning the gulag, Pol Pot's madness in Kampuchea and other ineffable cruelties illustrate a phenomenon that can reoccur in different ways! Absolute evil is indivisibly connected with the Jewish question, but it concerns all of humanity. Perhaps the Shoah of the Jews can serve as a grim indicator of the spiritual crisis of civilized peoples as the twentieth century comes to a close.

Absolute Evil

MISSIKA: *I would like to ask a question that is perhaps a little delicate: Can you understand a believer who, after the Shoah, rejects God or who considers that God has abandoned men?*

LUSTIGER: Yes, I understand. . . . I understand. I have known such people. I understand it very well.

MISSIKA: *Nevertheless, you would not say that God has abandoned men?*

LUSTIGER: No, but what happened is unbearably painful. And I can bear it only by seeing in it the mystery of the suffering Messiah and his compassion. That is the only way I can endure it.

WOLTON: *And those who do not believe in the suffering Messiah?*

LUSTIGER: I do not know. How do you expect me to answer for them? I am telling you how I can endure it. Serge Klarsfeld's book, *Le Mémorial des Juifs de France,* contains seventy thousand names: I have read through all those names perhaps five or six times. I was literally unable to separate myself from those names. You understand, all those people . . . What did they do? Who are they? I think that the Jewish consciousness, and thus the Christian consciousness—the consciousness of the suffering Messiah—permits us to understand the mystery of the human condition, or, at least, to enter into it by a way other than the "Buddhist" type of compassion, which would only be indifference. Perhaps touching the depths of horror allows a person to emerge from them by loving men. The question I asked myself: "Will I ever be able to smile again?" meant: "On what Good Friday, in what state of abandonment are we living?" I knew that God loves men, but I could not deny the tragedy; I wanted to shoulder it. All those clichés, those inane phrases about the "tomorrows that sing", the "sunshine after the rain", the "silver linings" were impossible to hear.

In spiritual and theological terms, I was able to smile again only when I understood that this annihilation is not an ultimate victory of evil over man. With the Resurrection given to the Messiah, God prevailed. Believing that the suffering Christ is the Messiah is not only to believe that the victim is the Savior but also that the victim, in the end, triumphed over his executioner.

WOLTON: *It was that conviction which made it possible for you to smile again?*

LUSTIGER: Yes, I think so. You may have the impression that what I am saying is the obsession of someone profoundly marked by his generation's experience. But this tragedy makes it possible to reach a true understanding of human history in its universality. And to be completely clear, what happened was a sign of the Enlightenment's extinction in man's heart. It spelled the end of the rationalist illusion, of a merely rational understanding of man. Nevertheless, we still have to struggle against this illusion, this temptation according to which the coming of the scientific era would bring about the elimination of evil in the world. The Bible teaches that evil is found first of all inscribed as a sin in man's conscience and freedom.

MISSIKA: *The rationalist or atheistic philosophers also have an interpretation. They talk about an eclipse of reason.*

LUSTIGER: For them, reason is an absolute, a gnosis. But who will redeem reason?

WOLTON: *Men.*

LUSTIGER: Well, that I would surely like to see! But it is illusory to think so, because we now know what man is capable of. And we also know that reason did not prevent anything.

MISSIKA: *But the philosophers say exactly the same thing.*

LUSTIGER: Then tell me why "men of goodwill" commit suicide when men with bad intentions triumph. Tell me why the German intelligentsia of the thirties caved in.

MISSIKA: *And you explain that by the devil? You say that it is all the devil's doing, and you call that an explanation!*

LUSTIGER: No, I am pointing out the mystery of evil that is active in human freedom, in the human condition. We are talking about a struggle against an evil that infinitely surpasses the means of technical reason. Evil is always connected with death, whether a person causes it, receives it or brings it on himself. This can be shown in a thousand brutal ways, such as drugs, speed or alcohol.

WOLTON: *Here you are getting close to a psychoanalytical explanation. Moreover, a person can evoke the death instinct without the devil's help.*

LUSTIGER: Really? Well, then, so much the better. Don't get discouraged on such a promising path . . . !

WOLTON: *Mind you, anybody can say that to someone else.*

LUSTIGER: No, because we have already seen reason at work.

WOLTON: *You are caricaturing. Today's reason is not the triumphant reason of militant atheism.*

LUSTIGER: I am not forbidding anybody to think whatever he wants! I am not out to destroy anybody's illusions.

WOLTON: *The word* illusions *is curious. You might have said "theories".*

LUSTIGER: No, I am saying that it is an illusion to think that reason can be saved by reason.

WOLTON: *You are responding as a man of faith, and you know very well—we have already discussed this—that the horrors committed in the name of reason cannot cause us to forget those committed in the name of faith.*

LUSTIGER: Anyone who thinks that reason can be saved by reason will end up in despair, once he sees that reason itself is lost.

MISSIKA: *You are saying that Nazism was absolute evil in action. But how can the problem of the double interpretation—profane and sacred—be resolved? There are historical explanations for the rise of Nazism or the development of communism that consider the economic, political, social and cultural factors. They come from serious scholars. How can they be linked up with your interpretation? If evil is the cause, then everything is determined in advance and there is nothing to do or say.*

LUSTIGER: No. Not all mechanisms of power are necessarily perverse. Not all conflicts, all dominating relationships or economic liberations are necessarily destructive. In every historical event, there is good and bad, and judging it in a definitive way is impossible for man, whether he does it as a contemporary or as a historian. History unfolds with its mechanisms and contradictions because human life is inscribed in time, and we try, by means of our reason, to gain a certain understanding of it.

But suddenly there open up beneath our feet—in the very heart of these conflicts and this progression of time—abysses that are all out of proportion to the causes and stakes, abrupt aberrations toward the irrational. The causes are no longer commensurate with the effects, and reason cannot control these forces. There is a break in the chain of causality. At first, people speak about madness; men become mad. The device of the scapegoat is put into place; the Jews or the Freemasons are accused.... Societies have to invent irrational explanations in order to grasp what surpasses a causal reasoning.

WOLTON: *You are doing the same thing when you speak about absolute evil.*

LUSTIGER: I am not trying to justify or prove anything! But there is a tragic depth of evil, a kind of chasm, in the human condition. I am not saying that only my generation went through it. After all, perhaps the generations who lived through the Algerian War saw things of similar scope and significance. That is possible. Who can compare one catastrophe to another? But just as there is an experience of freedom's existence, there is also an experience of freedom's impairment, of man's potential for evil, and the profundity of this evil can in no way be expressed by human reason. If the word *devil* shocks you, then say that we are confronting the Lie. We remain obliged to make a qualitative leap as far as a rational discourse is concerned, because we are observing such a rupture in the connectedness of events and life that human reason cannot grasp it. In order to exorcise it, reason is likely to resort to mechanisms of forgetfulness, transfer or substitution. In my generation, certain Jews have tried to forget by dedicating themselves to building the state of Israel; Frenchmen have been able to forget by devoting themselves to the reconquest of honor or the conquest of an American-style prosperity for France. As a believer, I can accept this tragic vision of human existence. I expect everything of man, but nothing about him ever surprises me.

MISSIKA: *Including the worst...*

LUSTIGER: Including the worst. That does not mean despairing of the human species, but simply accepting that the worst can arise at any moment. This vision allows me to face up to history. Of course, we feel shame, but to feel shame does not mean pushing the infamy as far away as possible. It means having compassion, an infinite pity and desire for healing, all the while retaining no illusion as to the risks we incessantly run. We have to estimate the evil of which man is capable as commensurate with the good to which he is called. There are not good people and wicked people; the worst of the wicked can become the best of men, because there is no damnation as long as God has not damned. To believe this is to refuse the Manichaean reasoning, to believe in man's freedom. A naïvely optimistic view of man seems impossible to me.

MISSIKA: *Certain rationalists do have a tragic sense of history.*

LUSTIGER: Then are they not in despair?

MISSIKA: *No, not necessarily.*

LUSTIGER: In any case, they must be stoical and skeptical.

MISSIKA: *Your interpretation of the Shoah is based on the power of evil. Other interpretations have been given—notably, that of divine punishment. There are Jews, for example, who have evoked . . .*

LUSTIGER: . . . Israel's sins.

MISSIKA: *Yes, and also in Solzhenitsyn's work there is a constant theme that consists of saying that Russia has been punished, through communism, because it was not sufficiently Christian.*

LUSTIGER: I approach this kind of thinking with extreme circumspection because one can say a lot of stupid things. It is not for us to pronounce God's judgment on the sins of history. Nevertheless, it is true that evil begets evil; even if spiritual responsibility is a personal responsibility, no human freedom is isolated in this world. There is a solidarity in evil, just as there is in the good, and the evil that results from human action always happens in sequences. The benedictions given to children and to the children of children have their opposite in the maledictions that are passed on from generation to generation. And benediction and malediction are not magic words; they take effect and demonstrate the spiritual solidarity of men among themselves. To me, there is obviously something missing in an individualistic vision of good and evil; solidarity in the good or complicity in the bad does exist, without implying, however, collective guilt. I refuse to get involved in the judgments you have cited.

WOLTON: *Yes, a part of the French Church said this kind of thing apropos of the defeat in 1940.*

LUSTIGER: I know, I heard it said.

MISSIKA: *Atheism, the republic, the Freemasons . . .*

LUSTIGER: I remember very well that kind of talk. Earlier I described the cartoon with the peasant who had read too much Gide. It expresses my reticence about this kind of thinking.

WOLTON: *But aren't you being tempted by this interpretation when you say that the political, economic or social explanations of France's moral collapse in 1940 are insufficient?*

LUSTIGER: I was speaking of sin, not of divine punishment. Anyone who evokes sin and the mystery of iniquity assumes his responsibility before God. He receives light from God, and such light is given in the grace of forgiveness. Anyone who called himself damned would surely be mistaken. He would be caught up in a fascination with madness; he would lack faith. Who among us would be able to pronounce a condemnation?

MISSIKA: *But is it not the same kind of thinking that concludes that, by forgetting God and believing too much in reason, there is a risk of sinking into evil?*

LUSTIGER: No. It is simply saying that if you are moving along the freeway at 150 miles per hour, it is likely that in a short time you will not be moving at all because you will have crashed into a tree or be lying at the bottom of a ravine.

The Spiritual Vocation

WOLTON: *How was your vocation influenced by historical events? Did you ever consider giving up the idea of the priesthood or even of returning to Judaism?*

LUSTIGER: The certitude of being called by God never left me, but there were temptations to botch it up in many ways.

WOLTON: *Did you have doubts about your capability for becoming a priest?*

LUSTIGER: No, simply whether I would do it. Whether I *could* do it or not made no sense if God had asked it of me. Later I wondered whether it was really the priesthood to which God had called me. But that was when I was already a seminarian, another period.

WOLTON: *Our question revolves around the conjunction between historically tragic circumstances and your spiritual vocation. Didn't the violence of history modify your spiritual itinerary?*

LUSTIGER: No, it only reinforced it. I mean, it confirmed it. I know that what I am saying can be given a psychoanalytical interpretation and reconstructed according to different schemas. But what is essential remains my determination and conviction that I had been called to make an absolute gift of my life to Christ, through the sacerdotal ministry.

I contemplated different forms of this ministry: when I was still in Orléans, for example, I had said to Monsignor Courcoux that I wanted to be an Oratorian. He laughed in my face and protested, "Oh! There! No!" Afterward, I said that I would like to be a priest in Orléans. His response was: "Out of the question! You are Parisian, go to Paris—what would you do in Orléans?" Years later, I thought that being Bishop of Orléans was quite an extraordinary answer! Then, I considered becoming a monk at Saint-Benoît-sur-Loire. I was attracted by the monastic life. I chose this particular abbey because of its association with Max Jacob,[11] whom I greatly admired and whose *Le Cornet à dés* I had read during the war. When I arrived, a very nice Benedictine showed me to a room and then, to give me something to do, he handed me a pair of large pruning shears and said, "You can go and trim the privet hedge at the guest entrance." He then demonstrated how it was to be done. Two hours later, he came back and exclaimed, "You have no vocation!" Given the state of the privet, he preferred to cut his losses!

WOLTON: *What was your reaction?*

LUSTIGER: I simply said to myself: Never mind, it is just as well! Since then I have been back to Saint-Benoît. There is still a privet hedge, but I do not know if it is the same one. I would like to think that the privet I trimmed survived!

[11] Max Jacob (1876–1944) was a French poet. A Jew who converted to Catholicism, he withdrew a few years later to the abbey of Saint-Benoît-sur-Loire. He died in the transit camp at Drancy.—TRANS.

But to leave the anecdote and return to historical events: at Toulouse in 1944, I was in hiding. As I told you, I had connections with an underground group associated with *Témoignage chrétien*—that is, members of the spiritual *Résistance.* Thus, there was no inconsistency between my reaction to history and my spiritual choices. We were in a period when arguments were violent because the stakes were awesome. At that time, argument meant war! Civil and international war. The clandestine authors of *Témoignage chrétien* showed a sense of truth, justice and law, a penetrating lucidity and respect for persons that were remarkable. They refused to be carried away by passions, to get entangled in unjustified controversy. I remember that the journal's subtitle was *La vérité quoi qu'il en coûte:* the truth, whatever the cost, and truth was not partisan. When I reread those texts today, I am astonished by their perspicacity, their eloquence.

MISSIKA: *Who were its prime movers?*

LUSTIGER: A group from Lyon, mainly Jesuits, among whom were Father Chaillet, who was its guiding spirit, and Father de Lubac, who worked a great deal with Father Fessard. There were also some academics, Mandouze and Marrou, and a few others. Abbé Charles Journet, who was later made a cardinal by Paul VI, sent articles from Switzerland under an assumed name which was, however, obvious. I remember, in particular, an issue devoted to anti-Semitism in which Journet and de Lubac wrote with exceptional clarity and veracity.

MISSIKA: *What was the position of these "spiritual resisters"?*

LUSTIGER: In a nutshell, they considered the victory of Nazism not only a German military victory but also the victory of a perverse ideology, of a fundamental perversion. They reasoned that if we were not victorious over this ideology within ourselves, we would be spiritually defeated, even if the Allies conquered militarily. Therefore, we had first of all to speak out against any complicity with totalitarian and racist ideology; otherwise, victory would have no significance. That meant eliminating all complicity in thought, judgments and conduct with a system of values that deforms man and destroys his soul. Father Gaston Fessard summed up this idea beautifully in the title of one of his books: *France, prends garde de perdre ton âme.*[12]

[12] "France, beware of losing your soul."—TRANS.

PART TWO

BELIEVING AND KNOWING

I

STUDENT AND SEMINARIAN (1945–1954)

Troubled Times

DOMINIQUE WOLTON: *You were in Toulouse when the war ended. What was it like? How did events affect you?*

JEAN-MARIE LUSTIGER: In fact, it was only then that I began to reason in political terms. What struck me, dumbfounded me, was the return of violence. Our feeling of relief, of freedom regained, was intense. At last, the beast had been beaten down. But at that very moment I witnessed scenes of incredible cruelty. I saw women with shorn heads being flogged and dragged through the streets. They were collaborators, people said, whores who had been kept by Germans. I saw men soaked in blood, their bodies torn to pieces, driven around the town on the hoods of automobiles draped with the French flag. . . . They were collaborators, people said. I was nauseated, and I kept repeating to myself, "No, this is not France; it is not for *this* that friends died, it is not to see *this* that we are still alive." I felt that we were falling into a trap; we were doing precisely what we had fought against. But at that time, these thoughts were only impressions. . . . I am not analyzing the way the inevitable purging was conducted; I am merely recalling the unbridled excesses, the things I saw happening around me that posed a brutal question: How can violence be resisted without resorting to violence?

A few weeks after the war's end, the Archbishop of Toulouse, Monsignor Saliège, called a meeting for Catholics on the Place du Capitole. At that gathering, Father Bergougnoux, a Franciscan, a professor of paleontology, a born speaker and a well-known member of the *Résistance,* let a Christian voice be heard above the clamorous fury. It was the Communists who were making the law in Toulouse then; they were trying to establish an autonomous base. The image projected by Father Bergougnoux and others who spoke highlighted the new position that the Church was going to occupy in postwar France. The Christian-Democrat argument for the reconciliation of the republic and the Church was out in the open; it took shape in French public life thanks to those legendary figures of the spiritual *Résistance* of whom Monsignor Saliège was the symbolic figure and among whom were all my friends in Toulouse.

How Can History Be Judged?

WOLTON: *How did you experience the relationship between the historical context and the spiritual pursuit?*

LUSTIGER: They were intimately connected. World War II was not an "ordinary" war that could be inscribed in the continuity of the wars of 1914 and 1870, of the Napoleonic Wars, the Thirty Years' War, the Hundred Years' War, etc. It was not a war "like the others". I felt that we had been plunged into an infernal abyss, a monstrous injustice. At stake in this war was an ideological victory or defeat. At the heart of the opponents' ideology was the persecution of the chosen people, the Jewish people, because they are a Messianic people. When as a child I spent time in Nazi Germany, I had understood: Nazism's aim was more than Promethean, it was Satanic. Even though its hostility to Christianity was fundamental, it could not dare to make a frontal attack because the Church represented a power that the Nazis were obliged to handle with care. But, as for the Jews, the Nazis charged into them headlong, lashing out ferociously. World War II unleashed the vilest of passions and worst of ignominies. It also gave rise to admirable acts of heroism and generosity on the part of ordinary people forgotten today. This utterly overwhelming conflict can be understood only within the mystery of the suffering Messiah and the redemption, with the struggle it implies. It was not primarily a war between two nations. A minor incident illustrating this comes to mind. Going to Mass in Orléans, I often found myself face to face with a German soldier.

WOLTON: *What was your reaction?*

LUSTIGER: It was very mixed. But his presence alone signified that a division had been bridged. I could not simply refer to "the Germans": I was forced to distinguish the Germans from the Nazis. What had been easy in 1936 in Heidelberg was unbearable in 1942 in Orléans. I endured that pain by concentrating on the spiritual dimension of events. The gift of faith allowed me not only to survive, but even more, to live with a certain assurance—in fact, to live without fear. In a word, to be . . . yes, to have confidence, not to feel afraid to die. Or rather, I was still afraid of dying, but I said to myself that if I had to die, it would be because God would have permitted it and that this event would be inscribed somewhere in the logic of history. It was not stoical resignation but confidence in God's goodness.

JEAN-LOUIS MISSIKA: *But don't people sometimes die in vain?*

LUSTIGER: No.

MISSIKA: *Even during a war?*

LUSTIGER: I have often thought about the following question. How many men and women, over the centuries, have lived and died on the very plot of earth where I am sitting, on this square meter of space that my feet are touching, whom no one remembers anymore? Who were they? Our civilization is built on remembering the names of heroes—is not much of the world of higher learning simply an immense labor of erudition regarding illustrious people? But what about the others? Is it worldly accomplishment that gives meaning to man's life? Can the academic discourse deliver the final judgment? What about all those people who have not been the object of scholarship? Those about whom we know nothing? Those about whom we shall never know anything? God alone knows them. Does life have a meaning? Through faith, I answer that my life is in God's hands. I have entrusted it to his hands. No one can take away my life, even if he kills me, because my life belongs to God.

MISSIKA: *Answering the question about life's meaning by saying that "God knows it" is more consoling when you believe in God than when you do not.*

LUSTIGER: Yes. But the real question is to want to live.

WOLTON: *Would you agree that it is more difficult to live without belief in God than with it?*

LUSTIGER: Perhaps . . . And some people would say, like the neo-Stoics after the liberation—Camus, for example: "It is more courageous not to believe in God because such a belief is a sign of weakness."

WOLTON: *No, no, I did not use the word "courage". . . . I was speaking of "difficulty".*

LUSTIGER: Believing in God helps a person to live; faith reveals the duty to live. God is not a principle—immobile on the horizon's wall—onto which you can hang your clothes or your rope. You are faced with an interlocutor about whom you cannot presume—before consenting to his presence—just how far he will lead you into places where you had no idea of going. What he asks of you is proportionate to what he gives you. Is it then easier or more difficult to live with faith? I do not know. Anyone who reads Christ's words based on Isaiah's, "the Son of Man has not come to be served but to serve and give his life in ransom for the multitude", without understanding them, can only be repulsed or frightened. He will look for every kind of justification that will support his attitude. And these words are indeed too stringent and absurd for anyone who does not receive their light and begin to put them into practice by following Christ. But there also exists a simple deism that guarantees the coherence of the world and human actions. All societies know this type of plausible image of life and death; it gives men the means of surmounting the anguish of human existence and permits them to go forward on the road to collective construction. When a society loses this coherence of socially acceptable images, it is threatened. From this point of view, Maurras and Hitler were correct in seeing the Bible as a threat to the internal coherence of their ideal societies and their notions of the divine or the sacred.

"Rationalist" criticism was inaugurated by the prophets (you find it in Isaiah) and by the writings found in the Wisdom of Solomon. And that polemic is worthy of a Diderot.

WOLTON: *You definitely have little fondness for eighteenth-century authors....*

LUSTIGER: I like Beaumarchais....

WOLTON: *Do you not have the impression that you are shifting responsibility when you impute everything you dislike to the rationalist mind?*

LUSTIGER: But I do not belong to the generation of the *petits marquis.* I was born after the nineteenth century. We have learned, along with the bearded Marx, Dr. Freud, Einstein and several others, that all that simply does not hold water. We have seen with our eyes, experienced at our expense why it does not!

WOLTON: *What? Religion or reason?*

LUSTIGER: This chimeric idealization of reason, this "self-sufficient" reason that ignores its own limits. If its authority is to be saved, then its pretension to sovereignty must be limited.

MISSIKA: *As far as method is concerned, I do not see how you can conceive of a break between Freud and rationality as it was constructed, in fact, well before the eighteenth century—because rationalism was not born in the eighteenth century.*

LUSTIGER: Suppose we introduce a simple distinction. There are, on the one hand, rules for verifying reason's functioning, rules concerning thought processes. But, on the other, there is a theory of reason. They are not the same thing. You are talking about the continuity between the "masters of suspicion" and the great rationalism. This continuity exists in the scientific usage of reason; but Marx, like Freud, wanting to be scientific, showed that somewhere reason was covering up a deception. I neither believe myself to be nor call myself a Marxist or Freudian, but the proven facts demonstrate that in this respect they were correct: reason has been duped, and its discourse has to be interpreted.

MISSIKA: *Yes, but the advantage of the scientific mind is to be able to construct refutable doctrines for which one can show that there is an error. . . .*

LUSTIGER: That did not stop the Enlightenment from begetting totalitarianism—that is, from making human reason divine and hence beyond all criticism. I am sorry for you, but . . .

WOLTON: *You are saying that, in the end, it is the Enlightenment that is at the origin of totalitarianism?*

LUSTIGER: That is a simplification . . . but I can justify it.

WOLTON: *It is a simplification, but there is a historical argument with which we can challenge that right away: the Enlightenment came after two or three centuries of appalling errors committed by the Church when she had temporal power. And at least it can be said that what happened in the seventeenth and eighteenth centuries, from the desire to construct a human reason without reference to God, can be explained primarily by the horrors that the Church's temporal power had perpetrated during the preceding centuries. Thus, I can make exactly the same argument as you, in the reverse sense. This no more justifies wanting to get rid of reason today than wanting to get rid of God in the eighteenth century. The errors committed for a hundred and fifty years in the name of reason cannot completely invalidate the atheistic thesis.*

LUSTIGER: The crisis of the Enlightenment already had a potential existence in what you call the history of the Church—but which is, more precisely, the history of Western Europe. The crisis of the West, of Western thought, does not begin in the eighteenth century. It was brewing much earlier.

WOLTON: *At the Reformation?*

LUSTIGER: Yes . . . during that century and even before. It is an internal crisis that can be identified and understood only as extending over a long period.

WOLTON: *After all, there was the Inquisition, which was hardly a bed of roses.*

LUSTIGER: No, but the origins and causes, religious or political, of the Inquisition have to be examined. Typically, the Inquisition is a part of the process of reconquest, the *reconquista.* There is a great difference between what Saint Dominic wanted and what the *seigneurs* of the *langue d'oil* did to lay hold of the region of the *langue d'oc.* The logic of power employed by princes, peoples and empires has also influenced Churchmen.

WOLTON: *But nevertheless the Church was also a participant and a very powerful one for a long time....*

LUSTIGER: Yes, but not without debates and contradictions. The clergy were no more able to escape from their times than we can from our own.

WOLTON: *You said the same thing earlier about the French episcopate's attitude during the war. It is true that churchmen are only men, but one can expect leaders to behave a little differently from other men, especially if they are Church leaders who speak out a great deal in the name of morality.*

LUSTIGER: How does one avoid becoming a prisoner of an anachronistic vision? How can we presume to say that men in the sixteenth century should have thought like men in the nineteenth and twentieth? The only epoch we do not criticize is our own, because it seems obvious to us. Our reference is what appears true and just now, but a distance of fifty or a hundred years suffices for the relativity of points of view to appear, even those deemed at the time to be most logical. It is an anachronism to judge an earlier society on the basis of what seems true to us today. The historical effort tries to see, or rather imagine, a bygone era. But there can be no "reconstitution of the past" without respect for others and recognition of their differences.

A highly placed government official recently remarked to me about the Bible, "How can you believe in that barbarous and bloody world? Did God desire the massacre of the Canaanites, the massacre of an entire people? Is it conceivable?" Citing the evidence of different civilizations, I tried to explain what this history means and brings to the revelation. Had he thought about all the massacres—oh, how much more monstrous and "rational"—committed in our own times? Can we project our present interpretation onto the past, as if we ourselves were above history and can sit in judgment on consciences of the past? In order to understand what has taken place, the historian strives to define the scope of series of events, to spot the differences within these series. But he is simultaneously working on himself as well as on the historical material, because history is the relationship of the present to the past.

MISSIKA: *But, despite everything, there are conflicting interpretations today. Dominique Wolton pointed out a few minutes ago that you were saying almost the same thing regarding the French Church or the Vatican during the Second World War as for the period of the Inquisition. If we are trying to avoid anachronisms, it should be noted that, in that earlier time, the Church had a great deal of power, immense power, and when you say that "Churchmen were led into this affair by princes", you seem to be forgetting that the princes were dominated by religion, by God—which was not the case with Hitler or Marshal Pétain.*

LUSTIGER: In most European countries, until all too recently, episcopal responsibilities were, if not venal, at least abusively monopolized by the powerful of this world and often diverted to their ends. For centuries (and still today), it was this control that was at stake in the main conflict between political powers and papal authority, whose independence is the guarantee of the Church's freedom. One of my predecessors as Archbishop of Paris was Cardinal de Retz. From time to time, I have leafed through his *Mémoires:* I confess that his literary reputation does not fill me with episcopal pride! How can it be explained that the Church in France, at the turn of the sixteenth century, could have accepted such a figure? But it was also the time of the great saints who set in motion the reform desired by the Council of Trent. Who is more Catholic? Saint Vincent de Paul or Louis XIV? In order to pass judgment on the Church's state at a given epoch, there has to be a historical study whose elements have not all been collected yet. But the Church's condition has always been the object of polemics. History is much too often an ideological and combative tool instead of one used for research that is—I will not say detached (that does not exist)—trying to be disinterested. The goal of research is to understand and recognize what has happened: What changes did the Christian Faith produce among men and civilizations that we would judge barbarian by today's standards? And at what price?

MISSIKA: *Yes, but that is true in two senses. When you say that the philosophers of the Enlightenment spawned totalitarianism, you are also using a polemical argument.*

LUSTIGER: That was an offhand expression. First of all, I was reacting against stereotypes: the Inquisition, the Borgias, obscurantism, indulgences and all the rest. I am simply asking for a minimal examination of circumstances. Above all, I am asking for integrity—intellectual integrity—and rigorous scholarship so that we do not end up substituting a facile ideological interpretation for history. Second, recognizing that the state of minds and morals among Christian peoples depends on the times in which they lived does not preclude passing a moral or even spiritual judgment on them. However, this responsibility does not belong to historians but to those whom the Church calls saints, canonized or not. Those men and women who have examined their epochs most freely and lucidly did so in the name of the Faith, by criticizing the perversions of the Faith. Throughout her history, the Church has known movements of self-examination, most of the time by a minority; they demonstrate that the spiritual combat takes place within the Church and concerns all those who in one way or another acknowledge her transmitted message, her spiritual reality, her rites and sacraments.

The Church of God produces her own renewal from within. What I am rebelling against is a shallow, simplistic vision that is often the fruit of the Enlightenment's anticlericalism. In the name of reason and spiritual exactitude, I am pleading for a deeper vision of history. I am asking that we recognize not only the grandeur of holiness but also—and it comes down to the same thing—the grandeur of the confession of sins and their forgiveness. In this light, it becomes possible to recall cowardliness and sins. Yes, it is abominable that certain Christian princes massacred the Jews! Yes, it is abominable that anti-Semitic themes were allowed to develop! Yes, it is abominable that innocent people were killed and persecuted! Yes, it is abominable that it was possible to abuse religion! Yes, it is abominable that Christians tried to impose religious acts that spring from personal freedom and can be accepted only in freedom! Yes, it is abominable that churchmen could ever think that recourse to political violence would allow them to attain the goal of evangelization to which they were dedicated! Yes, it is abominable that men are sinners!

Matriculation at the Sorbonne

WOLTON: *Since there is not much chance that we are going to agree on the analysis of the Church's historical role, let us return to your biography. You came back to Paris in the fall of 1944. What was the atmosphere like? What were your feelings, your reactions?*

LUSTIGER: There had been no news about my mother. Nobody knew anything. My father and I came back together, and we found our apartment occupied. It had been stripped. . . .

WOLTON: *Occupied by whom?*

LUSTIGER: By some unknown people. The store had been confiscated; we had nothing left. We went to live in a furnished room in a little hotel in the fourteenth *arrondissement* behind the Place Denfert-Rochereau. We stayed there for at least a year, maybe two, I do not remember exactly. My sister was still in Orléans. What could she have done in Paris under such conditions?

We had to pick up the pieces in order to survive. We certainly had to do something. . . . There are some things that cannot be spoken about. . . . I do not know how to say this. . . . I no longer know when the Red Cross . . . the Red Cross undertook the job of locating those who had disappeared—or maybe it was the *ministère des Prisonniers,* I cannot say anymore. . . . In the end we were told. . . . Two years after the war's end, in 1946, we were given an official paper certifying my mother's disappearance. As for my father's family, we did not dare to bring up their names. Almost all of them had been exterminated.

MISSIKA: *Why did it take such a long time to recover your apartment?*

LUSTIGER: I do not recall. . . . There were legal proceedings.

MISSIKA: *That means that the people living there denied that . . .*

LUSTIGER: No, they were simply occupants. There was a court action that lasted more than a year.

WOLTON: *But who were these people? Do you remember them?*

LUSTIGER: No, I no longer know who they were. For a year or so, my father and I lived in the furnished room on the Rue Brézin. During the following academic year, we returned to our apartment; my father regained possession of the store and started to work again. We collected a few scattered pieces of furniture, recovered a few things, not very much. We were wandering about in an empty apartment. . . . And there was the uncertainty about my mother's fate. Deep down, we knew that she would not be coming back, but as long as we had no proof . . . As a compensation for the stolen furniture—my parents had chosen it with taste, they had always wanted to have beautiful things—the government organized a warehouse containing all the stolen household belongings that the Germans had not taken away. People like us were given furniture that came from heaven knows where! I remember in particular a hideous rolling table, made of poplar but stained to resemble walnut. . . . We came home with all sorts of odds and ends, some pots and pans, a mattress and bed, a table, etc., for furnishing the apartment. When we stopped and looked at ourselves—my father and I—surrounded by that hodgepodge . . . It was really quite a difficult moment. . . . But we said nothing because, after all, we had to go on living. However, that gives you an idea of the depths of the bitterness that had to be purged. . . . It was probably about a year later that my sister, who had passed the first part of her *baccalauréat* in Orléans, came back to prepare for the final part in Paris. She took over the running of the household.

There was really not very much money. I started to work immediately as a *pion*[1] at the Lycée Montaigne where I had been a student. The world of *pions,* I discovered, could sometimes be very strange. And supervising the student cafeteria just after the war was quite a strenuous sport. I had seen school dining rooms at Conflans . . . but at Montaigne, it was a shambles! The children's aggressiveness, their savagery. . . . And there was not very much to eat.

I enrolled in the Sorbonne in October of 1944. You cannot imagine what a delight, an enchantment, it was for me to enter the university. But first I should speak about Paris. I rediscovered, or rather I discovered Paris, because I had only childhood memories of it. As an adult, I was free to move about. I explored Paris with love, with passion, but also with nostalgia. I paced tirelessly through the city, day and night. I roamed the streets, gazing at things, at people . . . marveling that we were all still intact, still alive.

And the Sorbonne! You others who knew the chaotic university of 1968 will find it hard to imagine my exultation on entering the courtyard for the first time! The Sorbonne was the temple of learning in the heart of the Latin Quarter. But it was also adjacent to my childhood haunts because, since the age of seven, I had considered the Luxembourg Garden as the locus of all my strolls. When I was a student at the Lycée Montaigne, I had ventured only as far as the Place du Panthéon; I had never dared go down the Boulevard Saint-Michel to the Sorbonne. As a child, I often meandered round the park's borders, and it had seemed to me that I had managed to circle the most sacred and civilized space in Paris. I had thought that the provinces began beyond the Closerie des Lilas, beyond Port-Royal! Saint-Germain-des-Prés had never tempted me: it was the territory of the "hepcats" and "existentialists" and was no longer the Latin Quarter. Past the Senate, there was another world. The Rue de Tournon was a frontier. And you had to stay clear of Saint-Sulpice with its horrible religious "trinkets" for sale in all the stores. . . .

WOLTON: *They are still there.*

LUSTIGER: Oh, no! It is not the same! You should have seen them in their heyday! Most of those little shops have disappeared, eaten up by the deluxe fashion boutiques on the new Boulevard Saint-Germain. The university restaurants marked the domain, Rue de Tournon, Rue Mabillon, Port-Royal. Beyond, it was almost the country! On the other side of the Luxembourg, the Rue Auguste-Comte with the Lycée Montaigne made a good border. If you went as far as the Jardin des Plantes, you were already on foreign soil.

[1] A *pion* is a student paid to supervise schoolchildren.—TRANS.

Entering the Sorbonne gave me an extraordinary feeling of exhilaration. I was in the temple of learning, of understanding.

MISSIKA: *Were you disappointed?*

LUSTIGER: Yes and no. I am never completely disappointed, because I always manage to find my intellectual nourishment....

WOLTON: *What did you study?*

LUSTIGER: I started out in *Lettres classiques,* although I am not a person with a literary bent. After two years, I left to spend two more years at the Institut Catholique studying philosophy. During that period, I did not set foot inside the Sorbonne. Finally, after having obtained a few diplomas, I finished my philosophy degree by following courses at the Sorbonne for a year.

I remember a course whose importance escaped me at the time. But it left a keen impression and influenced the continuation of my intellectual development. The syllabus for a degree in French literature included the *Chanson de Roland.* It is true that I did not find it fascinating reading. But its value came from the methodology used to analyze it. What were the origin and date of the text? The folklorist school had attempted to distinguish its strata by using historical hypotheses concerning the genesis of texts. The nineteenth-century German folklorist method, characterized by romantic interpretations of peoples' genius and their heroic creations, found this work ideal for showing off its properties. But the *Chanson de Roland,* once decomposed into several documents, became an absurd mosaic, impossible to make coherent. And furthermore, no certain conclusion could be drawn from any of the points in the contradictory hypotheses put forward by scholars. All that may seem of little consequence, but a few years later, in seminary, I was surprised to find the same problem in the approach to biblical exegesis, which was still under the intellectual domination of the German school with its folklorist and Hegelian origins. It was only at the beginning of the Seventies that it finally freed itself.

When I stepped inside the library at the Sorbonne for the first time, it took my breath away. And the Sainte-Geneviève library! And later, the Bibliothèque Nationale! That expanse of books, all those people who were reading... From that moment, the gates of knowledge were open to me.... I plunged frenetically into reading novelists and poets, limiting myself almost exclusively to the nineteenth-century and contemporary writers.

The Discovery of Art

LUSTIGER: During that same period, I also discovered painting. Up to then, I had been completely unaware of it. A painter, just a little older than I, used to take me along to museums. . . . He introduced me to the painting from the beginning of this century and to another way of feeling. My previous familiarity with the writings of Max Jacob and his friends from the Bateau-Lavoir had prepared me for this, as well as for surrealism. I began to learn to relinquish the image in order to let myself be seized by the painting, by the painted surface. That could be a purely sensualist or irrational abandon, or else an effort at trying to understand the logic of the process itself. Sometimes it was a formal logic imposed by the mind, sometimes a logic stemming from color. This is in striking contrast to academism, which imposed its own categories on the object. Here it is the object, the painting, that gives itself to be seen. Since I was not dealing with a philosopher but a painter, there was no conceptual tool to explain that to me. He helped me to perceive it on the sensory level, which, in the end, was probably the best level possible. "Look, look, let yourself be taken in by the color, look!" And that was very instructive. It was then that I understood that painting—like music, by the way—is a spiritual experience and that, in this respect, it is ambivalent.

WOLTON: *Ambivalent?*

LUSTIGER: Susceptible to good or evil—that is, the categories of good and evil are involved in it.

MISSIKA: *So you think that moral categories can enter into aesthetic judgment?*

LUSTIGER: Two anecdotes: when I was a student, I spent a summer vacation in Switzerland, in a guest house almost directly across from Gruyères. I struck up a friendship with an elderly gentleman (at least he seemed elderly to me in my youth) accompanied by an elderly lady, his wife. His name was Ossiasson. He is well known as a nonfigurative painter, and he died only a few years ago. A Russian Jew from Odessa, he had come to France at the beginning of the century. . . . He had designed stage sets for Diaghilev. Having learned to paint in the academic style, he subsequently followed the path of his generation. His erudition, both pictorial and literary, was prodigious. We spent the summer chatting away. He had taken a liking to me, and it was reciprocated. I would like to tell you about two conversations I have always remembered.

First, what he said to me about Picasso: "He is the devil. He is immensely talented, but his painting is malicious. He is spiteful; an evil spirit dwells in him. He is a genius, but he is nasty, bad." Hence, he considered the will, man's freedom, as a determining factor in the painter's act.

The other conversation was about the act of painting, which is, in the end, a spiritual and mystical act. Ossiasson brought up the search for the absolute, the almost impossible search for something beyond one's self, the act of a man who creates but creates something that destroys what is beyond himself because he thinks it is impossible. . . . On hearing this remark, I pronounced the name of God. I saw Ossiasson go pale, and he began to shout, "Don't ever pronounce that name!" (He knew very well that I was a believer.) "Don't ever pronounce that name!" It was as though, for him, God could not be called God. He had in mind so-called religious painting, the figurative paintings of the Italians, Spanish, even the French, and it seemed to him that the word *God,* a prisoner of this kind of painting, led one away from the mystery of God. He thought that he did not believe. Tragically, he felt as though God ought to exist and yet he could not succeed in seeing him. As far as he was concerned, what most people called God could not be God. The meaning of his nonfigurative quest consisted in saying, "Why do you expect us to paint faces that look like photographs? . . . This is not what has to be done. We have to search for that other reality that remains hidden. It is further away and it is precisely what I object to your naming."

Painting can be a spiritual adventure. When I look at the development of modern painting since the beginning of the century, I conclude that it is the painters who have been our cultural prophets. It was they who detected the subversion that was taking place: they even helped to create it. And it was an ambiguous subversion, sometimes diabolical, like Picasso's, sometimes desperate in its search for the unnamable good, like that of so many others. I remember that when I saw Picasso's paintings in the Museum of Modern Art in New York, I stood rapt, intoxicated. I found them extraordinary, but I kept asking myself what spirit possessed them.

MISSIKA: *That has nothing to do with morality. . . .*

LUSTIGER: But it does!

MISSIKA: *Why?*

LUSTIGER: Because to use the right color is a good act, it is *right.* . . . That is what we have to understand. It is not the fact of showing a nude woman or of taking such and such a subject that . . .

MISSIKA: *Good sentiments make bad literature. . . . They must also make bad paintings. . . .*

LUSTIGER: No, no. You are way off base! Miró writes about this in his journal. Painting for those people was a search for the absolute, a spiritual quest. But today's painters no longer have a common language. Each of them is obliged to create his own. They are hopelessly alone, and their art no longer has any social significance outside the galleries.

MISSIKA: *But there is a meaning for the artist....*

LUSTIGER: Yes, but it stems from a personal adventure without social meaning, except for the art dealers. Painting has become art for domestic consumption. Its only criterion is whether or not it will sell to private collectors or, in a pinch, whether it will be bought by a museum—that is, relegated to a cemetery.

WOLTON: *Why is the Church absent from contemporary art movements—painting, sculpture, music, indeed, architecture—when she was so present in the past and all those forms of artistic expression are much indebted to her? Why this abandon, and why is the Church witnessing only to the past?*

LUSTIGER: There are perhaps two sets of causes: those arising from the internal crisis of modern art and those coming from within the Church. If there is a disjunction of representation and figuration in aesthetics, that means that there is a spiritual crisis in the Church herself, in the various Christian cultures or peoples in which she is implanted. It is a sure sign. The divergences between aesthetics and spirituality are an indication of a brewing crisis. The popular religious art of the nineteenth century was characterized by an *art rétro*—that is, fake Gothic, then fake Romanesque, and finally fake Byzantine. This propensity for looking backward—it has been the case for almost two centuries—points to a widespread situation whose origins are to be found more in the depths of Christian life than in its social organization.

WOLTON: *Currently, with abstract art, it is something else.*

LUSTIGER: The social function of art, including religious art, is no longer the same. There has always been a re-utilization of elements from the symbolic heritage for new creation, but now people are content simply to imitate the past. Contemporary art went through a formidable crisis that called its social function into question. The refusal of figuration, in my opinion, is an overtone of the atheistic negation or at least of a certain distancing from God. Today, art has reached such extremes that artists are cautiously beginning to return to figuration. There is no mistaking the evidence: perhaps we are coming out of a certain phase and going beyond hyperrealism or varied collages. If artists are mystically inspired, there will be creative geniuses. There are two ways of seeing the Church's role. She can be a silent partner or a diffuser, but in that case, she is only a patron. But what is radically needed are artists who share the common faith and then express it in their original styles. At that point, art becomes something entirely different. In the nineteenth century, the Church was a patron, like the bourgeois state, but what she got was "pretentious" painting in the style of Saint-Sulpice, just as the state got its Flandrin.[2] If geniuses are to be produced, it is not enough to be a silent partner!

WOLTON: *Yes, but it has been a very long time since the Church nourished artists from within her bosom. For a period in the nineteenth century, she was at least a patron.*

LUSTIGER: From the moment that I came to know "artisan" painters and sculptors (some of them do not accept being called artists), I have observed that they are fascinated by the religious object. Today, the *art du chevalet,* art for exhibition to which the aesthetic function has been reduced, has resulted in a reduction of the artist's role, and we are suffering the consequences. In that more favorable era to which you allude, the Church offered walls and ceilings to painters and also sacred spaces to sculptors. In that case, art did have a social function. . . .

WOLTON: *But what is to prevent the Church from doing the same thing today?*

LUSTIGER: Nothing, nobody, except perhaps the interior crisis that we have been discussing . . . and lack of money! Today it is the state that has the wealth. And art has become an object of speculation. There are the prices and laws of the marketplace.

WOLTON: *True, but this interior crisis has certainly been drawn out: it started three centuries ago! In a rational and scientific society, the Church might have been able to claim or become responsible for the nonrational dimension of reality and express a spiritual pursuit. It appears that she has not done this.*

LUSTIGER: But beauty is not opposed to truth in the way that the nonrational is opposed to the rational. As classical philosophy said, the transcendental categories—the True, the Beautiful and the Good—communicate with each

[2] Hippolyte Flandrin (1809–54) was a French painter who executed large murals in a serious, correct and rather cold style.—TRANS.

other and are interchangeable: I think that the aesthetic approach to truth is extremely important as a basis for theological work. I consider that such a theoretical claim, which is being made today by intellectuals and theologians, is the dawn of a new, brighter era, both for society and the Church.

WOLTON: *What do you mean when you say that modern art symbolizes a society that is radically at odds with itself?*

LUSTIGER: I mean that it is a world closed in on itself, believing that in order to liberate itself it has to undergo a destructive experience—a nihilistic one, or at least one that refuses the canons that have shaped it up to now.

MISSIKA: *I do not understand the connection you are making between aesthetic or cultural history and the artist's social status or the art market.*

LUSTIGER: The aesthetic act is a spiritual act that can be borne only by the spiritual values prevalent in a given society. Whatever the originality of the artist, even though it may be hard to understand, it is supported by a social coherence. But there comes a time when society can be considered spiritually dead—or, at the very least, its strictly spiritual component can become disassociated from the aesthetic adventure. You have to be able to explain, for example, why Saint Thérèse of Lisieux, a great mystic, such a spiritual innovator and so prodigiously modern, is so disappointing on the aesthetic level—in her poetry and painting. It is the sign of an era in a state of disjunction, of breaking apart.

MISSIKA: *But an artist is never reconciled with society, whatever the society.*

LUSTIGER: By definition, the artist is "asocial" and independent. Fine. But so is the mystic! However, there have been periods and societies in which the act of commissioning and the act of painting were directly connected. Take Fra Angelico: both acts came from the interior. . . . But what happens when the painter finds himself alone before his wall and says to himself: What am I doing here?

WOLTON: *Hasn't that question been asked by every painter, regardless of the historical period?*

LUSTIGER: Certainly. But today, because of the revolt against art, because of art's mercenary character, there is an aggravation of the aesthetic crisis. Mind you, I am not advocating an ideological art subordinated to the Church.

I am simply saying that the aesthetic adventure led by artists at the beginning of the century, in breaking the shackles, turned them into blind prophets.

Religious Activity among Students

WOLTON: *Did students at the Sorbonne talk very much about religion, and how did you see religion's role in that completely secular world?*

LUSTIGER: It was an explosive period of apostolic witness—both fruitfully and controversially so—from within and without. My first concern, after setting foot on Parisian streets and enrolling in the Sorbonne, had been to find the chaplain of the JEC [*Jeunesse étudiante chrétienne*]. He turned out to be a Jesuit whose name was Jean Daniélou.[3] Thus, I fell on an extremely bright young priest, full of exuberance, with whom I was linked in a respectful and grateful friendship ever afterward. From the beginning of the academic year in 1944, I participated in a group motivated by politico-religious aims. Its intention was to respond to the Christian vocation by a kind of sociopolitical action, by getting involved in student unionism and various other activities available to us. The underlying theoretical question was to what extent our commitments to these activities could be defined as "religious". Was it an apostolic mission? In what sense? What was the relationship between this kind of activity and its stated end: the accomplishment of God's will and the coming of his reign? And even after forty years, we are still debating this question! At the time, however, it was posed in those terms.

The JEC proposed an institutional type of goal. As for myself, I joined right away what was beginning to be called "student unionism". At first, I belonged to the "classics" branch, which met somewhere in the garret of the Sorbonne. We were called the GEA, *Groupe d'Études Antiques.* A year later, I became the president. I was also the second president of the FGEL, the *Fédération des Groupes d'Études de Lettres de Sorbonne* [Federation of Arts Studies Groups at the Sorbonne].

In those days, there were two colleges at the Sorbonne: one for *lettres* [arts], the other for sciences. Thus, there were two sections of the JEC, two Catholic groups. The chaplain for the Catholics in the College of Arts, appointed by Cardinal Suhard, was Abbé Charles, vicar at Saint-Étienne-du-Mont. Abbé Charles immediately gave a very strong impetus to that group and subsequently brought about a merger of the different Catholic organizations—the main ones being the JEC and the GCL (*Groupe Catholique des Lettres*). There was

[3] Jean Daniélou (1905–74) was a specialist in the writings of the Church Fathers, and he was a brilliant apologist. Created a cardinal in 1969, he publicly defended traditional orthodoxy in the turmoil of the early Seventies.—TRANS.

also a Scouts group headed by Pierre Schaeffer, a graduate of the prestigious École Polytechnique, and a *Conférence de Saint-Vincent-de-Paul*[4]. . . .

Very early on in the academic year 1944–45, Abbé Charles—who was dealing with students whose ages ranged from eighteen to twenty-five, some of whom had taken part in the *Résistance*—used an extremely firm language. He urged the leaders of these different organizations to get together, and with a kind of premonition he said, "I am going to bring you together in a council" (that was the word he used) "so that united you can take on the responsibility for the Church to be built at the Sorbonne." He also succeeded in renting a small space for all these people to meet at 2, Place de la Sorbonne. This union of the various organizations took the name of Centre Richelieu, in memory of the cardinal who founded the modern Sorbonne, but even so the name was provocative. Almost immediately the *centre* gave considerable momentum to the Catholic presence, first in *Sorbonne-Lettres* and subsequently in *Sorbonne-Sciences:* it was a visible affirmation of the Church's existence among students. Later, a "council" was formed for each class in each of the colleges. It included an annual session of fifteen days, during which those who had participated in the activities of the ending year would assess them and help to plan for the year to come.

WOLTON: *Was there no conflict among the various tendencies? No opposition between progressives and conservatives?*

LUSTIGER: Yes, in general there were two positions between which I am going to make a clear-cut distinction, but, in fact, their differences were more *nuancées.* One stand consisted in saying that the Kingdom of God is the pursuit of justice, and hence every pursuit of justice is a pursuit of the Kingdom of God. Consequently, if you were working politically for the good and the true, you were working for God. This could dispense a person from any other form of activity or even rule it out.

The other group said basically that the Kingdom of God is not of this world; it belongs to a different order, the order of revelation, of fidelity to God, judge of everything. This order does and must shed light on everything, but it cannot be reduced to any of the temporal realizations in which man's responsibility is engaged. Furthermore, the reign of God belongs to God and not to man, even if man must work to make this earth more just and more in conformity with what he knows to be good. We who are mere men are incapable of meting out justice in the divine sense of the word—that is, of

[4] This was a branch of the charitable organization created in the nineteenth century by Frédéric Ozanam, under the patronage of the seventeenth-century saint. It was a spearhead of "Social Catholicism".—TRANS.

judging the profound probity, the internal honesty of consciences and hearts. We know neither the ultimate secret of good and evil nor that of human destinies.

I shared the latter opinion because regarding politics as sacred means being ripe for the holy war and all totalitarianism. I had a keen consciousness that, after Hitlerism, such an attitude was impossible. The history of communism is another affair. We shall come back to it, no doubt, because communism's attractions . . .

WOLTON: *Communism appealed to you?*

LUSTIGER: Yes. It represented a definite temptation for all my generation. But I was never close to succumbing to it. I remember once having interrupted a dignified theologian who advocated socialism to ask, "And what about original sin?" I could not have been very much of a theologian at the time, but it was precisely the sensitive point in the system he was talking about. It meant that if there had been no sin in the world, one would have been able to imagine an ideal city where man would have no need of a savior—and thus, of God—to bring about his salvation.

The theoretical theological position to which I adhered corresponded to that of *Témoignage chrétien* before its transformation, which was to take place several years later. Its editors Chaillet and de Lubac, as well as Fessard, were acutely conscious of the necessity for what was then called a "secular commitment", but they also spoke about the Christian implications and conditions for this kind of action. Their ideas were concerned with the defense of man and thus were antitotalitarian. In the background, there were Maritain and the whole range of eminent liberal figures from the prewar period. But simultaneously they affirmed that the political order could not become the decisive level of human existence and, therefore, could neither sum up its religious content nor determine the order of faith. The totality of human existence cannot be realized in the human city, in *la cité* as we always used to say. We considered ourselves to be living in a propitious period because, at last, the public and political position of Catholics seemed to be finding its place. We were doing away with centuries of conflicts and exclusions, those of clericalism and anticlericalism, all those conflicts from before and during the war.

MISSIKA: *But wasn't it also because the Catholicism of the right no longer had a voice? Those who had collaborated were discredited, but surely they had not disappeared as if by magic.*

LUSTIGER: Certainly not. But a part of the Catholic right had joined the *Résistance*.

MISSIKA: *The other part was simply reduced to silence.*

LUSTIGER: Yes. But, at the same time, there was a considerable revival of Catholic thought in France. Certain men from the founding group of *Témoignage chrétien* were among the initiators of the patristic revival and participated in the collection *Sources chrétiennes,* which had just been established.

As early as 1945, Father Daniélou had created the journal *Dieu vivant.* With an ecumenical open-mindedness that was surprising for the times, it prepared the ground for a revival of Christian thought in its biblical and Patristic categories. It rekindled interest in the earliest Christian literature and asserted that the reaffirmation of God's transcendence was "modern" indeed.

Dieu vivant was intended to take up the problems of Catholicism and contemporary thought, not as political categories—simplistic, in the end—but in their relationship to the meaning of history. It did not accept the super-interpretation of a progressive schema that aimed to say, "There are the progressives, and that's us, and since all the rest of you are not progressives, then you are reactionaries." Once it was accepted that Christians belonged to either one group or the other, then there was nothing left to do except pit one group against the other.

MISSIKA: *You have not yet replied to our question about the place of religion in the student milieu.*

LUSTIGER: I am badly placed to answer that because I am a convert. I was "out of step" and I remain so. I gauge this when I recall the situations and clashes, the numerous and repeated discussions to which I was witness—and in which I was sometimes a participant. What appeared obvious to me was not obvious to the others, and vice versa. To many of my fellow students, some of my strongest convictions seemed to come from out of the past, as though marked by a kind of—I shall not say traditionalism, but, in the end, something very close to it. . . . Some of them, reacting in just the opposite way from me, were obsessed by the desire to free themselves from what they had received from their upbringing, what they regarded as a constraint.

MISSIKA: *Their heritage, in a way.*

LUSTIGER: Yes, a heritage that was restrictive and had to be rejected so that they could be themselves. It seemed clear to me that this heritage, rather than being a constraint, was a great benefit, a hidden treasure whose plenitude and scope I was discovering. To me, it seemed insane to reject, without even being aware of it, what was not a yoke but a source of freedom.

WOLTON: *Then you did not share the general feeling toward the Christian heritage?*

LUSTIGER: The people with whom I felt most at ease were of two types. First, the unbelievers. I could well understand the exterior point of view: I had come from there. I had never had to go to Mass on an empty stomach, never been obliged to confess, nobody ever checked to see whether I was receiving Communion, no religious act had ever been imposed on me in any way. In my education, no ethical or moral standard had ever been forced on me. Yes, those standards had been taught by my parents; yes, they had been transmitted as a duty and an honor, since they came from our "election". But I had not been coerced. I had never been "forbidden" to visit the unorthodox or anyone else I wanted to see. . . . I had never had to eliminate anybody.

WOLTON: *And who were the others to whom you felt close?*

LUSTIGER: The converts. There were lots of them.

WOLTON: *Lots!*

LUSTIGER: Oh, yes, there were all sorts, a great mixture; it was more or less a continuation of the prewar period. Some were Jews; I was not the only one. There was a bit of everything represented.

WOLTON: *In comparison to your experience at Orléans or later during the war, did you still have the impression of an individual destiny?*

LUSTIGER: I was not a rare bird, not a unique one, in any case. The category existed: it was not a group, but many converts could be identified.

WOLTON: *The first Catholic postwar movement that you have mentioned was characterized by a political commitment on behalf of the excluded and the working classes, in contrast to the French episcopate, which was more to the right and more conservative.*

LUSTIGER: Not at all! The French episcopate, to a man, supported the MRP.

MISSIKA: *After the great majority had been Pétainist!*

LUSTIGER: It was not in those terms that the question was posed to our generation.

A Generation of Left-Wing Christians?

WOLTON: *How did you situate yourself on the political scene? In what ways were you involved?*

LUSTIGER: As president of the FGEL [*Fédération des Groupes d'Études de Lettres de Sorbonne*], I voted for the Grenoble charter.[5] I was one of the leaders with *"jéciste"* leanings; and it was this faction, allied with the Communists who pushed through—over the heads of the *corpos*,[6] whom we considered reactionary—the definition of the student as a "young intellectual worker". As for national politics, I did not follow it very closely. On the other hand, our generation was, as we said then, *"engagée"*. We imagined that we were building a new France that would in no way resemble the old one. It was going to bring about, at last, an equitable society in which we, the youth, would be the protagonists. As time went on, a certain disenchantment set in, and we began to remove ourselves somewhat.

However, the theoretical stakes of political action were linked with Marxism. They revolved around the question: Does history have a meaning? Marxism's appeal, at least for youth like us, stemmed from what we believed to be its efficiency, its coherence and its capacity to interpret reality. Would it be possible to salvage all that for Catholicism's profit, or could Catholicism produce comparable tools? I took this question along with me to seminary, and it converged, up to a point, with the pursuit of progressive Christians. In 1948, a group of six or eight of us met in a fellow student's apartment for a discussion with Raymond Aron,[7] who had very graciously accepted our invitation. After we had spent the evening talking about whether history had a meaning, etc., our distinguished guest treated us to quite an extraordinary session of *"rabotage"*![8] I do not recall all the details, but I do remember that although Raymond Aron was perfectly polite, he wasted no time in bringing our excessive statements down to size. He forced us to stop and think. The obsessive question revolved around commitment. Commitment was the supreme value. All that against an existentialist background. The existentialist-Marxist commitment, do you get the picture?

MISSIKA: *Did you ever consider joining the Communist Party?*

[5] The Grenoble charter marked the birth of the UNEF (*Union Nationale des Étudiants de France*—the National Students' Union of France).—TRANS.

[6] The *corpos* stood for a more strictly corporatist vision of student unionism.—TRANS.

[7] Raymond Aron (1905–83) was a French philosopher and sociologist who was an outspoken critic of Marxism.—TRANS.

[8] *Rabotage* is the French word for a "planing down a piece of wood".—TRANS.

LUSTIGER: No, not for an instant. Because I had the intuition that it represented a reversed "religious" image, raised to a frenzy of extremes by Stalinism, as Annie Kriegel subsequently described it.[9]

WOLTON: *Who were the others, those who were much more tempted than you to utilize Marxism as an analytical tool—indeed, to adhere to its political schema?*

LUSTIGER: They were often Christians who were called "progressives" in the technical sense of the word, or they were fellow travelers or even Party members. They had created the theory for supporting the Party or of the Party's integration into Christian action. And certain Christian groups pushed this theory quite far. Christian activity, pastoral practice, the situation of priests, including their professional work and relations with unions and political parties, were all formulated and implemented "dialectically". The hierarchy at the time was naïve and defenseless. These progressives did not let you off lightly, but they were divided, torn, unsure of themselves and unable to carry through their inherently contradictory positions to the end, precisely because of that part of the Christian heritage whose existence they continued to maintain.

As for myself, I belonged to the "party of progress", that was obvious. I saw myself as a progressive in all respects—I stood for renewal and was concerned with the future. . . . I would never have put up with being treated as a "conservative". When I had to situate myself politically, I would say that I was "to the left". It was even unthinkable that I could be "to the right". This is the way so many of my contemporaries and I saw ourselves! Everything associated with the hope for change and renewal was in the same perspective. The title of the journal *Jeunesse de l'Église* was significant. The first issue, devoted to its plan of action, came out in Lyon in 1942. Its drifting—and its disappearance around 1950—traces exactly the same evolutionary line as that of a part of French Catholicism. All of that generation was obsessed with an image of the senescence of rites, of a worn-out clergy, an antiquated religion that was in stark contrast to what we were living through. Everything that we were doing seemed to be full of life, youth, innovation, invention and *"créativité",* as people said later. In this context, the relationship to Marxism was ambiguous in that we were uncertain as to how to recognize, for Christianity's benefit, what seemed to be an advantage or a truth revealed by the tool of Marxist understanding. I remind you that we are talking about a period that not only preceded the Cold War but also the wider awareness of

[9] Annie Kriegel (1926–) is a professor of political sociology at the University of Paris and an editorialist for *Le Figaro.* The book referred to here, *Les grands procès dans le système communiste,* was published in 1972.—TRANS.

Leninism's real consequences in the USSR. I saw Soviet countries for the first time in 1950, in Berlin. I had certainly read Gide's *Retour d'URSS,* but nobody—the Communist Party was, after all, the "Party of the executed"!—at that time could have, would have dared to say . . .

MISSIKA: *Some people, like Souvarine,*[10] *had said and written it well before the war, but nobody would listen.*

LUSTIGER: Some said it, and they were not heard because they could not say it loudly enough. There was a kind of fascination exercised by Marxism in its most religious (most equivocal) aspects: its eschatology, historical logic, totalitarian or totalizing claims and its mixture of ethical values—justice—with the realism of action.

I observed Christian friends who, after completely rejecting the Catholic institution in the name of spiritual arguments, turned around and buried themselves more and more in an identification with the Marxist ideal, to the point that they eventually became "clerical-Marxists" and accepted constraints from the Party's discipline that they would never have tolerated had they come from the Church.

WOLTON: *Why were Christians, and Catholics in particular, tempted to that extent by Marxism? Did that temptation signify a total incapacity on the part of Christianity to produce its own analytical categories of social reality?*

LUSTIGER: Probably. But I am coming to that question, which I date from 1948 or '49. I had seen the choice: either the "progressive Christians" were right, and in that case you had to go further than they—because they had gone only halfway—and join the Party and cease to call yourself Christian; or else they were wrong and you had to be able to understand and demonstrate how they were wrong. In any case, you could not stay in midstream. Therefore, it was necessary, if not to retrace your course, at least to change it—that is, to change the problem's formulation.

That was my personal position in those years, but there cannot have been very many people who insisted on its clarification. In retrospect, I am very grateful to my teachers at the Institut Catholique, among whom were Daniélou and Bouyer, but also to those people whose words I read at that time: de Lubac, Fessard, Raymond Aron, Henri Marrou and many others. . . . The

[10] Boris Souvarine (1895–1984) was one of the founders of the French Communist Party. He was later a secretary of the Third International and, as such, collaborated with Lenin, Trotsky, et al., before being excluded from this organization for "indiscipline". After breaking with the Party, he wrote a biography of Stalin and a survey of Bolshevism that appeared in France in 1935.—TRANS.

accumulation of various intellectual tools permitted a certain number of people of my generation to have, if not a rigorously formulated position, at least a sufficient means of getting ourselves out of the "trap" of the characteristic issues of those years following the liberation, to clarify the confusions of the times, in particular those about the meaning of history—that question that people were dragging around like a ball and chain!

Seminary and Theological Education

WOLTON: *You entered seminary in 1946. Why so late? Why not in '44?*

LUSTIGER: Why so late? I would be tempted to reply, "Why so early?" In 1944 I was still quite young, only eighteen, and there was a family conflict to be resolved; it was not just going to take care of itself. I had decided to enter seminary only after reaching my majority. Relations with my father were very difficult, and Abbé Veuillot, whom I continued to see, had advised, "First you must get your degree, and then you will see." What is unusual is that I entered seminary before finishing my degree in *lettres.*

After two years at the Sorbonne, I sensed that the time was right, that I would gain nothing by waiting any longer. It seemed obvious that I had to make a decision because I still had ahead of me a minimum of two years of philosophy and four of theology—thus, six years of study plus a year of military service. All I can tell you is that I was determined to go ahead. There was again an extremely vehement clash with my father. It was very cruel, very brutal. I was not yet twenty-one, and my father took the drastic measure of cutting off all my means of existence, even the *cartes d'alimentation.* . . . It was very painful. The storm subsided two years later, but I did not see my father during the interim, and so I was alone.

WOLTON: *Who are the professors and what are the movements that marked you most?*

LUSTIGER: I went through two very distinct periods. In the first, I studied philosophy, and in the second, theology. There were different faculties whom I appreciated differently.

The other element to consider is my fellow seminarians. We numbered over sixty and all of us had previously studied at university. I met there—brought together in an atmosphere of intellectual freedom and freedom of speech that was apparently extraordinary for the times, but seemed normal to me—personalities as different as Marc Oraison[11] and the man who became the "Abbé de Nantes",[12] who is presently not in communion with the Church. It was an effervescent, fascinating environment, very lively and full of contrasts. There was surely nothing mediocre about it. During most of my time there, I was fortunate to have as a superior, Monsieur Enne, a man of faith whose keen sensitivity was as great as his general culture. He was a Sulpician who had been greatly tried by postmodernism. A fervent reader of Blondel, he poked fun at the successive theological *modes,* forcefully reminding us of the essential. But he did all this against a background of a skepticism and anxiety that had been overcome.

WOLTON: *Did the other seminarians know about your personal history?*

LUSTIGER: I said nothing about it. I have never felt the need to confide in people. I have a horror of playing the convert who has to tell his story. I have always had an insuperable sense of propriety, and when I was appointed Bishop of Orléans, it was really an ordeal to have to talk about myself. I have never hidden who I am, but I have never wanted to make it a subject of conversation. Exhibitionism offends me.

MISSIKA: *Did you ever hear any of the seminarians make shocking remarks about Jews?*

LUSTIGER: None that I can remember, none that hurt me. Perhaps I heard them and forgot, which would indicate a censoring mechanism, or else there were simply none to hear. I kept a very strong consciousness of my identity. There were other young men of Jewish origin at the seminary.

WOLTON: *Did you ever have a feeling of being something of an outsider?*

LUSTIGER: Maybe, relatively speaking. The problem came less from Judaism than from a sense of the sacred, the sense of the absolute of God.

WOLTON: *Did you ever lose your temper?*

LUSTIGER: I did. I could not help it. I am temperamentally incapable of suppressing those kinds of upsets. And later I realized that I was, in part, unfair.

[11] Marc Oraison became a famous and controversial priest-psychoanalyst.—TRANS.

[12] Georges de Nantes founded, even before the Second Vatican Council, an arch-conservative Catholic movement that he still leads.—TRANS.

MISSIKA: *You did three years of philosophy at seminary. What was the teaching level like?*

LUSTIGER: I was bedazzled by one or two professors, and by three or four others I was . . .

MISSIKA: *. . . disappointed?*

LUSTIGER: Yes! Compared to what I had known at the Sorbonne, they were not up to the task.

WOLTON: *What was the curriculum like?*

LUSTIGER: First of all, there was a remarkably interesting and intelligent nonphilosophical course, given by Father Louis Bouyer, that the seminary's superior strongly advised us to take. The lectures were later published as a book, *La Bible et l'évangile.* Father Bouyer described the state of biblical criticism in so far as it was then accessible to students at the university level, and he stressed a religious and theological understanding of Scripture. His vision agreed with what I knew to be true, but up to that time, it had had no confirmation other than my own naïve reading of Scripture. He emphasized the historical continuity of Judaism and Christianity as well as the spiritual *nouveauté* of the Gospel. Already in his book, published years ago, there was a supplement dealing with the link between the Last Supper and the Passover.

Some courses in philosophy were excellent. Father Dominique Dubarle—a specialist in the philosophy of science, an Aristotelian and Thomist and an outstanding *connaisseur* of Hegel—taught a course in cosmology that was an introduction to metaphysical intuition. In it he compared Aristotelian and modern scientific categories. The vision of the scientific world to which he bore witness and his philosophical reflections were on a very high plane. I was very far from feeling that I had plunged into an obscurantist world; on the contrary, I was made to see the most advanced aspect of contemporary issues.

Daniel Lallemant was a completely amazing person. With his Grand Inquisitor's face, ascetic and dogmatic, he had a very bad reputation among the liberals. A strict Thomist, representing that constellation of minds who had clustered around Maritain, he gave courses introducing Thomism and also some that he called sociology. His positions on society (just like Maritain's, incidentally) could be considered "to the left" while his Thomism and doctrinal rigor would have classed him "to the right". He made us think. I heard him dismiss Kant with one word: "Rotten!", and Sartre with: "Hum, hum, hum, hum!" (an inimitable snigger). You must excuse his blasphemy, but, after all, in 1946 it was a good thing to have the courage to show your nonconformity in front of young intellectuals. . . .

There was also Father Fillière, who presented an anthropology from heterogeneous but stimulating sources. His dominant idea was that the desire for God is instinctive to man. Man is a "mystical animal". Those words had a familiar ring! Fillière, like Lallemant, covered the problems of totalitarianism and social doctrines by trying to unveil the ethical stakes involved. Thanks to these professors, I read Sorel[13] and many other authors. Instead of being satisfied, as they were at the Sorbonne, with explaining the theories, they tried to diagnose the finalities by referring to the resources of Christian thought. This kind of procedure satisfied me, even if I was not always assured by the rigor of their criticism of various authors.

MISSIKA: *Are you saying there was a considerable gap between teaching at the seminary and teaching at the Sorbonne?*

LUSTIGER: Yes, and for two years, I struggled between the two worlds: between the world of contemporary culture from which I had come—that of Marxism and existentialism—and the neo-Thomist world of my seminary professors. At that time, I read Maritain, Gilson and the history of philosophy from a Thomist point of view. But I was questioning whether Thomism was a philosophy or a theology that assimilates the elements of a philosophy. I could not understand how men of the twentieth century could pretend, after the stringencies of the eighteenth and nineteenth centuries, to construct a philosophy on the basis of what was obviously a theological synthesis.

Consequently, I did not become a neo-Scholastic. The role given to rational demonstration seemed to be excessive. And, in my opinion, this type of thought does not give sufficient recognition to history's role, which is so important in the Jewish and Christian experience. Moreover, if carried to its conclusion, a certain affirmation of nature—of its specificity and sufficiency—could lead to the conclusion that the relationship to God is superfluous, indeed, alienating. The danger is not imaginary. Is it not true that the feeling that God is man's rival (what I give to God, I take away from man) has permeated the Christian West since the fourteenth century? I know very well that this is not Saint Thomas' position; it is even a nominalist theory that he opposed. But how many Scholastics (indeed, Thomists) are nominalists? The Lutherans and the Jansenists believed that they could affirm God's sovereignty only to man's detriment. And, conversely, rationalism thought that it could

[13] Georges Sorel (1847–1922), a French sociologist, was the author of *Réflexions sur la violence* (1908)—in which he advocates that the working class should use violence in order to gain power—as well as of many works on philosophical, economic and moral problems.—TRANS.

affirm man only by destroying God. Maritain saw this danger, and he speaks about it in *Humanisme intégral*. Paradoxically, it was he who invented the idea of a nonsacred Christianity. Thus, he was involuntarily one of the fathers of the so-called progressive movement, even though in those fifty pages he is setting forth a history of relationships between nature and grace in Western thought in which he criticizes and denounces these doctrines.

WOLTON: *So you were Augustinian rather than Thomist in this classic debate?*

LUSTIGER: I read Saint Augustine, but I find these distinctions dated. One great question was debated by our teachers: "Is there a Christian philosophy?" And, as always, I was inclined to think that the problems posed by the generation of 1930 had been superceded.

MISSIKA: *The question of your generation was rather: "Is there a Christian politics?"*

LUSTIGER: Yes, perhaps. In any case, when I was in seminary, I had the impression of being plunged into a set of problems dating from prewar days. I invested several years in them and then became indifferent. Augustinianism does not interest me. What does interest me are Saint Augustine and the Church's Tradition. If you absolutely insist on "labeling" me, I identified myself with Father de Lubac's writings.

MISSIKA: *Did you go back to the Sorbonne during your years in seminary?*

LUSTIGER: Yes, in 1948–49 I did a supplementary year of philosophy. At the university, neither psychology nor sociology was yet detached from philosophy as an independent discipline. It is impressive, when you think about it. Forty years ago, the chief part of what are now called "the human sciences" did not exist in France. But even so, many of the courses were stimulating. Unfortunately, in the name of scientific neutrality and objectivity, too many professors hesitated to take a stand, except under cover of an author's thought.

WOLTON: *Yes, that was contrary to academic tradition.*

LUSTIGER: Exactly.

MISSIKA: *Did you have the feeling that the teaching of philosophy at the Sorbonne was behind the times?*

LUSTIGER: Oh, yes! I was a part of that unfortunate generation of philosophy students—those before Hyppolite, hence before Hegel—who were nourished by classical French philosophy alone. It was understood and transmitted in such a way that we could no longer get our teeth into it. Actually, we disdained it, but we had no access to anything else. Camus and Sartre were on the intellectual horizon, and we "rehashed" Marx but without being able to understand anything at all about him, because on the one hand there was the Communist Party and on the other, the inaccessible Hegel. Students who came soon afterward could delve into Hegel and Heidegger, whereas we had only heard their names mentioned.

WOLTON: *Is it easy to go from philosophy to theology?*

LUSTIGER: I spent more than a year trying to understand what theology was all about: What was its object? What was its method?

The method then used to determine what is to be believed was initially historical. Using external and internal criteria, an enormous critical effort was made to establish the origin, authenticity and value of the witness given by scriptural texts, the councils, the Church Fathers and accredited theologies. This work was extremely frustrating for someone with a philosophical turn of mind. It became apparent that we were in a methodological area akin to the study of sources I had been taught in the literature course at the Sorbonne, but the reasoning seemed to be "blocked" somewhere. In fact, what was at stake in the debate was the renunciation of a philosophical kind of procedure and the acceptance that the study of theology, although it used tools of intellectual rigor, had its sole source in the act of faith. Intelligence had to be submitted to normative laws imposed not by a human standard but by the relationship to God, the personal and shared relationship of which the Church is the guarantor. Therefore, I needed an intellectual conversion to enter the heart of theology. Father Guy de Broglie helped me to make it. If theology is a science, as Father Chenu used to say in the tradition of Saint Thomas, it can be so only in a truly analogical sense.

The theological demarche is a demarche of faith. The truth revealed in it is not of a speculative order; it is given in the contingency, the concreteness and singularity of history. That God spoke to Abraham, I had known since childhood. Absolute Transcendence entered into a relationship with man. If God declares himself, lends himself to thought, he can do it only by revealing himself as one who remains beyond man's grasp. Abraham was ready to believe in God, who revealed himself in concrete and historical circumstances, according to ways that he, God, had chosen. God spoke in Christ, his Chosen One. In him, he continues to declare himself today. The documents of faith are not invalid certificates to be stored away in filing cabinets: they continue to touch us in the present. The Church, Body of Christ, who receives her existence from God, is the place where the Word of God made flesh is declared by his Spirit; the Church is the witness and guarantor. She is not some kind of academy whose regulatory role suppresses freedom and the creative mind. Theology's norm is not found in the human mind but in the Church's Faith, which recognizes God's revelation in Scripture and in her Tradition. For the theologian, Scripture is holy; it is recognized and interpreted by the Church. To wonder about the method of theology is to deal with history and Christology, faith and the Church. It is also to penetrate the theologian's domain.

MISSIKA: *You say that it involves something beyond reason or, in any case, that you have to make a mental operation that amounts to a leap when compared to a classical rational discipline. Under these conditions, are we not in a domain where the discipline's objective is to distinguish what is authorized from what is not and thus to approach something that is essentially normative?*

LUSTIGER: Yes and no. Theological activity cannot be reduced to making inventories of revealed documents and their authorized interpretation. It is characterized by an incredibly fecund and diverse productivity, an abundance of thought, research, speculation and discovery. Through all this, theological thought has developed, with great difficulty and effort, apparently incompatible concepts like those of person and nature, which now belong to the common treasure of universal thought. The theological concept of history also comes from the revelation. In order to make the biblical affirmation conceivable, the human mind was led to redefine useful and fruitful metaphysical notions and thus to go beyond ancient philosophy's contributions.

Theology has done more than produce concepts; in the nineteenth century it gave rise to the major attempts at rationality. Hegel, for example, undertakes the secularization and rational reduction of the historical representations of Christianity. He is trying to bring the historical contingency into a rationality conceived by man and, through thought, to appropriate everything that gives meaning to history. But, in the revelation, what gives meaning to history is precisely what escapes it: the Spirit of God. The Hegelian aim is to reintegrate the source and absolute norm of meaning into history and the human subject's freedom. His demiurgical undertaking has a theological origin. Even its terms often remain religious.

The development of experimental science in the West was made possible by, among other things, the affirmation of the concept of creation. Nothing escapes the condition of the creature. Nothing of what man can attain escapes his domination. In other words, man's intelligence is sovereign, capable of understanding our world. A priori, that permits the lifting of every taboo that would impede the human mind's curiosity, thwart its desire to understand.

WOLTON: *But, conversely, do you have the impression that contemporary thought has a contribution to make to theology?*

LUSTIGER: Reason's effort in regard to the revelation is not sufficient to define the theological method. The empirical approach places human reason in the face of objects or religious statements; it reduces theology to objects or statements subjected to human intelligence. But the key to productivity in theological thought is that it is situated in the face of the Subject whom it is questioning and who has first questioned it. In other words, it comes face to face with God. Theology becomes sterile if it forgets that God is the Person it is confronting, if it ceases to believe that God is the living God. This is a terrible asceticism, and I am coming to modern thought's contribution to it by this apparent detour.

MISSIKA: *Is it possible to be a good theologian without having faith?*

LUSTIGER: That depends on what you call theology. If, as I do, you think of it as the search for God with all the resources of reason, with all the resources of human existence and divine grace, then the response is: "No, one cannot be a theologian if he does not have faith." Of course, there can be men searching for God, theologians without realizing it—or in spite of themselves. Nevertheless, only the person who desires to fulfill a mission that comes from his relationship with God can be a theologian. Without this relationship, he is simply studying "religious science". Similarly, the study of literature will not make you into a poet nor of art history into an artist.

MISSIKA: *But there is a "logy" in "theology". . . .*

LUSTIGER: Yes, but what is this *logos,* what is this word and who uttered it? I come back to the question you raised a little earlier: "Does contemporary thought contribute to theology?" Yes! Quite obviously! Most of the concepts of contemporary thought have arisen from religious thought, and they return to it in secular form. To be reintegrated, they have once more to be subjected to an exorcism.

WOLTON: *An exorcism! Well, then, atheistic thought must be the devil!*

LUSTIGER: No, but how the devil does frighten you! Take, for example, the case of historical criticism. It is a major tool for the documentary approach. The revelation is presented as something inscribed in history, as an event. From this, biblical and Christian thought produced history as a rational discipline. But in time, this discipline, as a critical and "superinterpretive" tool, was turned against religion. At present, the theological effort is inscribed in the trend of modern thought that criticizes the criticism in the name of a new step forward in hermeneutic reflection. Too many people today have stayed with the positivist teaching! It is the "vulgate" of Western thought, conveyed by common knowledge. It is very sad because this popularization has imprisoned a whole generation in already outmoded categories. Take the similar cases of sociology and psychoanalysis: I cannot help thinking that their conceptual tools are actually derived from theological data coming from the biblical world. Freud was a rigorous scientist. But that did not prevent him from suspecting, on the basis of his clinical practice, that clear and distinct reason was not the supreme norm. He restored all of symbolic thought, the idea of interpretation, the description of reason as desire spread out in time, with its relationship to the origins. . . .

WOLTON: *You are attempting an analogy with the revelation?*

MISSIKA: *In that case, a real exorcism would have to take place because there is sexuality. . . .*

LUSTIGER: If you believe that sexuality is not a part of the revelation, go and reread the first two chapters of the Bible. . . . *Moses and Monotheism* is the first book to perform psychoanalysis. It is a wonderful work that shows the extent to which psychoanalysis is useful in analyzing Freud.

WOLTON: *Why?*

LUSTIGER: Well, because he is settling his scores with Judaism and his father.

WOLTON: *You see an analogy between what he says about the primitive father and his relationship to his own father?*

LUSTIGER: Yes, and to Judaism as well, it is obvious.

MISSIKA: *And* The Future of an Illusion?

LUSTIGER: It is the same thing.

WOLTON: *We are going to take up psychoanalysis later. Coming back to your theological studies, what were the dominant intellectual trends at that time?*

LUSTIGER: We were faced with the aftermath of modernism. In the nineteenth century, in order to adapt the Church to modern society, exegetes and historians of dogma applied the methods of the fledgling historical criticism to Christian documents. Their goal was to show the evolution of the Christian message and Christian institutions. Some did it to defend the Faith and the Church. Others wanted to clear away everything that appeared to be incompatible with what reason—in their opinion—could accept. German Protestants were the ones who were the promoters of this movement; some of them came to deny all historical value and factual significance to the affirmations of faith. It is this tragedy of liberal Protestantism that provoked pietistic or fundamentalist reactions and also the very influential one of Karl Barth.

As for the Catholic Church, she reacted abruptly and vigorously reaffirmed the dogmas of the Faith. But an entire generation had the feeling of being torn between an ecclesiastical authority, which was imposing a mode of thought on theological matters (by not hesitating to employ disciplinary and even religious sanctions), and the obvious facts of critical reason, of historical reason—indeed, of speculative reason. People who continued to be more or less believing were "obliged" to subscribe to statements to which they could not truly adhere. All of a sudden, certain intellectuals found themselves in an equivocal position in regard to the Faith. The religious society maintained a doctrinal normality, but those who were its defenders were not really in agreement with it.

Some people got themselves out of the predicament by a kind of *fidéisme* or blind faith; their act of faith was obscure; they were living a contradiction, an avowed contradiction, between faith and reason. Others, and this was more serious, played a double game, used a double language, mixed what they thought reasonable to say with what they prudently left unsaid—while letting the latter be understood by implication, by allusion.

WOLTON: *What were your personal feelings about the modernism that developed in reaction to Scholasticism at the end of the nineteenth century? That antagonism had substantial intellectual consequences that are still with us.*

LUSTIGER: Allow me to distinguish my feelings: they were not the same for the advocates of *fidéisme* as for those who spoke a double language.

Renan and Loisy[14] never inspired my sympathy. To the tips of their toes, they were decidedly too clerical to be credible. The current of ideas that they represented, at its peak at the beginning of the twentieth century, seemed as

[14] Alfred Loisy (1857–1940) was a priest and a leader of the modernist exegetes. He lost his chair at the Institut Catholique de Paris in 1893, had his works condemned in 1903 and was excommunicated in 1908. He was then given a chair at the Sorbonne.—TRANS.

far removed from the students of my generation as World War II is to students today. It had marked many of our professors, but we were fascinated and influenced by other masters. Modernism's challenge to faith reached us through critical exegesis, studies about Christianity's origins and philosophical rationalism. The same persons who had helped me to understand the war's spiritual stakes, to defend myself from Marxism's attractions and to resolve the question about the object and method of theology furnished us with the necessary tools for criticizing modernism's principles and also for detecting its positive aspects. Thanks to those who initiated the biblical, patristic and liturgical movements in France, we were brought into contact with the treasures of early literature. And we approached them freely, without hesitating to use a strict critical method. This new Christian current uncovered a fragment of treasure that had remained hidden in the Faith's legacy, covered up since the Enlightenment by human reason's claim to an absolute sovereignty. It also revealed to us that there was something valuable in reason that should be retrieved. Reason's salvation consisted in using it while being aware of its limits. This renewed approach guarded us from both modernism and fideism. Our attitude toward the latter's supporters was admiring and compassionate: "What a pity that their generation did not dispose of the intellectual tools necessary for criticizing the principles of what they took to be rationality." At the same time, we esteemed those men of faith, like our superior at the seminary, who lived through those contradictions in fidelity. I can appreciate the ordeal to which some of them succumbed.

My attitude toward those who used two languages, one for thought and one for discourse, or also one for thought and one for behavior, was much more severe: do they still have faith, I kept asking myself. I was profoundly shocked. Either you believe something is true and you say so, or else you think that you have made a mistake, and then again you have to say so. You are free not to believe, but if you do not, then admit it. Besides, if a person has faith, he has to find reasons for it. The ordeal of the dark night cannot be reduced to a sham. Certainly faith can lead to the most radical kind of questioning because no one comes into contact with the absolute in vain, and reason can sometimes be deranged, stunned by it.

Little by little, an impression was confirmed. In the clerical world, whether in the life of the mind or in the organization of the Church's life, the grounds for faith were too often perceived of as a "datum" to which one was "obliged" to inscribe oneself socially, something that could not really be renounced but that had to be contradicted if one wanted to be modern. It was as though this social datum had to be skillfully handled so as to make it evolve from the interior, as one would act to make a trade union change its policy, for example. That has always made me feel very uncomfortable. I saw no reason to struggle in a social world that was not mine: it had meaning only if it accepted what it was bearing—namely, the absolute and the truth of the Faith. It is not the life of the empirical environment that gives significance and values to the Church; it is the Church who gives that meaning, whose dwelling place and witness she is, to social reality. The Church can have meaning only as long as she maintains her prophetic role of witness. Men can claim to speak in her name only to the extent that they are faithful to this mission.

WOLTON: *Given your history, your education at the Sorbonne and the fact that you were something of an "outsider", didn't you feel angry with the Church who, after all, had considerably provoked the modernist crisis or had, in any case, not known how to manage it other than by condemnation?*

LUSTIGER: I repeat that modernism did not seem to be my generation's problem. We already had the scope of understanding that distance and history give. The Church had resolutely reaffirmed what had to be believed. In practice, the fear of modernism had been a poor counselor. According to Father de Lubac, it caused one of the tragedies of the French Church: the abandonment of the rational field. People threw themselves into social and pastoral activities. That was good, but too little was invested in the theological terrain and the cost was great. There were some courageous exceptions: for example, Father Lagrange[15] in exegetical matters.

But we cannot blame men of a particular epoch for not possessing the indispensable conceptual tools. Their ordeal was necessary for forging them. How can we reproach, for example, the first three centuries of Christianity for not having forged the theoretical concepts that could have explained the Church's dogmatic affirmations? I am not going to censure Descartes or Malebranche because they did not invent phenomenology. Were Churchmen faithful in their behavior? Certainly not all of them. No one is ever perfectly faithful, including us. There have always been, alas, many lost opportunities.

WOLTON: *I am surprised by the contrast between your hostility to the Enlightenment and the little irritation you show against the Church as an institution for having missed the boat in an intellectual evolution.*

LUSTIGER: What do you want me to do? Should I take a whip? Pound the walls? Resentment has never produced anything. What interests me and seems useful is to understand our present situation so as to do the least harm possible.

WOLTON: *But you cannot do anything about atheistic rationalism either! And*

[15] Albert Lagrange (1855–1938), a French theologian, was one of the initiators of critical studies of biblical texts.—TRANS.

yet that does not prevent you from expressing an unequivocal hostility toward it. The fidéisme *and double language of some of your former professors visibly got on your nerves. But the ecclesiastical hierarchy's repression of the modernist movement hardly ruffles you.*

LUSTIGER: I feel no rancor. I look on all this with a benevolent and critical eye. "Yes, it was too bad, but could they have done anything else?" I have no bone to pick, I have no desire to rewrite history, pronounce a judgment or rap anybody's knuckles.

WOLTON: *I am going to restate my question. Too bad if it makes you angry. There is not just a condemnation of modernism by the* Lamentabili *decree and the* Pascendi *encyclical, in July and September of 1907, respectively. The conflicts continued until the period between the wars, and, even after World War II, priests and theologians favorable to the "new theology" were called neo-modernists by their neo-Thomist opponents. Moreover, the encyclical* Humani generis *(1950) protested against the "new theology" and explicitly targeted certain French theologians. At the time, people spoke about an ecclesiastical "McCarthyism". But each time this point is brought up, you say only, "It's a shame, but that's the way it is."*

LUSTIGER: I have been thinking about the overall evolution in the Western world. I am not a *corbeau*[16] who is eager to defend the clerical party. I am simply trying to be honest. One of the products of Western culture is an exaggerated ambition for reason. I belong to that generation who gathered the bitter fruits of reason's claim to unlimited authority. In the modernist tribulation, in face of the Enlightenment's reason, some Christians yielded to its fascination, sacrificing what would have made it possible for them to exorcise and surmount the tribulation. In a way, it is the Enlightenment that remains in question. Marx criticized it in the social and economic domains, and a criticism of clear and distinct reason was made by Freud. But the religious question? The reproach to be directed at certain Churchmen of those generations is perhaps that they did not know how to stand back far enough to rediscover the Church's buried treasure.

What bothered me in the mid-Forties was the feeling that, in clerical circles, both the progressives and their adversaries perceived the problem in the same way. They were dealing with the same data, the same terms, whereas they should have been trying to understand why things had functioned so badly on both sides. What part of the Faith's legacy had been obliterated by the excessive pretension of human reason? How was it possible to recognize that

[16] *Corbeau* is the French word for "crow". It is used pejoratively to designate a priest, a "black coat".—TRANS.

part of reason that was not an enemy but a precious partner to be welcomed? That was the real question. Accepting the dichotomy between an identifiable "progressive party", which coincided with some of the modernist premises, and the "reaction" of its opponent prevents both an understanding of the question and a hearing of the responses. It is a manipulation of intellectual history.

WOLTON: *I agree, but it is within these categories that a number of conflicts—within the Church and between the Church and the world—have been interpreted. Allegedly there existed a kind of scission between the modernists taken over by the leftist forces committed to the century and the conservative movement that opposed it.*

LUSTIGER: It is true that this is the way some of the participants experienced it. I am not shirking a debate, but I never identified myself with either one of those positions. Never.

WOLTON: *But you do recognize that this is the way the history of the French Church between 1945 and 1970 is interpreted?*

LUSTIGER: It is at least the historiographer's—sometimes official—interpretation. Some of them continue to write unflaggingly in the same terms. I find that their vision does not correspond to reality. I prefer to deal with non-Christian observers who are detached from the conflicts and see the insularity of such language and categorizations. This overly simplified analysis proves just how deep the crisis is, since even certain participants and spokesmen for a given group have no words for declaring themselves other than those that deny their own specificity, strength and stakes. From that moment, they can no longer understand what is happening right before their eyes.

Army Officer in Berlin

WOLTON: *Did you do your military service?*

LUSTIGER: Yes, in 1950, when I was twenty-four. I went to Germany—to Rastadt—for basic training in an infantry regiment. It was made up mostly of young men from the north of France, *"ch'timis"*,[17] some of whom barely spoke French. It was then that I became aware of the diversity and cultural gaps, in all respects, that can exist in France. I greatly enjoyed those three months. Immediately tagged as a seminarian, I was surprised to find that these men had

[17] *Ch'timis* is what people from the working class in northern France called themselves. —TRANS.

a relationship to religion that, although crudely expressed, was rich and confident. Afterward, I attended a school for reserve officers in Saint-Maixent. Because I was a seminarian, I had been against the idea; but the pressure to rebuild the army officer corps was great, and I finally let myself be convinced. We numbered between four and five hundred, among whom a third were *instituteurs,*[18] another third were seminarians and the rest were various students. We all belonged to the war generation that had experienced dissensions, disappointments and the wounded national pride. Basically, underneath the political commitments that were mostly to the left—reflecting the prevailing mood of the times—we were quite ready to feel patriotic and well disposed toward the army. Of course, the war was already going on in Indochina. The officers and the NCOs recounted their heroic memories of the Italian campaign; however, our main concern was still the national humiliation inflicted by Germany. I must say that, as a result of the tactlessness—the stupidity at times—of the training, there was a turnabout in the group's generally positive attitude. Many of the candidates began to balk at the mindless drill of military training. I viewed this situation as a missed opportunity to heal the wounds of our generation who had suffered from the French collapse. Perhaps this happened because most of the officers and the NCOs had fought outside of France, and thus they were not really aware of what had gone on under the German occupation. And, on our side, we could not understand on what combat experience and military victory they were basing their lectures. I do not know if this personal impression is indicative of a more general phenomenon.

MISSIKA: *But if the army's morale was low, wasn't that precisely an effect of the national humiliation?*

LUSTIGER: We were dreaming of Leclerc and de Lattre,[19] while all we got was the tedious life of the barracks. I soon realized that the clerical world was liberal, intelligent and open in comparison to that confined military society. But it was an excellent post for observing the exercise, in its raw state, of the fundamental mechanisms of social functioning, all the rituals, like making the bed *au carré,* which were submitted to codification and an impeccable rationalization, but whose repositories had lost all meaning. It was a harsh omen and cruel apprenticeship for other institutions.

Leaving Saint-Maixent as an officer cadet, I was able to choose a post in

[18] An *instituteur* is a primary school teacher. Until the late Sixties in France, men traditionally made up a large percentage of the teachers in elementary schools.—TRANS.

[19] Jean de Lattre de Tassigny (1889–1952), *maréchal de France,* escaped from prison in occupied France to join the Free French. In 1944, he led the *Première armée française* from Saint-Tropez to the Rhine and the Danube. In the name of France, he accepted the German surrender at Berlin in 1945.—TRANS.

Berlin. It was 1950, before the wall and after the blockade. The French army units occupied what we nobly called *"le camp Napoléon"*, but which had been constructed under the name of Hermann Goering Kaserne.

MISSIKA: *Why did you choose Berlin?*

LUSTIGER: It was a unique opportunity! I would be able to go back to Germany. And I would be returning as a member of the French Army—hence, as a conqueror, no? And then to see Berlin, to get so near to Eastern Europe was an exceptional chance!

MISSIKA: *There are men of your generation who promised themselves never to return to Germany.*

LUSTIGER: Yes, I know. But at that time, I was wearing the victor's uniform. I asked myself that question only later and differently.

The material conditions were good. As officers, we were put up in private houses in the city, and we spent only our "on-duty" hours in the barracks. At that time, you could pass freely from one sector of Berlin to any other, including the Soviet sector. From their side, the Germans in the Eastern zone could easily enter the Soviet sector of Berlin; thus, it was child's play to meet East Germans. For the first time I saw, not Marxism, but the Communists in power. I saw real communism. So much so that if there had been scales on my eyes (which was not exactly the case), they would have fallen off. I went through Catholic groups to make contact with East Germans, but even so, people were wary. They wondered who I was and dared not speak. It took time for them to accept me. I was able to observe, in the daily details of their lives, a situation whose deplorable characteristics are now known to everyone.

WOLTON: *Can you describe how you felt?*

LUSTIGER: Berlin—in particular, the Soviet sector—was a landscape of ruins whose horrifying destruction had remained frozen. I felt a deep pity for the people: the terror they had inspired had rebounded to rain down on them.

The grip of the Soviet occupier, when compared to that of the Western countries, had been savagely brutal until the war's end, and it remained merciless. In the beginning, I asked myself if this were not the habitual consequence of every military occupation. Did we not have to understand the Russian attitude as the victor's revenge on a cruel enemy? But afterward, I was wiser: I realized that I had been looking at a system. The ideological grip of the police and military occupation had replaced political life. The crude takeover of religious symbolism served to support the ideology. For example, the Russians erected a monument honoring the Red Army. An enormously wide avenue, at least a kilometer long, lined with huge blocks of stone engraved with bas-reliefs and inscriptions, leads to a small Byzantine-style mausoleum, a rotunda decorated with mosaics representing Soviet heroes. One Sunday, dressed in civilian clothes, I joined the crowd of Germans who were visiting it. Amazed, I saw men and women crossing themselves as they entered, as if by reflex. The symbolism and style of the place were such that you had to look closely to realize that you were not facing icons of saints but the triumphant heroes of the Red Army. And the Germans went for it! In the Eastern sector, only the "historical" films of the Stalinist era were being shown. They were worth seeing for their fantastic mythology! Stalin was God the Father, serene and peaceable, determining in advance the places and times of battle and victory.... Christian themes had been entirely transposed to serve Stalinist mythology. It was grandiose! The most curious thing was to observe the Germans who filled the theater. I never succeeded in finding out what they were thinking. A large part of Nazi officialdom had been immediately re-employed by the Communist system—shamelessly. Everyone with whom I could talk confirmed it: "They took back the Nazis to operate their machine. They were simply given a thin coat of whitewash and trotted out again." The system from the Nazi period had not even been overthrown but had been literally caught in flight and taken over to function in the Party's service by a simple change of label.

MISSIKA: *Did you meet any Christians?*

LUSTIGER: The Christians with whom I was able to speak drew a terrifying picture of a police state. Every expressed deviation threatened the security of persons and property. They had been reduced to the systematic use of a double language. They described a schizophrenic generation who, in order to survive, would be obliged to maintain the Marxist language on the exterior and, in order to live the Faith, would have to keep the Christian language on the interior. The one thing that remained was the family; it was their only defense, if that. In 1950, I could still recognize the Nazi Germany of 1936–37, denuded of its proud springtime, which had been replaced by misery, political and economic disaster, famine, shortages of all kinds. The Catholic Church, very much in the minority in the East, was growing, with refugees who were coming from the western part of Poland recovered from Germany, or from Silesia or the Sudetenland. Germans were being driven back from all the countries of central Europe.

The Church in East Germany seemed to be resolute in her positions and vigorous in her faith. For both Catholics and Protestants, she was a rallying point of spiritual resistance. Under conditions that were strikingly different, the same logic recently appeared in Poland: the only way of facing up to political totalitarianism is by spiritual resistance.

WOLTON: *Can this remark be generalized?*

LUSTIGER: According to Péguy's words, the greatest political force is mysticism. Mysticism can decline into politics. But when politics declines into totalitarian tyranny, only mysticism can oppose the enslavement of citizens. You may think that my remarks resemble theories on the revolutionary role of active minorities, but I am convinced that totalitarianism's only true victory is the captivity of minds. A purely military tyranny is not, in the end, so formidable because sooner or later it is bound to collapse: power never dominates indefinitely. As far back as memory goes, there is no example of human history of an immortal power. It crumbles from within. True slavery is the subjugation of the mind, the enslavement that is in the head of the slave. The Bible describes this in flaming letters: when Israel left Egypt, the true danger was not the Egyptians, it was the Egypt that was in the Hebrews' heads. In order to be free, they had to accept not missing Egypt and trusting in God and God alone. The political role of mysticism, therefore, is to be a genuine mysticism, because then and only then does it know how to decipher and express the reality of political power.

Political power in democracies where there is a diversity of opinions, confrontation of interests and various conflicts is something completely different. But from time to time in human history, politics has monopolized all social sacredness, and that is totalitarianism. The removal of politics from its pedestal relegates it to its true human place, practical and contingent, where it grapples with history's hazards and reason's calculations. However, although politics relies on the sacred, it does not belong to the same order: only God is truly sacred.

MISSIKA: *Did you ever witness any skirmishes between the Soviets and the Western occupiers?*

LUSTIGER: Yes, notably on Pentecost in 1950, when the Communist Party organized a youth parade through Berlin. The Westerners feared a "peaceful" invasion of West Berlin and thus all allied military forces were mobilized, the Americans were on war alert and the intelligence services were operating at full capacity.

I have kept in mind a chillingly impressive scene: a mass of young Communists marching in rows of sixteen or twenty on wide avenues surrounded by ruins; they passed by for hours and hours before a high reviewing stand where a Soviet marshal sat. Those young Germans were marching with goose steps and had shovels or pickaxes on their shoulders! Rubbing my eyes, I asked myself: Where are we? In Nazi Germany? To the rhythm of the music the youngsters clapped their hands as they shouted: *Freundschaft!* Friendship! Friendship! Friendship! It was a terrifying sight.

First Trip to the Holy Land

MISSIKA: *You made quite a few pilgrimages to the Holy Land. When was the first one?*

LUSTIGER: In the summer of 1951 while I was still in seminary. That first trip, which Abbé Charles asked me to organize for Sorbonne students, played a crucial role in my life. We were far from affluent, and the accommodations were extremely unpredictable. It was just after the first Judeo-Arab war. Our tour took us to Beirut, with stops in Cyprus and even Greece. We crossed Lebanon, Syria and Jordan to reach Jerusalem.

I had an extraordinary shock—both emotional and spiritual—on seeing the land of Israel, the Promised Land of Abraham, the Holy Land. When you are studying the Bible at your desk, you can ponder indefinitely about what is said or not said by avoiding too many questions about the reality of a particular event and the way it touches you. But there, in the Holy Land, I could not put anything having to do with the truth of such events between parentheses. The question presented itself in a historical way, and history, with a brutal and indisputable objectivity, presented itself geographically. The soil itself, the Holy Land and its inhabitants became so eloquent that a decision became urgent. I could no longer dodge the question.

WOLTON: *What question?*

LUSTIGER: Whether I would decide to adhere unreservedly to the reality of God's gift. I knew, of course, that some questions would remain open: rationality, internal coherence, the agreement of reason and faith—in short, a whole series of interrogations.

At the ultimate stage of this spiritual journey, I arrived at the holy sepulcher and walked into the semidarkness of the basilica—rather dilapidated during those years before its reconstruction. You had to stoop to go through the sepulcher's narrow door, and a monk holding a little candle, which gave off some light, stood guard to keep visitors from knocking their heads against the lintel. In short, the setting was about as unmystical as it could possibly have been. It was very hot. I found myself touching the marble slab that covered the rock. I touched it with my hands and put my forehead against its cool surface. Then I said to myself, "Just as true as the fact that this stone is here, that you are touching it, that it supports your hands and forehead and compels the recognition of your senses, you must decide, yes or no, if you fully adhere to the resurrected Christ, to God the Savior, to God's call to his people for the world's salvation. Or else you must leave—it is but time!" And the light given to me at that precise instant, in a word, the interior experience, can be translated in this way: the reasons for and against exist, they are not of equal weight, but they resolve nothing. On the other hand, what determines everything is my personal relationship to the one in whom I recognize myself created, called, saved, loved and capable, by the gift he makes to me, of being a witness to what has been granted to me. Such were the question and the decision. And I lived through the remainder of that month in a mixture of joy and distress. And I discovered with pride the land of my ancestors and also the state of Israel.

MISSIKA: *When you say pride, is it historical or religious?*

LUSTIGER: The two! But it was both pride and a question. I remember a nightlong discussion with an old man of Russian origin who was the head of an agricultural school near Nazareth. Everything revolved around secularism. He represented secular Zionism, and I was protesting, "You are consuming the reserves of the traditional Judaism that you reject. But what reasons will your children have to fight and survive? What will prevent them from leaving if you do not recover something of Israel's spiritual heritage so that it becomes rich in meaning and coherence? You think that you are constructing an ideal society. In fact, you are promoting a European utopia." These questions remain fundamental to me, and I passionately hope that they will be answered.

WOLTON: *And how did he respond?*

LUSTIGER: The response was a little embarrassed. He conceded that "Ben-Gurion has started to pray again" and that his generation was "beginning to rediscover the spiritual question of God". But he said especially, "Have confidence in us; we are building a state. First of all, we have to be able to give every citizen a job and a place to live; we are building a democracy."

MISSIKA: *It seems curious to me that you have so little confidence in national identity, in the adhesion to democratic ideals, in culture. You seem to think that a people collapses if it ever turns away from God.*

LUSTIGER: We are talking about Israel.

MISSIKA: *But so what! There is no reason why Israel should be different from any other country! It is your interpretation of the term* election *that seems debatable.*

LUSTIGER: Perhaps, but underneath the audacious challenge that the state of Israel represents, there is the hidden part of the iceberg, made up of four thousand years of faith and sacrifices. And this long history was not endured simply to construct a socialist or petit-bourgeois state.

MISSIKA: *But why not? Why do you exclude a secular interpretation of what has happened? A certain number of Jews, especially those coming from Eastern Europe, have had enough of suffering and have sought a means to make it cease. Maybe there is a religious or sacred interpretation of this event, but maybe, too, we should just leave the Israelis alone.*

LUSTIGER: Leave them alone, yes! But how could they go on living if they were to forget who they are?

II

THE HUMAN SCIENCES

Attraction and Repulsion

DOMINIQUE WOLTON: *How do you explain the fact that, after the war, the clergy was much more attracted than ever before by the development of the human and social sciences: primarily, history—we have already discussed that—but psychology and sociology as well? Actually, it seems that the Church became quite deeply absorbed by the subject matter.*

JEAN-MARIE LUSTIGER: It is difficult for me to give a balanced response. Possibly not enough time has yet passed. As far as psychology is concerned, the Church has always had a great interest in the subject, precisely because of the development of Christian anthropology. The case of sociology is different. Its religious roots do not appear as clearly. Sociology's objective, as Durkheim expressed it, seemed to be something truly new. Besides, the sociologists were attracted by the Church. For them, she was a fascinating object!

WOLTON: *But she could also be their "enemy"!*

LUSTIGER: The question of the sacred is at the heart of sociology. The Christian Faith is a system not only of beliefs or images but also of practices, and it has a social significance. Let me say it differently: in the process of secularization, the nineteenth century had been tempted to dismiss religion as belonging to the private and, hence, subjective domain. The theologians on one side and the men of action on the other—priests or laymen—were therefore obliged to reaffirm that the Church has a social aspect. *Les aspects sociaux du dogme* is the subtitle of Father de Lubac's book, *Catholicism,* which had a wide influence. De Lubac has always known how to treat the essential questions at the essential time or, in general, a little beforehand. Faced with the attempt to make religion a private and individual matter—while secular culture, sometimes antireligious, was undergoing a hypertrophy as the collective and social became increasingly important—certain Christians turned toward sociology. It was something of a defense reflex: they were refusing to make the religious experience private, and they wanted to rediscover that determining part of religion, the social phenomenon, while simultaneously explaining the necessity for acting. It seems normal to me that the Church was interested in the sociological venture. All the more so because, at its origins, sociology was focused on interpreting and understanding religion.

WOLTON: *Speaking of that, can you comment on Durkheim's definition of religion: "It is an interdependent system of beliefs and practices relating to sacred things—that is, separate, forbidden beliefs and practices that unite the members of a moral community called the church and to which those who believe in it adhere."*

LUSTIGER: It is a good description of the religious event; obviously it omits any mention of contents and references. If it were a description given by an Iroquois—since theoretically, the sociologist is an Iroquois, plunged into an alien society, who is trying to see things differently from any of that society's members—then I would say that the Iroquois had a very astute perception of the tribe. However, it would be easy to take each element of the definition, word for word, and show how susceptible it is to another point of view, another understanding. What is missing from the definition are God, faith—its content and finality—and the notion of history. In a word, it is a formal description of religious functioning that, in principle, could be applied to religions in general, although I am not absolutely sure of that! I find nothing offensive in Durkheim's definition. It is a tool, an interesting one, but one that manifestly does not have a true grasp of religion.

JEAN-LOUIS MISSIKA: *You have brought up the issue of making religion "private". Is it not true that generally this trend is connected with secularization—that is, with the fact that when society becomes secular, religion is no longer the basis for the social link and thus becomes a private affair?*

LUSTIGER: Today I would say, in answer to my youthful reflections, that the social link belongs to the sacred. Even more, it is constituted by the sacred. The sacred is defined by the idea of separation, of course, but I would include other notions in it. First, that of symbolic patrimony—namely, the totality of realities symbolized in the social consciousness that belongs to each member of a given society and is also the soul of a culture. I would also include historical memory and the hope of a common future. Therefore, not all of the sacred is necessarily religious, in the technical and precise meaning of the word, just as everything sacred, or religious, does not necessarily refer to the unique and true God. But the idea of a complete secularization (in the sense of theologies of secularization or of the death of God, which arose hardly twenty years ago in the United States and Europe), even though it took me aback at the time, appears to me to be very naïve from the sociological point of view. It amounts to denying the "sacred" character of social phenomena and relations, to denying one of the most radical dimensions of social and human life.

Next, we have to look at what happened and is still happening in "our" Western societies. It cannot be analyzed in general and abstract terms. For example, the crisis of secularization in France cannot be understood without reference to the French Revolution and the subsequent history of anticlericalism and the clerical party. The same particulars in the Anglo-Saxon world did not bring about the same results. And in the United States, who made up the Catholic Church? They were workers, first Irish and Italian and then Polish, the poor. There the Catholic Church was identified with the poor. And if we look back to the Ruhr, indeed to certain regions in northern France, those high-flown theses—Franco-Marxist or Marxist-French—about the Church who lost the working class and about industrialization that produces de-Christianization do not fully reflect the reality. In the Ruhr, social Catholicism, close to the people, was a staunch defender of workers' rights. Up to twenty years ago, it was still a workers' country, where religious practice was greater proportionately than in the most Catholic regions of France.

WOLTON: *Then why is France a particular case?*

LUSTIGER: There are all sorts of working hypotheses. You have to blot out the Épinal images[1] and accept a meticulous inventory made by historians. I recall seeing a thesis—I only skimmed through it—on the origin of the urban proletariat in northern France. That proletariat was composed of peasant populations drawn to industrial centers by the possibilities for employment and another way of life. But the thesis carefully distinguished the rural illiterate populations from those who had been provided with some schooling. The former—because their culture, consistent in its way, was strictly oral and based on custom— became proletarian within one generation; they had been uprooted from the places and institutions that had allowed them to survive. The peasants with schooling, with a written culture, produced another kind of worker and a different religious and social behavior when they migrated to the towns. What was being called "the de-Christianized proletariat" was undoubtedly a peasantry that had never been either educated or Christianized.

WOLTON: *The people who had been Christianized and had had schooling resisted better....*

[1] Épinal is a town in eastern France that was a center for the production of popular eighteenth- and nineteenth-century prints depicting traditional scenes of French life. In today's language, an "Epinal image" means an outdated cliché.—TRANS.

LUSTIGER: They had been able to transfer to the interior of that new world, a harsh and competitive one, a certain number of values and to maintain them as an expression of their culture.

WOLTON: *Independently of the industrialization and urbanization that were relatively important factors in de-Christianization, hasn't the development of the human sciences since the beginning of the century also contributed to the process in a part of the population?*

LUSTIGER: I find that difficult to answer. I can see the violence of the anticlerical attacks and the violence of the clerical defenses, the stupidity of many of the arguments advanced by both sides, the ferocity of the combat and the fanaticism that it reflected. It must have been very hard to live in those times! It is not easy to respond, because I think that my response risks being anachronistic—that is, not explaining the excesses, the aggressions or abuses that the opponents engaged in. But I instinctively refuse the Épinal image as an outrageous and extreme simplification. It seems that, since the nineteenth century, the situation has evolved rather well in France.

WOLTON: *Yes, but on the whole, the Church has always resisted a bit. In 1864, it was the encyclical* Quanta cura, *which criticized rationalism and liberalism; people had to wait until 1890 and the famous "toast d'Alger"*[2] *to see her rallying to the republic, and until 1891, with the* Rerum novarum, *for an intervention in social questions. In 1907, she condemned modernism and the separation of church and state. The examples could be multiplied. Certainly each time the struggle was vehement, but one gets the impression from official texts that the Church always took peremptory positions that denounced society's evolution.*

MISSIKA: *In retrospect, it appears that she behaved as though she were a besieged fortress, as though she were defending a threatened territory.*

LUSTIGER: Not being a historian, I am hardly qualified to give a precise reply to your remarks. You have mentioned only certain pontifical declarations that have become symbolic of "reaction". But there were also evolutions and initiatives, often extremely fruitful, that preceded and prepared them.

WOLTON: *I can well appreciate your observation; however, the fact remains that*

[2] When the French navy made an official call at French-occupied Algiers, the Archbishop, Charles Lavigerie (1825–92)—who had agreed to back the call of Leo XIII for French Catholics to rally to the republic—received the officers and offered a toast to the republic.

we are dealing with a number of official texts and that the Church is also an institution whose declarations commit her.

LUSTIGER: There are not only those texts, there is also the effort, the work, and the signs of tremendous activity! And in this there is an initial element of response. The Christian social movement was not born from a single encyclical. The encyclicals were a result, in particular, of French and German social Catholicism. You have to look at numerous initiatives, at an overall internal thrust in the Church's life, coming from laymen like Ozanam[3] and Le Play[4] and all the social theoreticians of Christianity. You also have to try to understand the specific necessities to which the cited documents responded.

The second element of my response concerns the politico-religious crisis with which the Church had to cope from the beginning of the French Revolution to the war of 1914. Besides, that crisis was going to be succeeded immediately by another one coming from Eastern Europe, the Russian Revolution. It has to be repeated that these destabilizations were very violent. Not that I want to liken the French Revolution to the Russian one, whether in spirit, consequences or ideology. Nevertheless, they are comparable phenomena of social subversion, of the birth of a new society, including deliberate aggression against the Church as one of the structures of the ancient order. Furthermore, in both revolutions, this aggression was coupled with an attempt to take over the Church's imagery, symbols and rites. Remember the goddess Reason, the *décadi,*[5] the worship of the Supreme Being, the republican "baptisms"—all of these can be found transposed in Soviet Russia. The subversion in both cases was all the more cruel and mortal since it could build on a certain decadence in the Church's institutions and clergy; they had themselves been accomplices to this violence.... The crisis exterior to the Church, which was going to come crashing down upon her, was also an internal crisis "of" the Church. It was a crisis for both the Church and society.

[3] Frédéric Ozanam (1813–53) was a French historian and philanthropist, one of the founders of the *Societé de Saint-Vincent-de-Paul* in 1833 and an associate of La Mennais and Lacordaire.—TRANS.

[4] Frédéric Le Play (1806–82) was a French economist and engineer. A principal representative of a social Catholicism of conservative and traditionalist tendencies, he was a pioneer in the area of social surveys.—TRANS.

[5] The artificial "weeks" of ten days each, imposed by the revolutionary government in France.

Terrestrial Realities

WOLTON: *What do you think about the theological movement that originated between the two wars as a means of resisting the Church's official positions and that wanted to come closer to social realities by founding what was called at the time a "theology of terrestrial realities"? There were theologies of the body, work and society. Can theology and the human sciences be mixed in this way?*

LUSTIGER: The "theology of terrestrial realities" was not directly connected with the human sciences.

WOLTON: *But how can you create theologies of the body, work, city, society, etc., without referring to history, sociology or psychology?*

LUSTIGER: We could cite names, because behind almost all of those theologies you have just mentioned there are book titles and authors with their passions and polemics. We have to step back and look at these elements and analyze them calmly.

WOLTON: *To tell the truth, I was quite surprised when I discovered that there had been attempts to create a theology of terrestrial realities. It hardly seemed to be the job for theologians, but after all . . .*

LUSTIGER: Today, in asking how the vision of man is connected with the revelation of his relationship to God, one would turn to Christian anthropology. We must not ask theologies to play the role of an ideology. If, in order to organize a cosmological or anthropological discourse, you want to interpret symbolic material—its sacred character and function within the Church—then you should beware of surreptitiously changing the frame of reference.

Another remark: at the time it was a matter of responding to the accusation of Nietzschean inspiration that reproached religion for having emptied man of his substance, of having "vampirized" him. Furthermore, the accusation was the title of the second issue of *Jeunesse de l'Église,* which came out in 1943: *"Le Christianisme a-t-il dévirilisé l'homme?"*[6] The Hitlerian dwarf had put on Nietzsche's heavy boots. Some Christians felt that they had to prove something to themselves and then convince their contradictors. Remember all the Nazi writers and all the attacks of this type? For example, it was said that a Catholic could not be athletic because he despised his body. Remember Montherlant![7]

[6] "Has Christianity Robbed Man of His Virility?"—TRANS.

[7] Henry Millon de Montherlant (1896–1972) was a French writer who praised passions that develop physical and moral vigor.—TRANS.

The same thing was allegedly true for love, music and all the earthly pursuits. De Lubac had already replied to this charge in his book entitled *Le drame de l'humanisme athée,* which was published in 1937. But it was essential to remove this suspicion and respond to the unfair caricatures as well as to criticize the Jansenist kind of narrow-mindedness. You must not forget that the nineteenth century was still struggling with Jansenism. It is hard to realize the extent to which this doctrine was able to put its stamp on clerical and Christian education in France. In replying to the suspicions that it raised, its opponents highlighted the positive aspects of Christian anthropology.

Third, there was an internalization of the criticism. Certain Christians had been wounded by the suspicions. They kept inside the criticism they wished to refute, and perhaps some authors who tried to respond also thought, more or less consciously, that God does indeed "vampirize" man: "All the while remaining obedient to God (we are believers), let us arrange the interior space by pushing back the limits so that man is given a bit of freedom, so that he is allowed to breathe." But inasmuch as this secretly dialectic thought ideologically mobilized a nominalist concept of nature, there was a strong temptation to create a kind of Christian secularism—indeed, a Christian paganism. Tartuffe's phrase, *"Car pour être dévot, on n'en est pas moins homme"*[8] took on a cruel depth.

WOLTON: *In striking contrast to this sociopolitical entrenchment of theology between the wars, which lasted until a few years ago, you do find a Christian literature with Claudel, Bourget, Bernanos, Mauriac, Gilson, who are concerned with much more spiritual themes, such as sin, the soul, flesh. It is curious that the same Christian inspiration has produced a kind of sociopolitical deviation—indeed, a secularization of theology—on the one hand and, on the other, a literature that has not followed this evolution and remains much closer to traditional religious sources.*

LUSTIGER: The authors you named are varied, but they share at least one trait. In evoking the great Catholic writers who are a part of the heritage of contemporary French literature, what other names should we mention? Rimbaud and Verlaine, Léon Bloy and Francis Jammes, the poet, should be included, and there is the series Péguy, Bernanos, Claudel, Mauriac that you have already cited. And there are the still more recent authors: Stanislas Fumet, Pierre Emmanuel, Julien Green, etc. They represent diverse temperaments; however, they have a *petit air* in common. What is it? Ah, yes, I was about to leave out Maritain and Max Jacob. I am sure to have forgotten a good dozen. Cocteau belonged to the group at one time. And how many others? These authors, often converts, share one characteristic: having discovered God's

[8] "One is no less of a man for being pious."—TRANS.

absolute, they have shaken off the social conformity of the *bien-pensants* [self-righteous], as Bernanos called them. But almost all of these men have also projected the brilliant light of the Faith on their times and its political conflicts.

WOLTON: *Coming back to* réalités terrestres, *I have read several texts in which the expressed wish is to rediscover the Gospel's significance in politics, social action and the class struggle. So as to take a stand in the century's combats, some people have identified the Gospel's poor with the working class.*

LUSTIGER: This is the *"séduction du Marxisme"*, according to the title of a controversial book that was well known in the Fifties. Such thinking risks reducing Christianity to an ideology at the service of social objectives. Some Christians feel that, in order to be appealing, topical and strong, Christianity has to be adapted to what interests people—that is, the social struggle. Suddenly, Christianity has to be theorized in such a way that it conforms to this struggle. Religion is going to be gotten rid of, since it is charged with being "the opium of the people". Consequently, there emerges the exclusive valorization of *"la vie de tous les jours"* [everyday life]. There is no more magnificent clerical expression than "everyday life"; we use it so thoughtlessly. All the more so since a simple observation, familiar to sociologists, demonstrates that what marks a person's existence is precisely not "everyday life" but what American sociologists call "breaking points": unexpected events concerning death and love, evil and war, all the unpredictable aspects of freedom that provoke the emergence of rites and images in the continuity and routine of life. As for everyday existence, it is susceptible only to quantitative serial analyses. It reflects the constraints and determinisms in regard to which most people feel helpless.

WOLTON: *Do you think that there has been, within the Church, a break or divorce regarding Marxism?*

LUSTIGER: A disenchantment came almost simultaneously from two sources. First, from the surrounding culture, because the behavior of Christian intellectuals was not any different from that of the overwhelming majority of French intellectuals: the *air du temps* had to change before Marxism's followers could take another direction and, under the influence of a sounder criticism, finally accept the facts. The moment when the rupture was completed or completed itself was, I think, in 1968, contrary to what most people say. It was the generation of '68 who finally dared to spit in the idol's face. I saw it with my own eyes and heard it with my own ears on the Place de la Sorbonne:

Cohn-Bendit[9] called Aragon[10] a *"crapule stalinienne"*. Just imagine Aragon being scorned as "Stalinist scum"! It was grandiose! Amid that flurry of red flags and black flags in full Marxist-revolutionary mythology! "Today", I said to myself, *"le vase de Soisson est cassé!"*[11] And after '68 came Solzhenitsyn and Poland. The new *sacré* on which the French intelligentsia had been nourishing itself since 1917 in the magic "enchantment" of a new religion and eschatology was irreparably shattered. The world was "disenchanted", and Stalin was dead at last.

But the second reason for the break with Marxism was internal. In a word, it was the thirst for God. Because, after all, Catholic society is not just a society; the Church is also God's temple. It is normal that the fruits of holiness, the capacity for knowing God, for following and loving him should grow up within her. There was the personal call, the hunger, the thirst for what gives life, while Marxism's fruits were causing death. Moreover, the disillusionment with Marxism coincides with an era in which the Church's public stand in defense of man is taking on its full vigor and stature. It is not for nothing but for the glory of God that the Pope is traveling to the four corners of the globe. His positions—positive, energetic and courageous because they are always controlled and, more often than one would think, solitary—in favor of human rights spring from the recognition of God and of his worship in spirit and in truth. It is at the moment when these ideological tendencies have been exorcised that the Church, rediscovering her freedom of movement in her interior strength, expresses and broadcasts far afield her fresh and forceful message.

WOLTON: *Isn't there a kind of "competition" between the social sciences and religion?*

LUSTIGER: Look at the various social sciences that appeared between the eighteenth and twentieth centuries. Most of them, at their birth, had a totalizing ambition, as if it were necessary, in order to seize one objective, to absorb everything else and to produce a method that would be substituted for every other one. Each time, Churchmen criticized this all-encompassing ambition. You may say that religion felt itself to be the target of these totalitarian pretensions because it, too, has a totalizing ambition. I have

[9] Daniel Cohn-Bendit, a German, was one of the leaders of the student revolt in 1968.—TRANS.

[10] Louis Aragon (1897–1982) was a French poet and writer who became a Communist in 1927 and dedicated himself to the illustration of Marxist themes in his novels about French society.—TRANS.

[11] The well-known anecdote about the vase broken at Soissons originated with the victory in 489 A.D. of the French King Clovis over Syagrius.—TRANS.

already explained myself on this subject: faith is the only total integration that can never be totalitarian as long as it maintains that God alone is God and, hence, man is only man. Each of the social sciences has been born from systematic and all-inclusive plans. It is only normal that the Church has had a defensive reaction, and it is easy to see why the father of sociology, Durkheim, appeared to be an adversary. But her attitude is not in the least obscurantist—on the contrary! The idea that we had to explore this new field of knowledge and contribute to it was widely shared.

WOLTON: *But what about today? The social sciences are still competing with religion to provide a meaning to life.*

LUSTIGER: I would say rather that the social sciences are trying to take possession of a treasure whose inventory they have not yet been able to make and whose contents are far from exhausted. The treasure includes symbolic thought in the Freudian or ethnological sense, but it also contains the sacred, that which makes the heart of human memory and hope. But, in desiring to dispose of this treasure in their own way, the young rivals have forced the old heir, theology, to examine more closely what it has had in hand. Moreover, a good part of theological thought can be a considerable resource for the human sciences. Take the example of Paul Ricoeur, both a philosopher and a Christian, or of Father de Lubac's book called *L'Exégèse médiévale,* which contains a wealth of hermeneutical reflections on the sedimentation and interpretation of meaning. The thought of eminent theologians like Hans Urs von Balthasar may offer no immediate and direct contribution to the advancement of specialized knowledge, but it provides a more than helpful, fruitful background for the evolution of ideas. In the field of reflection on society's finalities, I am struck by the proximity of Hannah Arendt's thought to that of Father Fessard. Raymond Aron respected and esteemed Fessard. The originality of his political thought was to integrate the spiritual patrimony into political and social analysis. We ought to mention also Mircea Eliade and Georges Dumézil.[12] It would be entirely unfair to remember only conflicts between religion and the social sciences. There also exists a mutual fertilization.

The Religious Roots of Psychoanalysis

MISSIKA: *Psychoanalysis has cast an unfriendly regard on religion. Freud writes in* The Future of an Illusion, *"All religious doctrines are illusions; they cannot be*

[12] Georges Dumézil (1898–) is a French historian of religions who was a precursor of Levi-Strauss. He contributed to giving the study of religions scientific status.—TRANS.

proved and no one can be forced to hold them as true and believe in them. Some are so implausible, so much in contradiction with what we have so laboriously learned about the reality of the universe that one can compare them, taking appropriate account of psychological differences, with delirious ideas. It is impossible to judge the true value of most of them. They can no more be refuted than proved. We still know too little to be able to tackle them more closely from a critical point of view. However, the scientific effort is the only path that can lead us to the knowledge of exterior reality."

LUSTIGER: I find this message extremely moving when I think of Freud's path. It touches me deeply because it shows the great doctor's distress. He has only positivism as a tool for comprehension, and he is using it intelligently.

WOLTON: *I am going to insist: in the foreword to* Moses and Monotheism, *Freud writes, "Psychoanalytical research is in any case mistrusted by Catholics, and we shall not argue that they are mistaken. When our research leads us to conclude that religion is only a neurosis, when it shows us that its formidable power is explained in the same way as the neurotic obsession of some of our patients, we are bound to attract the greatest displeasure from this country's powers."*

LUSTIGER: Freud says that religion is a neurosis. It has also been called the "opium of the people", a means of social alienation. In a word, he is repeating the accusations of Feuerbach and Marx. I refer you to Paul Ricoeur who takes a considerable distance from those "masters of suspicion".

What a paradox! It seems to me that the fundamental inspiration, the hidden source of Freudian thought, can be found in the biblical tradition and the spiritual experience of prayer and reflection. Some people have detected a direct rabbinical influence in Freud's writing, and several books have recently been written on the subject.

MISSIKA: *There have even been allusions to its influence on two specific aspects of analytical technique: the fact that the patient does not see the analyst supposedly reflects the Jewish tradition's rejection of graphic representation, and the principle of listening would refer back to the "Hear, O Israel"!*

LUSTIGER: One can also point to the spiritual practices in Catholicism. In the monastic traditions or in the *Spiritual Exercises* of Saint Ignatius of Loyola, there are prescriptions and rules that resemble certain directions for psychological treatment—in particular, the one regarding the relationship of the analyst to the analyzed. Freud employs the tool of experimental investigation at his disposition, but he is referring to a heritage that he is tempted to underrate, although he does use it to explain himself in his unconsciously personal works such as *Totem and Taboo* and *Moses and Monotheism.* These works differ from all of his other writings; they represent an experimental field. With his scientific tool, he brings back to the fore something that positivism was denying. And this is his paradox, poor soul! He was not recognized by medical doctors, although he claimed to be one; he was not recognized by scientists, although he claimed to be one; he found himself being reproached as a Jew, whereas he wanted to be an atheist. In brief, he is the most complete of contradictions: he is martyred by himself! Besides, there is something tragic in Freud's work as there was in his last years. Basically, he restored to thought, to the contemporary secular intelligence, a domain of which it had been deprived. He gave back to Western thought the depth of the historical subject, the idea that there is always a problem in interpreting the spoken word and the unspoken and that this hermeneutic stems from reason. He allows one to see that man's consciousness is immersed in something beyond itself and that it is historical since it conceives of itself only in relation to the father and mother. As far as I am concerned, Freud has thrown a lateral light on my path, which, at the end of the twentieth century, is seeking to know God.

MISSIKA: *Then you think that psychoanalysis and, more generally, psychology have roots in the Judeo-Christian heritage?*

LUSTIGER: I have already mentioned the reference to Judaism. But I refer you also to the Christian tradition from which an entire body of anthropological thought has developed. Its modern form, especially from the sixteenth century onward, is that of morality and its analysis of the voluntary and involuntary. It was a matter of qualifying the responsibility morally committed in human acts relating to God's law. This branch of knowledge was fully developed by Catholicism, and the seventeenth century had already disposed of a considerable body of empirical learning for the practice of the sacrament of penance and spiritual guidance. Before becoming reading matter in anticlerical journals, an accumulation of its reflections and observations on subjectivity had remained ignored. As schoolchildren, we had to read the *Caractères* of La Bruyère or the *Maximes* of La Rochefoucauld, but they had themselves relied on an acquired lore, a considerable collection of moral and spiritual literature. Besides, all the Church's spiritual traditions led up to this attention to man's conscience and a discernment of the intimate stirrings of his soul. In this respect, the rediscoveries of the twentieth century can often seem to be a reformulation and codification, in positivist terms, of experiences and conflicts fully observed by the spiritual masters. The doctrine of Saint Ignatius' *Spiritual Exercises* on the movements of the soul is a valuable example of this. The practice of the "exercises" is inconceivable without recollection and interpretation. The idea that a mood or an inner impulse can have a hidden meaning is found in all the mystics from the time of the first hermits and the Church Fathers. I insist on this point, which the human sciences, naïvely, have failed to recognize. They have finally begun to turn to mystical writings. And they will find in them inexhaustible materials and a learning that has been forgotten. Are these writings not just as interesting as Zen for the self-understanding that Western man is seeking?

When modern psychology appeared, it was therefore completely predictable that Christian milieus would be keenly interested by it. As far as Freud and sexuality are concerned, the problem was first posed from the moral angle, but it also engaged man's self-understanding. Christians were fascinated, but at the same time they felt under strong attack, offended. And the success that Jung achieved in Catholic circles . . .

MISSIKA: *But, after all, Christianity can assimilate Jung much more easily than Freud!*

LUSTIGER: I do not know. For whatever reasons, Jung was not felt to be an aggressor. He did not provoke the same repulsion as Freud. But the point is that the conflict did not revolve around the principle of an exploration of the human psyche.

MISSIKA: *Does psychoanalysis allow a fruitful secular reading of the Bible? Can there be an analytical reading of the sacred texts that speak of father, mother and son?*

LUSTIGER: The Bible speaks of relationships between subjects and recalls unique histories. There can be points of continuity, but transcendence, just as a peoples' common history, eludes an analytical reading.

MISSIKA: *I must say that your argument does not convince me. Certainly the Bible is a collective history, but that history is recounted through singular destinies. It might almost be said that the analytical approach is more legitimate here than in the explanation of social and political problems.*

LUSTIGER: Except that the Bible speaks of transcendence and a people. Singular subjects arise, their history is narrated, their genealogy described, but, at the same time, there is the question of the election and consecration of a people and the salvation of all men. You say that the Bible is a magnificent terrain for analysis. Then why did Freud take Oedipus?

MISSIKA: *Do you mean why did he go looking in Greek mythology for something that he would have been able to find in the Bible? Perhaps because of what you brought up earlier, his denial of Judaism.*

LUSTIGER: Quite the contrary. The reason was that Freud could not ignore the fact that if he had taken the Bible as a symbolic reference, he could only have become a believer again, a Jew, even in his lack of belief. He could not afford to take the Bible.

WOLTON: *The role of analysts in our de-Christianized societies has often been likened to that of confessors. What do you think of the comparison?*

LUSTIGER: The psychoanalyst has a terrible job! Psychoanalysis is hell. I mean, it is fire, acid. It is an almost impossible profession. Psychoanalysts are always organizing themselves into cliques; they are obliged to quarrel in order to survive, simply in order to withstand all the negativity they receive: it devours them. Among my psychoanalyst friends, some have gone so far as to say that they do not know if a single cure has ever been achieved. Experienced analysts do not hesitate to depart from the purity of the doctrine and give precedence to their capacity to aid, to help someone. From this point of view, there is a sacerdotal aspect in the figure of the analyst. I remember with wonder Bettelheim's *The Empty Fortress.* It was controversial, much criticized, but I detected in it the face of the *kenosis,* of the Messiah. Bettelheim plunges into the abyss where the lost child is; he goes to find him where he is hidden. What a powerful love that demands! And what generosity: time, care, love of human beings, precisely those who are the most lost! What a great amount of intelligence, knowledge, attention to others is dispensed in this therapeutic undertaking! The labor is all the more moving since it offers none of the satisfaction of the surgeon's fastidious work, so quickly accomplished. In fact, psychoanalysis is the profession of a secular redeemer.

MISSIKA: *The Church has held a discourse on sexuality for a very long time. She has directed consciences, encouraged people to control their desires and master their drives, and she has condemned certain sexual practices. Psychoanalysis is not a theory of liberation, but it has stressed that a too drastic repression imposed from the exterior by an institution can have catastrophic consequences for the human psyche. Is there not something in this attitude that is intolerable for the Church?*

LUSTIGER: Catholic morality is no more a repression than psychoanalysis is a liberation. Quite some time ago, one of my analyst friends called to say that he was sending someone to me for spiritual guidance. When I asked him to suggest what might be helpful to his patient, he replied, "Make him feel guilty!" He was, however, an orthodox psychoanalyst! But he had concluded that it was absolutely essential to assist this person in structuring himself, and he was not confusing analysis and liberation.

Having said that, I admit that there exists an irreducible distance between psychoanalysis and religion. To study and treat the human psyche is one thing; to help a person develop moral freedom and responsibility is quite another. These efforts represent two different levels of acting and being human. If analysis claims to substitute itself for moral judgments or proposes a rule of responsibility, then it commits an abuse.

How can a person's feelings of guilt be treated while at the same time his right to spiritual freedom and a moral judgment of his acts are being encouraged? Therein lies the real confrontation. Human activity finds a resource in the spiritual domain and moral standards that can also be therapeutic. But, in general, psychotherapy cannot have moral significance, and morality must not be substituted for therapy.

In principle, the therapeutic procedure aims at the psyche and cannot draw a moral evolution from itself, just as moral judgment does not dispense psychological conflicts from either analysis or therapy. But moral standards and spirituality do offer human conduct resources whose fruitfulness can also be therapeutic in a supplementary way.

III

REASON, SCIENCE AND FAITH

Proofs for God's Existence

JEAN–LOUIS MISSIKA: *Can human reason demonstrate the existence of God?*

JEAN-MARIE LUSTIGER: The answer falls almost as swiftly as a guillotine blade, since your question was vigorously debated in the nineteenth century. And the First Vatican Council responded yes. Why? Because man is created in the image and resemblance of God. God has endowed man with a reasoning faculty for knowing the truth. It must permit him to accede to the supreme truth that is God; otherwise, man would not be truly free and responsible for his own life before God. God would not be God but a tyrant, an idol. In other words, this rational demonstration has to be possible. . . .

MISSIKA: *"Has to be" possible or "is" possible?*

LUSTIGER: Let that remain an open question for the time being. I shall return to it in a moment. But just now I want to point out the import of such an affirmation. It is a formidably audacious proposition, wholly "anti-obscurantist", because it accepts the ultimate consequence of the idea that God is good and Creator. The idea of "mystery"—that is, of what surpasses the grasp of human reason—is not to be confounded with the idea of "taboo", of forbidden knowledge. From the moment you admit that man is made for God and God gives him reason, freedom and intelligence, then it follows that man has been given the capacity to recognize his Maker. In the name of faith itself, the believer is led to affirm reason's power. It is extraordinary! This reversal, this paradox, never ceases to astonish me. It establishes the anthropological optimism of the revealed Tradition, and this doctrine is in the direct line of proofs for God's existence coming from Saint Augustine and Saint Anselm—the "ontological" proof—and from Saint Thomas.

We know that God exists without knowing what he is, who he is, because biblical and then philosophical thought understand that the only definition of God consists in renouncing all possible definition of him. In the terms of this "negative theology", nothing of what one can say about God is what he is.

Moreover, we have to consider reason in its true exercise—in human history. The revelation reinforces the fundamental optimism about the intellectual tool and its validity, but it also shows that men are impaired in their freedom, their conscience and their reason. "The fool says in his heart, 'There is no God' " (Ps 14:1, 53:1). Reason wanted to be sovereign, it wanted to define its own dimensions, whereas it remained called to receive them by respecting an objectivity given elsewhere and an inherent finality. Reason does not exist independent of wills, desires, choices. In order for man to be convinced by proofs of God's existence, his reason must allow itself to be purified. Reason's effort in affirming God's existence derives all its assurance from the act of faith, itself the fruit of a healing God, of a grace.

Then can reason attain its specific capability if it has not been healed by God? That capability is the frontier—or the union—of reason and faith. It is "an irritating frontier" for the believer as well as the unbeliever. The believer cannot give up reason, and yet he recognizes that faith surpasses reason, that there is a wisdom or light that goes beyond it and that, in giving him access to God, makes him accessible to himself.

DOMINIQUE WOLTON: *How is it possible for your conception of a reason ultimately in God's hands to be accepted by an unbeliever or an agnostic?*

LUSTIGER: Depending on the situation in which he finds himself, it can be a matter of humility. Because reason is obliged to concede what it cannot reach, even before it has been purified and restored. It is as if reason has to abdicate in order to admit what is eminently rational: that God exists. In fact, reason is called on, not to deny itself, but to relinquish itself so as to gain its most original truth. And the source of certitude escapes it.

WOLTON: *I suppose you need grace to cross over the threshold?*

LUSTIGER: In practice, yes. But I used the word *healing.*

WOLTON: *But to go from a rational demonstration to a more comprehensive perspective, a dimension connected with grace has to be introduced.*

LUSTIGER: You can say "grace", if you want to, but this word belongs to the technical vocabulary of theologians.

WOLTON: *"Healing" is hardly any better, since it is associated with illness.*

MISSIKA: *Does that mean that you think that reason is man's illness?*

LUSTIGER: No, but the inability to accept the truth is reason's illness. Man is wounded.

WOLTON: *Wounded by triumphant reason?*

LUSTIGER: No, he is wounded by his sin and his condition, including reason, has been torn apart. You probably will not like this romantic definition: "Man is a fallen god who remembers heaven." At any rate, it describes reason's wound or, rather, the human condition.

MISSIKA: *The argument that you are developing is equivocal, even contradictory. It leads one to think that a person must be a believer in order to demonstrate rationally God's existence. Would it not be simpler to say that although one can obviously discuss rationally the existence of God, it is impossible to demonstrate, and it is precisely this impossibility that traces the frontier between reason and faith? Why are you so set on having reason come into play?*

LUSTIGER: This discussion has two important stakes. The first is reason's status in modern thought. Today the most common model for reason is technical. This technical reason is extraordinarily powerful and inventive in all domains, but at the same time it lacks wisdom, the savor of the true and the joy of the good. The Church cannot resign herself to adopting this operative model under the pretext that it is dominant in our present civilization. She remains responsible and witnesses to a human intelligence nourished by Truth and its assimilation. This anthropological conception is itself connected with the revelation of God, his Word and his Spirit.

The second stake is theological. Man has been wounded in his dignity; however, we cannot give up hoping in him. Herein lies the paradox. The act of faith brings us simultaneously both the conviction that the initial goodness of creation is constitutive of man and the realization that man, in order to receive its benefits, needs—in concrete history—a deliverance, a liberation. To attain basic wisdom and goodness, man needs salvation. If believers have a service to render to all humanity, it is to protect this treasure that men are tempted to forget: facing the latent despair of the century of Hiroshima and the gulag, we keep the faith, we cling to the original affirmation: "It is good!"

WOLTON: *What is good?*

LUSTIGER: When I say "it is good", I am repeating the translated words from the Bible's first chapter. It recounts that, in looking at his creation, "God saw everything that he had made, and behold, it was very good." Here we get down to the problem of theodicy. Evil exists, but God is good. It is the scandal of Job and the vanity of Qoheleth. However, the Church keeps watch in hope; even in the worst of tragedies and darkest of insanities, she firmly maintains that God's existence can be accepted by everybody, that it is a reasonable affirmation. Why must this claim to universal truth never be renounced? Given man's misfortune, why does she not take refuge in mystical subjectivity or the arbitrary but consoling conviction of the *belle âme?* Simply because, as the Bible says, God is the Savior of all and not simply of those he chooses.

WOLTON: *Does atheistic humanism not offer possibilities for a belief in man?*

LUSTIGER: I am not saying, "Look at the perversity of the atheists and the grandeur of believers." Among my unbelieving friends, companions over the years, there are those who have an obstinate, desperate optimism—that is, I deem it to be desperate. Perhaps they think that my position is desperate. In any case, they uphold an unshakable conviction acquired from a noble struggle with every kind of profound repugnance and discouragement. The issues we are discussing are universal. Everybody is confronted with them sooner or later. But, most of the time, people have other things to do, and they cope with their lives as best they can. Nobody escapes these fundamental questions, and the various concrete responses that people make stamp their character on a society or a culture. Some societies commit suicide, become depraved or "sincerely" close themselves into behaviors that destroy man.

WOLTON: *Sometimes very Christian societies are the ones that have fallen into folly.*

LUSTIGER: What do you call Christian societies? Do you have a good gauge for judging one? Believing in God is not like being vaccinated against rabies or typhoid fever.

WOLTON: *Then I do not understand your reasoning. You are pointing out the dangers for men and societies who consider the sky empty, but I remind you that the same dangers exist for Christian societies.*

LUSTIGER: It is true that the greatest risks show up in societies that have been touched by the grace of faith. The most developed societies are the ones that are most threatened. They are just the opposite of archaic societies; they have tasted the intoxicating power of a reason that has seen in itself more than it contains. The peoples and cultures who have received the treasures of God's light are precisely those who are tempted by the worst perversions. You may conclude that, if this is so, then it would have been better not to have received them in the first place. As Job says, "Let the day perish wherein I was born, and the night which said, 'A man-child is conceived!'" But no, that temptation cannot lead to the pure and simple refusal to exist.

WOLTON: *It is the Christian societies that have committed the greatest massacres.*

LUSTIGER: It is Western society! Our own. Whether you like it or not, atheistic society is Christian society. But its atheism is specific. It does not involve the destruction of gods but the negation of God. It is not simply a rejection of gods who sometimes take revenge by coming back in force and en masse. Modern civilization is inescapably marked by the encounter with the true God. The consequence has been the contact of human intelligence with the absolute, and the Promethean temptation of man.

Apropos of this problem of reason and God, I would like to read a text to you: "For the idea of making idols was the beginning of fornication, and the invention of them was the corruption of life, for neither have they existed from the beginning nor will they exist forever. For through the vanity of men they entered the world, and therefore their speedy end has been planned." (First explanation:) "For a father consumed with grief at an untimely bereavement made an image of his child, who had been suddenly taken from him; and he now honored as a god what was once a dead human being and handed on to his dependents secret rites and initiations. Then the ungodly custom, grown strong with time, was kept as a law. . . .

"And" (second explanation) "at the command of monarchs graven images were worshipped. When men could not honor monarchs in their presence, since they lived at a distance, they imagined their appearance far away and made a visible image of the king whom they honored, so that by their zeal they might flatter the absent one as though present. Then the ambition of the craftsman impelled even those who did not know the king to intensify their worship. For he, perhaps wishing to please his ruler" (note it is always men's foolish craving to seduce at all cost), "skillfully forced the likeness to take a more beautiful form, and the multitude, attracted by the charm of his work, now regarded as an object of worship the one whom shortly before they had honored as a man. And this became the hidden trap for mankind, because men, in bondage to misfortune or to royal authority, bestowed on objects of stone or wood the name that ought not to be shared." Who do you think wrote that? Diderot?

MISSIKA: *Why are you always bringing up Diderot?*

LUSTIGER: Well, I was reading from the Bible, from the Wisdom of Solomon, chapter 14, verses 12–21. Still further on in the same book, another passage says this: "For when a potter kneads the soft earth and laboriously molds each vessel for our service, he fashions out of the same clay both the vessels that serve clean uses and those for contrary uses, making all in like manner; but which shall be the use of each of these the worker in clay decides. With misspent toil, he forms a futile god from the same clay—this man who was made of earth a short time before and after a little while goes to the earth from which he was taken, when he is required to return the soul that was lent him. But he is not concerned that he is destined to die or that his life is brief, but he competes with workers in gold and silver and imitates workers in copper; and he counts it his glory that he molds counterfeit gods. His heart is ashes, his hope is cheaper than dirt and his life is of less worth than clay, because he failed to know the one who formed him and inspired him with an active soul and breathed into him a living spirit. But he considered our existence an idle game and life a festival held for profit, for he says one must get money however one can, even by base means. For this man, more than all others, knows that he sins when he makes from earthy matter fragile vessels and graven images" (15:7–13).

Freedom and Grace

MISSIKA: *Is divine will so determining that man has neither freedom nor responsibility?*

LUSTIGER: Divine will gives man his freedom because man struggles in slavery as long as he has not been gathered in by God.

In the course of history, the debate over the divine will as opposed to human freedom has often been formulated in abstract categories. The power of human freedom versus God's initiative, damnation and salvation have been discussed without reference to historical situations. The Bible, on the contrary, poses the problem in concrete terms. The general, timeless idea of gratuity is verified in human history by choice, by the arbitrariness of a choice. Why does God reveal himself to a people, why does he speak to Abraham rather than to someone else? Why did he choose Hebrew, Aramaic and Greek for revealing himself and not Chinese or Sanskrit? Why did the Word of God become flesh in the uniqueness of a specific human existence? Because the universal is given in the concrete singular. Israel is chosen in view of the salvation of all nations, of all men in all times. Christ, Word of God and Son of God, born in the flesh, came for the salvation of all men. What is given to a part of humanity is not an exaggerated privilege but a mission that is a superabundant grace of God. Every man, like Abraham, can have access to God's friendship. What was given in the singularity of history is destined for all men.

The divine omnipotence is likely to be conceived of by man as that of a tyrant who is equivalent to man. The Old and New Testaments warn against the idea of reducing God to an element of the world or a partner to be handled with care. When God creates man, he creates a vis-à-vis. This man, in order to be truly himself, has to be able to behave freely before God. Behaving freely before God means recognizing oneself as a creature who, adopted in grace, is meant to serve God. Serving God means reigning with him. We are not debased in submitting ourselves to God. On the contrary, we receive our freedom from him who is its source. "The truth will make you free", Jesus says (Jn 8:32).

MISSIKA: *Why is forgetting history so detrimental?*

LUSTIGER: Especially around the sixteenth century, grace and freedom were understood as metaphysical categories, as if momentarily there had been an occultation of history and its account. That led to a metaphysical interpretation of the relationship between the divine omnipotence and created freedom. The implantation of these categories in the revelation and the history of salvation was obliterated. The way in which Paul's letter to the Romans was treated in the classical age attests to this shift. According to the interpretation of that time, the epistle has two parts: the first deals with grace and faith, or faith and works, and can be associated with the great debate that developed around Lutheranism and Jansenism; the second part deals with Israel's relationship to the pagan nations and also has a long exhortative conclusion on Christian communities. For a goodly number of modern commentators, these two parts represent virtually two letters, which can be commented on separately, whereas there is always a strong unity in Paul's thought. In fact, the word *works* suggests the observance of the law given to Israel, the *mitzvott,* while *faith* is the faith in Christ Messiah in which the law can be fulfilled by all nations. The dialectic of the Jew and pagan (chaps. 9–11) is that of the justice and mercy at the heart of God's love: it is a kind of demonstration by sacred history of the fulfillment of the law and its works through faith in Christ—that is, in the Messiah, Justice of God.

The metaphysical debate on freedom and grace is not in vain. But it can be resolved only by the reinsertion of its terms into the history of salvation, where these metaphysical notions are restored to their original meaning. On the philosophical level that would correspond to the problem of the relationship between metaphysics and history.

MISSIKA: *You say that freedom is given by God, but that does not answer the question. What is there of divine intervention in human affairs and the question of grace, as it is conceived by Saint Augustine, for example?*

LUSTIGER: Our idea of God is always too tangible or too abstract: we see him either as a partner whose interventions we can mobilize or as an adversary from whom we take flight. Nominalism conceived of God and man as two antagonistic forces; as though man can affirm himself only by destroying God and, conversely, that God can triumph only by demeaning man. Reducing their relationship to a power struggle indicates a dimming of vision, and a portion of the West's spiritual history has been marked by this image of conflict. But the spiritual struggle is one in which we have God as our helper; it is a struggle for God, against our own deviation, against the forces of darkness that dwell in us. At Gethsemane, Jesus enters into his "agony". The word *agôn* (Lk 22:44) does not signify the last instants of life but the combat, the clash of Jesus' human freedom with the Father's will: "My Father! If it be possible, let this cup pass from me; nevertheless, not as I will, but as thou wilt" (Mt 26:36–46). In his acceptance, human freedom is fully shouldered: it expresses horror in the face of evil and sin, compassion for all sinners and the worship and submission of the faithful son who wishes to obey the paternal will. "My food is to do the will of him who sent me", Jesus says (Jn 4:34).

To understand the union of a believing and loving human freedom with God, you have to reread Psalm 119. Pascal called this psalm about the law "the stairway to divine love". In Roman legal parlance, the word *law* connotes the subservience of man: *dura lex, sed lex.* But the Psalmist praises it as the union of two freedoms: it is "sweet . . . to my taste" and a "lamp to my feet. . . . I delight in it." It is by obeying God that man receives his freedom. He obeys him the way a son obeys his father, a wife her husband, a friend his friend. "No longer do I call you servants", Jesus says to his disciples, "but friends" (Jn 15:15). Biblical poetics employs all these relational images to show how human freedom is supremely exalted at the moment when it accepts receiving itself from something greater than itself, its source.

MISSIKA: *Would you say that Christ's words on the cross—"Father, forgive them; for they know not what they do"—exclude responsibility and human freedom? How can someone who does not know what he is doing be held responsible?*

LUSTIGER: The gap between immediate responsibility and judgment is expressly mentioned in the Bible. In the fourth Servant Song (Is 52:13–53:12), Israel says of the Servant; "For he grew up before him like a young plant, and like a root out of dry ground; he had no form or comeliness that we should look at him, and no beauty that we should desire him. He was despised and rejected by men; a man of sorrows, and acquainted with grief; and as one from whom men hide their faces he was despised, and we esteemed him not. Surely he has borne our griefs and carried our sorrows; yet we esteemed him stricken, smitten by God and afflicted. But he was wounded for our transgressions . . . and with his stripes we are healed." In other words, we did not know what we were doing. The truth surpasses men's immediate understanding; hence, it is like an immediate irresponsibility. But who can claim to have no responsibility whatsoever for what he has not seen or not wanted to see?

The parable of the last judgment in chapter 25 of Saint Matthew shows the same gap between what everyone knows and the significance of his acts. The Son of Man is represented by the figure of the King seated on his glorious throne: "Come, O blessed of my Father, inherit the kingdom prepared for you from the foundation of the world; for I was hungry and you gave me food, I was thirsty and you gave me drink. . . . Then the righteous will answer him, 'Lord, when did we see thee hungry and feed thee, or thirsty and give thee drink?' . . . And the King will answer them, 'Truly, I say to you, as you did it to one of the least of these my brethren, you did it to me.' " Therefore, the Messianic Subject who judges the world from the interior of history is not necessarily recognized. And the "least of his brethren" refers to Jesus' disciples who share his suffering and redeeming condition, the condition described in the Servant's poems found in Isaiah.

What is the significance of this gap between immediate responsibility and conscience? Immediate human responsibility, such as men can apprehend it, is not the ultimate judgment of all things. The ultimate judgment is made only by God. We are not discussing the civil liability that human judgment can pronounce: "The proofs are peremptory, such and such a person has committed such and such a crime." One thing eludes this juridical decision: the conscience, the moral responsibility. In order that men, all men, accede to full and total responsibility, they need to receive from Christ, fulfilling his mission as suffering Servant, the revelation of their sin at the same time as their forgiveness. The sinner can measure his sin only by the forgiveness he receives. Prior to being forgiven, he is a slave to his sin: his "eyes are dimmed", his "heart is hardened", as the Scripture says. At the point when the sinner is ready to ask for mercy, he has already been touched by it: his heart of stone has been broken, crushed. But the prophet also announces the total forgiveness of the New Covenant: "A new heart I will give you" (I shall not be satisfied with simply crushing it to make it more sensitive and receptive) " . . . a heart of flesh . . . and cause you to walk in my statutes and be careful to observe my ordinances" (Ezek 36:26–27; cf. Jer 31:33). Forgiveness is the gift of restored innocence. When I read what Pascal writes in his *Mémorial,* about having heard Christ say to him, "I shed this particular drop of blood for you", I feel like answering, "You wrote those words on that night; God bless you, that was the light he gave to you. But I hear something different: 'For you I shed all my blood, all my life.' " Every man, whoever he is, has the right to everything. In this deliverance, face to face, heart to heart, with the crucified

Messiah, we confess the revelation of God's supreme justice in the crucified Slave recognized King of Israel and thus King of the nations. The humiliated Messiah proclaimed as King gives man his royalty, his dignity, his responsibility.

But only a man of faith can speak in this way, I quite agree with you.

The Ways of the Lord

MISSIKA: *Can a person simply decide to believe in God, or is faith a force that imposes itself on the individual even against his will?*

LUSTIGER: Anyone who hesitates between deciding to believe or waiting to be struck by God's lightning is like someone who, in a darkened room, is looking for an unknown person to speak to and finds himself in a hopeless predicament. Why does the one toward whom he is shouting not respond? Whenever someone in this situation asks me what to do, I suggest that he or she pray conditionally: "Thou, O God, whom I am searching for or fleeing from, I do not know if thou dost exist, but let me meet and recognize thee." In fact, anyone engaged in this debate is already positioned in regard to God, even if he does not yet know what still has to mature in himself. "Thou wouldst not search for me if thou hadst not already found me." This sentence of Pascal aptly expresses the situation of someone who is hesitating before God. But it also happens that the believer can traverse a period of doubt or darkness. Anyone who, in faith, has already received something of God's light can recognize that there is more than a simple flaw in argument or a dizziness of the heart in his reason's sidestepping. He is sufficiently informed to recognize the cunning of the mind that shies away from God, of reason that does not accept its own limits, of freedom that has been tempted in one way or another. He is capable of suspecting himself, and in darkness he can perform the act of faith that repeats: I am deciding to trust in God, who has never been unfaithful to me. He has never betrayed me. Saint Polycarp, urged by his torturers to insult Christ so as to survive, replied, "I have been serving him for eighty years and he has never mistreated me. Why then should I blaspheme my King and Savior?"

MISSIKA: *Have you personally known moments of doubt and darkness?*

LUSTIGER: Fluctuations? Certainly. I have experienced such periods. The reasons for believing sometimes appeared strong and sometimes like plausibilities whose fragility was threatened in proportion to my ignorance and weaknesses. Faith is a vital relationship with God, but it is necessarily put to the test, sometimes by questions with no answers, sometimes by questions that surpass our intellectual capacities. In those dialogues, as in life, we cover a whole series of suspicions, from historical criticism to psychoanalysis. You do not go through such periods without suffering. And no person is capable of confronting all questions with equal competence. The martyr is one who bears witness to God in circumstances where the refusal to renounce his fidelity to God entails death. The book of Maccabees tells us about the death of an old man to whom it was said, "Sacrifice to the king's gods, to the king; then you will save your life." And the old man replied, "God has always been faithful to me; why should I be unfaithful to him?" There is a form of martyrdom that consists in putting oneself into God's hands because God alone is God and, in so doing, to move beyond the darkness of reason.

MISSIKA: *The other way that faith is discovered—it has almost become a stereotype—is illumination.*

LUSTIGER: Yes, many *spirituels* and mystics have described their relationship to God as an illumination that completely overwhelmed their lives. The divine Omnipotence, they say, took possession of their consciousness and swept through it with his gifts of grace, love, forgiveness, joy and light. This seizure allows a person to give much more than he had ever imagined that he could give in his life. The accounts of this experience that have reached us are only a minute part of what truly happened. My only reservation is that it is too bad that the descriptions that get the most attention are those that contain fabulous or extraordinary phenomena. One is tempted to interpret them in terms of psychical ecstasy and extrasensory or nonphysical experiences. At the beginning of the century, a great deal of research was done on what was called the psychology of mystical states. Some people questioned whether there was not a specificity to mystical knowledge; Bergson more or less sensed that there is. Some theologians defined mystical life as a way of knowing that could be added to other degrees of knowledge. A kind of chart of mystical states was drawn up. Undoubtedly, it made sense in a way because there do exist markers, special paths, and guidance is essential. But these reflections and accounts can lead to illusion and result in forgetting that the essence of mysticism is the intense communication in the Faith with the mystery of God. Mystical "states" are more common and frequent in the life of faith than you might think. Nevertheless, just because someone praying to God experiences a special joy, that does not necessarily mean that he or she is a Saint Teresa of Avila! Similarly, not every dark path is necessarily the "dark night" of Saint John of the Cross!

MISSIKA: *Pascal advised the freethinkers of his time to practice in order to believe. Do you think he was serious, or was he simply being ironical?*

LUSTIGER: He was not being ironical. There does exist a profound relationship between moral conduct—between the good and the true—and the discovery of God. I have met men and women who were circling all around that discovery, and I have quoted that Pascalian phrase or its equivalent to them: "I do not know how far your certitude will lead you today, but you can begin right away to try to put your life in harmony with what you think is good." There is definitely a connection between man's conduct and his reception of the truth. When Pascal says to those who are hostile or indifferent to religion, "Get down on your knees and you will believe", it is a jest, or possibly a gesture of exasperation with their pride, or licentious living or intellectual vanity. But I also see in such advice a path toward conversion, which begins—to speak like Pascal—by the reform of morals. I remember asking someone who was confiding in me, "How do you judge your life today? What is good in it? What is bad? Is it within your power to act according to what now appears to be good? If it is, try doing it. Perhaps it is God who is asking it of you. In doing good, you will be putting yourself in another attitude for discovering the One who is the Source of good and you will accede to another relationship with him." These words may sound quite banal. . . .

MISSIKA: *They contradict just a bit your preceding remarks that "works", doing good, do not guarantee salvation or access to God.*

LUSTIGER: Works and good deeds are ways to salvation insofar as they are a response and fidelity to God's gift and his mercy. Our acts are commendable, theology says, if they are received from God. . . .

WOLTON: *What do you mean by "if they are received from God"?*

LUSTIGER: So long as man does not give a Promethean content to his moral attitude, so long as he does not carve his own statue. Some people like to do good as a way of affirming themselves. Certainly, what is good is good, and it is much better that a person behaves virtuously! But even so, there remains one enormous step to be taken on the journey toward a relationship with God. It is not enough to conform to moral standards, even Christian ones: that much sought-after perfection has to be inscribed in the love of the one who is the source of all perfection. It is he who is the origin of all the good deeds we perform. It is his forgiveness that makes the sinner once again capable of righteousness. If we ignore this, we close ourselves into our own insufficient and unreliable virtue. Man must do good with the grace of God. But when he has accomplished all the good possible, he still has a supreme act to fulfill, one that is the key to all the others: he has to open up that interior "vault", where he has been gazing at himself in the mirror and whose door he has kept tightly closed, and emerge from the radical solitude of pride to accept communing with the one who is his vis-à-vis, his Creator and his Beatitude.

The Place of Science

MISSIKA: *It has become a commonplace to say that in Western societies science occupies the position formerly held by religion. Would you agree?*

LUSTIGER: Certainly not. If it does, then it is no longer science but an ideological image of science substituting itself for a certain sacred or religious idea.

MISSIKA: *Of course, we are talking about images. Do you consider that a bad thing?*

LUSTIGER: Oh, that is almost inevitable, like the rainy season in the tropics. This phenomenon is one of the endemic temptations of human societies. Man is incessantly struggling against the idols and gods of his own making. Every experience of faith is aimed at disenchanting the world, whereas man's temptation is to use his tools to make idols. Earlier I read to you a page from the Wisdom of Solomon. I find nothing new in our present situation; it is like the one described in the text: man, fascinated by his instruments, elevates them to the place of the sacred.

MISSIKA: *But, conversely, did religion not feel threatened by the scientific method at a certain period? I am thinking about Galileo's trial or the banning of the dissection of cadavers.*

LUSTIGER: You have to take into account the polemical and anticlerical interpretation of the history of science.

MISSIKA: *You are right, but things like that did happen. . . .*

LUSTIGER: But other things happened, too. For example, the development of experimental science originated within the Church. This is attested by Duhem and others. To come back to your examples, the dissection of cadavers raised real questions. Does it not any longer? As for the Galileo affair, historians have blown it up all out of proportion. Recent research shows that it is less obvious than we had been led to believe.

Scientific reason also claimed to denounce religion as an illusion, a trickery. I am like Cyrano about his nose: *"Je me les sers moi-même avec assez de verve, pour ne point tolérer qu'un autre me les serve!"*[1] As believers, we have the right to ask ourselves why the coming of scientific knowledge met so much resistance everywhere, just as much from scholars as from Churchmen—and the Churchmen were sometimes scholars, or the scholars, Churchmen—to ask why—yes, why—this knowledge set itself up as an antagonist to religion!

WOLTON: *Wasn't there a contradiction after a while? The Church had imposed a body of doctrine that was blocking scientific progress.*

LUSTIGER: Pascal was a good mathematician; he invented the calculator....

WOLTON: *Religion and science were very much mixed from the thirteenth to the seventeenth century, and, as you said, the clergy were often also men of science. But since the scientific revolution of the nineteenth century, there has been a break. The Church no longer intervenes in matters of scientific content because she considers that a separation took place, and she now steps in only on moral issues.*

LUSTIGER: Religion was not peremptorily interfering with scientific matters when Pascal was calculating probabilities or physicists were studying atmospheric pressure. But in its early stages, between the thirteenth and the seventeenth century, experimental science posed questions of a philosophical nature (cosmological, anthropological)—questions closely connected to theological ideas. Both scientific and philosophical thought tended toward a unifying vision of human knowledge and man's place in the universe. In the sixteenth century, there could be conflicts and quarrels between science and faith but not a rupture. The Jesuits went to China, where they taught astronomy and mathematics. Why was this evolution transformed into a combat? Where did the aggression come from? Why did science result in atheism? You are not going to make me believe that enthroning a comely young Parisienne in Notre-Dame and calling her the "goddess of Reason" had anything to do with experimental science.

MISSIKA: *That was different. It was a political, not a scientific, event....*

LUSTIGER: Exactly. The stakes went beyond science. It is absurd to reduce this situation to a conflict between religion and science. It was in the nineteenth century, after the revolutionary exigency, whose influence was not

[1] "I myself ridicule my nose to the point that I find all other criticisms of it unacceptably insipid."—TRANS.

limited to science, that the "spiritual crisis of the West" developed. At issue was the aim of the atheistic undertaking: the salvation of humanity by itself and the birth of a society enlightened by human reason alone. Science had more than a scientific objective; it had a social goal as well: the creation of a utopia. Today's scientists say, "We keep to our laboratories, we are researchers, we have nothing to do with the political problem." But can we forget that the entire scientific venture at that time was first directed toward finalities that are alien to science? It suffices to read the *Encyclopédistes.* [2] The Enlightenment's ambition was to save humanity! On that ground, the contest became formidable.

It is still going on, but the twentieth century has been led to re-examine the problem of reason's limitations—on two levels. First, that of humanity's goals. What does a "happy humanity" mean? Our century has experienced both the greatest of man-made catastrophes and the greatest technical achievements. We are becoming aware—and at what cost!—that reason has to learn wisdom. Second, on the level of methodology: each branch of learning has been forced to examine itself and determine its own limits, as much in terms of goals as in the construction of results. Our century has had to serve its epistemological and then hermeneutical apprenticeships of human knowledge. We are no longer completely in the stage of Auguste Comte's "Tree of Knowledge".[3] Science and religion have now entered a period of mutual recognition, as if an atomic bomb had exploded between the two factions, vitrifying the protagonists in a kind of intellectual desert, and some explorers, coming from elsewhere, had tried to go and see what had happened on the two sides of the explosion. During the postwar period, I was envisaging the end of scientism. But, in 1954, as chaplain at the university and in the university parish, I was stupefied to observe that the majority of twenty-year-old students were submerged in positivist and scientistic doubt. And we Christians had so few qualified interlocutors who were both truly scientific and truly believers—such as Louis de Broglie and Louis Leprince-Ringuet.[4] To give you an idea of the climate of the times, their names served as the authority's argument that one could be both a great scientist and a Catholic!

Since then efforts have been made. New generations have gathered the fruit of this intellectual upheaval, epistemological questions are beginning to be

[2] The *Encyclopédistes* (Diderot, Voltaire, Rousseau, d'Alembert) were the main proponents of the philosophy of the Enlightenment in eighteenth-century France. They expressed their thoughts in the *Encyclopédie,* a dictionary of modern knowledge.—TRANS.

[3] Auguste Comte (1798–1857) was a French philosopher who is known as the founder of "positivism". He conceived of a "logical" organization of all branches of knowledge, using the tree—with its roots, trunk, boughs, etc.—as a model.—TRANS.

[4] Louis de Broglie (1892–1986), French physicist, was awarded the Nobel Prize in 1929 for his work in the field of wave mechanics. Louis Leprince-Ringuet (1901–), also a physicist, is a professor at the Collège de France. He has specialized in the study of cosmic rays.—TRANS.

raised and we are benefiting from this commotion. But it is not certain that these new ideas are very widespread.

Biology and Ethics

MISSIKA: *For several years now, there has been a sharp controversy surrounding artificial procreation, genetic manipulations or genetic control. In the United States and France, at the initiative of the scientific milieu, ethical committees have been set up. Do you feel that priests should participate in these committees?*

LUSTIGER: The matter is so serious that the medical profession finds its own norms being challenged and is calling on society to establish a control that it can no longer ensure. The instinct of medical research is to go as far as possible, saying that, in any case, whatever serves scientific progress serves human progress. But what professional deontology must doctors or research scientists obey when they are dealing with human subjects? Until recently, the medical profession's response was based on the Hippocratic oath and a certain definition of man—his integrity and his rights—about which there was supposedly a universal consensus. The present recourse to ethical committees indicates the existence of a fissure in the frame of reference. It can have resulted either from an expansion of research beyond its usual sphere or from the internal disequilibrium of a society less sure of its convictions and unanimity. The fact remains, however, that sometimes the deontology is so much connected to the medical act's technical nature that only professionals, armed with a certain conception of man and a moral sensibility, can elaborate it. Nevertheless, lawyers, judges and moralists, although unconnected with medicine, must also form consciences and give advice. And the scope of problems has to be determined, the data defined and the ethical question clearly posed.

For this reason, I am, in principle, in favor of advisory ethical committees, with a few conditions. The first, that the representatives are competent and honest. Whether Catholics are represented by priests or laymen matters little so long as they are convinced Catholics and are sufficiently well informed to be authentic spokesmen for the Catholic Faith's point of view. Otherwise, it is absurd to say, "Catholics have a voice."

WOLTON: *But does the idea of representation make any sense in this matter? Who represents what?*

LUSTIGER: Certain questions are still debatable among Catholics. That is why the Catholic representation must strictly respect the Church's doctrine.

The second condition is that such committees must not claim to substitute themselves for the conscience or dispense any participant from his responsibility: not the doctor, the politician or the citizen. Third (since disagreement is inevitable), the political way of arbitrating between the majority and minority must not be applied to the ethical debate. We are facing a moral problem: the majority decision cannot represent truth, or the minority, error. If a consensus is reached, let it be stated. If divergences exist, let them also be published. If there is a debate, let its terms be given. And ethical committees should not be organs of political decision. They can give advice, clarify the risks, but that does not discharge political leaders or citizens from their own responsibility.

Given the grave nature of the questions and the breaking apart of the consensus on the definition of man and his individual and social rights, the debate can be healthy as long as it does not turn to factiousness, witch-hunting or manipulation. Ethical committees should not resemble purging committees. A majority opinion proves nothing as to the moral validity of what is decided. Even if carefully composed ethical panels had been set up in Germany in 1939, they would not necessarily have condemned the extermination of handicapped adults. The authentic moral debate is respectful. Its aim is not to hammer out a decision but to make people think. It takes nothing away from the freedom or capacity for reflection, but it simply probes more deeply into heretofore obscure questions.

MISSIKA: *What do you think is at risk in this debate?*

LUSTIGER: Science has developed by controlling increasing numbers of objects in an increasingly efficient way. My admiration for medical science is boundless. The ingenious and complex inventions of doctors and researchers are marvelous. The ultrasonic instrument that can pulverize kidney stones without surgery is prodigiously clever! The laser for ophthalmological surgery is fantastic! But that is just the point: this science progresses by laying hold of man's body as if it were an object, because it is true that the body is also an object and that there are affinities between the surgeon's work and that of the carpenter, the seamstress and, sometimes, the mechanic.

For a long time men have experimented with—more recently they have controlled—the reproductive mechanisms of vegetable and animal species. The innovation of recent years is that some researchers have dared to apply this know-how to the human species. Initially, it was for therapeutic ends, but it came to be used for treating infertility. At that point, a fearsome question arose: What is the relationship of man's humanity to his body? Until the middle of this century, there could be variations in the definition of man, but everyone seemed to agree that there was an impassable limit as to what man is and what in him is to be respected. Now technical prowess seems to extend beyond that definition and is saying, "To achieve in vitro fertilization, we are obliged to develop a series of embryos and freeze them. What shall we do with the unused ones?" Scientists have had the honesty to say publicly that they cannot make the decision alone.

All right, then, what are frozen embryos? Are they human beings? The problem is not new. The question of the precise moment that a human embryo can be considered a human being with a soul was discussed at length by ancient and medieval authors, but their knowledge was limited. Today, however, the accumulated scientific information about a human being's beginnings makes us more and more certain on this point. Here I am adopting a strictly scientific point of view: research and experiments that mark the progress in our understanding of human life from conception to birth maintain with increasing certitude that the embryo is not just a mass of flesh without a name or significance but that it is already inscribed in human individuality and life: "that" might well become a man. I simply wish to say this: that risk, that likelihood exists. And it demands an absolute respect. When it comes to respecting a human being, we have to be intransigent, even if it means that scientists have to make detours that may be more costly in money, energy, time and intellectual effort.

WOLTON: *Then you think that, in one way or another, some limits must be imposed on scientific research if the definition of the human being is to be preserved?*

LUSTIGER: Yes, we have to be ultrarigorous when human dignity is involved. And that applies to all domains. Bringing up these problems reminds us of the racist and eugenic dreams that tore Europe apart less than fifty years ago. I am thinking of the Auschwitz experiments and not just of Mengele's. Up to now, this madness, this rational delirium has served primarily to inspire science fiction, but we are now on the threshold of the plausible, the possible. It is no longer preposterous to think of doing literally "everything".

MISSIKA: *But, for the moment, not "everything" can be done.*

LUSTIGER: No, but it is not unthinkable that the time will come when, if not everything, then at least a great deal can be done.

MISSIKA: *Biologists do not agree on this point.*

LUSTIGER: Very well, let us take some realistic hypothesis—choosing a child's sex, for example. Neither biologists nor demographers have yet explained why there is a statistical balance between men and women throughout the world. Nothing prevents imagining a society whose desire is sometimes focused on the masculine image, sometimes on the feminine. This could lead to a disequilibrium as absurd as those existing in commerce or agriculture once the subsistence economies are exceeded. There could be fantastic uncontrollable disorders. Then would the question have to be settled by a computer? Would quotas be set? Another question: Are we going to practice eugenics?

MISSIKA: *You are mixing problems....*

LUSTIGER: Perhaps it is a gross confusion between culture and genetics, but I raise the question: At what moment must we say "no"? Once we have ceded on the respect due to human integrity, we know that we shall acquiesce to everything. Therefore, we have to maintain a tough, unyielding position that forces people to think. That is precisely what the Holy See has done with its instruction on *Respect for Human Life in Its Origin and the Dignity of Procreation.* I was struck to see that, in the debate surrounding surrogate mothers, many psychoanalysts joined the Church in adopting a position of firm hostility. They are not necessarily moving in the same direction, but ...

WOLTON: *It is an objective alliance....*

LUSTIGER: A completely objective alliance! Psychoanalysis has had the merit to situate the human condition in its historical continuity. Suddenly, it points out that a technical rationality risks destroying a determining element in this condition.

Do not get the wrong idea. I am not opposed to science. I am simply asking that it not exempt its technique from moral obligation. Until recently, medical deontology, on the whole, had been able to do this. Researchers dealing with the inanimate or infrahuman animated world did not have this kind of problem; however, in medicine, science is integrated into the service of the therapeutic art, and that gives it both its dignity and its limitations. Imposed ethical standards are the price science has to pay for its access to the control of the human person's biological condition. For science, this is a source of real progress.

Perhaps my education has been too classical, but it seems to me that constraints are a source of freedom and greater beauty. The day that the painter is no longer bound by his canvas or a determined surface, he is lost. To create a work of art, the sculptor must respect his oak or his stone. When the constraint disappears, the result becomes completely undistinguished. Look at reinforced concrete! You can do whatever you want with concrete and, hence, you lose the formidable advantage of discipline, convention and order that, in fact, structure the human mind. By analogy, I consider ethical standards and their restrictions as a condition for scientific progress. The question being posed to our culture and civilization is about man: What is man's good? It is a metaphysical question.

MISSIKA: *In the United States, certain religious groups are insisting that a scientific type of explanation of man's creation by God, "creationism", be taught along with neo-Darwinism in the natural history courses given in public schools. What do you think of this demand?*

LUSTIGER: What I know about the matter makes their position seem at the very least naïve, if not abusive. They are substituting one order of knowledge for another. The biblical account says that God, the Unique One, is Creator of all things, that nothing escapes his benevolence by which the world exists in its genesis and history, its completion and hope. And it also declares that man has a divine vocation in the world. This message merits being taught. But substituting it for empirical scientific knowledge and thus exempting the human mind from its research on the spatiotemporal evolution of life and man would be distorting the Faith, and it would also be a misuse of reason. But one must not be lacking in civil respect for religious beliefs.

Take a look however, at the biblical story of creation. The creative act causes the entire world to enter into history, and it situates man, who receives his being from God, in the totality of history: the human species is unique in its vocation, and all men are brothers. I recently read an article by a widely respected paleontologist for whom the variety of human differentiations is dissimilar to that found in the animal species. Thus, scientifically also, one would be dealing with a unique species. It is impossible to insist too much on the beauty of the account of creation that opens the Bible. It lacks neither eloquence nor polemics. For example, instead of naming the moon and the sun, which were divinities for the surrounding people, the author speaks of the greater and lesser lights. That amounts to saying, "You take them for gods, but they are only small lamps. God has placed them in the canopy of heaven to serve man: they indicate the seasons and the days, the days and the nights so that man can praise God." The description of creation is full of splendor and remains meaningful to man today. It is far from irrelevant whether man loves creation, respects its diversity and beauty and does not consider it merely as exploitable resources to be used for his own ends. Creation speaks. It is fascinating to think about the kinship between mind and matter. A fragment of stone can be analyzed on a molecular and geological level, and if it has been carved into a work of art, a message or a weapon, it can also be read as a trace of mankind's history. The same object can have a prodigious plurality of meanings and purposes. The place of science is on another plane, objective and formal. Today, it confronts us with concepts that are incomprehensible on the commonsense level. For example, a curved and finished space. Or the discoveries of a universe in expansion. The average person will ask: Expanding toward what? In what? Similarly, the theory of the original Big Bang—what does it mean? And before it took place? Should a temporality prior to temporality be imagined?

The description of creation given by Genesis teaches that each element of the whole refers to the Creator. The cosmos, with man at its center, is incessantly held under the sovereign creative freedom of God, who gives it meaning and substance. "And God saw everything that he had made, and behold, it was very good." And although the problem of evil and death has inescapably tormented the conscience of every human being, Genesis acknowledges the scandal and affirms that life is good since it is a gift from God. We must love and serve it, our own and that of others.

WOLTON: *Therefore, Genesis is not to be seen as a chapter in a natural science textbook?*

LUSTIGER: It is absolutely essential to distinguish scientific knowledge from religious instruction! Substituting one for the other seems to be a "concordism" (to use a term from the beginning of the century) that is dangerous, to say the least. And to follow my train of thought through to the end—without wishing to offend anybody—it strikes me as slightly ridiculous.

PART THREE

THE CHURCH AND SOCIETY

I

CHAPLAIN AT THE SORBONNE (1954–1969)

Getting around Paris on a Solex[1]

DOMINIQUE WOLTON: *You served as chaplain at the University of Paris from 1954 to 1969. Was this your choice?*

JEAN-MARIE LUSTIGER: No, I did not choose the post, but I had hoped for it. During the seven years that I was in seminary, I kept in close touch with the Sorbonne chaplains, in particular with Abbé Charles, the creator of the Centre Richelieu, and with several of my former classmates. I had also come to know other students from succeeding generations. Some of them have remained close friends in spite of geographical distance and the passing years. But above all, I wanted to serve there because I was in complete agreement with the way the university chaplains were living and exercising their ministry as priests.

To tell the truth, I had had practically no contact with a traditional parish. Many of my fellow seminarians were dreading it. They thought of it as an outdated form of the Church's life, lacking in apostolic and spiritual inspiration. The majority looked with envy on the well-known examples of renewal in the parishes of Saint-Séverin, L'Haÿ-les-Roses, Colombes, etc., that were provoking quite a lot of controversy.

It was only later that I realized just how ignorant I had been then of the parish world. But in 1954, when I was appointed by Cardinal Feltin[2] as a student chaplain, I found myself in familiar company, one in which I felt most at ease. However, my uppermost concern was to establish a well-defined way of living and acting as a priest, a way of living in a community. At that time, there were five of us sharing an apartment and our meager financial resources. We lived like "monks": each of us had a very small room and we took our meals together. Our days were punctuated by prayer services, and all our apostolic action was planned and reflected on in prayer. Personal preferences were subordinated to the priority of our common mission. And, in particular,

[1] A Solex was an inexpensive, popular moped, always black (like Henry Ford's Model T), with a small engine over the front wheel; nevertheless, it occasionally had to be pedaled.—TRANS.

[2] Maurice Cardinal Feltin (1883–1975) was Archbishop of Paris from 1949 to 1966.—TRANS.

our shared faith nourished the enthusiasms of our relative youth—I was twenty-eight—and made it possible for us to take all the hard knocks and overcome numerous obstacles. Our ministry to students was marked by the basic intuitions of *l'Action catholique* in encouraging the vocation of laymen. I was able to see and live through the implementation of those systematic and successful intuitions that Vatican II was going to explain and motivate so forcefully. The young laity, about equally divided between boys and girls—which was rather unusual at a time when coeducation was not yet widespread—received their share of apostolic and spiritual responsibility for the Church. It was an organized discipleship in which the preaching of the Gospel, focused on the university environment, went hand in hand with spiritual life and theological education. Our plan was directed toward young intellectual apprentices. There were no traditions and, hence, none of the lethargy of adult parishes to hamper our freedom of action and invention. Outside of the academic setting, we would have had to cope with resistance and inbred customs.

As a member of the team of Sorbonne chaplains, I was in charge of students in classic and modern literature, philosophy, psychology and mathematics. I was also responsible for the Institut National d'Orientation Professionelle,[3] the École des Chartes[4] and the École Spéciale d'Architecture—as well as all the foreign students in Paris, with whom we organized many meetings, bringing together believers from different religions. It was then that I began to discover, other than through reading, the diversity of Islam. Furthermore, Cardinal Feltin had named me as chaplain for the Académie de Paris[5], which is made up of public school teachers grouped into what its founders, Joseph Lotte and Father Paris, had named the University Parish. My superior there was a towering figure, Father Dabosville, an Oratorian, who was the national chaplain for Catholic teachers in public schools. He had also entrusted me with the chaplainship at the École Normale Supérieure in Saint-Cloud[6] and the one at Fontenay.

WOLTON: *But how on earth was it possible to take on so many jobs?*

[3] The Institut National d'Orientation Professionelle (I.N.O.P.) aimed at helping students choose a career.—TRANS.

[4] The École des Chartes specializes in the study of ancient documents.—TRANS.

[5] The Académie de Paris was then the administrative body for the system of education in the greater Paris region.—TRANS.

[6] The Écoles Normales Supérieures were formed for the education of an "elite" corps of teachers. The two oldest (and most prestigious) are the one located on the Rue d'Ulm in Paris (for men only, until recently) and the one in Sèvres (for women). The schools at Saint-Cloud and Fontenay were raised to the same status after World War II.—TRANS.

LUSTIGER: Well, I did it, thanks to my Solex, and it was fascinating. There were in all twenty priests who were serving—in various ways—the Paris university community. Some of them were full time: the Jesuits were at the *grandes écoles*[7] and the medical schools, the Dominicans covered the law schools, and our group dealt with the students in the humanities and sciences. There were other priests who, in addition to their regular activities—often teaching and research—were part-time chaplains.

At the same time, I was also the chaplain for the JEC at the Sorbonne. There had been a stormy period prior to my arrival, and since I was a former member, it seemed that as a new man I could help in settling the acrimonious dispute....

WOLTON: *Dispute between whom?*

LUSTIGER: Between the Centre Richelieu and the JEC. The rupture dated from 1948. My task was to bring about a meeting of the two groups, who no longer understood each other.

When I had left the Sorbonne in 1949, nothing had changed since the beginning of the century. And when I returned in 1954, everything was still the same, except that degrees in psychology and modern literature had been added. The same *appariteurs*[8] staunchly looked after the university. It is true that the halls already echoed to the pounding footsteps of the increased influxes of new *bacheliers.*[9] The *année propédeutique*[10] was about to be invented, and the first death knell of the old university was soon going to sound.

So, I spent my years of chaplain apprenticeship at the Sorbonne—between 1954 and 1959—on a solid foundation. My reference points from those days are all connected with the university.

WOLTON: *Yes, you have not spoken at all about Vatican II and especially about what was leading up to it in those years.*

LUSTIGER: We all welcomed Vatican II with the serene feeling that it was obvious. For us, it seemed to be putting an end to the debates—indeed, the

[7] *Grandes écoles* (including the Écoles Normales Supérieures) are prestigious state-or privately run schools at the university level with highly competitive entrance examinations. —TRANS.

[8] The *appariteurs* acted as janitors-guardians and saw to law and order on the campuses. Originally, their job was solemnly to usher in professors before their lectures.—TRANS.

[9] *Bacheliers* are the equivalent of high school graduates.—TRANS.

[10] The *année propédeutique* was a one-year preparation course, offered until 1966, for entering students, who had to pass an examination before being admitted to departments leading to specific degrees.—TRANS.

quarrels—that were dividing Catholics; and we felt that it reinforced our own orientations while obliging us to enlarge our views. We greeted Vatican II with joy, but we were not really surprised. An example: every year the pilgrimage to Chartres, made on two weekends, attracted about 12,000 students, of whom 6,000 were from our branch of the Sorbonne. In 1962, the theme was "the Church". For the occasion, a close friend, a priest and musician, composed some very beautiful songs that were particularly suited to a liturgy involving a large crowd. One of the songs took as a refrain a verse from chapter 21 of Revelation: "Behold, the dwelling of God is with men / He will dwell with them, and they shall be his people / And God himself will be with them." "People called together by the word of the prophets / People gathered round Christ the Lord / People who listen to their God / Church of the Lord". Chapter 2 of the Constitution *Lumen gentium* was already being condensed in the verses of this song, which enumerated all the biblical images designating the Church.

JEAN-LOUIS MISSIKA: *Did you ever meet John XXIII?*

LUSTIGER: Yes, I did. It was during the years of the Council, when we went to Rome for Holy Week with a thousand students from the Sorbonne. He met with us in the Sistine Chapel where we had sung for a service—it had been a "premiere". In his talk, the Pope praised our singing of the Psalms in French. We took an immediate liking to each other. Later, as he lay dying, he asked after us in a deeply moving way. He saw those French students as a "model" for youth in the Church's future.

Anticlericalism at the University

MISSIKA: *Were you confronted with anticlericalism at the university?*

LUSTIGER: Yes, we were, much to my surprise. For my generation, anticlericalism and the simplistic rationalism of prewar France, of the Third Republic, were completely outdated. I was stupefied to discover that the young Catholic generations, as well as all those who called themselves more or less unbelievers, were still profoundly marked by a conflict that no longer interested me. Although unresolved, it was a closed matter for me, at least. But I was obliged to deal with it by responding to the incessant objections of those eighteen-year-old boys and girls who were just entering university. It had to be demonstrated that faith is not in contradiction with science, or with man's development, or his freedom, or his personal and collective success or with social effectiveness—with which, at that time, Marxism was credited. We had to take up the most persistent nineteenth-century hypotheses on the collusion of the clerical party with the forces of "reaction".

We also had to show that the most rigorous moral standards were not incompatible with emotional and sexual development. In a way, we were required to exhaust all these issues before going on to the most important and vital questions—namely, that knowing God and living with him, discovering the gift of communion received in the Church, is a call in the strongest sense of the word and that it offers us the joy of living a human life as a divine vocation. We had first of all to set forth all the students' objections without ridiculing them; otherwise, the questions bothering them would have been doomed to silence.

WOLTON: *Was there anticlericalism among the faculty?*

LUSTIGER: In this respect, too, I was greatly surprised. When I was studying at the university, I felt that I was meeting only free men and women who were intellectually independent and who usually had very well defined opinions and were aware of their choices. I never noticed any harassments or persecutions for religious or political reasons. In a word, I held the most idyllic vision possible of tolerance in the public school and higher education.

In 1954, however, the reflections of professors and confidences of elementary school teachers led me to discover a difficult situation. This kind of conflict went so far as to compromise the careers of Catholic faculty members who, nonetheless, loved their work and were faithful servants of public education. Thus, as a chaplain, I saw that it was essential to reforge a conception of the laity that would be acceptable to both Catholics and the secular party. A number of highly respected academics worked assiduously to do it intelligently, and, in my opinion, they succeeded.

At the time of the quarrel over the schools in 1982–84,[11] I was dumbfounded to see a resurfacing of the most archaic and outmoded ideas of thirty years earlier.

[11] During those years, in what is called the *affaire scolaire,* the Socialist government attempted to nationalize all private schools in France, most of which are Catholic. It had been a traditional priority on the leftist agenda, but popular reluctance (voiced by Cardinal Lustiger, among others) and even mass demonstrations forced the government to abandon its plans. As a result, Education Minister Alain Savary and Prime Minister Pierre Mauroy were forced to resign.—TRANS.

The Great Patience Required for Scientific Research

MISSIKA: *In a more general way, what did you derive from the company of scientists and academics?*

LUSTIGER: I witnessed numerous discussions and even angry disputes among scientific researchers. I learned that real science takes place in day-to-day research. There are men and women who devote their entire lifetimes to repetitive experiments and dogged explorations in order to make an inventory of one short segment of knowledge and, sometimes, to demonstrate that there is nothing to demonstrate—which, of course, can also be an important result. The verification of a hypothesis can take a lifetime, an entire lifetime! ... You have to have a lot of patience and a lot of honesty to go about accumulating such concrete knowledge. It demands at least as much stubborn determination and solidarity as, for example, the clearing of the Gallic forests by monks in the Middle Ages! We often have a mystical, magical vision of the scientist and science. In fact, his everyday work is very ordinary, often slow and rather "tinkering". The reality of scientific research is very different from the public's image of it.

Those years at the Sorbonne were exhilarating for me. The Latin Quarter was my village—a village that had been home since I was ten years old.

MISSIKA: *You certainly seemed to like it there!*

LUSTIGER: I fitted in as naturally as the chestnut trees in the Luxembourg Garden.

WOLTON: *Did you consider yourself an intellectual?*

LUSTIGER: No, I was simply a native of the Latin Quarter. That does not suffice for making an academic, much less for making an intellectual.

WOLTON: *What is the difference?*

LUSTIGER: To become an academic worthy of respect requires an effort of considerable austerity. I am too lazy for that! In any case, it is not in that domain that my willpower asserts itself....

MISSIKA: *But were you ever attracted by such a career?*

LUSTIGER: I have devoted my energies to something else; there were people more competent than I to do it: it is a matter of a division of labor.... What really interests me is experienced as much in action and reflection on that action as in academic pursuits.

The Algerian War

WOLTON: *You were chaplain during the Algerian War. How did it affect your contact with students?*

LUSTIGER: I was close enough to them in age to feel myself involved. I could have been sent off to Algeria as an officer. Some of my friends—seminarians and priests—were. The students' reactions were not fundamentally different from those of French youth in general. The divisions and clashes were the same as those found in national opinion, except that they were much more exaggerated and ardent. With students, everything assumed an extreme and drastic intensity, whereas the majority of Frenchmen simply "absorbed the shock". As time passed and the war took a more brutal turn, passions were aggravated. The young *pieds-noirs*[12] studying in Paris—their numbers were increasing every year—posed the problem shrilly and dramatically. The left took a stand against torture, and the debate began to center more and more on moral questions. Then, from the Church came the army chaplaincy's report on torture.

WOLTON: *Cardinal Feltin is known to have passed on a document on this subject to government officials. Do you think that the radicalization of certain Christian groups could have been avoided if he had made his position public?*

LUSTIGER: In the end, the contents of the report did become known. I later learned that Cardinal Feltin, who was the vicar of the army, had not wanted to dramatize the debate. He was seeking to prevent the report from being used for polemical ends. Was he wrong or right? To answer that question, we would have to ascertain all the circumstances of his decision. Should I ever find myself in a comparable situation—which is not impossible—I simply do not know what I would do. That is the problem with action and responsibility. A public declaration is not the best solution in every case. In circumstances where it appears that the law or morality is not being respected, it is sometimes more effective to speak directly, with conviction and authority, to those who are in a position to remedy it. It is even the most logical way of doing things, because the end being sought is not to discredit whoever might be involved but to act so that the moral law is upheld.

[12] *Pieds-noirs* is a familiar appellation for the European inhabitants of Algeria. Its literal meaning is "black feet".—TRANS.

WOLTON: *Your attitude here is the same that you expressed about the episcopate's conduct during the Second World War. Does that mean that you are not surprised that there was no public intervention by the Church?*

LUSTIGER: The Church's role is not to score points. Taking a public stand indicates that the only remedy left is making an appeal to the public conscience, or else that the evil being committed risks perverting the moral judgment of a nation or its leaders.

In situations of this kind—common in this world, alas—the credibility of witnesses poses another problem. High-level authorities can be the objects of involuntary or partisan poisoning. Controlling and verifying accusations take a great deal of time, while it is quick action that is needed. When the Church speaks out publicly, she risks making her authority a "tool" and, hence, feeling the need to adopt strategies for conquering public opinion. On the other hand, she must never shy away from an intervention because she fears being "used". Her leaders must create conditions for taking a stand, conditions that will protect their independence in the verbal war that politics has become. Political parties see their various partners only within the context of their strategies, as being "for" or "against". For those who want to gain power, a spiritual authority such as that of the Church, with the adhesion she inspires from a certain number of her faithful, can appear to be a bonanza.

The Church has the duty to make her opinions clear, not only from the point of view of morality but also from that of faith. She claims no monopoly on moral sensitivity. In our country, other religious groups, other institutions, can and should express themselves in its name. A nation needs moral magistracies. Montesquieu said that democracy was the regime that required the greatest virtue. But, for the Church, there is still another consideration: the light of faith. It is God's primacy over everything human to which we must bear witness. That does not mean that theocratic power should be established over political, economic or social power; "God's primacy over everything human" is an expression of the grandeur of God, Source of the personal and moral grandeur of man. Thus, the equal dignity of all men is based on the fact that we are all created by the unique Heavenly Creator and redeemed by the unique Redeemer. Furthermore, no adversary can ever be considered someone to eliminate, because Christ says to us, "Love your enemies."

MISSIKA: *But all moral intervention is done in the name of values. In what way is the Church's action different?*

LUSTIGER: Sometimes, the difference is striking. But to understand its validity, you have to know about the substantial but hidden spiritual effort it requires from the faithful. If we want to "speak out for what is just", it is not sufficient to write an article or make a public declaration; we must pray, if only to purify our hearts from hate and to elucidate the problem. Formal statements of the Church's views seem obvious once they are made, and yet it is not so easy to express them before God and men. Even the affirmations that seem to be the most simple require patient prayer and a great personal effort. This specific and singular contribution of the Church places her at the crossroads of all human problems. Of course individual Christians can—at their own risk—take sides on political issues. But they cannot claim that their particular choices exhaust that source of courage, reflection and freedom that is, in the communion with God, the light that the Church brings to men.

WOLTON: *Do you have the impression that all bishops have the same ethical code regarding the Church's public pronouncements?*

LUSTIGER: It seems to me that the Catholic position is expressed quite clearly by what I have just said. During the Algerian War, moral questions arose again in a very acute way. Torture is totally unacceptable. In my view, that moral judgment is obvious. But certain officers responded that "if a guy is going to blow up the Casbah, you have to use every possible means to find out where he put the bomb"....

MISSIKA: *And you do not accept this reasoning?*

LUSTIGER: My response is simple and categorical: No! The end never justifies the means. The degradation of one man by another, whether by torture or enslavement, for whatever reasons, is a moral and spiritual scandal. Certainly, it is a difficult deontological problem for those responsible for security to determine that thin boundary where a "tough" interrogation ends and torture begins. The law's objectivity must protect everyone from arbitrariness. It is by that standard that a civilized country is recognized. Laws, regulations, are necessary to avoid justifying the behavior of a petty sadist who happens to be on duty. Gangsters' morals must not become models to imitate. And, by the way, it seems to me that crime novels and sadistic accounts of torture are far too prevalent and extremely dangerous.

MISSIKA: *What would you want to do about it? Are you in favor of forbidding an author to write such books or for a system of censorship?*

LUSTIGER: No, but I remind you that every person is morally responsible for what he says, writes and does in regard to others. If not, society falls apart.

WOLTON: *But now you are talking about the problem of freedom of expression. You have gone from one problem to another.*

LUSTIGER: Not at all! I am simply pointing out the seriousness of a cultural phenomenon that is directly related to your question about torture. The fact is that, for mercenary reasons, sadism has been made commonplace. When this kind of reading matter is sold and diffused with such success, it is a disturbing symptom. Do you think that a person can give in with impunity to the sadistic urges that can spring up in anyone? During the Algerian War and later on, I heard the confidences of so many draftees who were witnesses to acts of violence and torture or who had let themselves be led into committing it themselves in order to get revenge for killed or tortured buddies. They had been caught up in a system of which they were ashamed and could not speak. As chaplains, we sensed that this generation was being subjected to grave traumas. No one had the key for helping them to express themselves. It is this kind of evil and open sore in society that the *Action des Chrétiens pour l'Abolition de la Torture*[13] wants to heal. It acts by trying to unite its members, who come from various religious denominations, in Christ's suffering through a common prayer. The exterior action on public opinion is nourished by the interior commitment. And that seems to be very sound.

MISSIKA: *What activities were you involved in during the Algerian conflict?*

LUSTIGER: We not only had to listen to the young *pieds-noirs,* we had to help them to become integrated into the national community and give them a chance to have their say. Their despair was absolute, heartrending! There were four serious moral problems that were clearly having political repercussions: the Algerians' right to independence; the rights of the *pieds-noirs* on that same land; the French problem of national unity and civil peace; and, finally, the question of the "means" being used: revolutionary war, violence, terrorism, torture. The Church could not stay silent.

We were asking ourselves how we could do our part. We wanted to encourage acts of reconciliation. A latent war, a religious war, was developing among Catholics, and a common language no longer existed. The spiritual reference to faith had been emptied of meaning. Only enmity remained. In practice, that amounted to saying that God does not exist, because even if each person continued to believe in God, he could do it only by excluding those

[13] This organization is a French-based federation of interdenominational Christian groups in Europe committed to abolishing, by means of prayer and efforts to increase public awareness, the use of torture.—TRANS.

who did not share his convictions. That violence was denying God, and we had to lead those who called on God and Christ for their inspiration to meet again and recognize the truth that they shared and that surmounted the inexpiable and apparently unsolvable quarrel in which they were engaged. Faith is futile, meaningless, if it is not also capable of facing up to mortal conflict.

Every December, for three years in succession, we organized a series of vigils whose theme was peace. The first one was really quite "heroic": we suggested to three well-known Christian laymen, whose disagreements concerning the Algerian War had been publicized, that they pray together at Notre-Dame. Each of them was asked to compose a prayer and to stand side by side with the others. You can imagine the difficulty of negotiating with the student leaders—we were organized in such a way that their responsibility was considerable. I can still picture two of them who came, one after the other, with tears in their eyes to protest against the plan. One was a *pied-noir;* the other belonged to a leftist organization. They were being torn apart because they knew that they would be regarded as traitors by their comrades in the struggle if they joined in prayer with the enemy; meeting the adversary would be tantamount to disowning the ally. The three personalities who accepted our proposal were François Mauriac, Georges Bidault and Edmond Michelet.[14] It was not at all easy to carry through. On the night of the vigil, police surveillance was heavy because they feared outbursts of violence: it was physically dangerous. I shall not name, because that information is confidential, the other personalities approached whose reaction was: "Me, go and sit beside that man? Never!" The texts written by the three men who did accept were very beautiful. We even made the front page of the *Canard enchaîne,*[15] which printed a cartoon showing three men kneeling in the cathedral with this caption: "Lord, do unto the others what they are asking that you do unto me." I was delighted that the *Canard* had understood and had said it *à sa façon.*

It was not our intention to try to mediate between the adverse parties. We simply hoped to provoke a reflection that would go farther and deeper. We knew that there would be repercussions. As priests, our objective was to prepare for them.

[14] François Mauriac was the leading French Catholic novelist at the time. He had denounced the use of torture in his well-known column in the *Figaro littéraire.* Georges Bidault had been a *Résistance* leader and was one of the founders of French Christian Democracy (MRP). He defended a "French Algeria". Edmond Michelet, a *pied-noir* politician, was torn between the opposing solutions. His beatification is currently being considered. —Trans.

[15] The *Canard enchaîné* is an anticlerical but respected satirical newspaper founded in 1916.—Trans.

WOLTON: *Did you ever meet with any representatives of political power and, in particular, with General de Gaulle when all this was taking place?*

LUSTIGER: I met General de Gaulle once. At the time of the Peace Vigils, we solicited messages from government leaders around the world, as well as from the Pope. There were quite a few responses. At one point, I had envisaged that some of those leaders might come and speak at Notre-Dame. In connection with this undertaking, I had met with President Senghor[16] when he was passing through Paris. The discussion ranged over many subjects, including *africanité,*[17] Senegal and Islam. It was fascinating. A short while afterward, when there was to be a reception at the Élysée in his honor, President Senghor arranged to have me invited.

And so, for the first time in my life, I entered the Élysée Palace. Dressed in my best soutane and running late, I was about to jump on my Solex to get across town, but my friends advised me not to play at being Don Camillo! And yet I could easily picture myself arriving in that way. In the reception line, General de Gaulle kept me for quite a long time, considering the number of people who were waiting behind me. I had carefully prepared what I wanted to say to him. It concerned the fate of African students in Paris—I was, as you will recall, the chaplain for foreign students, and the Africans' problems were particularly distressing to me. I spoke about them in a detailed and precise way: How and under what conditions should French-speaking Africans have access to higher education in France? What attitudes should France adopt, and what could be expected from the authorities? I had developed my thesis quite forcefully, and the general listened to me very attentively—at least, so I thought. He asked me two or three questions and encouraged me, having taken note that I was a chaplain at the Sorbonne. I later learned that my words had had some fallout in the ministries of *Coopération* and *Éducation nationale.* For me, de Gaulle was a fabulous individual, one who had given back to us the honor to be French. I was surprised by the attention he gave to the remarks of a young priest who came up to him in the middle of a crowded reception.

The Centre Richelieu

MISSIKA: *You took over as director of the Centre Richelieu in 1959. What were its activities?*

[16] Léopold Sedar Senghor (1906–) is a Senegalese statesman and poet. He was president of the Republic of Senegal from 1963 to 1980.—TRANS.

[17] *Africanité* refers to the specific character of African culture.—TRANS.

LUSTIGER: It would take much too long to describe them. I can give you only an overall impression. For those who were participants, the witnesses who took part enthusiastically or else left in disgust and hostility, what I am going to say will seem very summary and probably unfair.

The Centre Richelieu was an exalting experience of the Church. By that I mean that it was beautiful, generous and possibly well ahead of its time. There was an expression that I often used to characterize it to foreign visitors: "We are", I would say, "in a Church that is just coming into existence, the way one speaks of hydrogen in a primordial state." I could not use the most apt expression, *jeunesse de l'Église,*[18] because everybody still remembered it as the title of a journal, but those were the words that always came to mind.

Why? First, a sociological remark: we had none of the usual institutional constraints. As a group of volunteers in the same age bracket—I was hardly older than the students—we did not have to deal with the passivity, the impenetrability, the resistances that can exist in a neighborhood or village parish. Next, we were also exceptionally homogeneous as far as language and culture were concerned. The incessant replenishment of student generations, by the way, is both exhausting and stimulating because it never lets you settle down; you must always be starting over.

Even if the term *de-Christianization* is ambiguous, too simple to be precise as to the situation in France, it is true that the Christian fervor in which we lived did not reflect society as a whole. We were well aware that by adopting faith's point of view, with all that it conceals as to obligations, riches, joys and restraints, we belonged to a minority. Too few people were immediately convinced that the spiritual effort of Christians to see and acknowledge the gift received is a normal task for the Church. The same was true for apostolic witness to unbelievers. It was still an acceptable idea that you could be a Christian and act just like everybody else: we knew that this was not so! Our first job, then, was to prepare young people to live in the Church as missionaries. That attitude corresponded to my personal experience. What had been said and written during the war with books like *France, pays de mission* or *Paroisse, communauté missionaire* corresponded to our perception of a Church who needed to be all the more fervent since she could not be that of the "upright and God-fearing" stigmatized by Léon Bloy and Bernanos.

WOLTON: *Were you in agreement with the analysis of France as a* pays de mission *—that is, that a new evangelization was needed?*

[18] *Jeunesse de l'Église* means "youth of the Church". The expression came from a famous convert at the turn of the century, socialist essayist Charles Péguy. *Jeunesse de l'Église* later became a movement with its own journal by that name.—TRANS.

LUSTIGER: I had sensed that on the basis of what I had observed for a short time at Decazeville when I had been a part of the workers' world. But I was too much of a "cocky Parisian", a child of Montmartre and Montparnasse, to accept completely the description given to unbelief. . . . However, I quite agreed with the diagnosis that the Church was in the minority and could no longer rely on an acquired social position. The frontier of unbelief is both everywhere and nowhere. There is not the Catholic fortress on one side and a "no-man's-land" on the other. The border crosses the interior of consciences. All of a sudden, this missionary situation became obvious in the university world, even if not all Catholic students were aware of it. However, if they agreed to speak about religion with their fellow students in the *amphi,* they could not avoid realizing the distance that separated them.

We lived through a period of renewal, a life of intense religious enthusiasm nourished by a revived interest in the liturgy of which we were passionate artisans. We had the firm conviction, borne out by what happened later at the Council, that we were participating in the Church's reawakening. As far as the liturgy was concerned, we were audacious but always obedient, faithful to what the Church was asking. We wanted to respect the rules, not through fetishism, but because we realized that the liturgy did not belong to us.

WOLTON: *What kind of audacity, for example?*

LUSTIGER: After Vatican II, community liturgies of penance were considered a second normal form of the sacrament's ritual. In them, the faithful come together to pray, and they ask God for the grace to be touched by his love and to recognize that they have sinned; they can then go and confess in secret to one of the priests who is there and receive personal absolution. We had already "invented" that—we were not the only ones, of course. There had been numerous endeavors of this kind after 1945. In order to "invent" this form while respecting the ancient discipline, we had found, in a book of rites reserved for a bishop, a public rite of reconciliation for penitents on Holy Thursday that had not been used habitually since the eighth century.

I had taken the text of this ritual as the theme for a talk given to students. The beauty of this early gesture of reconciliation found its topicality revived: an entire congregation gathers round the bishop, pleading for and awaiting the return of the excluded. The bishop sends the deacon to say to the penitents who have publicly confessed their sins and are standing patiently at the door, "Do not weep . . . be patient." The congregation intensifies its supplication. Then the bishop goes forward to meet the excluded who, now reconciled, are led by him into the Church. They enter in long weaving lines, holding hands, while the congregation cheers: "Our brother who was lost has been found! . . . ", and the deacon chants the verse from the prophet: "I do not wish the death of the sinner but that he may convert himself and live. . . . " We were searching the Church's documents for the elements necessary for a faithful renewal.

We were also thinking ahead of our times in giving laymen access to theology. And there existed an initiation to prayer and communal life that corresponded to what present generations have been discovering. Some people thought that it was out of place or inappropriate, but there reigned among us and the students a brotherhood whose memory is indelible. I still remember the faces and names of those I knew then, and there were hundreds and hundreds! The big occasions, like the pilgrimage to Chartres and the Peace Vigils attracted thousands of students, not all of whom were regularly practicing or even believers. At that time, assembling such numbers was no small achievement. The lay mission was taken seriously, and the priest's first job was precisely to find students who were ready to share the apostolic responsibility for the Church wherever they happened to be.

MISSIKA: *But what were your objectives in an environment that was, after all, de-Christianized and more often drawn to politics than to religion?*

LUSTIGER: Another of our major objectives was to help students to unify what they were learning in the light of faith. That required a deep intellectual effort spread out over time. There was hardly a question of doing it in their first years at university when they needed time to find a new equilibrium. But very soon each of them became marked by the scientific or literary discipline he or she was following. You would force me to give an encyclopedic discourse if you asked me to talk about the questions raised by students in the *troisième cycle*[19] of mathematics, geology, history, etc.

We insisted on the finalities of education, both the social ones (a career? which kind?) and the more theoretical, speculative ones (the only learning is done by man for man—but what is man?). I could give innumerable examples of debates or sessions— from seminars on Hegel for the *agrégatifs*[20] in philosophy to spirited exchanges between mathematicians and philosophers on the subject of logical positivism, not to mention all the durable "classics": science and faith, psychoanalysis and religion, etc. This effort allowed for a permanent and free confrontation between students and their older professors or researchers. Such debates did not take place anywhere else in the university. And there were also discussions between Catholics and non-Catholics, believers and unbelievers, including Marxists.

[19] The *Troisième cycle* is the level at which students begin to prepare for a doctorate.—TRANS.

[20] An *agrégatif* or *agrégative* is a postdoctoral student who is preparing to take the examination for the *agrégation,* which was designed for recruiting tenured professors for *lycées.* —TRANS.

WOLTON: *To return briefly to the Algerian War: Did any of your group take part in demonstrations?*

LUSTIGER: We always refused to do so, on principle.

WOLTON: *Why?*

LUSTIGER: Precisely because we placed ourselves on a different level from political movements.

WOLTON: *Was there agreement on this matter at the Centre Richelieu?*

LUSTIGER: Yes, but it had to be negotiated. That did not prevent students active at the Centre from belonging to other organizations—quite the contrary. We were determined, however, to be "the Church for the Sorbonne". The stands we took were carefully thought out and parsimonious, even if we were sometimes mistaken in saying either too much or too little. What was said for our group as such had to be acceptable for the Church as such. That imposed a demanding and formative critical discipline on all of us.

WOLTON: *What were the Centre's relations with the different archbishops of Paris?*

LUSTIGER: They always encouraged us. Not that they were *au courant* as to everything we were doing or invariably approved when they were. But they intervened positively during critical periods when the stakes were high, when the very existence of our activities risked being called into question. When I was named director, I immediately went to see Cardinal Feltin, and in the ensuing years, I met with him on several occasions, honestly reporting our situation, estimating the possible gains and losses and asking him for an endorsement of our mission.

When Cardinal Veuillot was named Archbishop of Paris, the fact that I had known him personally and had never ceased to see him freely did not result in any "favoritism" on his part. On the contrary, he was more stringent with those he loved and knew. But I never had to control my reactions, sure that he would always know how to interpret matters. He expected frankness from me, even if it was brutal, and he, in turn, did not mince his words. He strongly reinforced the Centre's orientations. All this was taking place during Vatican II, and it was in its light that Cardinal Veuillot sized up and evaluated what we were doing.

When Catholics Look at Themselves

MISSIKA: *You have mentioned conflicts between the Centre Richelieu and other institutions. What was this all about?*

LUSTIGER: Some of the clashes were very bitter. If seven is the metaphysical age, then eighteen has to be the sectarian age or the age of guerrilla warfare. It is a time of the most definitive disputes in which people tear each other to pieces for ideological reasons. Some students thought that we listened too much to young people; others thought that we were too much concerned about our roots in Tradition and Christian fidelity. We could, it is true, appear strangely contradictory.

WOLTON: *Were you accused of lacking a commitment to twentieth-century issues?*

LUSTIGER: The reproach was made. Why? Perhaps because some students looked on spiritual activity as alienating, diverting us from secular efforts. Perhaps, also, because they were attempting to identify the substance of Christianity with secular tasks. From that point of view, any emphasis on specifically religious activities was open to criticism.

MISSIKA: *Can you be more precise? Who were the critics?*

LUSTIGER: The criticism was a widespread tendency expressed in different ways. We were living in a period of searching and questioning. Positions were very fragmented and sometimes confused. Some people theorized that the Church had to keep in the background, since her mission could be realized only by her ultimate disappearance. Her death was becoming the symbol of the redemption she was supposed to be announcing. They were calling for the extinction of Christian identity even before the American theologians published their theories about "the death of God" and "the secular city" (at the beginning of the Sixties).

WOLTON: *Meaning that the Church should become less visible?*

LUSTIGER: No, that she should not be visible at all. For many students, the mere fact of proclaiming the Gospel, Christ's message, could be an infringement on somebody's freedom. Later, after 1968, the idea re-emerged that a person can say what he thinks and that even if he contradicts someone else, he is not to be considered offensive. But we were still very far from that attitude then!

MISSIKA: *You were supposed to keep quiet....*

LUSTIGER: There were those who said and wrote that. Spiritual and theological theories of obligatory silent witness had been elaborated: the Gospel as lived by the Christian ought to become readable not by his words but by the humble difference in his behavior.

WOLTON: *And were there not those who felt that the difference ought to be seen in his engagement in the twentieth century, in the class struggle?*

LUSTIGER: That was another aspect of the dispute. The ideas I have just cited were sometimes lived in a remarkable way, as a religious vocation: men and women buried themselves in the anonymity of the large city or in the impoverished layers of the population, just as others buried themselves in the solitude of the desert.

WOLTON: *A kind of monasticism...*

LUSTIGER: If you wish. There are many possible interpretations of these convictions. But once they are made into a general theory of the Church's discipleship, they become worrisome. They sometimes end up in absurdity. Such ideas, however, were often shared either by laymen or the clergy and were considered to be more advanced. In fact, their influence was a result of a repulsion felt by many Catholics—a repulsion, moreover, that I too felt—for a caricatural and mythical representation of the nineteenth-century Church....

MISSIKA: *Sure of herself and dominating...*

LUSTIGER: It is not easy to explain how we reached that point. Was it a fear of too much self-assertion, after the rejection of what was later called the Church's triumphalism? Or was it, on the contrary, guilt or "resentment" for having been repeatedly accused since the nineteenth century of missing our chances for a reconciliation with modern society? Or maybe it was the unavowed desire to get into step with a world in which the visible signs of Christianity are diminishing, so as to be recognized by it at last?

MISSIKA: *More precisely, where did this desire for moving into the background come from?*

LUSTIGER: Once again, I propose an explanation that extends over a long duration. A permanent problem of Catholic leadership, both lay and clerical, has been the gap between their image of the Church's place in French society and the actual place she occupies. The image was that French culture coincided with the religious identity or that the national identity coincided with religion. The reality was very different. Since the birth of France as a nation-state, the Catholic Church has never truly been in complete accord with the totality of French culture. In the historical, cultural and political construction of France, the Church and political power were objectively allied by the same implicit analysis: both wanted to obtain social and cultural legitimacy, and each one counted on the other to ensure its own victory, since it could not be obtained by any other means.

WOLTON: *A friendly exchange of services?*

LUSTIGER: A relationship of rival complicity. The will to centralize and unify the nation requires the bringing together and equalizing of different cultures under a strong and centralized power. In order to do this, political power has continually asked for recognition from the Catholic Church. It has never hesitated to serve her so as to use her. Conversely, Churchmen observed that the lack of unity between the national culture and the Faith resulted not merely from local resistances and refusals but from the persistent paganism of entire zones of society. And many clerics were, in turn, fascinated by the prince's power, hoping that if the prince were converted, the nation would follow.

WOLTON: *But, during those years at the Sorbonne, you were not in agreement with the position advocating the Church's self-effacement. Why?*

LUSTIGER: I was striving, with difficulty, to formulate the elements of the problem. The plan for occupying the social centrality in a culture, an epoch or a nation is not a perverse ambition of Christianity, unless it is reduced to a strategy for the conquest of political power. The reflection on evangelization consists in identifying the heart of a culture and trying to find out how the Gospel can reach it.

WOLTON: *You will admit that, for an atheist, the difference between "evangelization" and "taking control" is minimal.*

LUSTIGER: That is the opinion of quite a few historians and sociologists who see only the socially visible contours of the Church and what results from them as factors of strength and influence. These scholars see the Church as only one of the forces at work in society. But an honest examination must also study the contents that this institution conveys and her role in civilizations and cultures. It can happen that the system becomes an end in itself, betraying what it is supposed to be serving. In that case, there remains only a subversion or caricature of the Christian message, and the Church leaves herself open to radical suspicion. Throughout history, some Churchmen have succumbed to political ambition—that is, to the temptation of interpreting their religious function politically. It also happens that princes interpret their political functions religiously—not without abuse.

WOLTON: *Even today?*

LUSTIGER: When one is possessed by the ambition to occupy the center of the social system, all means and hypotheses become conceivable. After their many trials, the failed attempts to seize power, the lost anticlerical battles and the bitter lesson that emerged from them, Catholics in a sense renounced a position of politically organized strength. They looked for other ways of occupying the social space. If they had wanted to recapture a central position, in spite of everything, they would have been forced to renounce their specific identity.

WOLTON: *Are you saying that it was the continuation of the struggle by different means?*

LUSTIGER: The price to be paid was a kind of suicide.

MISSIKA: *An exorbitant price.*

LUSTIGER: Too many Catholics looked at themselves just as the sociologists did, as if basically they agreed to see themselves as "the Catholic party" —until the moment when, precisely, they could no longer put up with the appellation. Thus, they had to destroy themselves as a social group in order to destroy the reflected image. And since it was necessary to justify this abandonment, a theology of annihilation also had to be fabricated: it was the *kenosis* of the Church. *Kenosis* is the Greek word for annihilation, and it is used in reference to Christ's humbling himself in his Passion (Phil 2:7). This self-destruction, this emptying out of oneself, became an interpretive scheme that provided the grounds for the Church's disappearance as an exterior institution—perforce oppressive, offensive, and laden down with every kind of sin—to be replaced by a hidden, vague and secret presence. And those who totally committed themselves to this path lost everything, including their own identity.

WOLTON: *The point of view you are describing, one favoring a kind of hidden presence, would have been championed by those who wanted to keep the Church in a central place in society. But how about those who, on the contrary, conceived of the Church as more of a minority? Did they want to assert their difference?*

LUSTIGER: Such an operation, if it was not to be suicidal, implied the conviction that, in spite of the institutional disappearance of the Church, Christianity remained the thing most commonly shared in our nation; however, that was to forget the social fragility of the Christian heritage. It was a recklessness comparable to that regarding the environment: rich countries lay waste their landscapes and squander their natural resources as if they were inexhaustible. But they are not, and unless they are constantly managed so as to be able to renew themselves, they vanish.

Spiritual capital, too, is exhaustible. To remain productive, it cannot be wasted. Of course, it is historically inexact to say that "France is in need of missionaries" in the way that a pagan country is. It is clearly a mistake to liken a civilization that has been marked by Christianity to one that has not. France is still deeply impregnated with the remnants of Christian culture, even though, of course, the French are far from being a nation of believers. Nevertheless . . .

WOLTON: *It is especially for that reason that some people have refused to accept that "missions" are needed for an already Christianized country.*

LUSTIGER: Yes, but we accepted that assessment because it corresponded to a fact: we were very conscious of being a minority, and it is obvious today that we were correct. We were not alone in thinking that way—there were similar perceptions in many sectors of Catholicism.

The Death of Cardinal Veuillot

MISSIKA: *You have alluded to your friendship with Cardinal Veuillot. . . .*

LUSTIGER: Archbishop Veuillot's arrival in Paris represented a great hope for many people who knew him. He was a symbol of Vatican II; a new vigor was going to be infused into the Church in Paris and in France. He had the energy required for attacking problems whose elements had already been enumerated by a number of us: clerical and parish life, discipleship—in a word, everything that could be considered a part of Vatican II's program. Consequently, Veuillot plus the Council, the Council plus Veuillot, seemed to have created the ideal conditions for our mission. His death was incomprehensible and very distressing. We knew, of course, that an archbishop is mortal and can always be replaced, but we had put so many concrete, immediate hopes in him; he inspired so much confidence and was such a good friend. Moreover, he was so courageous that our grief at losing him was all the greater.

He died of cancer in February of 1968. John XXIII had died five years earlier, and his mortal agony had been a "media event", which was deeply moving but also disturbing. The world had perceived the message of a man who gives the supreme witness of putting himself completely in God's hands during his final ordeal. But, at the same time, this *médiatisation* did provoke critical reactions in certain Catholic circles. People had used such terms as *spectacle,* and sometimes even *immodesty.* When Cardinal Veuillot learned that he had cancer, he bravely took the decision to continue working as long as his strength held out. Then came the day when he had to be hospitalized, and we knew that he was soon going to die. It was only a matter of weeks, if not days. There was no vacancy at the head of the archdiocese: two auxiliary bishops, Daniel Pézeril and Robert Frossard, had been ordained earlier. They were then my superiors—they both subsequently became my auxiliary bishops—but above all they were my spiritual fathers and friends. When the cardinal fell ill, his closest associates tried to protect him so that he would not be uselessly solicited. Perhaps they also wanted to avoid dramatizing, making a "media event" of his death. Besides, during his illness, Cardinal Veuillot had been constantly waited on and surrounded by his relatives, and no one else could see him.

One morning, one of his secretaries sent me a message: "Father Veuillot is asking for you; come." He was in Saint Joseph's Hospital. His secretary showed me in and I stayed about an hour, I cannot really say how long. It was a typical hospital room. Father Veuillot was lying on his bed. His face was emaciated and showed the traces of his long battle with illness. Near death, he still had all his faculties, and he was fully conscious. He spoke almost without stopping. As I left, his secretary whispered to me, "You must make a note of what he said to you—for yourself. You will need it someday." I was much too overwhelmed to follow his advice. I was incapable of writing down anything at all. Thus, that hour passed, and I have retained only an extremely vivid impression and a few phrases. I was deeply moved by his intense integrity, the intense spiritual combat in which he was engaged. I felt that he was struggling to communicate something to me.

Spiritually, he is one of the men toward whom I feel the greatest filial duty of respect and love. I do recall that he talked a great deal about the mystery of the Cross and suffering. His sentences were short, broken by silences. He spoke about his ministry, about the meaning of human existence in the light of Christ's Cross and about the scandal and folly of the Cross. He had to approach his own death in order to receive a new understanding of what he had so often preached. Nevertheless, in making me a witness to his spiritual journey, he was not pretending to dispense anyone from having to make it in his turn. Quite the contrary.

I had known Father Veuillot very well. He had a devastating temper. He usually controlled it and kept himself from being malicious, but sometimes his words shot forth in spite of him and hit their target head on! He was very cheerful, even though he often appeared rather cramped in his person. Some people were critical, saying that "when Veuillot walks by, it is always with the air of 'I am the bishop' ". Actually, he was good-humored, exuberant and unaffected. You might say that he had the Parisian spirit. In any case, he was open and direct. When he was named a cardinal, however, I observed the emergence of just a touch of vanity—or, at least, that is how it struck me. Since I felt at ease with him, I told him so. He did not take it too badly, but I was certainly made to understand that it had been somewhat out of place to make such a remark to a cardinal of the Roman Church! As he lay dying, it was as though he had been purified, and I was saying to myself: This is the kind of archbishop we need; he is completely mature. And it is just at this point that he is being taken from us. That was very difficult to comprehend. I remember that he said something else about the Church. Three times, he repeated a phrase that is engraved word for word in my memory: "Pure, pure, pure. Everything must be pure." And he added, "We have to make a true spiritual revolution. The Pope realizes it; few people have; but that is what the Church needs." Then he blessed me and I left. I was deeply distressed, beside myself, and in spite of his secretary's advice, I wrote down nothing. How much I regret that today!

I will not hide from you that in 1981 when I was named Archbishop of Paris, he was the first person I thought of. Nothing had prepared me for the position, and his words came back to me in a forceful flash. I felt a responsibility for what he had passed on to me. I consider his words a guiding light for what I have to do, and I have the impression of having received from him—in advance, in a way that was inexplicable for me and perhaps also for him—a very precious treasure.

The Beginnings of May 1968

MISSIKA: *You had a privileged observation post at the university. Did you sense that May '68 was coming on?*

LUSTIGER: I am certain that, from 1965, we had a foreboding of the crisis. At that time, I was heading all the student chaplaincies in the Paris region. It was in the years 1960–68 that the university began to expand. Plans for the new School of Sciences on the site of the Halle-aux-Vins[21] were taking shape. The District of Paris[22] had been created some time earlier, and it was known that there would probably be other universities scattered through the capital or its immediate surroundings. Ideas for educational reform reappeared in force. And reform was definitely becoming urgent. I was very much concerned about the university's future and the chaplaincies' future within it. It was essential that Christian communities be created as soon as new faculties were established, and that meant having places to meet and chaplains.

In the Sixties, I learned about many grandiose plans and shared the enthusiasm of those who conceived them. The officials of the EPAD [*Établissement Public d'Aménagement de la Défense*],[23] and the new towns in the District of Paris led me to discover other ways of thinking about the future of urban life. I became familiar with their methods, and I mixed with an amazing variety of people who work on such projects: top-ranking civil servants, leading architects, financiers and property developers, construction contractors and workers. Far from being indifferent to the Church's place in the urban landscape of the future, everyone—whatever his personal religious views—saw it as an indispensable element of the social symbolic system. I had a more modest goal: to find space for the chaplaincy in those yet-to-be-built universities. I hung on with tooth and nail to get something done, and the effort paid off; there were some disappointments but also some successes.

As for the university itself, it was about to be "ripped apart". It was like an infernal time bomb; you could hear it ticking, but there was no way of making any of the political leaders understand what was happening. We knew it was going to explode! We even knew the date, but we had no idea what the explosion would be like and what it was going to bring about.

WOLTON: *Why was the explosion foreseeable?*

LUSTIGER: As I recall, there were two academic gatherings—one at Caen and the other at Grenoble, in 1964 and 1965, respectively—which predicted that the university would blow up for mechanical reasons. And I wish to mention two additional indications among others. First, what happened at Berkeley with the hippy movement was an obvious presage of what was going to take place in France. Several professors and students who had been

[21] The former Wine Market was located on the Left Bank a couple of miles up the Seine from the Sorbonne.—TRANS.

[22] The District of Paris was in charge of urbanization for the greater Paris region at the beginning of the Gaullist era, at a time when the foreseeable growth of the capital required planning.—TRANS.

[23] *La Défense* is a new high-rise business center, northwest of Paris, at the end of the perspective of the Champs-Élysées.—TRANS.

there gave us detailed accounts. Next, there was the preparation of new theoretical bases for political agitation. While the notion of "psychological action" was burning out its last rage over the war in Algeria, the psycho-sociologists took control of student unionism. In 1962, two articles appeared in *Les Temps moderne*[24] under the title *"Vers un syndicalisme étudiant?"* The authors, Kravetz and Peninou, were already theorizing a new type of revolutionary activity, incomprehensible to the classical left but in agreement with the future Maoists' mode of thought.

We were closely observing the university's statistics, which reflected the influence of demographic growth. An institution built on a social and cultural elite, more cultural than social, was bound to explode when the masses flooded in. Up to that time, the French university had produced a certain type of cultivated man adept at a number of functions that, other than in university and secondary school education, were exercised mainly in the political and cultural domains. Industrial and administrative prospects were reserved for graduates from the *grandes écoles.* It was a closed system. Then, all of a sudden, as a result of compulsory schooling, a large number of young people who until then would not have gone beyond the *certificat d'études*[25] turned up at the university, and the institution simply did not withstand the shock. It was incapable of understanding that the quantitative change required a qualitative one. Unable to transform its logic, it had no desire to be anything other than itself and to pursue the task it had set for itself—that is, to last forever with its methods and goals. Hence it was in contradiction with the public for which it was responsible. The new wave of students did not espouse its goals and was unfitted for its methods; all of this bred a considerable number of breakdowns resulting in the depreciation of diplomas and a lowering of teaching quality.

At one point, some of my colleagues and I began writing a white paper on the *propédeutiques* of the arts and sciences, collecting facts to demonstrate what a waste of time they were for that generation of students. Unfortunately, we did not follow through this initiative to the end. I did, however, attempt to warn the faculty members who seemed to be the most open-minded. But the young and brilliant *normaliens,*[26] who were at that time already associate professors and were to be among the theoreticians of 1968, completely refused to face the facts when they concerned their personal conduct in teaching. They were ready to make a revolution but unwilling to make the slightest

[24] *Les Temps moderne* was an intellectual journal founded by the influential existentialist philosopher, Jean-Paul Sartre (1905–82), who progressively ended his long flirtation with the Communist Party and eventually supported radical Maoist theories, although he drifted back to "humanism" in his last years.—TRANS.

[25] The *certificat d'études* was a diploma created in 1874 for students who have passed a state examination at the end of primary school.—TRANS.

[26] *Normaliens* are graduates of the École Normale Supérieure.—TRANS.

effort for the students who had been entrusted to them. With one of them I almost lost my head. Or, rather, I did lose it. I began to shout at the young and brilliant person with whom I was conversing that he was being inconsistent and that his revolutionary speeches were irresponsible. I pointed out that he should stop treating his students like *Khâgneux,*[27] when what they needed was a different kind of pedagogy— but that, even so, he had no right to look down on them. So much for the attitude of the younger faculty members, those who were going to direct the upheaval in the universities. As for the older ones, the full professors, they were often generous and conscientious but out of their depth. They hardly understood what was going on. Most of the big names did not teach the *propédeutiques* courses, and, therefore, they were insensitive to situations they had not encountered.

WOLTON: *What was your perception of the ideas of May 1968?*

LUSTIGER: They were liberating in the sense that they criticized ideologies. You might even say that they were religious, in that ideology is the worst degradation of faith and religion: it prevents the calm development of the experience of faith. Like a termite, it eats away at everything from the interior. But May '68 was also the result of planning by groups of leftist students whom we had known for several years.

MISSIKA: *How did you know them?*

LUSTIGER: We were in touch with everything that was going on at the Sorbonne and the other universities. Certain members of those groups used to come and talk with us—they were always trying to recruit Catholic students. There were meetings, discussions. I could not believe either my eyes or my ears: Where had those students come from? From another age, it seemed to me! Even my generation, which had been strongly attracted by Marxism, would not have dared to use such an overweening verbosity. Their verbal radicalism reminded me of literary *souvenirs* from the nineteenth century. It was hard to understand and even harder to take seriously. Moreover, later when students told us about what was happening at the École Normale Supérieure on the Rue d'Ulm, we were astounded. They described a reign of terror established when different leftist groups, like the *"Althussériens",*[28] seized power and began using methods from the cultural revolution: omnipresent slogans, public trials, indictments and all kinds of similar proceedings

[27] *Khâgneux* are members of a post-*baccalauréat* class preparing for the rigorous entrance examination for the École Normale Supérieure. —TRANS.

[28] *Althussériens* were followers of Louis Althusser (1918–82), a French philosopher and professor who proposed a scientific reading of Marx beyond the ideological one.—TRANS.

that were assaults on basic freedoms. (We later learned that Pol Pot's future second-in-command had belonged to one of these groups.) As for myself, who had been marked since childhood by Nazi and fascist persecutions, the resurgence of the same irrational and totalitarian phenomena was inconceivable. The ill treatment, the attack on basic rights, the lack of respect for persons, the intellectual tyranny—all this was profoundly shocking. But even so, we failed to see the full significance of what was taking place.

MISSIKA: *What influence did radical leftist ideas have on Christian students?*

LUSTIGER: During that same period, at Strasbourg, the *situationniste* movement took control within the *Fédé,* the Protestant student movement. We knew about it from their publications and from the Protestant students in Paris on the Rue de Vaugirard. They were applying the same system of provocation and disobedience to religious conceptions and moral standards, which they were labeling Puritanical but which are simply Christian. Their position was very strange: it espoused a Christianity that had become a political surrealism. I had no more sympathy for that than I had had for Lautréamont[29] in my youth: when I was nineteen, I had opened his book and closed it almost immediately. It may have been intellectually dazzling, but it was indisputably blasphemous.

WOLTON: *Did you go often to the university at Nanterre?*

LUSTIGER: During the school year 1967–68, we opened a Catholic center there, with a full-time priest. I knew the main Catholic leaders personally. Nanterre was at that time a strange little academic "paradise". Perhaps this blessing came from its being a newly created institution, although the physical setting was most unfavorable. The campus was surrounded by an impoverished suburb and was near to a large shantytown. And yet the students were upper-middle class: the new academic policy obliged the high school graduates of the well-to-do western section of Paris to enroll at Nanterre. The Christian community often invited a Jesuit theologian, Father Jean Daniélou, a truly loyal friend, to speak in one of the biggest lecture halls. Invariably, he had to cope with radical leftists, and his response to their verbal aggression was always brilliant. He had a genius for making himself heard in those overheated, tumultuous student meetings; in particular, he had a knack for brushing aside unexpected or unfair objections. All this could look

[29] Isodore Ducasse Lautréamont (1846–70) was a French writer. The strange character of his work and premature death caused him to be ranked among the "accursed poets", and led the surrealists to claim him as one of their precursors.—TRANS.

rather quaintly picturesque, but many people were beginning to wonder what it would lead to. Nanterre was drifting after the surprising outcome of the strike in the fall of 1967. The students were fascinated and happy about the closer ties with the faculty that had resulted from it. Then came March 22. I knew several students in the sociology TP[30] from which that acting out"[31] departed. Shortly before Easter, some of them, no longer knowing what to think, came to inform me of their reservations over the plans put forward by the most radical leaders of the "March 22 Movement": their strategy was one of provocation-repression, which had already been tested in Berlin and which, in May, would be used in Paris.

MISSIKA: *Yes, but the fact that some groups, or* groupuscules,[32] *were making subversive plans is not original. What is hard to explain is their success.*

LUSTIGER: There were several subversive strategies, but it happened that one of them worked and was able to catalyze the rest. I sent word to the university administration and political leaders to beware of treating the student crisis with contempt. There were two kinds of responses. The first: "You're dreaming! You're letting yourself get carried away by the students' dramatizations"; and the second: "It's all a conspiracy. They're working for the Chinese secret service"....

MISSIKA: *Who said that about the Chinese?*

LUSTIGER: I cannot say.

MISSIKA: *Was he a politician or an academic?*

LUSTIGER: A politician. You have to remember that at that very moment peace negotiations between the Americans and the North Vietnamese were taking place in Paris.

WOLTON: *In general, how did you feel about the events in May? I get the impression that you did not appreciate them very much....*

LUSTIGER: No explanation of these events was ever satisfying; not one linked up logically with the preceding one. Society exploded by a phenomenon of sympathetic vibration of the entire social body. Some people called it a

[30] TP stands for *travaux pratiques*—tutorials where a limited number of students assimilate the lectures of a full professor with the help of junior faculty members.—TRANS.

[31] This phrase is in English in the French text.—TRANS.

[32] *Groupuscules* is a pejorative word for small groups of people.—TRANS.

"spiritual event". I did not keep company with Maurice Clavel,[33] but I understand his point of view. I consider it incomplete, but it is no further from a part of the truth about '68 than any of the other interpretations. It may be even closer.

During the upheaval itself, we chaplains chose a very precise attitude. Our first thought was for the students: all the rest, strictly speaking, was not our business. We did not feel directly responsible: let everybody protect himself and his own. We were striving to remain adults in a period when so many people completely lost their heads. It was not so easy to remain calm and critical interlocutors—close to the students through the experience of events, distant by judgment and the call for reflection. We tried to be persons to whom the students we knew could appeal, because to enclose them in what they were living through would have driven some of them to despair.

We always celebrated Mass; we were constantly praying, giving students the possibility of praying and of confessing, if they wished. By contrast, the Masses were plunged into silence, whereas normally the liturgy was sung. This kind of respiration and withdrawal was necessary for rediscovering the fundamental Christian affirmations of the Gospel: the respect for the other person, the love of neighbor, the refusal to regard violence as legitimate except as a means of defense.

WOLTON: *Did you have the impression that you were being heard? Were you in contact with the events and the actors?*

LUSTIGER: We were certainly in contact with those who approached us. We were trying to give priority to the stakes for the university, to render a little coherence and reason to those who were beginning to drift, to help those who could not hold out.

WOLTON: *What do you mean by "those who could not hold out"?*

LUSTIGER: I mean those who gave in to the revolution, or suffered depressions or simply ran away. The effects of the psychic, moral and social destructuralization were awesome.

MISSIKA: *What was your political analysis of events?*

LUSTIGER: It was a difficult experience. I clearly remember a discussion in the presence of Cardinal Marty. I had said that there were two possible

[33] Maurice Clavel (1927–79) was a French writer and professor of philosophy. He was known as a Christian leftist intellectual and said that the "events" of May 1968 had been prompted by the Holy Spirit, in rebellion against the hypocrisy of the bourgeoisie.—TRANS.

hypotheses for the outcome: either the Communist Party or de Gaulle would emerge as the winner, and it would certainly be de Gaulle. The other factions would not hold together politically.

WOLTON: *Were you never afraid of a revolutionary crisis?*

LUSTIGER: I never believed it could happen. The relationship of forces within the power structure was not to be seen at the university but in society as a whole, and that ended up with the Grenelle compromise on wages. On the other hand, I immediately interpreted the student crisis as a resurgence of the revolutionary phantasmagoria of 1848. I found that astounding, unimaginable. You just had to read the graffiti with its mixture of blasphemy and the sacred. For me, that was tragic. I spoke about it with a few frustrated academics: "It's the revival of the irrational", I said, "they are not aware of the symbols they are handling. This can be the beginning of a real fascism; nihilist leftism can be the reverse image of Nazi nihilism."

WOLTON: *That was a very harsh judgment.*

LUSTIGER: The irruption of the irrational opened up the way to blind power and the tyrannical domination of the mob. It made it possible for violence to appear in a pure state.

MISSIKA: *But you seem to forget that there were also elements of rational criticism.*

LUSTIGER: Yes, the consumer society was criticized. Everybody was quoting Marcuse and Reich and the "Frankfurt School"—but nobody had read them yet. It was all the more strange that these ideas spread so quickly. They encountered themes of Christian inspiration, as Clavel pointed out. Some Christians also spoke about an experience of the Spirit. Every experience of the Spirit, of God, leads to a deconditioning because it is an experience of freedom; but every experience of deconditioning is not necessarily one of the Holy Spirit. Between licentiousness and liberty, or between uncontrolled orgies and the mystical explosion of joy, it sometimes takes virtually nothing to make things swing to one side or the other.

WOLTON: *In the end, you were more sensitive to the unfavorable elements in May '68 than to the favorable?*

LUSTIGER: I do not know. I did, however, find that the simulated violence was insufferable. For me, violence had a face. What was the point of feigning the worst? Playing at a revolutionary carnival, shouting "CRS = SS!"?[34] We who were older knew what the SS had been; those students did not. And some adults were accomplices in this confusion. It was criminal because it made a travesty of history, debased words and memories and prevented a generation from understanding the past and, hence, from being on guard for the future. By depreciating symbols in this way, one empties them of meaning and lowers defenses: I consider that a moral outrage. Another thing that surprised me was to realize just how fragile our society is. At times, we had the feeling that there were no more adults to be found!

MISSIKA: *Do you mean people who know how to say no, who know how to oppose?*

LUSTIGER: I would not necessarily say "oppose", but who at least refuse to use the language of demagogues, who refuse to say, "We are ready to do whatever you want. . . ." My idea of politics, of the arbitration of reason in the sense of the good and the true, is too noble to tolerate manipulation and demagoguery. I saw intellectuals, eminent minds, completely defeated, shattered, by verbal attacks. This crisis appeared to bring to the fore something I have mentioned elsewhere: the absence of fathers. There was a kind of scraping of the bottom, and everything rose to the surface: the best and the worst. On some days, I was exultant with amazement in suddenly coming upon some surrealistic slogan or marvelous poetic invention of youth, but everything was done in such a climate of violence, disorder and destructuralization! I was especially sensitive to the price that the young people were paying.

WOLTON: *Did you ever consider intervening publicly?*

LUSTIGER: I refused to do it! From the day that tourism was organized in the Sorbonne's courtyard, we were urged in umpteen ways to open a "stand". We had every access to it, more than all those people who turned up there overnight, after having shed their ties and jackets. But I said no. The Gospel would have been out of place in that madhouse.

WOLTON: *Was it like the merchants in the Temple?*

LUSTIGER: I have no regrets about not doing it.

MISSIKA: *What repercussions did 1968 have in ecclesiastical circles?*

[34] The CRS are the *Compagnies Républicaines de Sécurité.* They were created just after World War II and served as riot squads in May '68.—TRANS.

LUSTIGER: I was caught completely off guard when I realized that a part of those circles was entering into the same folly, utilizing the same notions, transposing the same categories and manipulations onto the ecclesiastical institution, taking the Church herself and her functioning as targets. I remained utterly stunned. I had not seen it coming and was scandalized by the fact that some priests and laymen were treating the Church and her hierarchy in exactly the same way that students and leftist groups were treating academic institutions. It was completely illogical and contradictory. They were deserting their posts just at the moment when the young people needed our presence and freedom. And the effects of that lunacy are still with us, because a large part of what some people have pejoratively called "post-Council", at least in France, has nothing to do with the ecumenical Council of Vatican II but is an outgrowth of "after '68"—its mythology and slogans.

MISSIKA: *Since you have said that you think the student upheaval highlighted the absence of fathers, could the analogy be stretched so that the same thing might be said for the Church and the "ecclesiastical May '68"?*

LUSTIGER: I believe that the Catholic body's internal crisis remains an open question. How far back does the analysis have to go? I do not believe in the theory of a "cunning genius" who could subvert a well-established edifice in eight days. It is impossible. Upheavals only show up already existing weaknesses.

WOLTON: *Then they existed within the French clergy?*

LUSTIGER: They did, but not so much in the clergy as in French Catholicism as a whole, and they had for a very long time.

WOLTON: *You mentioned that you were worried about the price to be paid by that generation of students. What price did they pay?*

LUSTIGER: First, a word about what they gained: although ideologies that were thought to be dead reappeared in a flamboyant fashion, and mythologies and irrationalism re-erupted, we did witness the dispelling of the Marxist-Leninist illusion and the first criticisms of consumer societies. People dared to say aloud a great many things that no one had ever said up to then. But the cost was the experience of a drastic destructuralization. Young people who should have been learning about freedom learned instead about deconditioning.

MISSIKA: *What do you mean by "deconditioning"?*

LUSTIGER: A personality is structured by many elements that function as obvious facts, and, in deconditioning, all that flies to pieces. I have said that "a true experience of God and freedom is a source of deconditioning", but there are precisely deconditionings that do not go in the direction of freedom but toward destructuralization. A psychologist or a psychotherapist can very well help someone to construct and assume his freedom—and that will entail the effects of deconditioning. He can also, by a clumsy or heavy-handed intervention, make him conscious of the precariousness of his defenses and his points of reference. Then the subject can collapse and believe that he is liberated when, in fact, he is only disunited.

MISSIKA: *Would you call the generation of '68 a "lost generation"?*

LUSTIGER: No. Some of them suffered serious wounds that have never completely healed: hopes were raised that were impossible to satisfy. Others have paid the price in disillusionment and cynicism. Perhaps these events brought something to society. Perhaps the shock was essential for some people to find a greater intellectual freedom. But I am convinced that the price paid was too high for the socially reinvested result. Furthermore, it was then that our society tasted the drug of political terrorism whose effects and countereffects are still with us.

MISSIKA: *Did these events modify your political convictions?*

LUSTIGER: I have always been interested in politics, but never in a political way. The *"politique d'abord"* of Maurras, which later found its exact replica on the left and which consists of demanding not only the autonomy of politics but especially its primacy and hegemony, is a grave error and an offense. Maritain's book, *Primauté du Spirituel,* which I read very early—in Orléans, I think (it dates from 1937 and is later than Rome's condemnation of *l'Action française*)—had struck me as brilliant. In substance, this is what he said: in opposition to all theocracy—i.e., all ideas of religious or clerical parties taking over political power so as to subordinate it—it must be proclaimed that man's freedom is guaranteed by his relationship to the Absolute that is God, and no one can appropriate God. He is subordinate to no one, because only God is God. It is from this Absolute, of which he is the trustee and the beneficiary, that man receives his freedom. When politics claims to substitute itself for this source of value judgments, it becomes not only idolatrous but tyrannical and perverse. Faith makes ideological or political positions relative, not to reduce them and take away their substance, but to allow them space for movement and freedom. The collusion between a religious faith and a specific political position leads either to clericalism or a crusade. In our century, more than ever, the Church is wary of these confusions. The condemnations in France of *Le Sillon*[35] and *l'Action française* are two symmetrical examples. A part of the most recent warnings of the Holy See in regard to certain "liberation theologies" or to priests' roles in political parties or functions can be explained in the same way.

[35] *Le Sillon* was a journal that reflected the opinions of a movement of the same name led by Marc Sangnier (1873–1950). It advocated a democratic and social Christianity. It was reprimanded for "social modernism" by Pius X in 1910.—TRANS.

II

POLITICS AND THE SACRED

"Render unto Caesar the Things That Are Caesar's"

JEAN-LOUIS MISSIKA: *Can you comment on these words spoken by Christ: "Render unto Caesar the things that are Caesar's and unto God the things that are God's"? Are they the basic and best expression of the division between the political and the sacred?*

JEAN-MARIE LUSTIGER: We are often told that they are, but I am not satisfied with the classical explanation from which a division of domains and powers has been deduced. An example: *"Messeigneurs, occupez-vous de vos oignons!"* Or in a slightly more dignified style: *"Les curés, à la sacristie!"* Or in the vernacular: *"Mais de quoi se mêle le Pape!"*[1]

The parable is aimed at Caesar's pretension in putting himself in God's place, just as it sometimes happens that God's representatives try to occupy Caesar's place. In fact, it is a polemical response, since Christ is catching out his interlocutors. . . .

MISSIKA: *. . . who are trying to trip him up . . .*

LUSTIGER: Perhaps I should explain a bit. When the Jews paid their taxes to the Temple, they had to change their Roman coins for the Temple's money. In presenting the coin with Caesar's likeness, Jesus is reminding his questioners that, if they are free before God, it is because the authority of the empire does not extend to the Temple, where God is present. Caesar's authority over Israel, although real and burdensome, is not divine authority. Therefore, Jesus is not putting God and Caesar on equivalent levels, in the way that the priesthood and the empire were in the old pagan quarrel. He is not dividing the world between God and Caesar. He is declaring that everything belongs to God and everything is to be given to him. Then, only afterward, is Caesar

[1] These three comments can be freely translated, respectively: "You bishops should mind your own business!", "Priests belong in the sacristy!", and "Why is the Pope meddling in this affair?"—TRANS.

to be given his due, and only that; simultaneously what is owed to God, and that is everything, must be given to God.

God does not behave like Caesar, and Caesar must not pretend to behave like God; otherwise, he becomes a tyrant and an idol. In fact, we find here the principle of freedom that opposes all totalitarianisms and all imperialisms—in the strongest sense of the word, since it concerns the emperor. The Gospel affirms that the guarantor of man and his freedom is precisely the one who is his Creator, God himself. No creature can demand that man turn over his freedom to him, unless he is ready to do it voluntarily. Authority is always delegated and comes from God; thus, it is accountable to him. Its role is to ensure both the autonomy of the political order and its relativity, to affirm that no subject of any emperor is ever his slave or property. Subjects have inalienable rights.

DOMINIQUE WOLTON: *Then collusion between the two authorities ends up in a theocracy?*

LUSTIGER: It has existed, and the Church has always been wary of it or else has forbidden it. In theory, the Popes' temporal power was justified as a condition for exercising the papacy's spiritual power. It brought about obvious deviations and abuses, which historians can relate in detail. But simultaneously, each time that the temptation of theocracy, in the strict sense of the word, arose, the Catholic Church checked it by drawing attention to the danger and illusion that it represented. One very well known instance of this was the pontifical authority's banning of the ideal societies that the Jesuits had undertaken to construct in South America. In other words, the ideal of a Christian political society merging with the Church is a formidably ambiguous temptation, and that has been true in all Christian empires. This does not mean that the Church challenges the idea that a people, in its culture and institutions, can draw its inspiration from Christianity. But to draw one's inspiration from it to the point of claiming to identify a historical, social and political realization with the Reign of God is not possible. Certain theoreticians of the nineteenth and twentieth centuries called "Christendom" such a politico-religious system. In earlier Christian language, the word had a more concrete meaning: it designated the totality of baptized people, members of the Church, those whom today we would call "God's people". Christians must never confuse the life of the world, which is transient and changing, with the coming of the heavenly Kingdom. Even if, at a certain time, all the inhabitants of a country were to be sincere believers, baptized and desiring holiness, that would still not mean that the hazards of sin did not exist: history is not yet finished.

WOLTON: *But, conversely, once the secularization or separation between the two "cities" has been admitted, do you think that there can be a "Christian politics"?*

LUSTIGER: There can be political conduct that is more or less in opposition to or in conformity with Christian aims . . .

WOLTON: *That is not the same question. . . .*

LUSTIGER: . . . but even so, this conformity or disaccord is not sufficient to guarantee a good policy. Several factors must converge: first, in a given situation, the "good" solution—that is, the wise and efficient one—must be determined; second, a moral discernment of the acts and goals pursued must be ensured; third, the citizens' consensus has to be negotiated—and there are still other conditions that must be met. Do not ask me to make a complete analysis of political decision making. In any case, in politics, good moral intentions—even if they are obligatory— are not enough. Sufficient information, stamina, decision-making ability, intelligence, understanding of the factors at play, the calculation of the opponents' strength are all indispensable for sound political judgment.

MISSIKA: *This corresponds to the contrast—or distinction—between politics and morality: that is, politics is not necessarily an activity concerned with morality. Let us go a little further: there are historical examples of political choices that, apparently, clashed with moral principles, and yet they proved to be good ones, acceptable from the point of view of what Weber calls the "ethic of responsibility".*

LUSTIGER: We can never know what might have happened if leaders had acted differently. The peculiarity of history is to be irreversible, and it can never be experimented with, as the physical sciences can. Each act, each destiny is unique and irreversible. One man does not replace another. Every human being is responsible for his own life, as he is also responsible for all humanity.

I am coming now to your question: what is meant when we say that something is "good politics". In fact, any political decision costs something; somewhere there is both a debit and a credit, an account to balance. The person who does not look beyond *Realpolitik* or a state's will for power as the sole principle for action can say, "It was a good choice, it was good management." But what is the human and sometimes moral cost? If a nation or party obtains authority or a kind of "imperialist" victory—i.e., domination—over a great number of men or vast territories, what is that victory worth if it has been gained at the price of the moral or spiritual degeneration of the conquering nation or party? If you engage in a war of conquest and if, in the process, generations of young men learn about brutality, torture and everything else that is humanly degrading, the nation will have to pay for it, sooner or later. Is that good politics? Was it "good politics" for Spain or Portugal to encourage the conquest of the New World by *conquistadores* with questionable ambitions? ... What should have been done? Would it have been possible to act differently? Perhaps. What would it have cost? These are complicated questions, but they illustrate the nature of political action whose rationality is much more complex than that of the exact sciences. The rationality of political behavior must reckon with the irrationality of violence, and it inevitably includes ethical judgment.

MISSIKA: *Yes, but you are presenting things in an overall way. The problem with politics is that it is always a matter of making decisions "here and now". It is the timeliness of the decision that counts. There is a relatively classic example: that of France's reaction to the remilitarization of the Rhineland in 1936. Some historians assert that if France had reacted militarily, Hitler would certainly have retreated. However, at the time, the choice not to intervene was interpreted by some politicians as a morally courageous act.*

LUSTIGER: It could just as well have been a cowardly act. In what way was not retaliating for Hitler's move a morally superior act? The difficulty for the conscience and judgment is to determine where the good lies and what good there is to be done. The basic rule of morality is that you must do what is good and avoid evil. In that case, it could be said that it was good to desire peace. But it could also be argued that it was good to defend the law and, through the use of limited force, compel respect for a treaty.

WOLTON: *Yes, but, precisely, the question revolves around the weighing of circumstances.*

LUSTIGER: Moral judgment is not to be confused with a sentimental reaction that can superimpose itself on a political judgment but cannot withstand the calculations of *Realpolitik:* from one day to the next, the same politicians, the same people, can swing from noble feelings to craven cynicism. A political behavior faithful to ethical standards requires much more lucidity and courage from citizens and their leaders. At what point do you say, "No, it is better to obey God than men—whatever the risk, whatever the cost"? When men are clear-minded and honorable enough to respond, "Now", then they have to be ready to pay the price—with their lives. "It is better to lose your life than the reasons for living it", our elders used to say.

Can There Be a Christian Politics?

WOLTON: *For a long time in Christendom, the spiritual order was superimposed over the temporal. Today, Church and state are separated, and Christians have become a minority. Could they not be tempted by what we saw emerge in France between the two world wars and continue into the Sixties—that is, the construction, within the framework of a political party, of a Christian policy supporting principles of action and political objectives based on religion? Do you think that this is possible, or is it only a temptation?*

LUSTIGER: First, a preliminary remark about Christians having become a minority. In fact, throughout the course of history, they have never ceased to be in this situation. To cite only a few examples, I remind you of their confrontation with other religions, notably with Islam, and their conditions in the Near East in the Turkish and various Islamic empires. . . . The minority positions are not only characteristic of modern times and the tragic circumstances in Lebanon. The idea that Christendom was completely closed and finished is a modern reconstruction. The evangelization of Persians, Anglos [English], Slavs, etc., never ceased both beyond and within the frontiers of what was once called Christendom. Historians have pointed out that what seems to be a new occurrence in France has existed for centuries. The "missionary" contributions of the seventeenth century (Saint Vincent de Paul, Saint Jean Eudes, and how many others) and the parish "missions" of the nineteenth century are proofs of this.

Now, to return to your question about the temptation to identify Catholicism with a specific party in a democratic regime . . .

WOLTON: *This need for identification can exist just as well within a minority Church when there is a desire for a more effective mobilization of political behavior particular to Christians.*

LUSTIGER: It arose in Germany, first with the *Zentrum* and then with the Christian Democrats. In the nineteenth century, the creation of a Catholic party could signify the fear of harassment or persecutions from state power. The Catholics organized themselves defensively. But, at the same time, their position was ambiguous since the price to be paid is obvious: letting it be supposed that there is only a single political attitude possible for the life and survival of the Catholic community.

It runs the risk of identifying a religious position with a political party. Contemporary democratic governments have allowed the political domain to become relative. Divisions and debates do not necessarily coincide with confessional adherence. The same moral principles that direct a Christian attitude can result in different policies. Politicians, if they are Christians, can acknowledge the same source of value judgments regarding human acts and ultimate goals for society, without necessarily having their conceptions of social evolution coincide. The Church proposes a doctrine constructed on anthropological foundations of social life and the evolution of civilization: this is her social doctrine. Wishing to make the Church's social teaching not only the heart and framework of a political undertaking but its program as well is forcing that teaching to play a replacement role in regard to economic doctrine and the hazards of political choice.

MISSIKA: *Do you regret that there is no Christian-Democrat party in France?*

LUSTIGER: It really is a matter of circumstances.

MISSIKA: *Solely? You could say that what is happening in Italy and Germany is, after all, not so bad....*

LUSTIGER: Our national history is very different.

WOLTON: *Nevertheless, it was attempted: that was the objective of the MRP [Mouvement Républicain Populaire] founded in 1944.*

LUSTIGER: Yes and no. In France the *démocrate-chrétien* party was actually founded before the Second World War. Its political orientation fit into Catholicism's internal debate since it was opposed to the Maurrasian right. After 1940, when they were in the *Résistance,* its militants made plans for an important "Christian-Democrat" party. Thus—thanks to the *Résistance*—this movement ended up in public at the liberation. But, in spite of its electoral success, the MRP did not call itself the Christian-Democrat party. Its leaders, in a France still close to its rural character of the nineteenth century, did not dare to do what De Gasperi did in Italy or Adenauer in Germany. Why?

Although their program was inspired by a Christian vision of man and society, they realized that it was both intellectually and politically sound to recognize its contingency. One of the party's eminent figures was Robert Schuman,[2] the "father of Europe". He was an exceptional man of exemplary integrity, a man of prayer and faith; some people have been proposing his canonization. He was keenly aware that his party's political action was not to be confused with the spiritual and institutional reality of the Church. The fact

[2] Robert Schuman (1886–1963), French statesman, was Minister of Foreign Affairs from 1948 to 1953. He was one of the founders of the European Community of Coal and Steel (1950), the president of the European Movement in 1955 and the president of the European Parliament in Strasbourg in 1958.—TRANS.

remains, however, that the idea of a French Christian-Democrat party has not completely disappeared, since the label has recently been taken over.

MISSIKA: *Are you alluding to the very small* "démocrate-chrétien" *party? There is also, you know, the CDS*[3] *in France....*

LUSTIGER: They do not call themselves *"chrétien"....*

MISSIKA: *No, but they are nevertheless the inheritors of that movement.*

LUSTIGER: Even if there are inheritors of Christian-Democrat trends in several political groups, the *épiscopat français,* on principle, has taken a stand in favor of a clearly displayed pluralism. The Church refuses to be identified with any political party whatsoever. There are convinced Catholics in almost all of the nation's parties.

WOLTON: *Therefore, you would say that the idea of "counting" Catholics politically is not really such a smart idea?*

LUSTIGER: I can understand that a simplified view of the "Catholic vote" interests the experts in political marketing. But since they take no account of the nature of the religious phenomenon and of its effect on social life, they risk serious miscalculations even in their electoral forecasts.

MISSIKA: *And yet you say that the sacred and the political are not completely separated. I quote a remark you made during a talk at the École Militaire: "Political power touches on the essence of a people, its unity. And* that *touches on the sacred." Hence, my question: In what way is the sacred involved in politics?*

LUSTIGER: In this instance I was using the word *sacred* in its broadest sense. There could be a temptation to think of politics as a purely rational practice, a simple strategy for action, a calculation of probability whose data could—in a pinch—be fed into a computer! In fact, from the moment that the social domain is touched, something else intervenes: What is the reality of social life? Can it actually be "calculated"? Or else does it not rather possess a hard nucleus that directs the rest and can be called the "symbolic patrimony" (or the "sacred" or "collective imagination" or "historical memory") because it constitutes the unity and consensus of a people at any given moment? The

[3] The CDS (*Centre des Démocrates Sociaux*) was created after the MRP dissolved itself in the early Sixties. (It had lost much of its constituency after de Gaulle's return, and it disagreed with his new policies.) The CDS later joined the UDF coalition that supported both of de Gaulle's successors, Georges Pompidou and Valéry Giscard d'Estaing.—TRANS.

goals and values pursued by a civilization are expressed in this patrimony, and every citizen participates in it with more or less adhesion. Of course, it remains difficult to define. When historians try to do it for past societies, their hypotheses are numerous, their approaches vary and the essential is never really grasped. The human social phenomenon remains extremely enigmatic, and it is in this sense that it relates to the sacred.

The sacred is man's relationship to whatever it is that, among men, surpasses human beings and permits them to exist and form themselves into a society. It can be given a purely sociological definition as Durkheim did. Other expressions of the same idea are found in Mauss and the sociologists who observe the so-called primitive societies. But this attribution of the sacred to a primitive state of society—from which the modern theory of secularization arises—leads to a total misunderstanding of modern societies. If secularization is made to be the negation of the sacred, known as "archaic", it shows an ignorance of the fact that, in secular societies, the sacred is simply vested elsewhere. In fact, men do not cease to be free, they do not cease to combine their freedoms and they escape neither moral value judgments nor the memory that precedes them. And, in one way or another, the sacred is related to this symbolic patrimony; it is involved in this historical memory. The Christian revelation gives an incredible scope and dignity to humanity's memory, once that memory is not merely ethnic or tribal but universal. It includes the smallest child who, in reciting the *Credo,* inscribes his destiny in human history, from the beginning to the end of time. That child forms a link in the solidarity of all mankind, people of every imaginable civilization, because he is proclaiming the unity of all generations and God's Covenant with humanity. His act is one of memory and anticipation. Now politics also, in its temporal way, dispenses memory and freedom. True statesmen are capable of mobilizing this symbolic legacy and of revealing to a people what it possesses within itself.

The Sacred and the Social Link

MISSIKA: *For a long time—at least from the beginning of the century until quite recently—people were saying that, with society's secularization, the sacred was in the process of disappearing. We now realize that this analysis is somewhat insufficient: the sacred has not disappeared but is being directly incorporated by society into the social connection. After all, aren't contemporary societies distinguished from earlier ones by the fact that, before, the sacred had an authority that belonged to a separate domain (for example, traditions: what the ancestors did that had to be reproduced identically, etc.) and that now that authority is no longer autonomous? From the moment that our societies enter into history and produce the social connection, there is a kind of fusion or incorporation of the sacred into the functioning of society itself, entailing the disappear-*

ance of any exterior authority that, in an extrasocial way, could offer meaning to the social.

I would very much like to know what you think about this analysis.

LUSTIGER: I would be ready, subject to further reading, to agree with a part of that thesis. It seems to throw light on the Church's role in the so-called nonsacred societies that reinvest or rediscover the sacred somewhere else. But the question remains: "What are the nature and source of the sacred in this case?" When political power made use of religious symbols in the coronation of kings or, as it happened—without people being aware of it—in the nineteenth century with the imperial or republican power, there was collusion, confusion or competition between the Church's power and temporal power. That is what occurred in the past. You might even say that the princes wished to be Church leaders: Constantine presided at the Council of Nicaea; Charlemagne saw himself as the Church's protective father; that attitude was supported by the medieval theory of "the two swords".[4] Even today, when the sacred has been reduced to social functioning, it finds a reference or a face: this is the way that Caesars begin to imitate God, wishing to restore the ancestral religions to their profit in the crudest of ways. The uniforms, parades, social rites, holidays, the pledges of allegiance—all of this has not disappeared from the functioning of political regimes as we approach the end of the twentieth century. The journalists who generously use Christian vocabulary to describe political events realize this. Never before in this domain have there been so many references to *"grand-messe"* and *"état de grâce"*. . . .

In such a perspective, the symbolic richness of the Church's memory, in contrast with that of mythologies, is all the more striking, and one sees more distinctly the differences between secular mythologies and the history of salvation given from on high. Nineteenth-century Westerners thought that they were relegating the Bible to the shelf reserved for mythologies; it would, they reasoned, die in the same way that the gods had died. But the end of the twentieth century shows that they were all wrong. Even though there are mythical and legendary expressions in the Bible, it remains that memory of humanity which, precisely, can embrace all fragments of culture. It resists the world's disenchantment[5] and the loss of fascination with the sacred after it has been identified with social life.

[4] The theory was based on the mention of two swords in Luke 22:36–38. The swords were said to represent spiritual and temporal power, both of which had been deposited with the Church, who exercised the latter through emperors or princes.—TRANS.

[5] This seems to be an allusion to Marcel Gauchet's thesis, presented in his essay entitled *Le désenchantement du monde* (Gallimard, 1985), that the sacred has "logically" disappeared from modern Western societies as an end result of Christian criticism of the sacralization of politics.—TRANS.

It was not without reason that at one point the Church Fathers reintegrated Plato, Homer and Virgil into sacred history; and it was not without reason that, in the Renaissance synthesis in the Sistine Chapel, the pagan sages—Socrates, Plato, Aristotle and the sibyl—were joined to the prophets; and it is not without reason that we can hope to see the memory and diversity of pagan nations collected, welcomed and maternally transmuted by the keen memory of God's people. This is something entirely different from collecting and preserving artifacts in the Musée de l'Homme or the Musée des Arts et des Traditions populaires. It is the inclusion of a living memory.

WOLTON: *How do you explain the fact that, in the last forty years or so, the Church has finally begun to catch up with the ideas of civil society? She was called conservative, but her action, like her reforms and discourses, seems in retrospect to have been much more in unison with than in opposition to civil society. How do you explain what can in the end seem to be the Church's lack of autonomy in regard to society?*

LUSTIGER: Is it a defensive reaction? Many Catholics have wanted to justify themselves in the face of criticism and respond to the attacks of the modern mind on the Church.

In previous epochs, the contradictions and conflicts came from within Christianity. Theologians and Christian thinkers were occasionally divided by important quarrels and disputes that could lead to deviations or heresies. But each time, even though the intellectual and spiritual costs of these dissensions were considerable, they provided an opportunity for progress or reformulation. But, with the modern mind, criticism has consisted in saying, "You are behind the times, you are"—as we would say today—"obsolete, antiquated, finished"; and Christians were always vaguely reproaching themselves for having been left behind! The Church and Christian thought had been at the source of progress—at least, they had always been a fertile source of thought—and then they found themselves brusquely dispossessed of spiritual and intellectual initiative. The following generations wanted to re-occupy a position from which the Church had been dislodged.

At the same time—and this is the other side of the spiritual crisis, it seems to me—the Church, tempted by something other than herself, in order to show that she was keeping up with the times, was bound to risk losing something of her specific identity. Too many pastoral, apostolic and spiritual choices were made with an eye on the exterior. In reality, the great movements for the Church's internal reform, which brought her additional holiness and grace, have always been born within her. The remarkable founding figures clearly demonstrate this. It was evinced in the sixteenth century by all the spiritual masters of the modern epoch: Saint Ignatius of Loyola, Saint John of the Cross, Saint Teresa of Avila, the French School, Saint Francis de Sales, Saint

Vincent de Paul and the resurgence that followed the Council of Trent with the extraordinary flourishing of the mystical century. It was true already in earlier times with the great charismatic figures of Saint Bernard, Saint Francis of Assisi, Saint Dominic, et al.

WOLTON: *Do you mean to say that all these movements arose within the Church and were not "imported" from the outside?*

LUSTIGER: These new categories of thought were born at the heart of Christian substance, whereas today it seems that exterior shocks are the ones that provoke the Church into making changes. At least, this is the image that many Christians have. They insist that the Church must, at least, "adapt" herself to the "modern world", without realizing that it is up to Christians to respond to this demand, not by adjusting to the requirements of fashion, but by a renewal of their Christian identity. It is not for them to adapt but to call forth meaning, not to conform but to create ways of thinking and living springing from the Christian *nouveauté.* That is where their responsibility lies. With the convocation of the Second Vatican Council, the Church, as a constituted body, has vigorously undertaken this task, and this is exactly what John XXIII meant when he spoke of *aggiornamento.*

III

THE CHURCH AND POLITICS

Individual Rights and Personal Rights

DOMINIQUE WOLTON: *Why is it that by and large the Church is reticent about individualism, and what difference does she make between personal rights and individual rights? We know that rights of the individual grew out of the secular thought of the eighteenth century and that rights of the human person stem rather from the Church's vocabulary. What is the difference between these two notions, and if there is a difference, why does the Church give the impression that she is going over to modern individualism?*

JEAN-MARIE LUSTIGER: Individualism makes a sovereign of every subject, without regard to the historical conditions in which he is called to live. Without regard, also, to his fundamental relationship to God, his Creator. This singular relationship to God—that is so admirably summed up by Newman's words: "Myself and my Creator"—is specific to each person; and this tête-à-tête between every man and God includes the solidarity of all men among themselves. Thus, human solidarity seems to be a basic element that distinguishes the two conceptions. Society is not just a collection of individuals: its aspect of initiation to a communion must not be forgotten. Father de Lubac made this point in his book *Catholicisme,* whose subtitle was *Les aspects sociaux du dogme.* At a time when the most serious threat was that of totalitarianism, he discerned the social and communal aspect of dogma in order to demand—in the name of the Christian notion of person—the defense of individuals.

Moreover, the individualism stemming from the Enlightenment, with which the Church clashed, affirmed itself as an abstract right independent of the conditions for the concrete exercise of this right.

JEAN-LOUIS MISSIKA: *That is precisely the strength of individualism as it arises from liberal thought.*

LUSTIGER: But it guarantees only a theoretical right to the individual. By not taking other factors into account—the common good, the inherent dignity of each person as a creature of God, etc.—the liberal theory, in practice, deprives the weaker of this right, to the profit of the cleverer and stronger. In other words, a formal affirmation of equality does not ensure the actual defense of the right, because the individual exists concretely only as a subject relating to others.

WOLTON: *Do you think that there are other differences between the concept of the person and that of the individual?*

LUSTIGER: Yes, because the concept of person has a theological origin. Please forgive me in advance if what I am going to say sounds too technical. In theology there is an ingenious and rigorous definition of *person.* It is linked to singularity, and, concurrently, it implies an idea of relationship. In christological dogma, the term *person* designates the unique divine Subject, the Son of God who was made man for us. According to the trinitarian confession, there are three Persons in God. Saint Thomas Aquinas defines the person as a "subsisting relationship". In Catholic doctrine, the word *relationship* is a part of the notion of person. There is only one God in three Persons, even though by saying "three" we are already introducing an abstract word.

The most common and fundamental symbol is suggested by the very names that Scripture has given to God: Father, Son and Spirit. They are all "worshipped and glorified", and that is why the Christian faith speaks of God in three Persons while it confesses the unique God who spoke to Moses like a friend. So as to relate the mystery in agreement with the Scripture, which tells of the "sending" of the Son and the Spirit, theology uses the words *missions* and *origin.* The Father is the Source who eternally begets the Son, who is not created—this begetting must not be confused with human begetting—and the Spirit proceeds from the Father and the Son, or from the Father through the Son. Thus, there is a *taxis,* as it is called in Greek—an order, following the origin. But "order" does not mean "subordination": in the communion of love, the divine Persons are equal in dignity. This is one of the logical difficulties for human thought; it is the mystery of divine life and love, and only God reveals God.

This revelation, however, finds a reflection in creation, including the human creature. Man searches in his understanding of man for elements to help him understand something of the mystery of God as it has been revealed to him. And the idea of person cannot be disassociated from the revelation of God as generation and love. Going further, I remind you of the first page of Genesis: "Then God said, 'Let us make man in our image, after our likeness.'" The human creature is made in the image of the Image that God gives of himself, his own Son. The human condition is filial. This filial dignity and vocation mark the human being as a unique person called to communion with God. It is in the relationship of man as person to God, Trinity of Persons—by the communion in the Spirit with the Person of the Son—that we reach the heavenly Father whom no one has ever seen. The eternal order of life and love is reflected and repeated, if I can put it that way, in the historical access of humanity to the relational, personal life of God. God's plan for deifying man is foreshadowed in man's discovery of himself as a person because, in doing so, he becomes aware that he is capable of a personal relationship with God. And when the mystery is revealed to him, he recognizes God as his Father; he hopes in the Son who is given to him as a partner, as a brother; and he believes himself called to love as God loves, in the Spirit.

What I have been explaining is a part of the common heritage of the Christian churches before the great divisions and schisms in the medieval and modern epochs. Perhaps our civilization has consumed these concepts more avidly than it has absorbed their richness. It is remarkable that all Christian mystics have, in one way or another, attained this mystery of personal union in God and with God. This is the vital center where the discovery of God in Christian mysticism, the reality of the Church as a communion and the dignity of the human person are joined together. When Saint Paul, himself a Jew, writes before 70 A.D. to those who have no rights in the Roman Empire, to those considered the dregs of humanity, the slaves: "Your body is the temple of the Holy Spirit within you" (1 Cor 6:19), it is a tremendous affirmation of the dignity of every person and of the respect due to him.

WOLTON: *But to return to history: for almost a century the Church denounced the illusions of political and economic liberalism. To be exact, she also denounced the socialist conception. In reality, she was in a perilous position in regard to the two major movements of the nineteenth century, and she never succeeded in making her own ideas prevail, other than in the tendency to back conservative regimes that she would never support today.*

LUSTIGER: If each human individual is defined as a person, it is because he is a responsible subject who has a value in himself, and his spiritual identity is a part of the definition. To speak of person does more than convey the notion of the individual, an extrinsic and juridical definition, guaranteed by the positiveness of the law; it also recognizes the individual both in his dignity as a creature desired for himself by God and in his most profound integral vocation. If only individual rights were acknowledged, human rights would take on an arbitrary character: in particular, they could be defined as whatever the majority—in any given country, at any given time—considers them to be. Thus, the question inevitably arises: "What is the basis for the right? Is it universal?" I am well aware that the relativity of civilizations and concepts makes us hesitate, because what has appeared acceptable or unacceptable has varied according to the centuries and cultures.

MISSIKA: *Yes, it is like the well-known phrase: "Not human rights, but English rights and French rights."*

LUSTIGER: The fact remains, however, that the concept of person is fully realized here. We do say "human rights" and not "individual rights". The expression implies that, in one way or another, men are human enough to have humanity—that is, to recognize that a man is a man and cannot be reduced to something else. This natural dignity inherent to all human beings shows them to be persons whose condition and destiny are common. The personal dignity of humanity, therefore, compels recognition from everybody, and that means that men can neither arbitrarily remove one of their own from humanity nor deprive him of his fundamental rights.

MISSIKA: *There is one element in the definition you give that makes it distinctly different from the liberal definition of individualism: you speak of the common good of mankind. In political liberalism and individualism, on the contrary, people speak of the pluralism of values. It seems to me that your definition has the underlying idea of a happiness common to the people as a whole, while in political individualism the collectivity has the unique function of defining rules from which each individual manages to cope in his quest for his own happiness, since there is a pluralism of values and finalities. This would suggest that there is an insuperable divergence between the two definitions.*

LUSTIGER: One of the inalienable rights of the human person is his freedom to choose or reject his end: the Sovereign Good. No one can force somebody else to choose freedom or opt for the Good. This self-determination of man is not opposed to God in a Promethean way. In the believer's vision of the human condition, each person is ultimately responsible for his freedom "before God". God is the supreme and absolute guarantor of human rights, the supreme defender of man. In this vision, there is a completely prodigious faith in man. In using this expression "faith in man"—which is susceptible to misunderstanding and a blasphemous interpretation: "I believe in man; hence, I do not believe in God"—I mean to say, "I believe that God bestows on man his personal, irrevocable dignity." My love for mankind and my hope in the destiny of the human race is based on the faith that I have in God who created us, who takes us in his hand and makes it possible for us to recognize ourselves as persons called to communicate his life. When I meet a human being, I hope to discover my fellow man, or rather my brother, precisely because we have the same Father.

Remember the extent of slavery in antiquity. If you note the way Paul speaks of slaves and slavery, you will realize that, from that moment, the principle of equal dignity, already inscribed like a watermark in the biblical revelation, was being forcefully emphasized by Christ's teaching and by Christian practice. The Bible had already rejected slavery among the Jewish people.

MISSIKA: *Yes, but only for Jews . . .*

LUSTIGER: But, henceforth, because of the pagans' entry into the people of the Covenant, it was a matter of affirming human dignity and the unity of the human race in Adam, a message already included in the beginnings of the revelation from the opening pages of the Bible. The first readers of Saint Paul's letters know already that slavery will eventually be condemned if his religion imposes itself in the hearts and minds of those who administer cities, kingdoms and empires.

The Church in Search of a Third Way?

WOLTON: *Since the nineteenth century, the Church has condemned liberalism, then communism, and as far as trade unionism and politics are concerned, she has for a long time advocated a third way, which she has had some trouble in finding. Can she continue to propose the search for a path between liberalism and Marxism, while she seems to be defending, notably through human rights, a more and more liberal position?*

LUSTIGER: The Church's perspective is different from that of her interlocutors. Marxism needs capitalism to exist, if only for its theory of the proletariat. And liberalism needed socialism, if not Marxism, to exist as a concrete and coherent theory. They are, in fact, antagonistic brothers who depend on each other, apart from the fact that Marxism will say that liberalism does not exist, while liberalism challenges Marxism as a totalitarian ideology. These falsely reflected positions, with which the two great powers, the Soviet Union and the United States, are respectively identified, seem to have divided up the rule of the world. Can both of them simply be dismissed as being no good? The Church is wary of such a step. The two models are not symmetrical. Furthermore, the Church's own position has progressively developed different expressions. The major social encyclicals at the beginning of the century were influenced by the state of economic theories and the sociopolitical circumstances of the times. They were not intended to set forth a timeless doctrine.

WOLTON: *But you do agree that, at that time, the Church repudiated both the liberal and socialist models?*

LUSTIGER: She repudiated liberalism insofar as it ignored the implanting, obligations and incarnate condition of human freedom. She condemned and challenged Marxism for being atheistic, totalitarian and "dialectic"—that is, for making the class struggle and its violence the driving force of history. However, the rejection is not symmetrical since the theories are not symmetrically opposed. They are not contradictory, they are enemies: that is not the same thing. And to the extent that the Church was trying to present a point of view that was respectful of the human person's duties as well as his rights, she adopted a critical attitude toward both of her interlocutors. But she was not putting them on the same level by saying, "You're both wrong!" She said to one, "You are forgetting the common good", or "You have systematized the principle of individual liberty in such a way that we cannot accept it, since, at least practically speaking, it does not recognize the Creator of us all"; and to the others, "You deny the person's moral dignity, and, in the name of violent acts, instituted or not, you ignore the forces of communion at work in creation."

WOLTON: *The Church did more: she tried to inspire a political model, the Christian-Democratic one, by going quite far in the search for an alternative political organization.*

LUSTIGER: Christians have attempted to realize operating models based on this source of inspiration. And these operating models were not unique. Salazar and Franco, as well as their Christian-Democrat adversaries, claimed to draw their inspiration from Christian principles. The facts prove that the general principles set forth by the Church do not constitute a program for political action or the systematization of an economic and political theory. She could never pretend that they do. On the other hand, in specific domains, she has articulated a doctrine recognizing rights and duties, to help leaders in making certain concrete decisions conforming to moral standards. For example, the Church says that it is morally legitimate in some circumstances for workers to strike; it is legitimate to insist that a man's salary should allow him to provide for his family's needs. It is a matter of expressing specific rights and moral judgments, or of more general principles about the organization of social life. This ethical doctrine is not limited to the strictly political program. Similarly, recalling that the so-called laws of economics are not determinisms that impose themselves in the same way as laws of physics and the fact that they must be subordinated to the respect and right of human persons is characteristically one of the Church's moral interventions.

Some people have made a banner of the Church's doctrine—perhaps unduly—and have wanted to see in it more than is there: Paul VI pointed this out precisely in his letter to Cardinal Roy in 1971. And when John Paul II expressly uses the term *social doctrine of the Church* to characterize this teaching, he is well aware of the modesty of our words in the face of the accelerating scientific progress and formidable problems that modern society is trying to deal with, but his intention is to underline, as forcefully as possible, the rights of the human person. He does this all the more resolutely since we are facing a totalitarian economism that poses a serious threat to man. The person possesses fundamental, objective and inviolable rights that must be recognized. Those who are responsible for the Gospel are saying that they want to become spokesmen for the voiceless, to present their justifiable demands and to ask all reasonable men to respect them, even if the problems are never definitively resolved and every solution begets a new difficulty. Only utopians claim to have drawn up the blueprints for the future city whose construction will resolve all problems.

WOLTON: *We are presently living in a "secularized" society dominated by the democratic model and one in which the Church is much less influential than she used to be. In this society, the weight of public opinion is important. What does the Church gain, in the eyes of that opinion, by becoming one actor among others?*

LUSTIGER: The Church must not see herself solely in the image that the public has of her. A society of opinion depends on its reflected image. The best example is found in the interacting and instantaneous polls presented on television. The way you think is suggested to you in such a way that you are delighted to find that you look "so beautiful in this mirror".[1] The regulation of opinion by opinion itself is self-conditioning: you may not now know what you think about this question, but you will in an instant since we are going to tell you what the majority is thinking.

WOLTON: *But we are not obliged to think like the majority.*

LUSTIGER: But it is the majority who are right, since they are the majority. The phenomenon is new because of its scale, extent and the means that it employs.

WOLTON: *How do you feel about the growing influence of public opinion?*

LUSTIGER: It has always existed.

[1] This is an allusion to the well-known "Jewel Song" from Gounod's *Faust* and also to the comic strip character called Bianca Castafiore, "the Milanese nightingale". She keeps singing this aria most energetically in the adventures of *Tintin and Snowy,* who are the creation of Hergé, a Belgian, and whom Cardinal Lustiger, like most Frenchmen, enjoys immensely.

WOLTON: *Of course, but we are talking about the present model.*

LUSTIGER: In the model functioning at present, there is something extremely valuable, which can become a condition of freedom, and also something extremely perverse, which can provoke a decline in reflective capabilities. I refer you to—it may sound a little erudite—the sociology of knowledge. I have Peter Berger and Luckmann in mind; they explain how all knowledge is a social fact. To be recognized as "true", an opinion must be socially acceptable. From the moment that it no longer is, the one who holds it feels himself becoming asocial, "crazy". The importance of social support to knowledge explains the advertisers' role today; they can sometimes condition public opinion.

MISSIKA: *I have an objection: you seem to think that people are at the mercy of media manipulation, but numerous sociological studies have shown that, most of the time, the manipulative effort fails. Although widely accepted, the idea that opinion—whether for marketing or political purposes—can be controlled has never been demonstrated.*

LUSTIGER: Of course, but it is a strange game that consists of utilizing trends in opinion for the adman's profit, just as the surfer uses the wave. In a social system subjected to public opinion, there is a missing link: that moment of reflection and argument, the critical moment. Those who are familiar with voting in deliberative bodies—academic, ecclesiastical, political, economic and social—know very well that there are games and stratagems in those assemblies; in a truly serious deliberation, you must have prepared what you want to say and have thought about the questions being debated so as to know what position to take. Otherwise, you are at the mercy of the better rhetorician, as the Athenians understood. In their case, however, rhetoric, which was the capital art of politics, still included a critical mediation. In this era of instant opinion and polls, critical authority is lacking. Protagonists pelt you with arguments; no one is capable of verifying the assertions being made. If an expert is brought in, he must be trusted simply because of the subtitle "Expert" that is flashed on the television screen.

WOLTON: *But, more generally, what is your analysis of the public opinion that plays an essential part in the functioning of a democracy? Is the concept of public opinion secular? To be specific: I am referring to the judgments made by citizens of a democracy who inform themselves by means of mass communication.*

LUSTIGER: The mirror system of the mass media allows for a steering of public opinion; the dominant opinion becomes the criterion for truth. The accepted "truths" are locked up and sealed, until great surges of grass-roots views force the system to react or swing over to an opposing interpretation. In the political domain, for example, it happens that governments conduct themselves on the basis of polls. Catholic as well as non-Catholic opinion is inclined to demand the same thing of the Church. Not to adjust one's opinion is to shy away from democratic judgment, is it not?

MISSIKA: *There is a very old expression:* Vox populi, vox Dei.

LUSTIGER: Everything depends on knowing whether the opinion is the *vox populi.* Is it the same thing? That is the question.

MISSIKA: *On the other hand, you do agree with the adage?*

LUSTIGER: Unreservedly. In the way that Saint Vincent of Lérins interpreted it: God's people are the totality of the Church, including the hierarchy and its Tradition.

WOLTON: *That can apply to the Church, but not to public opinion!*

LUSTIGER: Just as it is necessary to consider trends in public opinion, it seems to me that it would be abdicating one's responsibility and downright demagogic to make it the principal criterion for judgment and evaluation. I see examples of it day after day in the deliberations in which I take part. When a lie is printed in 500,000 copies, it becomes a "truth" that no denial can weaken.

Our civilization has to develop the moral and intellectual mastery of the marvelous means of communication that it is producing. That, I am afraid, will be a great deal harder than trying to control nuclear energy. The communications civilization that is installing itself under our eyes will have either positive or negative consequences on the physical, psychic and emotional existence of everyone. These consequences can be brought under control only by a personal apprenticeship of freedom. The alternative is to allow large groups of humanity to become subordinate to the economic interests involved in these enormous investments.

Liberté-Égalité-Fraternité: Is It a Christian Expression?

WOLTON: *The Gospel contains the principle of equality among men, but when the claims for liberty and equality appeared in the eighteenth century, they were considered the fruit of secular thought and were even lived in complete opposition to religion.*

LUSTIGER: When Pope John Paul II made his pilgrimage to Lourdes and was welcomed by President François Mitterand at the Tarbes airport, he commented on the motto, *Liberté-Égalite-Fraternité,* by pointing out the Christian origin of the three terms. Your objection, which is valid, illustrates the extent to which the crisis of the French Revolution and the Enlightenment can be understood as a new schism within Western history. But it remains an affair internal to Western thought and, hence, a Christian affair.

MISSIKA: *But even so, will you admit that a system of thought can exist outside of religion? You seem to be saying that all secular thought is schismatic. Will you concede that a new thought can be atheistic or areligious and dispassionate as far as religion is concerned?*

LUSTIGER: Perhaps it is dispassionate today, but it was not always so. The fact remains, however, that this "new atheistic or areligious thought" is a product of our culture, which is Christian. It carries its indelible mark. As proof I remind you that you define this "new thought" by the negation—a-theistic, a-religious—of what brought it into existence.

MISSIKA: *But individualism as it is conceived of in the liberal thought of the eighteenth century is, after all, relatively autonomous in regard to the definition that you have given to the person in Christian thought. It is legitimate to look for roots, but not to the point of stifling new ideas.*

LUSTIGER: I repeat: I do not deny the ruptures, or the negations, or the incongruities or that these can one day become lasting in people's minds. But whoever studies the "history of Western thought" is certainly obliged to re-establish relations between Christianity and "secular" thought. Even philosophy conceives of itself as a history of philosophy, because it must have this perpetual resumption of thoughts and their origins in order to understand where it is heading.

The tragedy of modern times is that the demand for human rights has never been so urgent, so insistent, so universal as at the very moment when the inconsistencies concerning their definitions and their concrete denial are more striking than ever. It is as if man were caught up in an infernal contradiction with negation being proportionate to the claim and the incertitude proportionate to the affirmation. Eugenics, euthanasia, economic crises, victims of famine or wars of extermination attest at every instant to this ambivalence.

WOLTON: *It is one thing to say that there is a difficulty in implementing the defense of human rights, and it is quite another to say that the difficulty is a proof of the unsound nature of this concept.*

LUSTIGER: Well, what was thought to be obsolete—namely, a religious definition of human rights—is at the source of their existence and reappears today with a youth and topicality that no one suspected. The "staging" of reason's triumph was done by announcing the death of God and expelling religion to the wings among the abandoned stage sets of history. And now it becomes evident that in the scene being acted, a partner is lacking, a partner whose presence is essential if the performance is to reach its completion.

In other words, to ensure its triumph, reason is now obliged to live through an episode that it does not understand. It is not that the curé who went out by the left exit is entering by the right one, but it is rather, it seems to me, a consequence of the fact that reason has begun to reflect more deeply on its powers and vocation. We must—using an expression that shocked you earlier—"save reason from itself so that reason triumphs". That is the issue. As a witness to the Faith and to the dignity of man, I repeat: the revelation of what man is as creature of God is the ultimate foundation of his dignity.

WOLTON: *Today, after so many wars and massacres, we have finally reached a kind of consensus on the principle of human rights. Then, just at this juncture, the Church speaks up: "Yes, we agree with you completely about human rights, we think the same thing, and moreover, you must rediscover their ontological definition, which we have known all along." I get the impression that the Church, after having opposed the two philosophical systems of liberalism and socialism for so long, has now, with Vatican II, integrated modernity and agreed with a certain philosophy of human rights—with, however, the assertion of a supplementary dimension. You accept the modern world after having fought it for a century: it is as though you have at last been won over by 150 years of secular thought!*

LUSTIGER: No, honestly, I cannot subscribe entirely to your description of history. The concept of Christian humanism, as historians of French thought have shown, is much older. The idea of the eminent dignity of man finds more than enough of its substance in biblical roots. You are saying what many people think, I know, but I consider it an ideologized vision of history. It overlooks our roots and projects on the past the present conflict between contemporary parties.

WOLTON: *Take another example: the relationship between community and society.*

The Church has always spoken of relations between the person and the community. Since the end of the nineteenth century, however, Western society has been profoundly transformed. We have gone from a society of small groups and circumscribed communities to one that is much more anonymous, a society of the masses. The Church condemned this transformation and continued to speak of the connection between the person and the community. And then, suddenly, for the last twenty years, just as the société de masse *has become a fact, one gets the impression that the religious discourse has accepted the transformation and is adapting to it. It is the same problem as the relationship between individual and person.*

LUSTIGER: In theological language, the words *community* and *society* are very old. You find them already vigorously asserted by Saint Thomas; hence, they were being used in a completely different historical context from our own. The word *community* had logical and metaphysical meanings; it could also designate specific religious communities. It had become a juridical concept and, not strictly speaking, a political one. Between the two wars, Emmanuel Mounier[2] highlighted its present use for the precise purpose of confronting the contradictions of liberalism and Marxism. He wanted to reintroduce a personalist social vision; the temptation in those days was of a totalitarian type. Caught in the "individual" and "mass" dilemma—these were the terms used ("totalitarianism" was not necessarily a pejorative word in all languages)—he developed a "personalist and community" doctrine. Then Gabriel Marcel brought his original contribution to it. When contrasting the words *person* and *individual, community* and *society,* European languages have different resonances. German, for example, is richer and has more nuances in this respect than French.

The Christian Origin of Human Rights

WOLTON: *The theme of human rights—as we have just pointed out—does not come from the Church but from secular political thought growing out of the revolution of the eighteenth century. The Church seems to have entered the picture just a little late. What is the particularity of her position in comparison with the way modern political thought poses the question of human rights?*

LUSTIGER: The first declaration of human rights based their inalienable character on the affirmation that each person receives them from his Creator. Humanism is theistic. It remained so in the United States whose revolution

[2] Emmanuel Mounier (1905–50) was a French philosopher who was one of the principal representatives of personalism. He founded the journal *Esprit* in 1932.—TRANS.

preceded ours. In France, in a highly polemical and antireligious context, human rights were very quickly set up as opposed to God's rights. They appeared to be a weapon in the struggle against the Church on both the French and continental philosophical and political scene. Europe was then in the full crisis of giving birth to modern atheism; consequently, the Church's first reaction was defensive, negative as to the expression itself. Then, with two centuries of distance—which is not long in intellectual history—we see a complete turnabout as to the concepts and their foundation. John XXIII, Paul VI and John Paul II have given the expression a meaning that is respectful of history and in full agreement with the most traditional doctrine. I am forced to come back to the same events. We are living in an age of totalitarianism and manipulation of human rights by the most contradictory ideologies. In such a context, the notion appears to be very fragile. It is invoked by all governments, even totalitarian ones, to justify their conduct in the eyes of international public opinion. But everything is justified, even the lie; rights are denied in the name of rights. The sole unshakable foundation of human rights is precisely man's creation by God. But even so, that does not mean that those who wish to respect these rights have to believe in God. The confession of faith allows for the protection of the statement of these rights. It ensures their justification against the arbitrariness of bad faith and the power of the states, the *raisons d'État.* There is something absolute in man: it is his reference to the Absolute that we call God. For believers, serving man and his rights is obeying the divine law, which is "to love thy neighbor". This conviction and respect do not result simply from common sense, logic or rationality but, for the believer, in any case, they are based on the observance of the will and commandments of God. Therefore, the *raison d'être* of human rights can lead the Christian as far as martyrdom.

WOLTON: *You repeatedly refer to the foundation for human rights in a religious perspective, but as far as content is concerned, what is the Church's proper role in the current defense of human rights?*

LUSTIGER: That would require long expositions. First of all, there are ignored rights that the Church enunciates with great force.

For example, the freedom of conscience that includes the freedom of worship, the freedom to be able to fulfill one's duty toward God. That can seem strange to someone who regards religious freedom as a private right permitting each individual to do whatever he likes in his own home, and not as a socially acceptable and civilly recognized right. In fact, the state's respect for this fundamental and objective right of the human person constitutes a test in the eyes of the Church and, in the end, of all religions. Man is a religious being; religion puts him in contact with something beyond himself. Recognizing this means respecting the transcendence of the human person. It is this principle that prevents the state, nation, tribe, race or party from substituting itself for the absolute and, by this substitution, alienating man. Such a right can be defined in a positive manner, as the Church does, by insisting on the moral obligation for juridical respect of religious freedom; but it can also be defined negatively by recalling that nothing in this world is God, and, hence, a man cannot be forced to worship anyone or anything because that would be a horrible tyranny. The guarantee of that freedom of persons and respect for human rights is that a state, nation, culture or empire can neither utilize nor deny the exercise of that freedom. This is truly the guarantee of guarantees, the absolute condition of all other liberties. I repeat, there are two formulations of the right: the positive one of the Church, which refers to God, and the negative one for unbelievers. If people think that there is no God, then it is certain that the state is not God, that Caesar is not God, and that alone is enough to establish the freedom, for those who wish it, to worship God.

For the Church, recognizing human rights includes a special vision of man in his relationship to himself, his existence, his body; to the world, his close relations, other men, his fellow creatures. Without wishing to include an entire ethical code or Christian moral doctrine in human rights, the Church insists that man's right to life is based on his corporal condition as a creature of God. From his conception, the weakest of persons has the right and the duty to live, because he has received life. There can be no question of defining as a "right" only that to which the majority rallies. Even if the majority in a society were to find torture legitimate, neither the Church nor the conscience could admit that being able to torture is a right. Speaking of human rights implies the respect for what man is and for the supreme guarantor of his humanity! Thus, the right to dispose of his body by committing suicide is not a human right.

MISSIKA: *Why?*

LUSTIGER: Because man must respect life, his life.

MISSIKA: *But can he be truly free if he does not have this final freedom?*

LUSTIGER: Is it really being free to deny the concrete state in which we receive our freedom? The person who accepts himself in his historical and carnal condition accepts his life as a gift of which he is not the master. I understand completely that this reasoning does not convince everybody, but the right to suicide cannot be a right: it is absolutely contradictory.

MISSIKA: *Would you go so far to support legislation to prohibit suicide?*

LUSTIGER: I am not envisaging any legislation, or prosecution or penal sanction. On the other hand, the moral responsibility of a society that advocates the right to suicide would be grave. It would develop the death instinct and once again encourage a lack of respect for life. It is not unheard of or impossible in the human species, including advanced civilizations: Stoicism commended suicide, and Japan raised it to the level of an art.

MISSIKA: *But only under specific conditions.*

LUSTIGER: So suicide, too, has been codified. But it is precisely here that the difference you are questioning me about is found. There is no exhaustive enumeration of all possible and imaginable rights. One can conceive of a future state of civilization where reflection could bring about a new requirement linked to a concrete determination of human existence. But today and always, there has existed an "unwritten law", an internal rule engraved in the heart of man, conforming to his personal nature and expressive of his dignity as creature.

I am convinced that in this fascinating and sometimes terrible century in which we live, men of faith have received the mission to testify to their fidelity to God not only by loving and serving him but also, because of the light they receive from him, by protecting man from himself. And this mission applies to all who have received the light of revelation. It is not a matter of an illegitimate intrusion of the religious into the rational. In reason's self-determination, it is absolutely necessary that somewhere there be a "north" because it can self-determine itself as freedom only if it accepts to receive a freedom greater than itself.

WOLTON: *I do not think that a rationalist will accept reason's dependence on a freedom coming from somewhere else. He will say that it is up to men to arrive at . . .*

LUSTIGER: Yes, to go as far as and including—and we have the experimental proof—self-destruction. We have had our fill of that, thank you!

MISSIKA: *I confess that to blame reason for genocide, for Nazism—indeed, for Stalinism—seems to be exaggerated; it really is unthinkable!*

LUSTIGER: I am not inventing anything. Hitler wanted to be scientific, just as Stalin wanted to be rational. To save reason's honor, we have to recognize the dangers to which it is exposed. I chalk them up to sin.

MISSIKA: *Well, you are a great help! The fact that technical means, in the service of a political madness that has always existed, permitted crimes of unprecedented scope cannot be attributed to reason. . . .*

LUSTIGER: Yes. But reason can be a sinner, because it is always the reason of a particular man, enjoying his freedom. Reason can become blind, can commit errors.

MISSIKA: *Argument for argument, I say that the totalitarianisms of the twentieth century are the fruit of the quest for salvation. . . .*

LUSTIGER: I could possibly agree that they contain lost hopes, but they are nevertheless sins. They are the consequences of man's ruin, which occurs when he misuses the gifts he has received from God. I am not attributing these faults to abstract reason taken in its universal essence or imagined as a sovereign deity beyond all real context. But reason resides in men, who use or abuse it! And the exercise of reason is obviously subject to illusion and error—not only to experimental error but to the erratic course and perversion that stem from freedom itself and the goals it pursues or impugns. Reason does not function independently of the ends man is searching for. Conceiving of reason as independent of "intention" makes it something like a computer (you program it, feed in the data and it will say anything at all and yet remain logical). But the process is very different with men of flesh and blood. We come back to the same point, concerning historical reality. My aim is not to belittle reason; on the contrary, I have a very elevated idea of it, because it is one of the noblest faculties that distinguishes the human species, and we must rejoice when it triumphs. But, like my believing brothers, I also know—from having verified it in my conscience, from having observed it in the social achievements of my times, from having recognized it in my reflections on mankind's history—that it is the confession of faith, the acceptance of revelation, the entry into communion with God that permits the human person to be protected in his dignity and to exercise his most noble faculties.

WOLTON: *What is bothersome in your way of thinking is that you consider all attempts to maintain a social organization, other than with Christian values, as either impossible or else as owing their inspiration to Christianity. As to these attempts you say, for example, "Yes, they are difficult struggles, but when you come right down to it, you can see that the concepts of* liberté, égalité, *and* fraternité *are closely akin to Christian ones; they are less of a rupture than a continuation." Moreover, the inevitably nuanced appraisal of these 150 years of secular society leads you to say, "All the defects of the human rights movement can be explained by the fact that a transcendent principle has been rejected, and reintroducing this principle would give meaning to society's pursuit!" The roots on one side, the ultimate meaning on the other: I get the impression that it is impossible to escape this cherished Catholic, apostolic and Roman Church.*

LUSTIGER: Whether people like it or not, it is clear that the Bible and the Gospel are irrevocably inscribed in Western civilization. In saying this, I am only making a simple observation that it would be absurd to deny. Those who have tried to uproot Christianity in the most drastic ways, including the use of force, could do it only by borrowing concepts and words from that which they wanted to destroy. But as soon as the storm has passed, the plants that were thought to have been ripped out sprout up again.

WOLTON: *So you feel that, even in the East, that uprooting will not triumph?*

LUSTIGER: No! It is clear....

WOLTON: *You think that it is already clear?*

LUSTIGER: It is very clear if you pay attention to what is moving behind the iron façade of official ideology.

MISSIKA: *Including the Soviet Union?*

LUSTIGER: Yes, including the Soviet Union! The only force that is capable of withstanding the ordeal to the end is spiritual, the mystical force of faith in God. I am not much surprised—although it is remarkable when you know the depth and the duration of the persecution—to see that faith, sometimes completely uncultivated, is flourishing there, whether in Judaism, Catholicism, Orthodoxy or Protestantism. It is in exact opposition to all the theories, to all those innumerable predictions.

Ought we to criticize the practical materialism of the West equally severely? I have spoken of "sin". Call it infidelity, if you like.... It is in the end the category that best expresses the West's errors. But the fundamental faults, those that bring about division, are permanent: they do not date from the eighteenth century! I detect no rupture at all in 1789.

MISSIKA: *And yet you are presenting things as if there were.*

LUSTIGER: No.... I just do not think that the conflict between the *Ancien Régime* and the *République* is pertinent to what we are discussing.

MISSIKA: *But by attacking the* Encyclopédistes *and reason so vigorously you gave the impression that . . .*

WOLTON: *. . . that they were the devil!*

LUSTIGER: When, by reintroducing the state's absolute right, Philippe the Fair's jurists made the Roman jurists' definition available to French kings,[3] they were going against the current of Christianity's entire effort to reinterpret Roman law. They were reinserting into medieval law a secular principle that was already totalitarian, since it made the state the absolute sovereign of the human condition. In other words, they were making the state man's God. The state was already being deified. That is not the same thing as the separation of the temporal government of peoples from ecclesiastical spiritual authority.

WOLTON: *But you know very well that it is easy to pass from one to the other.*

LUSTIGER: Admittedly. But from the moment that the pagan *raison d'État* is reinvented, it introduces such a radical principle into the thought and political ambitions of Western nations that the old idea of arbitration in the name of common values is going to fall apart.

WOLTON: *Would you say that the foundations of Western democracy as we conceive of them today, at the end of the twentieth century, can exist only if society accepts their connection with Christian values?*

LUSTIGER: Yes, in a way. On the other hand, there is a work of liberation, of further development that remains to be done, and Christians have a specific role in this task. Just a word about international law: we have mentioned the nineteenth-century nationalism to which internationalism was opposed. What is the Church's place in this affair? She defends the legitimate right of nations to exist, and yet she intervenes as an element that upsets nationalism's claim of self-sufficiency. Nationalism's defect is to have established a coincidence between the national affirmation and that of a sovereign state, to have reintroduced the *raison d'État* for which the nation and its government become the absolute value and to which everything must be sacrificed, including man. Just as the Church recognizes the nation as a cultural phenomenon to be respected in the way the family is respected, she cannot accept, even in the name of man's liberty, that a national authority allow itself to ask everything of man without subjecting itself to moral law. The nation or the state can ask a man to offer his

[3] This occurred at the beginning of the fourteenth century.—TRANS.

life in the name of solidarity or the good to be defended, but it cannot ask him to go against his conscience in the name of a "reason" for which it gives no explanation.

WOLTON: *We are always coming back to what you might call the absence of an ultimate reference.*

LUSTIGER: There has to be an ultimate reference and a rule of morality so that the human and Christian conscience can advocate insubordination to a morally unjust law. The state is neither the absolute sovereign nor the absolute norm of consciences and societies.

IV

TRIUMPH AND ILLUSIONS OF INDIVIDUALISM

Interdictions

DOMINIQUE WOLTON: *I know that you disagree with liberalism and individualism on at least one point: since the Sixties their demands for rights regarding contraception, abortion, homosexuality and more sexual freedom in general have become increasingly clamorous.*

JEAN-MARIE LUSTIGER: Is the body an object, a commodity to be used, or is it an integral part of the human person? And, in the latter case, does it exist outside of the realm of human freedom and, hence, beyond good and evil? That is the fundamental debate.

WOLTON: *For you.*

LUSTIGER: And for everybody.

WOLTON: *Yes, but no one in favor of more sexual freedom would ever think of his body as merely an object.*

LUSTIGER: The point is to know if the human being can dispose of his body as something independent of his freedom and, therefore, independent of the notion of good and evil. If the sexual domain, like other distinct areas of human activity, remains extraneous to the determination of freedom, to the moral category, then it is true, I admit, that there should be no limitation on the right to use and abuse one's own body and its capacities for sensual enjoyment, just as no one can forbid me from taking my watch and smashing it to pieces if I want to.

WOLTON: *Of course, but I do not think that the advocates of contraception or abortion or a certain idea of individual liberty are challenging the concepts of good and evil.*

LUSTIGER: Stating that good and evil exist can be done only on the basis of two criteria. Either the categories are determined by a completely exterior social taboo or legal measure, or else man finds in his conscience—in the universal determination of good and evil or in his faith—the ability to choose the good and avoid evil. If sexuality is joined with man's freedom, with that part of the human conscience that is noblest and most specifically human, then anything that applies to economic, political or human relations also applies to sexual relations. Nothing human should remain isolated from freedom and thus from moral choice. Man has the ambition that nothing should escape his deep desire to make decisions for himself. But his personal vocation is to integrate the totality of his existence—including, of course, his body and sexuality—into his humanity, which is capable of choosing the good.

From the first pages of Genesis, this affirmation is made repeatedly throughout the Bible. Christ cites it for clarifying moral conflicts to which objections are being made. "So God created man in his own image . . . male and female he created them" (Gen 1:27). Animal sexuality is regulated by instincts and drives, depending on the equilibrium of the species and their needs. The Bible teaches us that sexuality in man and woman is a reflection of God, of God's image. Therefore, it is endowed with a sovereign dignity. Since man is made in the image and resemblance of God, he must act as God acts.

WOLTON: *There is not much chance that referring everything connected with sexuality to God will be understood as a freedom. It is more like being dominated!*

LUSTIGER: But the Bible's moral commandments do not proceed from that reasoning. A key precept explains the logic behind them: "You shall be holy, for I the Lord your God am holy" (Lev 19:10). Jesus repeats the precept and comments, "Be perfect as your heavenly Father is perfect." Man is meant to conduct himself "with divine morals", as the Church Fathers said. Human sexuality is an area of life where man expresses himself not only according to his natural condition but also according to his divine vocation. Sexuality is not just an arena for exercising one's freedom. Through it man can express his resemblance to God.

And the sovereign other who institutes man as relation and difference is God himself. The Ten Commandments are always relational in regard to God and to one's fellow man. That is why human fertility is essentially different from animal reproduction. In the human species, each individual has a personal relationship with God. It is not simply sexual attraction and specific reproduction that make him or her a person in communion with other human beings; it is also the dignity of a personal love and a procreation in which each person has been chosen by God himself. In other words, when a person is conceived by his parents, he is desired for himself and created by God.

WOLTON: *That is just what I was saying: introducing God into a domain that is already formidably complex is not so simple.*

LUSTIGER: Look at the Bible. The promise of innumerable descendants made to Abraham is already a prophecy of the ultimate victory over death, a guarantee of the human person's vocation for life. Human fertility has an absolutely sacred and unique character, because it is not the conservation or statistical multiplication of the species that are involved but the birth of unique beings. And God's personal responsibility is engaged since it is he who gives these beings the possibility to exist as persons. Parents are not creators: they procreate. They do not give life; they transmit the life they have received. And it is God who "gives" them a child. The expression (which may seem archaic) is found in the Bible—where the child is perceived as a gift from God. Is it a naïveté, an anthropological naïveté? If the child is seen as God's gift, it is because he is a new person whose dignity—unique—completely eludes the powers of the man and woman who "make a child", according to the current expression, which, by the way, seems to me to be quite excessive: a couple does not "make" a child. They give birth to him, they bring him into existence. They procreate, but it is God-Creator who makes the child exist as a person. This is what is meant by the conjunction of human fertility and man's divine vocation.

WOLTON: *But I repeat my question: What is the connection between the explanation you are giving and the question raised about the Church's refusal of a certain idea of freedom?*

JEAN-LOUIS MISSIKA: *Because, in the end, what you are saying is expressed by the Church in her declarations that consist of interdictions, condemnations. . . .*

WOLTON: *And there have been so many of them! It is the domain where they have been most numerous.*

LUSTIGER: Sexuality is an aspect of human life that has extraordinary meaning and values; it is a crossroads and a stake of human freedom and morality. It is not exhausted by interpersonal relations any more than freedom is, and, like freedom, it refers to the One who instituted it in difference and communion.

Good and Evil

WOLTON: *But since man is free—that has even been reaffirmed several times by the Church—why not allow him the full exercise of that freedom? Why must he a priori be judged harshly for some of his acts, notably sexual ones, performed in the name of that freedom?*

LUSTIGER: Man is free, but it is the duty of the Church—speaking in God's name and repeating the received Word—to point out good and evil. The Church pronounces no civil or penal sanctions; she instructs the moral and religious conscience and gives a name to good and evil.

WOLTON: *What is something good, for example?*

LUSTIGER: The proposal of monogamy and the indissolubility of marriage as the fundamental vocation of man.

MISSIKA: *Since you have cited it, I would like to look more closely at the binding character of marriage. It has always seemed really strange to me that as far as the Church is concerned, the question of whether the conjugal relationship can be dissolved should not arise. Is marriage really forevermore, even if the partners cease to love each other? What happens when a woman no longer loves her husband or when a man no longer loves his wife? Can you imagine that?*

LUSTIGER: Well, such a situation does not need to be imagined because it is a common occurrence, and I have been the saddened witness to or confidant of it. Your question rests on an obvious fact: according to recent notions, the marital union of a man and a woman is based entirely on a certain emotional experience that our societies call love.

MISSIKA: *Aha, I should have known! Once again, we have the individualism of the eighteenth century to blame!*

LUSTIGER: But you know very well that a person's feelings about "being in love" are influenced by the way "love" is presented, not only in literary and theatrical forms but in the sensational images—ever so much more powerful—of movies and television.

WOLTON: *But what does this have to do with the matter?*

LUSTIGER: When the sole criterion for the stability of a couple's union is what is currently called love and when you see the way our society represents that love to adolescents and young people, you grieve for them! A man and woman can be joined in marriage in the name of what they experience as love and yet know full well that their feelings for each other may not last.

WOLTON: *But why not respect the individual's freedom? Why not trust his experience?*

LUSTIGER: Does this feeling of being in love suffice for establishing the happiness proposed to a couple? For establishing a home and starting a family capable of transmitting, along with life, culture and morality? Does it suffice for creating the indissoluble union that human marriage is?

WOLTON: *But surely you must know that, in the end, many children of divorced parents prefer the situation created after the divorce—even if it is inevitably painful—to the one preceding it, very often fraught with conflicts, in which there is an attempt to preserve artificially the sacred family life that you have mentioned.*

LUSTIGER: Now you are posing the question under the narrower angle of how to cope with failures, given the present functioning of the couple. In the most developed Western countries, marriage is the object of an inordinate hope and thus the source of great disillusionments and suffering. But the law of life that the Church proclaims is not an illogical censure falling from on high and imprisoning people in their wounds without their having truly chosen or wished it. She is simply maintaining and recalling a principle in an epoch that is not dealing with the problem very well. . . .

WOLTON: *Has there ever been a time when this kind of problem was well regulated?*

LUSTIGER: But when has it ever existed on such a scale?

WOLTON: *It is rather less dramatic now than it used to be, even if there are many fewer illusions about marriage and perhaps precisely because there are fewer.*

LUSTIGER: Our present culture compares itself to the more or less mythical state of the society immediately preceding it. It is in rebellion against the puritanism and a certain hypocrisy of the nineteenth century. Although, from my literary acquaintance with those morals, I am not ready to idealize the bourgeois society of those times—or that of the subproletariat portrayed in particular by Zola who describes the worker's world and the condition of both sexes in it—I nevertheless know that the previous century was also characterized by tranquil family happiness and virtues. Whatever the case with past generations, a moral problem does exist today. Perhaps we cannot approach it in the same way. The anthropological tools and values are culturally different. Dr. Freud has left his mark in this field. There has been a subversion of acceptable rites and standards; moreover, there has been a deliberate will to transgress—as if to recognize, in spite of oneself, the connection of human existence with the sacred.

The Church's Painful Duty

WOLTON: *The Church stopped defending the nineteenth-century model of the individual and his freedom quite some time ago; nevertheless, she remains opposed to certain practices: she condemns divorce, condemns contraception, condemns abortion, condemns homosexuality—that adds up to quite a few condemnations. It is one thing to speak out against a headlong flight toward hedonism or an illusion of individual freedom; it is quite another to take—systematically—a position that is contrary to all attempts to exercise individual freedom. You are saying, "No, the Church does not condemn", but, on the whole, not only does she make harsh moral judgments, she invariably takes a negative stand each time that liberalizing legislation is proposed.*

MISSIKA: *May I add a word to make the question more precise? What is equally striking about these condemnations is the extent to which they focus on a problem's exterior aspect—hence, the less important one. In the end, what should be decisive is the authentic or inauthentic character of what a person does. A relationship between two men or two women can be a genuine and beautiful love, while a very Catholic marriage can be contracted for sordid reasons. I get the feeling that the Church remains on the surface of things, that she fails to take account of the unique character of a relationship, of the fact that each time there is a particular problem, whereas she is condemning across the board.*

WOLTON: *In short, might there be ways of reminding people of her fundamental positions without resorting to condemnations?*

LUSTIGER: They are not condemnations. The Church is simply recalling the intrinsic requirements for human existence: life, love, the natural dignity and divine vocation of man. Nobody is saying that these standards are always easy to live up to or that the problems can be resolved by mere social conformity. Unfortunately, our epoch has introduced a very great confusion among the several levels of understanding involved in moral choices.

The first level is the one I mentioned earlier: the Church's reminders that there is a standard of conduct whose basis is linked to creation and God's plan for man. The second level—quite different—is that of civil legislation, at a given time in a given country: laws are passed to regulate certain acts and arbitrate their relationship to the socially permissible or impermissible. The third level is the existing state of morals in a specific society—that is, what is collectively considered socially admissible and normative: "Everybody does it; thus, there can be nothing wrong about it." Finally, there is the subjective level of individuals, the consciences of people caught in particular circumstances.

All of these aspects have to be considered: the moral law as it is understood in the divine light, the state of civil legislation, the moral climate and public opinion, and the personal situation.

WOLTON: *But the aspects you mention are practically never mentioned in the Church's stand on these matters....*

LUSTIGER: They are always mentioned and are to be respected. If I have enumerated the elements that enlighten the conscience, it is because all too often people depend exclusively on a dominant social opinion when making a moral decision. Many of them find it hard to accept the distinctions and discontinuities connected with the simple statement that there are distinct levels of moral perception. Consequently, they insist that the terms of a commandment received from God be transformed so as to accommodate it to the majority opinion in a given society or to the subjective judgment of an individual conscience. It is the Church's painful duty, in this matter as in many others, to be faithful to the teaching God has made known to her, even if it is hard to hear—indeed, hard to say. She does not speak with a pretentious hypocrisy that censures but with compassion, mercy and genuine love of human beings. She has a duty to maintain the strict standard of conduct that she has received as a mission to be proclaimed for men's own good. All the more so, since she knows that personal participation in the act of deliverance that God has made in sending the Messiah to mankind makes it possible for sinful man to live up to this standard. This mystical "experience" is salutary in the ethical domain, both for the individual and for society. God's grace is given to man for attaining the ideal proposed from on-high. It would be the height of duplicity to pretend to impose by social or coercive means what can be attained only by the power of God's gift received voluntarily. Holiness cannot be promulgated by civil law! On the other hand, we ought to be dubious when a society makes socially normative—and thus legal—behavior that is contrary to the dignity of man.

WOLTON: *What is this behavior that is contrary to human dignity?*

LUSTIGER: I have mentioned contraception, divorce, abortion.

MISSIKA: *But, after all, contraception, divorce and homosexuality cannot be considered detrimental to human dignity.*

LUSTIGER: The crux of the matter is to know what a society can or cannot legitimately authorize or propose as a social model for its own good and the good of every individual who belongs to it.

It is not the liberalization of morals after the prudery of the nineteenth century that is the real problem for contemporary society, but the control that scientific and technical knowledge now have over the human condition, and here I include, along with biology, the tools of psychological and social analysis and even of ethnology. Through the means of comprehension and intervention that the present state of learning attributes to man about himself and his sexuality, our societies find themselves in the same situation as that of the European nations in the nineteenth century in regard to labor and the worker's condition in the industrial revolution. Until rational mechanisms began to control some of the excesses of technical and economic progress, the price paid for it by the most developed countries—not to mention the underdeveloped ones—was enormous and has had brutal and lasting effects. Today, thanks to scientific progress, formidable powers over life and human procreation have been acquired, and if the harm to humanity is not to be just as cruel as it was in the economic and industrial revolution, it is crucial that societies be enlightened by an increasing fund of wisdom. I realize that the Church's warnings can appear just as archaic to present generations as those of the Churchmen at the beginning of the industrial revolution did to their contemporaries. But it is of primordial importance to repeat the ends and moral values that must govern the integration of this new control that man has over himself, his body and sexuality.

WOLTON: *Why not? But there is at least one objection: although it may be the Church's duty to warn against dangers such as those of the industrial society and, today, those regarding genetic engineering or the control of human reproduction, why does she persist in doing it from a condemnatory stance or, at best, in using a Cassandra-like tone?*

LUSTIGER: Christians have a paramount contribution to make in this domain, even if they are not always heard or followed. The Church's teaching cannot be summed up by interdictions. It is much more than that. She is earnestly asking researchers in all disciplines to extend their efforts to integrate moral standards into the solutions they propose. In a word, by insisting that technique be subordinated to man and his vocation, the Church attests that man is called to commune with God who is life and love. But the question remains: Why is her message heard as a law of doom, when it is proposing holiness and light? Saint Paul was already pondering that contradiction.

PART FOUR

TOWARD A SPIRITUAL REVIVAL

I

FROM THE LATIN QUARTER TO THE SIXTEENTH *ARRONDISSEMENT* (1969–1979)

Fifteen Years as a University Chaplain

DOMINIQUE WOLTON: *You were appointed curé at Sainte-Jeanne-de-Chantal in Paris in October 1969, after having served for fifteen years in the student milieu at the Centre Richelieu. What assessment did you make of those years at the time when the form of your ministry was about to undergo a profound change?*

JEAN-MARIE LUSTIGER: My experience had convinced me that, in its permanent confrontation with the innovations and convictions of our times, the Gospel remains fruitful. Having witnessed the conversions of numerous intellectuals and artists—young and old—I had seen how the Church is constituted. Moreover, I had had the grace to celebrate several of those adult baptisms. I had been not only an observer but a partner in the decisive debates of the era, and the strength and topicality of the Christian message had been verified for me. My theological understanding—more as a result of discussion and reflection than of bookish study—had matured a great deal. I had encountered a wide diversity of social activists and calculated the risks and fragilities of social and political life. Finally, I had lived through what I thought to be the most beautiful period of my life in a realization— authentic, in my opinion—of Christian fraternity and shared responsibility.

But I also knew that I was an adult who was gradually growing older and that if I continued to serve at the university, I risked enclosing myself into the relative irresponsibility of a youth that had not yet dealt with life's limitations. Youth is exalting because everything is possible, at least verbally. That could have been a source of illusions for me, a source of immaturity, to tell the truth.

I had learned the price to be paid for loyalty to what one thinks and believes to be true. I knew that it was essential to maintain the internal dynamism of a consistent Christian life, in danger of falling apart as young people in our society became the sounding board for every emotional or ideological contradiction, Christian or not.

WOLTON: *Are you trying to say that your faith encouraged you to assume a collective ecclesiastical function?*

LUSTIGER: The Centre Richelieu was where I had been placed, and my incentive was to remain, even though the discipleship was not easy. You cannot organize an annual pilgrimage to Chartres with five to six thousand students by putting a small ad in the newspaper! A militant determination was required, but it was of a different nature from that of the organized political minorities whom we were never tempted to imitate. At the same time, we had to beware of the opposite kind of temptation: an outright stance of keeping in the background, which would have been an unpardonable cowardice. Many of those young people found themselves utterly lost and anonymous in that impersonal, urban and academic environment. They had to be helped to adjust to the cultural effervescence offered by the large schools of the arts and sciences. Our job was very different from that of the chaplains at the École Polytechnique or the École Centrale who were dealing with classes of a hundred or so students previously selected, first from *classes préparatoires* and then by highly competitive examinations. We were facing thousands of girls and boys who were flooding into the *propédeutiques,* coming from everywhere and nowhere. Having left the relatively stable world of the *lycée,* they were plunged into the vast gulf of the university, without supervision, without anything to help them get their bearings; in a word, they were "deconditioned". I looked back and compared my own days as a student in the same classrooms, on the same benches. The experience of freedom had been exhilarating for me and the greatest of benefits. But that kind of freedom was precisely what many of them did not like: they saw it as an abandonment.

JEAN-LOUIS MISSIKA: *Their perception was not false, because circumstances were different.*

LUSTIGER: For me those first years had been so very stimulating. I was discovering culture; they were bored by their studies. . . . I had been hardened by the war and other circumstances; they had just emerged from adolescence and felt very insecure. We would have failed in our function and mission if we had not done everything possible to help them to adapt to the university, that vast space of lost footsteps, more like a cavernous railway station than a place of learning—especially the arts section.

WOLTON: *Let us come back to your spiritual itinerary and your ministerial choices.*

LUSTIGER: During those years my sacerdotal ministry brought me a joy that no one could take away, but I was also subjected to its restrictions, fatigue and contradictions. We had to treat students as equals and yet not abdicate our roles as priests and adults. The right balance was not always easy to achieve.

WOLTON: *Speaking of this, there is a theme that up to now has not been much discussed—that of the students' "emotional frustration" or "sexual frustration", as it was called then. Protests were just beginning. How did you view this problem at the Sorbonne?*

LUSTIGER: As normal for young people between seventeen and twenty-five who are attaining control of their sexuality and emotional life.

WOLTON: *Then, in your memory, it did not present a particular problem?*

LUSTIGER: It held an important place, but not any more or less than when I was young, even if it was expressed differently.

WOLTON: *That is not, however, the way the historical and social imagery of the Sixties has been constructed. With the emergence of demands for sexual liberation, it seems that there was a break with the generation of students who came immediately after the war.*

LUSTIGER: The break was more evident in the behavior of society in general. The student world was a reflection of this changing behavior. It exaggerated rather than created it.

But to come back to the apostolic mission: those young people whom I served as priest became a marvelous and irreplaceable gift for me. Helping them to discover themselves and God was an invaluable stimulant for spiritual life. The mission of urging others to pray reminded us of our own duty to pray, even when the prayer is poor. The mission and desire to celebrate the Eucharist led to an intense reflection on its place in the Church's life. But it was also a period of harsh clashes. The questions you have been asking were constantly being posed by all sorts of interlocutors, sometimes ferociously, sometimes connivingly, sometimes ambiguously. And there were still so many other questions! I was obliged to deal with them even when they no longer interested me—because there does come a time when you turn the page, when a question seems to have been superseded, even if it has not been exhausted! Really, I loved all those students passionately. I realized it when I left them.

WOLTON: *But it was a rather uncertain period for the Church. There was even a growing indifference to her.*

LUSTIGER: I felt that I was living in a time of prodigious grace, even if elsewhere it was considered a time of disintegration and destructuring. It is true that evidence shows that there were issues raised then that prefigured later movements. Was I blinded, or did God protect me and keep me out of things? I do not know, but I did not share the feelings of doubt that surrounded me. I committed myself with all my heart to the struggle that involved the welfare of students and their world. But I believe that all those disputes, that polemical atmosphere—connected in part with the age group and the setting—would have worn me out eventually. On the other hand, there was no chance of falling asleep from boredom!

The Perception of Vatican II

WOLTON: *In this context, what was your reaction to Vatican II? Were you more impressed by the christological refocusing of* Lumen gentium *or by the missionary thrust of* Gaudium et spes?

LUSTIGER: The Council was a phenomenal grace, a time of great gifts from God. I have described the Church's minority position in society as a whole; however, it was not noticed by most Catholics, or only partially so. Those who had the intuition of it were most often those with the most outspoken missionary aims. However, some of them had adopted ways that were not ours. We held fast to the vision that the Church must receive herself from God in her sacramental reality and in the Faith. Other people, in their desire to join up with those who had drifted away, seemed tempted to abandon what seemed essential to us.

MISSIKA: *For example?*

LUSTIGER: We felt that sacramental life, faithfulness to the sacramental form of life (which was regarded by too many people as a sociological adherence) was fundamental. What was being called "the cultic", in a reductionist way, was sometimes placed in opposition to the living witness to the Gospel. For us, the sacramental reality was not only of a ritual nature: it constituted one of the privileged places where the mystery of God appears, making itself accessible to men.

MISSIKA: *Nevertheless, you have alluded to your feeling of solitude. . . .*

LUSTIGER: It was more like a feeling of difference, of being in disagreement with commonly accepted ideas, with the accepted "truths" of the moment. There were compensations, albeit rare—but that simply made them all the more valued: having my mission repeatedly confirmed by the archbishops of Paris, having my preoccupations converge with those of personalities as different as La Pira, Mauriac, Guitton, Ricoeur, Lichnerowicz and so many others who were wonderful interlocutors, and having the opportunity to meet Pope John XXIII and then Paul VI. The Council shattered the provincialism of the Church's life and enlarged horizons. We were particularly impressed by the evolution of ideas and practices in the Church from a twofold point of view: that of spiritual and Christian coherence and that of intellectual rigor, in particular in the use of Scripture. Help began to come between 1963 and 1965. Currents of thought began to take shape among the best-informed theologians, and, in the name of an epistemological type of reflection, they criticized the confusion of concepts and the too-simple identification of the contents of the Gospel, even the absolute, with the events of daily life.

MISSIKA: *You spoke about the influence of May '68 on the Church, but you have not told us what your personal thoughts were. Did you feel the effects of this upheaval?*

LUSTIGER: We were in the post-Council period. The "death of God" and "secular city" theologies were just beginning to reach France. I was sensitive to the trend, but I was hardly a good observer of what was going on in the Church. I was too much absorbed by my mission in the privileged but circumscribed canton of French intellectual life and scarcely ever kept company with other ecclesiastical circles. An important contact took place when we asked a hundred or so priests to help us out on the pilgrimage to Chartres. Those who responded more or less agreed with what we were doing. But a gap in sensibilities was already striking in '68—and how much more so in '69 when I changed ministries.

WOLTON: *You disagreed with the prevailing mood of the "sharing and communing" kind. . . .*

LUSTIGER: I agreed with the feeling but not the pathos, with the earnestness but not the woolly thinking! The "fusional" aspect seemed questionable. The company of psychologists teaches one to pick out the "archaic" aspect—in the psychoanalytical sense of the word—of phenomena that are in principle religious but that are uncertain—if not suspect—from the point of view of equilibrium and rationality. My idea of the mystical event, the spiritual event, is too elevated to be mixed up with everything else. The research on the state of religious consciousness was a great preoccupation during the prewar and early postwar periods. The fusional itineraries were more like substitutes for religion.

MISSIKA: *You have not spoken about your reaction, in this context, to Vatican II.*

LUSTIGER: The Council brought a call for more freedom and Christian responsibility. For some Catholics, it was the occasion for a "deconditioning", according to a word I used earlier. And for them, 1968—when, for large sections of society, deconditioning was experienced as a freedom—was like a confirmation that they had chosen the right path. I recognized in the Council old premonitions, more or less obscure, and, at the same time, the reaffirmation of the common Faith. Take the declaration concerning the Jews: I had never seen the Church as a persecutor, but, knowing that persecutions had existed and that Christian nations bore the responsibility for them, I deemed it to be in conformity with the internal coherence of the Church and with Christians' honor that such a statement be made. Similarly, we knew the weight of history, knew that in the past the Church could be oppressive. One of the most contested declarations, the one on religious liberty, represented—in spite of possible imprecisions—a finally recognized, finally attested obvious fact. These texts brought the confirmation of what the Church, the one in which I had believed, actually was. The constitution *Gaudium et spes* seemed to elucidate fairly the relationship between the temporal and the Church; it taught us the respect for all and the sense of pride in the Faith; it was a word of freedom addressed to the whole world. The visit of Paul VI to the United Nations was a brilliant illustration of this, just as his meeting with the Patriarch Athénagoras was an illustration of ecumenism. And the constitution *Dei verbum* brought to light Christian sources that had been long buried. Something was definitely changing. . . .

As for myself, I was ready to change ministries. Cardinal Veuillot's death had upset my plans. In fact, from the time he had arrived in Paris, Monsignor Veuillot had said, "You were named director of the Centre Richelieu in '59; you will leave it no later than '69, more likely in '68. What are you prepared to do next?" I had replied, "Urban life, in spite of its monstrous side, fascinates and attracts me. I love the city, I love Paris. How can Christian communities be made to thrive here? Given the new constraints of urban life, what changes can the Council's call for revival bring about?" I was wondering whether the intense experience of lay participation in Church life that I had known in the student world could be transposed outside to the parishes. Cardinal Veuillot had requested that I see him again on this subject one year before the foreseen termination of my duties as chaplain.

MISSIKA: *Did you find that there was a connection between Vatican II and May '68? How did the Church manage May '68?*

LUSTIGER: The Church, both its members and pastors, was going to relive what I had been through in the university. The effects of May '68 transformed the Council's hope into its exact opposite. Instead of renewing the institution by an effort of interior conversion and rejuvenation, there was a deconditioning of people who felt their heritage to be an oppression and an alienation. They "alienated" themselves and were in a sense going to change dramatically. They "decompensated", as psychologists say. It was plain to see that the same mechanisms that had been used at the university were being reproduced in the clerical institution.

MISSIKA: *Did this negative judgment on the Church's crisis lead you to have doubts—I mean serious ones—about your choice of vocation? Did you experience a personal crisis at this point? Did you ask yourself if you had taken the wrong road?*

LUSTIGER: Not in the terms in which you pose the question. I had begun to make various plans, all quite vague, to present to Cardinal Veuillot. But he died, and I had to apply myself to the tasks at hand, especially since the events of May '68 occurred at that juncture. It was not a time to dream but to hold fast. In the meantime, Monsignor Pézeril, Auxiliary Bishop of Paris, said to me, "You should become a parish priest." Initially, I put up a fierce resistance; then in the end I accepted, without any discussion, the parish proposed to me.

WOLTON: *How old were you?*

LUSTIGER: I was born in 1926; thus, I was forty-three. It was an abrupt change. For the first time since my ordination, I had a free summer, a vacation, since I no longer had a summer camp or a pilgrimage to the Holy Land or anything like that to prepare. I turned over the Centre's key to my successor at the end of June.

A Trip to the United States

WOLTON: *How did you spend this vacation?*

LUSTIGER: I went on a two-month tour of the United States. It was tremendously interesting, especially after what I had witnessed in '68. I had only one question in my head: What was urban life like there?

MISSIKA: *You were alone?*

LUSTIGER: Yes. I met some fascinating people who helped me to understand what I was discovering. The country was a mirror of Europe and also, it seemed to me, a certain anticipation of our future, in some domains at least. The American Catholic church could give me a foretaste of what was likely to happen here, in spite of obvious differences. I saw the devastating effects of a turbulence comparable to May '68 among certain laymen and a part of the clergy and the religious; but I also saw spiritual resources, a human and religious potential that we were lacking. I also observed, in conflicts that were sometimes harsher than ours, a greater mutual tolerance.

WOLTON: *Was the American voyage a success as far as your interest in urban problems was concerned?*

LUSTIGER: It was all the more so since, in Europe and especially in France, the intellectual fashion of the times would have had the Church model herself on the functionalism of planners who were proposing separate areas for the main urban activities: residence, workplace, commerce, leisure, etc. It was alleged that distances no longer imposed the same limitations as in the past. Suddenly, the parish, based on the model of the rural village, seemed completely outdated; the city of the future was going to regroup a freer and more mobile population by centers of interest. This functionalism had already been applied to the reorganization of several worship centers in a few large European cities. But American urbanization, which was surely not lacking in means, had already demonstrated the drawbacks of these theories. The appropriation of space was, on the contrary, the most important factor of an urbanization that had been much less planned than ours. Territorial communities were inescapably being reformed in the urban fabric, adapting to mobility and composing megalopoli with functionality.

WOLTON: *What was your intellectual discovery?*

LUSTIGER: American sociology with its fantastic system for conducting surveys. I was particularly interested in religious sociology. I brought back a huge crate of books, very well known in the United States, of which the greater part had not been translated into French.

The debates on the subjects of the "secular city" and "the death of God" were the *dernier cri* in France at the time. Imagine my surprise at finding that the matter was already passé in the United States. There were also many other things to discover: a reflection on the past and present of European culture and its relationship to other civilizations, something that is more "legible" in that country of immigrants, the relevance of psychological practices: I learned that they are staggeringly abundant and have a strong influence on the new American culture. In the spiritual domain, I had a close look at the Catholic charismatic renewal then in full expansion and as yet unknown in Europe. As for the life of the churches, among other fascinating experiences, I was very much interested by the results of an experimental project conducted by the Protestant churches for the creation of "new types of pastoral ministry". Everything that we would imagine and attempt to do in France in the next ten years had already been done and assessed by this project, whose conclusions were more or less negative. The only "pastoral ministry" that was working was the one defined by these structural circumstances: relationship to the community, service of the Word, worship, organization of charity, personal relationship to the faithful, etc. All that saved me a lot of time in the following years.

WOLTON: *What were the arguments on the death of God?*

LUSTIGER: It was a matter of theorizing the disappearance of the religious and the transcendent in a world dominated entirely by rationality. Thus, to be true to itself, Christianity had to announce its own death. The advent of the human spirit went as far as the self-destruction of all figuration of the sacred or of the divinity in man.

Paradoxically, it was the Americans who produced this theory of secularization, whereas their civilization is deeply impregnated with religiosity and the biblical tradition—much more so than ours. And in comparison, our culture seemed to be much more cut off from its biblical roots and explicit references to Christianity.

MISSIKA: *Were you not swayed by these arguments?*

LUSTIGER: No. I was trying to diagnose what we were living through, what this shock meant for us. It seemed to me that the effort of renewal that the Council had hoped for was turning into the nightmare of a society in crisis, an identity crisis. I had become acquainted with this adolescent stage in the academic world; but when it was applied to social bodies like the clergy or traditional Catholic milieus, it took on fantastic proportions in depth, scope and risks. I could not understand how it was that, in a trial whose terms were relatively easy to name, some people would remain steadfast while others got carried away. It was then that I felt a need to reroot myself in what was the very foundation of my choices in life. I began to re-examine many things that since my ordination—absorbed by other pressing matters—I had not forgotten but had more or less laid aside. I had never known so much external questioning of culture, of society and especially of the Church. I often mused in those days that my fidelity was a gift. I could in no way take credit for it; it had been paid for by the history that I had inherited. I also recalled these words: "If we are faithless, he [God] remains faithful" (2 Tim 2:13). "For the gifts and the call of God are irrevocable". That is a quote from the Epistle to the Romans (11:29), itself taken from the Old Testament. Paul reaffirms it at the moment when he wants to describe the irrevocable gifts made to Israel. "God is faithful" was the episcopal motto of Monsignor Courcoux in Orléans. It seemed that our faith was being put to the test by that part of paganism, in every person, that had not yet been converted. I had the impression that I was facing the temptation of being unfaithful to God rather than the temptation of a meticulously articulated intellectual objection. Yes, it was like being tempted to worship idols. That was symptomatic of a profound crisis in Western society whose ins and outs we were unable to discern. We were living with the illusion of an optimistic society.

WOLTON: *But do you associate the shock you have been speaking about with a crisis in the Church or in society?*

LUSTIGER: The doubts brought about by '68 did not seem to disturb modern reason at all; scientific rationality and technical progress were never in danger of being seriously subverted by this "sneeze". But there was a crisis concerning society's goals. People began to see that the tide of technological expansion was not irreversible. And the enthusiasm provoked by the Council did not seem to be sufficiently shared in a France that had suddenly entered an unforeseen critical period and was hardly capable of welcoming the promise that the Council represented.

Arrival at Sainte-Jeanne-de-Chantal

WOLTON: *It appears that the change from the Latin Quarter to the Sixteenth* arrondissement, *from student chaplain to parish priest, was not so easy, given your personal situation and the social climate in the aftermath of May '68. . . .*

LUSTIGER: Finding myself on the Right Bank, at the far end of the sixteenth district, I felt uprooted and longed for my beloved *Rive gauche.* It happened that on some evenings I would ride across Paris on my Solex just to take a turn, ever so quickly, around my old haunts, the streets of the Latin Quarter, not daring to stop for fear of being recognized. Sainte-Jeanne-de-Chantal was like a foreign land, a land of exile. Ten years later when I had to leave my parish, I wept once again: I realized just how much I had come to love that group of dissimilar parishioners from whom I was about to part. I had come to know them, and I was bound to them by a mutual friendship, strong and indelible.

But in 1969, the title of curé had theoretically disappeared from the official nomenclature. Thus, I was appointed *"Responsable d'une Équipe Pastorale"* [Leader of a Pastoral Team]—I believe that the words *de base* may even have been included in the title. That produced the initials REP . . . , which in my memories of military service stood for *Régiment Étranger de Parachutistes* [Foreign Regiment of Parachutists].

WOLTON: *How do you explain this* basiste *behavior that dominated the Church then?*

LUSTIGER: After 1968, the refusal of institutional hierarchies was a common phenomenon in clerical circles as well. Hence, the vocabulary had to be changed. That indicated that there was a strong desire for *nouveauté* which, in theory, could be justified as long as there was a respect for what had to remain and could not be sacrificed to novelty for the sake of novelty or difference for the sake of difference. So I docilely began to say to the parishioners that they no longer had a "curé" but an "REP".

MISSIKA: *And how did they react?*

LUSTIGER: It very quickly became clear that it was wiser to accept the title of curé, which the parishioners used spontaneously. The fact remained, however, that having come from the Latin Quarter, I was from another world. I felt that I was having to make a leap backward of at least one generation. I discovered not only students' parents but their grandparents. And I began to understand something that I had not seen so distinctly when I had been a student chaplain: their family roots. I came into contact with the slowness of human life and with society's inertia.

MISSIKA: *You discovered conformity?*

LUSTIGER: I knew about student and academic conformity, but I discovered another kind that struck me all the more because it was completely unfamiliar. I also encountered different sacerdotal life-styles. There were wide gaps in the clergy's ages. I became the leader of a group of priests who were markedly unlike those with whom I had lived and worked until then. My "vicars"[1] —I was not used to that expression—represented a great diversity not only in age but in experience, origins and education. . . . Very quickly I began to detect the self-denial specific to the Parisian clergy. Each priest, in his own way, had carried out his mission, faithful to his vocation. Heaven alone knows

[1] In France, the parish clergy consists of a *curé* (pastor) and *vicaires* (assistant pastors). —TRANS.

at what cost! The older ones, in particular, introduced me to the beauty of a sacerdotal life entirely and humbly devoted to the service of the people. Nevertheless, that first year was difficult!

Moreover, I took over my functions just at the moment when the decrees for applying the liturgical reform came into effect. Quite a few of the parishioners were not prepared for that transformation. Nobody attributed the responsibility for the changes in rites to me personally, but perhaps I did follow the official texts a bit too strictly. Even so, I drew on my previous experience of liturgical innovation only parsimoniously! I ran counter to the customs, to the ways of doing things, in so many domains. I was "maladjusted"! And, as always, in situations of this type, one has a tendency to shift the blame for one's own failure to adapt to those around—in any case, to be unfair.

WOLTON: *Ultimately, what is the most important thing you will have learned from your experience as a curé?*

LUSTIGER: I was struck by the continuity that exists in a parish. Most of the parishioners had lived in that peaceful neighborhood for a long time, whereas in the student world, I had been dealing with generations who were replaced every two or three years. There are certain experiences that can be understood only over the length of a lifetime, from birth to death. In the parish, I became acquainted with the deep wellsprings of memory, the lasting influence of events and their transmission from one generation to another. I was only the third curé of that parish, which was just my age since it had been founded in 1926. . . .

I listened with a growing interest to what so many people in the neighborhood told me about what had been going on there for half a century. I strolled through streets that were often empty, getting to know, little by little, the real life behind the façades. Certainly, I was in the fashionable *seizième* [sixteenth], just to the south of the charming old village of Auteuil, and there were a few prestigious and tranquil streets lined with solid bourgeois apartment houses dating from the nineteenth century and inhabited by families with deep roots in Paris. But the parish was more varied than it had appeared at first sight. There were also the remnants from the time of the *fortifs* and the *zone*[2] and what remained of a suburb of small houses, still rural before the war, I was told: it was an early housing development for the working classes, some of whose first occupants were still living there. The postwar construction boom had erected apartment buildings that had been filled by a wave of young

[2] The old walls of Paris (*fortifications* or *fortifs,* for short) were torn down only at the end of the nineteenth century. The area just outside the walls was known as the *zone.* Many social outcasts and marginal people had settled there in hastily built slums that had to be progressively destroyed.—TRANS.

couples twenty years earlier: in '69, their children were just starting to leave the nest. Woven into all this were the various layers of immigrants, beginning with the Alsatians after 1870, the Russians after 1917, the Spaniards after 1936, and finally the Portuguese who were then coming to France in great numbers. I was given epic accounts of how the church had been built; it had been finished just before my arrival. It was a large structure standing before the Porte de Saint Cloud, and for several decades it had mobilized so much energy and generosity on the part of all the parishioners. . . .

MISSIKA: *Given the reluctance with which you had gone there, how did you succeed in transforming the situation?*

LUSTIGER: Following 1968, a seething caldron of ideas, which had been accumulating for more than twenty years, had shaken up many long-held assumptions about the parish. In short—and I shared these prejudices—it was felt that everything or almost everything that had been classically thought of as making up parish life had to be questioned: territorial priority rather than joining elective groups; the development of private and family life to the detriment of professional tasks and social commitments; a preponderance of acts of worship over other forms of Christian life, etc. Moreover, it was being predicted that more and more urban parishes would be emptied, since increasing numbers of Parisians were leaving the city on weekends. And added to all this, there was the dissatisfaction expressed by the active minorities about the anonymity, the formality of the large Sunday congregations. The *grand-messes* were no longer very well thought of. . . .

I was wrestling with my thoughts, groping around to find a mission for myself in this section of Paris, whose social and religious coherence I had not yet been able to grasp from the assortment of jobs I had taken on.

WOLTON: *What did you do that differed from the fashion of the times?*

LUSTIGER: The point of departure and the heart of my action was the Sunday Mass. I had been led to it by a conviction and an observation. All my previous experience had taught me—from the time of my own baptism—that God's action in the sacraments has an extraordinary power. My anthropological reading also supported this. Thus, I was unable to accept for very long that worship in a parish should be depreciated in the eyes of those who were participants. On the other hand, I said to myself that every Sunday, several thousand people in the parish were choosing to devote one or two hours to "go to Mass". The Church was not empty. In fact, after the post office, it was the area's facility that had the most "customers". . . . And they were "customers" whose motivations must have been strong, even if they were not very explicit.

I soon began to focus all my efforts on making the Sunday Mass a privileged time, rich in meaning, joy and spiritual beauty. It did not seem exaggerated to spend a whole day preparing it by reflection and prayer. I felt that I owed that assiduity to the faithful. The conditions in which the Mass takes place (the songs, music, participation of the congregation, involvement of the celebrant, etc.) ought to permit each individual to hear the call that God addresses to him personally and to respond to it together with the other members of the community. It was important to break down the barriers and solitude of city dwellers who ignore each other, but to do this without depriving them of the freedom that they were justifiably looking for. Anonymity in itself is not negative. It can be a favorable occasion for a free decision. Each Sunday came to be a *fête,* for me and for the parishioners. As the years passed, the efforts and talents of many (musicians, etc.) were pooled for this celebration. We lived with the rhythm of these weekly rendezvous where the Word of God created the event. Over time, the congregation's attitude changed so much that the joy of our meeting became visible, even for someone who was only passing through. I was, as you can imagine, very happy about this.

The configuration of the parish was discernible in that group, so diverse, who had decided to be a part of the Sunday congregation. It remained to be seen whether they could do more, something other than meeting for these weekly celebrations of the Eucharist.

WOLTON: *Did you continue to keep in touch with the intellectual world of the Left Bank while you were at Sainte-Jeanne?*

LUSTIGER: No, I was at the other end of Paris. For ten years, my participation in the ferment of ideas was only from afar. I immersed myself in a more personal undertaking. I went back to disciplined reading and chose a few special interlocutors in the domains of the human sciences and theology—among the theologians, I read Hans Urs von Balthasar in particular. I read and studied the Scripture more intently. That required a long and slow effort of internalization and meditation spreading over the entire time I spent there. Actually, I was sheltered in "the cleft of a rock". I was able to make new acquaintances. I began to explore Judaism again, and I reread many works that I had gone through too quickly. Finally, after a few years, I found an environment that was as stimulating as the one I had known before.

WOLTON: *How did you manage to make the parish more active?*

LUSTIGER: The difficulty was to find an adequate form of mobilization. In the preceding thirty years or so, all sorts of models had influenced the

French pastorate. Everybody was trying to open up the parish boundaries so as to improve the organization of evangelization. But, in the end, I realized that the parish, which had been criticized for so long, was and still is the foundation for that mission. However, it was clear that it could no longer content itself with routine ways of doing things. Changes had to be made, as had been pointed out by a whole generation of priests who, after the war, had been variously marked by the fame of Saint-Séverin, by Michonneau's book, *Paroisse, communauté missionaire,* by Jacques Loew's[3] reflections on his Marseilles experience and by so much more.

WOLTON: *What were your criteria for measuring your effectiveness?*

LUSTIGER: Of course, we looked at numbers: counting those who participated in the Masses, in catechism, in the sacraments, in other activities, etc. But these quantitative criteria were not at all sufficient or suitable for what we were trying to measure: our fidelity to the content of the Faith—not just the fidelity of the priests but of the laity as well. That is why there was a high priority in putting our common heritage—the Word of God and his love communicated in sacramental life—in everybody's hands.

In the practices then current in France, this spiritual, scriptural and dogmatic patrimony was usually accessible only to the clergy. It was more the custom for laymen to share certain jobs so as to "give a helping hand to Monsieur l'Abbé" than to share the common treasure of the Faith. The access of laymen to real responsibilities implied that we priests were placing ourselves with them before the gift of God's Word. The criteria for measuring our effectiveness did not depend on anyone's social standing or abilities. Everyone was led to ask himself, "Am I being faithful to the Word received from God?" Thus, it is God who determines the criteria.

MISSIKA: *Why must fidelity to God's Word lead to action? Why not simply to contemplation? All the more so since there is no standard for judging your success. If the only question is fidelity, it is hard to understand the logic behind the Church's action.*

LUSTIGER: This is precisely where the originality of the Christian faith is found. The Word of God is not a poem, a collection of elevating thoughts or a book to be left to the meditation of believers. It is God himself who is speaking and acting so that I will act and respond to him. God gives me life

[3] The old parish church of Saint-Séverin (in the Latin Quarter) had pioneered the liturgical renewal. Father Michonneau's work in a suburban parish had produced a model for Sunday Masses. Father Joseph Loew was one of the faithful "worker-priests" in the early Fifties.—TRANS.

because he loves me. He has me share his love for all men, my brothers. He unites me with his action. This act of God that I have just described in subjective terms, in the first person singular, is given to us by Christ in the objectivity of the history of salvation. When members of the Church—priests and laymen—receive, share and transmit this Word, they are letting themselves be seized by God's action, which leads them to transform all domains of existence—social, cultural, familial, etc. Most often this action provokes clashes within the Christian community and with the society surrounding it. There is nothing new in this: from the Sinai desert to the martyrs of Korea, the living Word gives to those who listen and put it into practice the lucidity necessary for remaining faithful to the light in a world plunged in obscurity.

For example, when parents come to present an infant for baptism, it is very easy to say that it is merely a social rite, inscribed in the family tradition, in the French tradition, without any particular significance. But how can we appreciate what happens in the secret of consciences? Is it not somewhat presumptuous to judge the authenticity of somebody's religious request merely on the basis of his personal opinions and the limitations of his language? Some parents can have a different religious language—indeed, one that is much less refined than ours. But sacramental behaviors, acts of faith cannot be reduced to a social habit inscribed in customs. We would not be believers if we were not convinced of this. In fact, the infant brought to be baptized is called by God; he is chosen, must I add, in the same way that every person has been called and chosen. This child was already loved by God in his mother's womb, and he is to be enrolled among those who will bear the face of the Messiah in this world.

MISSIKA: *But what about all the others? What do you make of all those who have not been brought by their parents?*

LUSTIGER: All men are called and loved by God, but even so, not all will resemble the Messiah during their lifetimes. Those who do have a particular role in history, in spite of their weaknesses and limitations; they become one with Christ to work with him so that all men will know the filial love of God, their Father. Israel's election has been enlarged to include all nations, and those who are visibly associated with Christ fulfill the eternal mission that God has given his beloved Son. It is the children of God who must attest that God loves the world and that the world is not lost or left alone with its nothingness. As for knowing who, among those to whom we are sent, will or will not respond to his call, that remains God's secret.

II

WHAT DOES IT MEAN TO BE A CHRISTIAN?

The Parish

DOMINIQUE WOLTON: *You were a parish priest at a time when the parish as a source of identification for Christians was often criticized, because the apostolic movements, specialized by age groups or professions looked more effective, more promising. What is your position in this debate that has been going on for a generation?*

JEAN-MARIE LUSTIGER: It was not so long ago that the parish was coming in for sharp criticism: "It's archaic, it belongs in the village! There's no point in continuing to use it in cities with their diversified functions, public transport, etc." But this seemingly sociological reflection hid a difficulty: one can "canonize" a functional and conflictual organization of society only by renouncing its "restructuring" and providing a minimum of communion, which is earnestly desired by everybody. The Catholic experience of the Church does not deny human differences but embraces them, insisting that they be recognized and accepted in a fraternity that overcomes divisions. Hence, it is very important for Christian life, as it is for contemporary societies, that there be places for Christian "recomposition" of a fragmented and scattered social body. By his participation in this process, each Christian has access to the source of unity and communion with his brothers and sisters whoever they may be: there is only one Body, just as there is only one Spirit and one God and Father.

JEAN-LOUIS MISSIKA: *You are criticizing the functional division of society, and you think that the parish could serve as a remedy for this. Is your position shared by the clergy and some of the faithful?*

LUSTIGER: People who have civic, trade-union, professional or political responsibilities like to find places for meeting each other. From the Church's point of view, the specialization of movements according to their objectives, methods, options and spirituality remains valid. But, at the same time, a strong feeling has resurfaced: this legitimate diversity can be fruitful only if it recomposes itself with a confrontation and dialogue that are not simply the equivalent of the high-level negotiations that take place in the prime minister's office! The dialogue must be continuous and sacramental. It must be accepted as normal that the same Eucharist with its symbolic power brings together people who otherwise would tend to organize themselves into separate churches. There is but one Church.

Since around the time of Vatican II, there has been an interesting evolution in France. There used to be a widespread doctrine encouraging the division of functions. The parish took care of the "ordinary" Christian life: administering the sacraments, educating the children, looking after the elderly, celebrating the Mass, marriages, funerals, etc. And then there was the militancy—that is, the Christian presence in the world as it was, with its social organization. However, during the past twenty years, a reversal has taken place. The majority of the most committed Christians have become much more aware of the atheism or religious indifference in France; they have re-evaluated this division between the parish, the traditional place of worship, and the "movement", the place of discipleship and commitment. The movements have been trying to find the key elements for sacramental life within their own structures. This trend is very general.

WOLTON: *Then have we arrived at the second stage, which is a reawakening of interest in the parish?*

LUSTIGER: Conversely, in the parishes, Christians who had not wanted to get involved with organizations that were too rigid or to be subjected to overly restrictive precepts have now taken on responsibilities in various domains of social activity. The crisis that followed 1968 challenged classifications whose inadequacy had been discovered.

Today, it is plain to see that sacramental life—prayer, which forms the heart of Christianity—cannot be reduced to a worship that is cut off from activity: it is the Christian life that makes it possible for believers to act in the world. The parishes must be places where people who have these different commitments and responsibilities are brought together in the true unity of the Eucharist and the sacrament. Without this, there is no longer a Church.

Liturgy, Symbolism, Sacraments

WOLTON: *You have often mentioned the importance of the liturgy for you—just as important when you were a chaplain as when you were a curé. Is that because it allows for a mise-en-scène of the invisible?*

LUSTIGER: The liturgy is not a presentation of the invisible; it is the actualization of what has made itself visible. No one has seen or can see God. But he gives himself to be heard. Through the transmission of his Word, he gives himself to be seen: his presence is inscribed in human history. The people whom God has called to become one with Christ participate in his eternal mission during their temporal lives. We are meant to share in this action by which God has given himself to be seen, and the liturgy is the act by which those who have been called to do so receive as a grace and experience as a "thanksgiving" what God has given once and for all. The Eucharist that Christ celebrated on the eve of his Passion is the ritual of the Jewish Passover. Jesus, the Messiah, gives a new meaning to this celebration, an eternal value in that he identifies himself as the Lamb offered for the world's salvation. For him, the Messiah, and for Christians, his disciples, the Eucharist is the sacrifice of reconciliation and deliverance, it is the entry into the Promised Land; it gives access to God who has been merciful to us. Regarding this act, Jesus himself, according to Tradition, said to us, "Do this in memory of me." So when Christians celebrate the Mass, the memorial instituted by Jesus, they become participants in his offering and share in his revelation. Thus, what is his becomes ours, and what is ours becomes his. It is the presence—at every moment of history and to every human being—of the unique act of Jesus Christ fulfilled in history during his mortal life.

WOLTON: *The Christian liturgy is linked with a particular symbolic system. How is it different from other such systems that have punctuated human history?*

LUSTIGER: In the first place, the Christian symbolic system, like the Jewish one, is historical. However, the symbols are always connected with man's natural and biological condition. Cosmic symbols are universal and are found in all civilizations: the sun and the moon, fire and water. . . . The Jewish and Christian tradition reinterprets these cosmic symbols as a memorial of the historical events of salvation. In that respect, it is completely original.

MISSIKA: *Do you have examples?*

LUSTIGER: Ritual baths, acts of sacred ablutions, exist in all religions. The baptism given by John the Baptist was a rabbincal act that admitted pagans into the Covenant. Already it was a symbol of the Children of Israel's crossings of the Red Sea and the River Jordan in order to reach the Promised Land. Jesus Christ wanted to receive John's baptism before being, as the Gospel says, baptized with the baptism of his own death. Since then, when anyone—adult or infant—is baptized with water in the Church's Faith in the risen Lord, the priest's sacramental gesture recalls what John did when he baptized Jesus in the Jordan; it was a baptism that prophesied and testified to the death and Resurrection of Christ. Consequently, Paul teaches that through baptism "we have been plunged into the death and Resurrection" of Christ. The cosmic ritual of the bath (purification, engulfment, rebirth) has become secondary; it has been appropriated by the Messianic significance and the life of the Holy Spirit given by Christ's death and Resurrection.

Another example described in the Bible is the Passover celebration, which combines two rituals: one is agrarian, the offering of bread at harvest time; the other is nomadic, the offering of the lamb, the firstborn.... These rituals are found everywhere—among Africans, among the Peuls.... But in Israel this ritual taken from the agrarian and nomadic traditions became the memorial of the exodus from Egypt and the Covenant made at Mount Sinai. Then in the Christian tradition it becomes the Passover memorial celebrated by Jesus in his unique sacrifice, and the cosmic rites are made even more historic.

I insist on this point because we have entered a period when the relationship to the cosmos and sacred antiquity has been destroyed by the rational and scientific domination of the world. The moon is no longer the one of antiquity: man has walked on it. Even the human body has become the object of technical control. Many people have made these observations and concluded, "The symbolic world is disenchanted; it has lost its primitive magic. Man continues to use the original symbols, but he no longer knows quite what to make of them. It has become a game. The symbol has lost its fascination and power, and suddenly the world is emptied of the sacred. The gods are dead, the great Pan is no more,[1] the ancient world is no more. How can poetry and religion fit into a world deprived of symbols?" But, in fact, man's symbolic rooting in his corporal and cosmic condition is a part of his inalienable heritage. Even if that heritage has lost its power of immediate attraction and repulsion, the symbols remain the fruits and seeds, the guarantors and witnesses of what surpasses everyone and makes him live. What the symbol has lost in naïveté, it has gained and gives in reason and wisdom. The idea that the world is "creature" of God and hence an intelligible language has led the astronaut and the astrophysicist to marvel along with the Psalmist: "The heavens are telling the glory of God; and the firmament proclaims his handiwork."

Cosmic and anthropological symbolisms, no longer regarded as sacred, are re-absorbed by historical memory and integrated into the history of salvation, which has kept its meaning and continues to convey it today, even for the modern rational mind. The biblical and Christian symbolic systems for the sacraments have not been weakened by the fact that the cosmos has lost its sacredness, because they are a historical and spiritual memorial.

[1] This is a reference to words from a song by the popular French folksinger, Georges Brassens.—TRANS.

Furthermore, they restore to the cosmos the beauty that it has received from its Creator.

WOLTON: *Do you feel that now that reason has triumphed, the Church is rediscovering the necessity of this assumption and the importance of symbolic systems?*

LUSTIGER: We have hardly begun to be aware of this because, in the liturgical reform, we have succumbed to the fascination with rationalism. The intoxication with modernism has resulted in the elimination of too many of the natural symbolisms that were considered pagan, as though they had nothing to say; hence, they had to make room for a "new language" still to be invented, notably for the young. But this new language can be very deceiving when it has no historical and eschatological dimension. There was too much of a tendency to think that reforming meant tearing out all roots and starting over again. This is as incomprehensible—and also as opposed to man's condition—as the attitude of the most radical revolutionaries who, in urbanism or elsewhere, say, "Tabula rasa with the past!" It shows a great misunderstanding of history.

MISSIKA: *But is it not true that symbolism, even when it is linked with history, loses its savor in a disenchanted world?*

LUSTIGER: It cannot have the same savor, because history is irreversible. But can it acquire it? Or have you lost hope in creation?

WOLTON: *What has been lacking—I am completing Jean-Louis Missika's question—is an effort to reinterpret those symbols.*

LUSTIGER: In the Jewish and Christian tradition, the cosmic symbols have become historical acts. In fact, it is the biblical revelation that conserves the pagan heritage while rejecting its idolatrous fascination. The Bible delivers man from pagan idols, but at the same time it saves paganism's debris and restores its symbols.

MISSIKA: *Yes, but that does not answer the question I asked: modern man, when he accomplishes a symbolic act, is completely aware of what he is doing, and that constitutes a difference between him and the ancients.*

LUSTIGER: Certainly, it is not the same thing. Today, when the Passover is celebrated with matzos, when the Mass is said with unleavened bread and a cup of wine, the fruit of the vine; when we take branches on Palm Sunday or when water, the symbol of ablution, is used for baptism or for sprinkling the congregation at the Easter vigil, we may not understand the gestures and words in quite the same way as earlier generations understood them, but we still repeat the gestures and pronounce the same words, and by that very fact a part of the early heritage is reintegrated into our present consciousness. What we derive from those symbols is not measured by our interpretations. The ritual that keeps them in memory is preferable to the crude, irrational reprocessing in which our superrational but Dionysian civilization risks foundering. The salvaging of ancient symbols is salutary, whereas their uncontrolled reappearance, in a strictly superstitious sense, could produce the contrary effects.

WOLTON: *In a word, why did you place so much importance on the liturgy when you were at Sainte-Jeanne?*

LUSTIGER: Because the Christian liturgy is not primarily the fulfillment of rites; it is a historical act as a time and place of redemption, of salvation and God's presence; it is an act in which Christ's disciples participate in his unique history. There is no Christian existence without the sacraments and the liturgy; without them, Christianity becomes only an ideology.

WOLTON: *Then the liturgy is what prevents Christianity's transformation into an ideology?*

LUSTIGER: Certainly. That can be proved negatively: every ideological deviation from Christianity deforms or eliminates the liturgy and the sacraments. It is the liturgy that is the occasion for the Word of God to be given as a transmitted life, as coming from God and pronounced by Christ through the Spirit's power.

WOLTON: *And that is why the sacramental life is important?*

LUSTIGER: Every culture needs the sacred, and many of them have adopted the Catholic Faith; but at the same time the sacraments are the guarantee that this appropriation is not going to close in upon itself. Take the example that is a part of the major stakes of Catholic universalism. The Christian religion was born in the Mediterranean basin, a geographical area of bread and wine. Everywhere, from its origins—whether in the countries of central Asia or the mists of Scotland—the Catholic ritual has retained the elements of the Passover rite, bread and wine, in reference to the exodus. Today, once again, Christianity finds itself in very different civilizations, those of rice and millet. In this case, why not use these simple and fundamental nourishments to celebrate the Passover ritual? Why keep the bread and wine? Is it through narrow-minded conservatism? No, but the rite obliges all people, in their diverse cultures, to recognize that the Absolute, which was given to them as the hope of their salvation, appeared at a specific point in space and time, to a specific people in history. We have said it already: Jesus was born in Bethlehem of Judea. He was not born in Timbuktu or Tibet or Caen. He was born during the reign of Augustus Caesar, not that of Tamerlane or Napoléon. . . .

WOLTON: *Do you mean to say that access to universalism comes by the acceptance . . .*

LUSTIGER: . . . of that singularity. Hence, no one people can appropriate him for itself.

MISSIKA: *Yes, but that did not stop Westerners from appropriating him during at least ten centuries.*

LUSTIGER: True, but they have more or less disowned him in recent times.

WOLTON: *Perhaps, but it has not been all that long since they relinquished their exclusive possession, and then not willingly.*

LUSTIGER: No one ever does it willingly.

WOLTON: *Therefore, there was a universal access by the intermediary of a particular identity, that of Westerners. They, for reasons of power, took control of that access for ten centuries; and you would say that today there is a certain disappropriation?*

LUSTIGER: The appropriation has taken place twenty times, thirty times, a hundred times in fifteen centuries. You ask that question because you have forgotten the past. When the people of Israel had to accept that the pagans were entering into the Covenant, this did not mean that their Messiah was taken away from them but simply that the family was larger than they had thought. After the Greeks had finally accepted this Messiah in their language, they had to accept the fact that it was the Latins who were giving their language to the Church and changing her theological perspectives. In the first six or seven centuries of Christian history, outside of the Greco-Latin zone, there were liturgies as original and distinct as the Syriac, Chaldean, Armenian, Coptic and eastern Syrian rites, with different languages, reaching as far as India. Then came the Germanic liturgies and the evangelization of the Slavs with the invention of their alphabet by Cyril and Methodius. How difficult it was for all these people to feel dispossessed in their turn!

WOLTON: *But, to come back to the sacraments, do you feel that they are less important or more visible today? Since Vatican II, there has been a tendency to make them less mysterious, more intelligible, just when the* intégristes[2] *are reaffirming the necessity of the mystery.*

LUSTIGER: There is a perpetual temptation—it does not date from Vatican II but from the origin of all liturgy—to explain the liturgy, like those literary critics who take a poem by Baudelaire and claim to explain it from A to Z. If they were to succeed, there would be no mystery. But neither would there be a poem nor any other interpretations! The liturgy is a concrete act that calls on the symbolic and historical patrimony. Its meaning cannot be reduced to what the one who is taking part in it thinks about it. The rite carries a mystery whose symbolic richness is commensurate with the Word of God and the mystery of history. To reduce the liturgy to what any one generation can understand about it is to put it on the level with a ceremony for the Olympic Games or a Bastille Day parade. All you have to do is find a commentator with a warm and agreeable voice; he will explain everything you want to know!

WOLTON: *Consequently, you are rather more in favor of Latin for the liturgy?*

LUSTIGER: Not necessarily.

WOLTON: *Not necessarily, but you are not hostile to it?*

LUSTIGER: No, Latin marks a certain continuity in a specific cultural zone. The Germans and the Anglo-Saxons, who were much less affected by *latinité,* very quickly adopted other languages for their liturgy. And, in the ninth century, the Slavs—who were strangers to Byzantium as well as to the Greek and Latin worlds—kept their own language. Liturgical language is not a matter of doctrine, but the celebrant does not communicate better with the congregation simply because he speaks the vernacular.

MISSIKA: *In general, you are rather more favorable to preservation and opposed to changes in the rites?*

LUSTIGER: That depends on the changes. We have not witnessed the first liturgical reform in history, far from it; but it is the first to have altered the Latin rite so radically.

[2] The critics of the Second Vatican Council in general and especially of the liturgical reforms are called *intégristes* because they claim to preserve the integrity (that is, the purity and totality) of the old rites and beliefs.—TRANS.

WOLTON: *In what way was it radical?*

LUSTIGER: The Council's Constitution on the Liturgy set forth only general principles, but you have to consider the subsequent applications. It was academics, professors, who conceived this reform, which was preceded by a very remarkable scientific effort. Modern historical scholarship on the liturgy began to take shape in the eighteenth century. Little by little, it instituted a historical and "genetic" criticism of sources. Between 1930 and the Council, liturgical specialists pointed to the basilical liturgy of the *belle époque,* the period between the fourth and fifth centuries, as a model. It was the ideal that had to be reconstituted! And the reconstitution was made. It was intelligent, but perhaps a slower evolution, less resolute and more respectful of permanence and continuity, would not have resulted in such a serious traumatism for many believers. If the significance of the rites as historical memory inscribed across generations had been more accurately measured, the progress in reform would probably have been much more gradual.

WOLTON: *Yes, but some people saw a "democratization" in this determination to make the liturgy and sacramental life more accessible, involving more participation.*

LUSTIGER: Democratization? That was surely contrary to what the majority of people wanted.

WOLTON: *Possibly there was a kind of popular ignorance that the liturgical reform was meant to diminish.*

LUSTIGER: But it ran counter to the desire of most of the faithful. In the end, what they wanted most was silence, music and the rite anchored in memory. The idea of "active participation", which was one of the Council's objectives, definitely reflects a certain resolution. But must that objective be carried out like Mao's cultural revolution, by forcing people to take part? Would it not have been wiser to introduce it much more gradually? Perhaps we handled this transformation so willfully and arbitrarily that an effect opposite from the one desired has been produced, and that, it seems to me, reveals a lack of historical sense.

The architects of liturgical reform felt, not without justification, that the rites had become obscure because no one knew anymore why they were there and what they signified. The language was blamed, but translation alone was not sufficient. The idea was to make the rites come alive again, to give them more transparency. But often, the explanation was substituted for the rite, the commentary for the symbol. A rite, a symbol, must be historically grounded and have a certain social universality. It is not a priest or a group of laymen who can invent a symbol. Besides, inventing symbols literally makes no sense. All the great revolutions have wanted to invent symbols; the only ones that "worked" were those that were salvaged from and enriched by history and the people's memory. The use of the cosmic symbols in the Jewish and Christian tradition comes from history, and if this tradition has become a carrier of symbolic strength, it is because the history of human generations led by the Spirit has, in memory, an incredible power of identification and percussion.

MISSIKA: *Would you be in favor of returning a corporeal aspect to faith, by practices like fasting that have been very much on the decline for the past twenty years?*

LUSTIGER: Everything in contemporary culture is pushing us in that direction. The renewed attention to the body, a new sensibility based on the perceptible modes of expression—song, gestures, painting, etc.—making them accessible to everyone, all this allows us to regain an understanding of the high spiritual value of man's corporeal existence: God became man. The flesh speaks the Word. Consequently, Christian asceticism, far from being contemptuous of the body, assigns it its true destiny. It is the temple of the Spirit. The young generations are rediscovering what we had thought to be outdated—even though they do not always reinvent it well. Why has our generation been traumatized and wounded by these practices that were transmitted to it, to the point of getting rid of them? What has happened in the West during the past fifty years?

WOLTON: *Do you agree with Cardinal Ratzinger's statement concerning the liturgy: "For the Catholic, the liturgy is the common homeland, the very source of his identity. That is why it must be predetermined, invariable, so that through the rite the holiness of God is revealed"?*

LUSTIGER: Yes, fundamentally. But "invariable" does not mean uniform. From the beginning, the liturgy has taken on multiple forms, and it will continue to do so. But it has a particularity in that it is an objective expression of God's gift to his Church. A singer, an artist, projects his subjectivity onto his audience, who either identify with him or not. That determines his success; his strength of expression comes primarily from his subjectivity and the way in which he is able to translate it. But, in the Christian rite, the celebrant is the bearer of a significance that does not belong to him; it does not depend on his subjectivity. It is an act to which those who are gathered together consent. When the priest celebrates the Eucharist, it is he who speaks and makes the gestures, but it is in the name of Christ, head of all the faithful, that he is doing it. People do not come to see the priest but to celebrate the Lord's Eucharist. The theatrical performance is divided between the actors and spectators, but in the liturgy, all are both actors, collaborators with God, and spectators of the work of God in themselves.

MISSIKA: *But do priests always know how to explain the significance of the liturgy?*

LUSTIGER: If the priest has not reached a vigorous understanding of the Faith, he can feel that he is only a producer of ceremonies for social rites, one performer among others. For example, in the celebration of a marriage, it can seem, either rightly or wrongly, that the primary thing required of him is a certain decorum and that the strictly religious aspect that involves his most profound conviction is of secondary importance.

WOLTON: *But didn't the idea of liturgical reform arise because some believers were no longer aware of the sacraments' richness of meaning?*

LUSTIGER: In part. The simplification should have allowed the priest to become involved in a more authentic dialogue. But it turned out that the faithful thought that the clergy were doing too much in the way of dialogue, were asking too much of the congregation. When I was curé, I heard this said to me: "Just be glad that people come to see you. If you annoy us too much, we won't come at all." Our objective, and its difficulty, were to restore life to the ritual, thus to insert it more solidly into the lives of the faithful. But how? And to what extent? We had the feeling, not always correct, that the sacristy was on one side and the *place publique* was on the other. Had faith, worship and fidelity to Christ become prisoners of the sacristy? If they had, then they ought to be freed among the public, and the unity of life and faith recreated.

A second attempt consisted in increasing the emphasis on everyday life, *la vie de tous les jours,* that all-purpose expression in ecclesiastical language. Daily life was thought to be the place where the sacred and God could be revealed. And, by the way, that is not altogether false. However, we must not forget that the modern world knows other models of everyday life: *"métro, boulot, dodo."*[3] It is the factory, the supermarket, the office. It is life organized according to the life-styles of contemporary society: frozen dinners, hours spent in front of the television set, household tasks, wash-and-wear, the weekend here or there. But this social life does not create itself. It is organized on the basis of choices and rationalities that do not necessarily give up their places to other meanings. Take the factory, for example. It is created to produce goods at a lower cost for higher profits—in a word, to make money,

[3] "Subway, work, sleep": after '68, the words became the derisory term for the dull, laborious existence imposed by the social and economic system.—TRANS.

and just possibly to increase employment or perhaps to improve social relations, but it is definitely not there for expressing *états d'âme!*

In the end, individuals have to find a refuge in their private lives if they are to regain a little freedom. The different areas of human existence are caught up in an organizational network where the symbolic systems of life are reduced, measured and polarized on the basis of well-specified goals, of demanding plans and objectives that are often economic. When, as witnesses to Christ, we adopt such a rationale, pretending to bring faith and its symbolic structure into this practical world, we have taken the most difficult way. In these circumstances, there is no appropriate place for the expression of religious symbolism, since, by hypothesis, it will be either expelled or appropriated by the system.

MISSIKA: *Then you are more in favor of maintaining separate sites and times for the expression of religious symbolism?*

LUSTIGER: But we are obliged to do this! There are only a limited number of events, such as birth, death and marriage, that break the continuity of everyday life, times when men and women who are driven by a merciless routine can rediscover something that is not found anywhere else. A human being has so few moments of freedom in his life, instants where choices seriously influence the future. And these moments we have just mentioned certainly form a part of them. We pastors look on passing lives from the side of the road. In those secret but decisive moments, we see men and women asking for something that often they can barely express. Such a situation demands a great deal of receptivity on the part of priests, because such moments are brief—even if they have a tremendous significance for those who come to us. Therefore, we must do and give something that is not, precisely, what these individuals have elsewhere in their ordinary environments.

WOLTON: *Then you are opposed to what could be called the ideology of participation, which for a few years tried to reduce the separation between daily life and the places and times for prayer.*

LUSTIGER: There can be genuine participation only if there is first a differentiation. Otherwise, the participation is archaic, fusional, regressive;[4] the participation we ought to hope for and toward which we ought to strive unceasingly presupposes precisely the accentuation of differences.

[4] "Fusional" and "regressive" are borrowed from the psychoanalytical lexicon. "Fusion" reflects the inability to accept differences, whereas "regression" is the opposite of mental progress or development.—TRANS.

WOLTON: *However, only rarely are communion and differentiation associated. In general, communion is understood as a synonym for fusion.*

LUSTIGER: One of the aspects of our mission is to prevent this regression, especially if we pay attention to what the symbolism of the Church and parish represents.

WOLTON: *Yes, but priests have played a considerable role in fostering the desire for participation and secularization. The idea was: "Down with the archaism of rites and worship services, incomprehensible to the public. Let's make them commonplace, open them up"....*

LUSTIGER: That ideal or practice was spread not only by the clergy but was demanded by some of the faithful. It is the grave error of a society that, in its confusion, risks self-destruction.

WOLTON: *You are aware that, by saying that, one can justify a society that is, shall we say, more hierarchical. It is easy to go from the necessity of maintaining differences to the vision of a much more rigid and hierarchical order—one we have already known.*

LUSTIGER: I well understand how my remarks could be understood in that way. Similarly, the fusional discourse could be understood in an anarchical or fascist way. But I am pleading, on the contrary, for a true democracy in the strongest sense. Democracy—at least my conception of it—means the ideal of responsibility and hence of personalization. And personalization means distinction and differentiation of roles—differentiation also of the sacred. There can be no communion without acceptance of "the other". To consider that the distance in which the other person constitutes himself is a negation of communion is literally to deny the other person, and that amounts to reducing him or her to oneself. There can be no real communion with another person without the acceptance that he is different and without respecting that difference. It is true of men and women. It is true of parents and children. If parents fail to play their role as parents, the children cannot exist as children.

Christian Practice and Morality

WOLTON: *What happens during the Mass?*

LUSTIGER: The Mass is the act of a congregation: an *ekklēsia,* the Greek word that translates the Hebrew *Qahal* and that gave us the word ecclesiastic.

Everyone in the congregation has been "convoked" by God. The Church congregation is a structured body with a head and members, and its structure is "apostolic". Through Christ's Apostles and their successors, all acts of the Mass allow us to share in acts historically accomplished by Christ himself and deeply rooted in Israel's tradition. The Christian liturgy of the Mass combines the liturgy of the Word borrowed from synagogal worship and that of the meal taken from the family ritual for Passover.

The celebrant faces the congregation. He presides over and greets it in Christ's name. After having asked for the forgiveness of sins, the congregation listens to the proclamation of the living Word of God: readings from the Old Testament, the apostolic writings and the Gospels.

MISSIKA: *And the sermon?*

LUSTIGER: The priest who has read the Gospel elaborates on the passage by a commentary. Then the assembly professes the Church's Faith by reciting the *Credo* and intercedes for the needs of the world and the Church.

The celebrant presents the bread and wine and blesses it: "Blessed are you, Lord, God of all creation. Through your goodness we have this bread to offer, which earth has given and human hands have made. It will become for us the bread of life." "Blessed are you, Lord, God of all creation. Through your goodness we have this wine to offer, fruit of the vine and work of human hands. It will become our spiritual drink."

The altar is both the table for the feast and the place of sacrifice. At the beginning of the eucharistic prayer, the celebrant calls on the congregation to give thanks to the Heavenly Father in Christ's name, recounting the history of salvation from the creation to Christ's coming into the world. Next, the prayer invokes the power of the Spirit, and the celebrant, following the New Testament accounts, repeats the words that Jesus spoke over the bread and wine at the Last Supper. The congregation bows and remembers Christ's sacrifice made present by his Body and Blood. The memorial of the free offering of his life includes the living and the dead in a supplication for the Church.

The rite of Communion begins with the recitation of the Our Father, the prayer of all Christians. The celebrant breaks the consecrated bread and partakes of it before distributing it to the faithful. He then drinks the consecrated wine. After a prayer of thanksgiving for the gift received, he sends the congregation on its mission: those who have been incorporated in Christ through the eucharistic sacrament are to fulfill in their lives what they have received from this sacrament.

WOLTON: *What happens during Holy Week?*

LUSTIGER: Egeria, a fourth-century woman, kept a journal on her pilgrimage to Jerusalem and told about the Holy Week liturgies in which she took part. These same liturgies have spread throughout the Catholic world. On Palm Sunday, the Jerusalem liturgy brought together that city's Christians at the summit of the Mount of Olives. From there, they walked to the city, just as Jesus did in the Gospels' accounts. The procession ended up at the holy sepulcher, the site of Christ's death and Resurrection.

The last three days of Holy Week—Holy Thursday, Good Friday and Holy Saturday—allow us to follow historically, step by step, the last Passover that Jesus celebrated. On Holy Thursday, the liturgy of the Mass includes the washing of feet (Jn 13). By this gesture, Jesus made himself the slave of his Disciples, thus taking on the face of Isaiah's suffering Servant. During the night of Thursday to Friday, the Church remains in prayer, sharing what Jesus experienced in those hours: the descent to the Kedron valley, the struggle at Gethsemane, his arrest, his trial and the insults heaped upon him.

Friday, the day the Lord died, the liturgy is austere. First the congregation hears an account of the Passion according to Saint John, after which the celebrant invites them to share in a solemn intercession for the Church and all humanity. This is followed by the veneration of the Cross. The cross was the common means of execution for those condemned by Roman law as criminals, but, enlightened by the story of the Passion, Christians see Christ's Cross as a sign of love, life, victory and plenitude given by God. Since Christ's death, it has taken on an extraordinary symbolic richness. Its wood is linked with the tree of life in Genesis, and its four dimensions assume a cosmic meaning. After the veneration of the Cross, Communion takes place with the Eucharist, which has been consecrated the previous night.

A silence of twenty-four hours precedes the great Easter Vigil on the night of Saturday to Sunday. The vigil begins with a liturgy of illumination. The Easter candle symbolizes Christ's rising from the dead to become the light of the world who gives spiritual understanding to all his brothers. The liturgy of biblical readings, very long, starts with the narrative of the creation and goes on to the Resurrection by way of Exodus, the prophets and Saint Paul. It is on this night that catechumens are baptized, and along with them all the faithful renew the profession of faith made at their own baptisms. Then comes the eucharistic liturgy.

MISSIKA: *How do you identify a Christian?*

LUSTIGER: I call anyone who has been baptized a Christian. Through the act of baptism, he has been identified with Christ, because in sharing in Christ's baptism—that is, his death and Resurrection—he has been born to the condition of a child of God. At that moment, the Christian receives irrevocably the vocation to become what he has been called to be. He has been reborn: now it is up to him to live. That is my definition of a Christian. Whether a person practices or not does not make him any more or any less a Christian. Once baptized, he remains a Christian.

MISSIKA: *But sociologists and political scientists would reply that they have discovered significant differences—for example, in the vote of practicing and nonpracticing Christians, or in their opinions on fundamental questions such as abortion and marriage. . . .*

LUSTIGER: The question is to know what is determining: Is a Christian adherence identified with a certain form of culture? At one time, the Latins, the people of the Roman Empire, were Christians and the barbarians were not. Thus, one might think that the difference between the barbarians and the Romans was simply that the former were not Christians. But later, when the barbarians were baptized—indeed, became Catholics—the difference remained in spite of their shared Faith.

WOLTON: *But can a Christian be recognized "phenomenologically"?*

LUSTIGER: A Christian must never try to give himself the "air" of being a Christian. He would only be an actor, a Tartuffe, a blatant hypocrite. You know the great challenge: "I would find it easier to believe in their resurrection if they looked as though they were saved." In face of this Nietzschean accusation, some Christians have tried to look as though they were saved! But appearances do not count: you have to *be* a Christian. And when Christians are recognized as such, it is because of what God makes of us and not by any air that we may give ourselves. In the Gospel, Christ says to his Disciples, "By this all men will know that you are my disciples, if you have love for one another", and he adds, "Love one another, even as I have loved you." These words are completely decisive and correspond to the response already made, but they are likely to be misunderstood: What does it mean to "love one another"? If you look at Christian societies throughout history, you will notice, not that they had the monopoly on hate and division, but that they *also* had hate, divisions and conflicts.

WOLTON: *Shall we say that their differences from other societies were not exactly obvious?*

LUSTIGER: Agreed. In any case, a Christian society is not a paradise. The example of love given to us is not a fusional model of good-natured understanding, of a society whose conflicts have disappeared as if by magic, thanks to the improved behavior of its citizens.

The model, the archetype of the love proposed to us, is the one that Christ lived—that is, his Passion, his death on the Cross, which bears our hates and refusals to love—i.e., our sin. "Greater love has no man than this, that a man lay down his life for his friends." These words that Christ spoke are not to be understood as urging us to make the suicidal sacrifice of heroes who destroy themselves to defend honor. On the contrary, they teach us that we must forget ourselves to the point of giving our lives.

Similarly, when as Christ's disciples we are called on to love one another as Christ has loved us, we have to surmount all the sources of division that exist among men and, thus, among ourselves—all the conflicts that separate Christians ethnically or nationally. We may ask ourselves why humanity should all of a sudden become any different when it is Christian. The answer is that Christians receive the Messianic strength to struggle against divisions. The sacraments are the source, the guarantors, the signs and instruments of this strength. They make it possible for us to endure the disunity and to transform it as we become, as the prophet says, "repairers of the breach". The key words are love, forgiveness, mercy and passion, Christ's Passion. The sign by which Christians recognize each other, the one by which they are sometimes discerned by the world, is that they have become similar to Christ in their mutual love, which identifies them with Christ in his Passion.

Chapter 25 of Saint Matthew, devoted to the Last Judgment, presents us with a parable on the judgment of nations to whom the Gospel will not have been announced. They will be judged by the way they have treated the Messiah's brothers who were hungry, thirsty, suffered, were in prison and persecuted. At the end of time, the Messiah says to the pagan nations, "Come, O blessed of my Father, inherit the kingdom prepared for you . . . ; for I was hungry and you gave me food, I was thirsty and you gave me drink, I was a stranger and you welcomed me. . . . " And the nations, the *goyim,* reply, "But when did we do that? We never saw you, we do not even know you." The Master answers, "As you did it to one of the least of these my brethren, you did it to me." And another group will be told: "Depart from me, you cursed . . . for I was hungry and you gave me no food . . . sick and in prison and you did not visit me." And they will protest, "Lord, when did all this happen, we do not know you." The answer follows the same logic: "As you did it not to one of the least of these, you did it not to me." The Christian is identified with Christ and must fulfill the Messianic function on which the world revolves and is judged.

WOLTON: *Is there a Christian morality?*

LUSTIGER: The first rule of Christian morality is to rely entirely on God's commandments. Because he has been created in the image and resemblance of

God, man must live as God lives, act as God acts, and the Covenant's commandments set forth standards for man's behavior that are commensurate with his divine vocation, which is to become similar to God, united with God, in communion with God. The believer must follow God's commandments: that is the fundamental, permanent requirement in our changing and precarious human condition.

MISSIKA: *Is there an absolute in morality?*

LUSTIGER: There is: God's commandments given as words of life and standards for conduct. They reveal to men just how helpless they are, whereas Jesus fulfills them perfectly, to the point of giving his life. And, in so doing, our Lord has made it possible for us to fulfill them through him, with him, and in him, thanks to the strength of the Holy Spirit that is given to us. The Christian can be assured that holiness is possible on earth, even if men are sinners, because forgiveness is perpetually being offered by God.

Such an ideal of human life, in communion with Christ by the gift of the Spirit, is specific to Christians and is endowed with a universal significance. Christians must never impose it by force or constraint on those who do not share their convictions, but at the same time they do have the duty to announce to all men the moral principles that dwell in them as a revelation and grace given by God for all humanity.

III

THEOLOGICAL QUESTIONING

Speaking about God

DOMINIQUE WOLTON: *Speaking about God assumes that one can address him and thus have an image of him. The image men have has evolved in history, going from a purely symbolic representation to one that became more and more anthropomorphic. What is the meaning of this evolution, which includes several forms of representing God? We all know that they have an effect on the way one talks about God and conceives of his role. Communication, even when it is sacred, presupposes an identification of the other.*

JEAN-MARIE LUSTIGER: I prefer not to get involved in a discussion of images of the divine in various civilizations. Ethnologists have become very cautious, and I doubt that they would subscribe to what you have just said.

I shall limit myself to the problem posed by the symbolization of God in the Jewish and Christian tradition. Figuration in the Christian tradition has changed across the centuries and has involved some ambiguities. It even produced a crisis, resolved in principle at the Second Council of Nicaea in 787, which ruled on the legitimacy of icons (or images). There had been fierce controversies over whether the characters of sacred history—Christ in particular—could be represented. This spiritual, aesthetic and symbolic crisis is not without resemblance to the present question in the West about nonfigurative painting. I think I have already said that abstract art and the demolition of human figuration raise a similar problem. The present debate on figuration can probably be clarified by referring to iconoclasm,[1] because there is a correspondence between the figure of God and the figure of man.

In the Jewish tradition, God is never depicted, whereas all the pagan religions of the Near East made images of their divinities. However, contrary to what is frequently said, the Jewish tradition does have a certain representation. The proof can be found in the mosaics of the Near East, between the second century before Christ and the second century after. For four centuries, there was a Jewish art that was surprisingly different. I am thinking of a particular mosaic discovered in Galilee. It portrays the sacrifice of Isaac and dates from

[1] Iconoclasm considered the cults of icons to be illegitimate.—TRANS.

the Hellenistic period, somewhere around the second century. In striking contrast to the Hellenistic art of the neighboring synagogues, it bears a certain resemblance to the Roman frescoes of Catalonia. And it is obviously not primitive art because it shows a considerable aesthetic savoir-faire, as if the artist had deliberately made the figures hard to recognize, so as to avoid producing a mere image. This is exactly the same problem as the one existing in modern painting.

Until a recent period, beginning with the baroque in the seventeenth century, God the Father was always represented by a sign: the sacred tetragrammaton (the four Hebrew letters of the divine Name), the ray, the sun, the hand—in other words, by abstract symbols, because the Father cannot be depicted. On the other hand, Christ, the Son of God, who took on human flesh and form, is shown according to a symbolic aesthetic, rarely realistic before the thirteenth and fourteenth centuries when, in the West especially, this began to change. All Byzantine iconography presents a highly symbolic human figure. What is represented in this way is a sacrament and a mystery, because the acts and words of Christ in the flesh are prophecies of what will be fulfilled in his brothers across time and throughout history. This portrayal contributed to the mystery of the Word of God made flesh. It is inscribed in the continuity of the eucharistic celebration. Until the Renaissance, the Church's iconographic program obeyed very strict rules based on a theological coherence. Painters and sculptors were subjected to a very rigorous spiritual discipline that governed their apprenticeships and the exercise of their professions. They were not "artists", but believers—most often monks—who created signs, "icons", just as others copied Scripture.

In ancient Judaism, showing scenes from the Bible in synagogues was not considered blasphemous as long as those assembled there had no intention of worshipping the image, which was there only as a sign, a reference, linked to the living Word. It was a painted word, not an idol. In medieval times, it was the Western tradition in particular that dared to represent God the Father according to the names by which he is designated in Scripture: Creator, Lord, pre-existent (hence, ageless), Lord of the Universe, etc. A threshold was crossed in representing the invisible Father by the image of an old man. The evolution is interesting from a cultural point of view, but it in no way weakens the Church's Faith.

JEAN-LOUIS MISSIKA: *Are you shocked that God is represented physically in human form?*

LUSTIGER: The Father, yes. Because that strikes me as being less respectful of the economy of salvation. You know the sentence from the prologue to Saint John's Gospel: "No one has ever seen God" (1:18).

WOLTON: *Then you prefer the symbol?*

LUSTIGER: Definitely. The monastic milieus of the fourteenth and fifteenth centuries developed an extremely refined symbolic system.

WOLTON: *There is not only a problem of representation but one of addressing him, of the mental image one has.*

LUSTIGER: If God is reduced to how we conceive of him, he is no longer God, Saint Augustine says. The problem has to be turned around. It is God who gives man the possibility of existing and of placing himself before God as a personal subject. He gives him speech, which permits him to address God. In revealing himself, God allows man to call his name, and in giving man his name, God gives man his speech and the words for addressing him. Right from the beginning of the Old Testament, God speaks. His words are heard, and from the moment that they are heard and accepted, they become human speech. The Word, who gives himself to man, allows him to know the invisible God and to call his name. It is the Spirit who opens ears and gives speech: he creates a language for man who without him would not be able to call God's name. In the Christian tradition, if we can address the invisible Father, it is because we are united by the Holy Spirit's power to the prayer of his Son, of Jesus in his humanity. Christ himself, when he tells us how to pray, says, "When you pray, say 'Our Father' ", and we use that noble expression taken from the Bible. Jesus used a word that has never been repeated, one that the liturgy has never dared to use. He said "Abba", the Aramaic word for "Papa". Thus, in the Messiah's person there is a kind of unheard-of familiarity, unique in respect to God the Father. Jesus instructed us, "You will say, 'Our Father who art in heaven, hallowed be thy name, thy kingdom come' ". These expressions, taken from the "Eighteen Benedictions" of the Kaddish, a ritual prayer of Israel, assume their Christian significance because they are said with the Son in the presence of the Holy Spirit.

MISSIKA: *Does one pray in the same way to the Father as to the Son?*

LUSTIGER: We do not pray to the Father as we pray to the Son. The Spirit gives us access to the Son and permits us to recognize God, Father. We approach God and his mystery as Father through the Son and in the mysterious familiarity of the Spirit. When we are introduced into this filial relationship, we are occupying our true position: we are one with the Son, through the power of the Spirit turned toward the Father. Whoever turns toward Christ, even without knowing him very well, will eventually recognize in him the invisible Father who is revealed by the Spirit. There is an order of divine economy and of access to God. Prayer is not a mental or fanciful visualization, it is first of all an act; it is joining Christ's act of turning himself to God, his Father and our Father. Christian prayer is specific, in contrast to a contemplation of a noetic type or to an introspective meditation. In the Jewish and Christian tradition, prayers include these dimensions but they are marginal; prayer is primarily the participation of man in the life and action of God. It is an act of freedom and love, of cooperation in God's work in history.

MISSIKA: *Do you consider that when a Christian prays, it is not he who is addressing God but rather the reverse?*

LUSTIGER: If man is to know God, then God must make himself known. Our first knowledge of him comes as a revelation; man has been created in the image and resemblance of God. The meaning to be drawn from the first pages of Genesis is inexhaustible. It is the creative Word who gives substance to man and who is also what makes man capable of speaking—that is, of speaking to God. As to the knowledge of and access to God, man is a paralytic who can neither walk nor advance along the route. He is mute, his vocal cords are silent, he can say nothing, he is totally deprived of language. He is blind and cannot see. He is deaf and cannot hear. He is wounded and almost lifeless. He is impure in the biblical sense. God has to make himself known before man can become what he was originally: he who has become blind must be made to see again; he who has become deaf must be made to hear again; he who has become paralyzed must be made to walk; and all this must be done in a way that leads him to speak. In short, language must be bestowed on him. This is the meaning of the miracles of Jesus who, according to Isaiah's words, restores sight to the blind, hearing to the deaf, speech to the mute, movement to the paralytics, life to the dead. The miracles are words in action. In the revelation, the problem of language is paramount. The word cannot be detached from the one who is speaking, not from God, not from man, even if the human speaker is tempted to say something completely insignificant. In saying "Let what you say be simply 'Yes' or 'No'; anything more than this comes from evil" (Mt 5:37) or "I tell you, on the day of judgment men will render account for every careless word they utter" (Mt 12:36), Christ is restoring dignity to human speech as the expression of man's freedom and action—this is so true that, conversely, there are words that kill. The Word of God gives life, it gives us speech and forgiveness, it is stronger than death.

Truth and Freedom in Discipleship

WOLTON: *Apropos of the relationship between morality and truth, I would like to know what you think about this sentence from a Vatican II declaration: "Christian truth must be imposed only by the power of the truth itself."*

LUSTIGER: Whenever men believe that they possess and control the truth, they are always tempted to impose it, whereas it is the truth that possesses men; hence, they can never claim to own it.

The Vatican II statement says what should be only a truism: from the moment truth is evoked, freedom is involved. Jesus said, "The truth will make you free." One can accede to truth only by respecting freedom, and no one becomes free other than through access to the truth. Every coercion of the human conscience, even for its own good, produces the opposite effect.

WOLTON: *The Church's Tradition considers the Christian vocation as necessarily apostolic. But every unbeliever wonders how the Church can authorize herself to attempt to transmit to all men the Good News of the Gospel and the salvation brought by Christ.*

LUSTIGER: Trying to lead everybody to the same opinion by all means of persuasion, including open or clandestine manipulation, is a caricature of proselytism. Such an attitude may be characteristic of totalitarian systems and ideologies, but the divine truth that gives itself to man does not work like that. It cannot be reduced to a formal definition of what is true and what is false. Since it is not an abstract and hypostatic truth, it calls for a completely different "definition": God is the source of life and meaning! In him, there is neither shadow nor darkness. From the moment he snatches man from the lie, he places him in truth and permits him to communicate with the eternal source of all wisdom.

Jesus' statement, "The truth will make you free", implies that when the truth attests itself, it reverses man's will for power. "The Son of Man came not to be served but to serve, and to give his life as a ransom for many. . . . You know that the rulers of the Gentiles lord it over them, and their great men exercise authority over them. It shall not be so among you" (Mt 20:28, 25–26). And these are also Christ's words: "Whoever would be great among you must be your servant, and whoever would be first among you must be your slave" (Mt 20:26–27). The truth attests itself by the absolute negation of the will for power. It is to his condemned victim that Pilate asks, "What is truth?" (Jn 18:38), and when the centurion contemplates the dead Christ he says, "Truly, this man was the Son of God!" (Mk 15:39).

Witnessing to the truth, discipleship, is not clandestine persuasion or propaganda or the establishment of a system for controlling opinion; it is not a conditioning or a "commercial" for marketing. It means "bearing witness to the truth" (Jn 18:37), like Christ, at the cost of one's life if need be. The prophet, seized by divine truth, accepts being put to death for it and for his brothers. Truth is affirmed by such an act, and it touches men's hearts only by setting them free. Discipleship is first of all love, love of brother, wanting him too to experience freedom. It is the desire that the treasure one has received will bear fruit and be equally available to everyone. But there can be no Christian adhesion unless it is a voluntary adhesion. Anyone who would want to use coercion and worldly means to impose Christian truth on consciences would be in error.

MISSIKA: *That temptation is stronger when the Church is in the majority.*

LUSTIGER: When the Church is in the majority in any society, the first temptation is to identify that society's form of culture with Christianity as a whole, but we know through historical memory that this confusion does not hold up. Israel had already had this experience, and the Church repeated it. Israel never knew an ideal period, never; the desert where God reveals himself and man revolts precedes the entry into the Promised Land. David is a sinner. After Solomon comes the schism. The Kingdom is eschatological and cannot be realized in an immediate and terrestrial form, even though everyone must work for it incessantly within the historical context.

A second temptation of a socially powerful Church is to utilize human power as a means of furthering what she believes to be a good cause. The reform movements from within the Church have always had the aim of escaping this temptation.

WOLTON: *But there is that persistent question of proselytism. What authorizes Christians to carry the Good News to those who have not asked for it?*

LUSTIGER: Simply this obvious fact: man needs to be saved. There is only one love: the love of brothers that brings the love of God to life, because he so loved us that he gave his Son for our salvation. Spreading this Good News is the manifestation of the love that comes from God and is expressed in fraternal love. It must never be coercive.

Old and New Testaments

WOLTON: *Why does Catholicism give a more important place to love than do Judaism and Protestantism?*

LUSTIGER: But love is at the very core of the biblical revelation and, thus, of Judaism! These words form the heart of all the commandments: "Hear, O Israel: The Lord our God is one Lord; and you *shall love* the Lord your God with all your heart, and with all your soul and with all your might" (Dt 6:4), and also: "You *shall love* your neighbor as yourself" (Lev 19:18). The revelation of God as love forms the basis of prophetic predication just as it does in Deuteronomy.

In the New Testament, Jesus comments on these two commandments by saying that all the law and the prophets depend on them (Mt 22:34–40). The definition "God is love" suffuses all of Saint John's writing, and Saint Paul eloquently sings about divine charity (1 Cor 13). I would also say that it is inexact to assert that Protestantism places less emphasis on love, to the possible profit of faith, than Catholicism.

MISSIKA: *As soon as we try to have you be more precise about the specificity of Catholicism when compared with other religions, you vigorously challenge all divisions. But, in general, do you consider that as far as love is concerned, there is no break between the New Testament and the Old?*

LUSTIGER: I understand your surprise, because the difference, I ought to say the *nouveauté*—and the separations that followed—are not found where they are usually alleged to have occurred.

History is too often judged on the basis of subsequent polemics that have created opposing images by the interplay of mutual caricatures. Vatican II called for a re-evaluation of Jewish-Christian relations, so as to restore their authenticity. Where is the difference? Where is the newness? It rests in the One through whom the promise is kept and the prophecy fulfilled.

The Bible sometimes expresses this awaited fulfillment in terms of a "new creation". To quote Isaiah: "Remember not the former things, nor consider the things of old. Behold, I am doing a new thing; now it springs forth, do you not perceive it?" (43:18–19). The prophets announce the ultimate intervention of God as a new creation; it will renew both the first creation of man and the liberation of the people and will make available to all the gifts promised to the people of Israel for the world's salvation.

The newness of the Gospel is that "the time is fulfilled". These are the words of John the Baptist and of Jesus himself. "The Kingdom of God is at hand; repent, and believe in the Gospel." Through faith, we have entered into the ultimate phase of history when man has met his God, who came to dwell among his own. For those Jews who did not accept him, time has not found its Messianic fulfillment; similarly, history remains indefinitely in abeyance for the pagans who have not been converted from their idols to the living and true God. When Jesus says, "The Kingdom of heaven is at hand", he is proclaiming that the time has come when God reveals in his Messiah what he has previously announced. This announcement is borne by Israel, even if Judaism does not recognize in Christ's Gospel the real and immediate presence of its hope. "The time is fulfilled", "the Kingdom of heaven is at hand." The notion of the "reign of God" is absolutely biblical, and its content is determined by faith. It is the time when God makes known to all people who he is by unveiling his divine Kingdom, so unlike earthly kingdoms. The reign of God is the time when man is saved by God and restored to plenitude as sovereign of the universe, because God alone is King and man receives from him the strength to fulfill the divine will; it is the time when man is delivered by the resurrected Christ from slavery to sin. The Kingdom of God is the place where the Holy Spirit is given, because it is promised as the ultimate gift; it is the place where all peoples of the world receive and recognize the unique God. As the prophet Zechariah says, "The Lord will be one and his name one."

One of the painful enigmas for Israel's conscience is that the unique God has not been recognized among the pagan nations; one of its sufferings is caused by its own infidelities in serving God. The Church experiences the same suffering and is confronted with the same mystery of incomprehension. Or, rather, the mystery in her eyes is intensified and the suffering is immeasurable because so many zealous Jews have not believed in the One sent by the Father, and so many nations have not yet acceded through him to the promised heritage. Israel has a filial relationship with God. It is the elder son, a much-beloved son, and this filial relationship is lived in its mysterious plenitude through the Messiah, the only Son of God. With him came the spiritual gift of divine adoption for all sons of Adam. The hope of nations, the object of Israel's supplication, was disclosed in Jesus' person.

WOLTON: *Then Christians consider that the coming of Jesus Christ brought a New Covenant into existence.*

LUSTIGER: What Jesus preached had been expressed in advance, in Deuteronomy and by Jeremiah and the other prophets. But the eternal *nouveauté* is that Jesus renewed the Covenant with his blood, restored it with his own life. Jesus lives, actualizes, gives flesh and blood to the words of the eternal Covenant by submitting himself to it. He makes the Covenant to be the everlasting standard for his disciples, a source of meaning and understanding. The same act of the Covenant that constituted Israel is renewed and fulfilled in the Christ-Messiah. It does not disown Israel and God's steadfast love for those whom he called first, but it opens the Covenant to all whom God now calls from every nation—as was promised. Christ, whom God has made Lord of all and the Firstborn of the resurrected, is not substituted for Israel but is, in his person as eternal Son, its redemption and exaltation. And if somebody protests that proof of the fact that the Kingdom of God is not at hand is that death still exists or that justice does not reign in the world, that men remain sinners, that humanity is still the victim of its own errors and idolatry, that Israel is still persecuted or that it is not holy and that its children who were scattered abroad have not yet been reunited, then we cannot deny the strength of their argument. But when we hear this heartrending lament, we see it as a part of the suffering borne by the Christ-Messiah in his Passion. For those who have recognized him, for Christians, Jesus resurrected, Christ and Lord, is the sign and guarantor of a new era. The Jews heralded it, and yet so many of them do not believe that this new era has come.

WOLTON: *There is no longer an "excommunication" of Jews who convert to Christianity. What is the rabbincal attitude from a theological point of view?*

LUSTIGER: The Halakah says that the Jewish condition cannot be abandoned; it is given once and for all by birth to a Jewish mother. The Judaic heritage is not an ethnic privilege but a part of a vocation. It is a historical grace and is irrevocable.

WOLTON: *So no exclusion is possible?*

LUSTIGER: None. The rabbis have preserved Judaism in its specificity, and they are entirely justified in saying whom they consider to be a Jew in agreement with the synagogue, but they have no power to exclude someone from the people of Israel.

WOLTON: *Do you think that it is possible to be both Jew and Christian?*

LUSTIGER: If the affirmation of Jewish identity depended on denying the particular grace Christ has given to his Church, then obviously it would be incompatible with Christianity. But there are Jews who believe in the Christ-Messiah; they call themselves Jews, and they are. Do they belong to the Church? Some refuse to join. Others want to be a part of it and are baptized and become Christians.

Sin and Freedom

WOLTON: *From the point of view of faith, what is the relationship between sin and moral error?*

LUSTIGER: Sin can be conceived only in its relationship to God, in regard to God, in the eyes of God. "In the eyes of God" means that God is looking at us, and we are looking at him. The definition of sin does not depend merely on an individual's appreciation of his own conduct, even in respect to a socially acceptable moral standard. The reference to the law and to the conscience's judgment remains fragile. Why? Because, in the Christian vision, the conscience that, in principle, is a light given to everyone and on which men must be judged by God, can itself become blind. Sin can be understood only from within the Faith, as a lack of response to the love whose revelation has already been given to us. And to become aware of our sins is to understand that we are loved by God and that we have not truly loved him.

Take a comparison. Infidelity in the relationship between a man and a woman is conceived of only when they have initially wished to be faithful to each other. If they loved without the ideal of mutual fidelity, then infidelity would have no meaning. It is the revelation of love that brings about the revelation of sin. And whenever sin and consciousness of a personal sin are invoked, so is the hope of forgiveness.

WOLTON: *And original sin?*

LUSTIGER: Man's conscience has been obscured, his will has been wounded. His communion with God has been interrupted and his strength diminished. He is capable of desiring the good, but his will falters. He is capable of glimpsing the light, but he heads on toward darkness. All men are like this; from their origin they are deformed in their historical condition. Man, created by God, has turned away from his Maker, and, marked by degeneration and dereliction, he cannot live up to his original vocation. It is God himself who takes the initiative to deliver man from this situation, which is, by the way, just the opposite of a naïve Rousseauism.

WOLTON: *Can there be a soteriology that would not first focus on the wrongdoing? Quite often we see an Eastern conception of error that is more Platonic, less centered on the transgression, and, hence, is in contrast with the Western notion, which is more linked with salvation as redemption of sin.*

LUSTIGER: Human intelligence moves irrepressibly toward the divine as toward a distant horizon. And the man who aspires to the divine as his Other is tempted to free himself from everything that is not divine. Such a temptation, which might be called gnostic, is nourished by the secret suspicion that God is completely different from us and that, in order to find God, we have to renounce the best of our humanity. This impossible plan perpetually fails, just as much in the field of philosophy as it does in religion. It is a desperate attempt, one that Pascal described perfectly and succinctly: *"L'homme n'est ni ange ni bête, et qui veut faire l'ange fait la bête."*[2]

WOLTON: *Speaking of what you call "man's risk" in thinking that he can save himself, do you believe that original sin should be restored to a more prominent place?*

LUSTIGER: Discovering the meaning of man's "wounded condition"—another way of describing original sin—can be done only by admitting a tragedy: man has lost his way by distancing himself from God. He is lost for himself, lost for his brothers. Original sin clarifies man's historical condition, because man is an insurmountable enigma to himself. He unravels the enigma only when he accepts the grace of salvation; he has first to recognize that he has been found and refound by God in order to admit that he was lost. The knowledge that men have of themselves is so horribly pessimistic....

MISSIKA: *But this pessimism can be explained without referring to sin.*

LUSTIGER: It can be explained in many ways, but the naïve optimism that sees a "naturally good" humanity with happiness ahead on the horizon, or in any case within reach, is not shared by the men and women of today's different cultural areas! Contemporary man is more aware of contradictory hopes, of the despair and calamities that oppress him; humanity's historical consciousness is a wretched one. Man must not be given an illusory hope; he has to be told about the salvation thanks to which the understanding of his wounded condition becomes accessible to him. And to speak of original sin is to announce that man can be saved. Otherwise, he would be without recourse against the fatalities of history, whereas sin can always be redeemed.

MISSIKA: *Are you saying that the condition for hope is being conscious of one's sins?*

LUSTIGER: Not in the way that someone might say, "The present miserable state of humanity is normal; it will always be the same because such is the inescapable human condition. Everything else is just a utopia or a pipe dream. The only hope is modest and short term, always counterbalanced by secret despair and resignation." Speaking of the human condition in terms of original sin signifies, on the contrary, that man's vocation is not to be confused with the destiny that he is capable of formulating for himself and living out. It means affirming that at the origin of humanity an area of freedom was opened

[2] "Man is neither angel nor beast, and whoever tries to be an angel becomes a beast." —TRANS.

up somewhere and that by God's grace this freedom remains constantly offered to us as a hope.

WOLTON: *Yes, but—and this is a classic philosophical objection—what is human freedom's role if, when all is said and done, it depends on God's grace?*

LUSTIGER: Freedom's specificity is that it is not abstract, outside of history. Today we unreservedly accept the idea that human freedom is limited by sociological determinisms that can be set forth, codified, observed and indeed manipulated. We have to dare to say also that human freedom is wounded, that it is imprisoned and needs to be delivered from evil. "The truth will make you free." In other words, God will restore your freedom to you. And salvation gives man a freedom purged of false guilt; it informs him of the true measure of his sin and, hence, of the bounty of God's grace and forgiveness. It is not denying man's freedom to recognize that it is partially alienated, not only by economic causes but also by spiritual ones.

WOLTON: *On the contrary, one would think that this spiritual alienation is much more serious!*

LUSTIGER: It is, but at the same time, in saying this, one sets forth the possibilities for ending his alienation: through salvation and redemption.

WOLTON: *That presupposes believing in God.*

LUSTIGER: Yes.

MISSIKA: *But that is not always so easy!*

LUSTIGER: No one is asked to believe what he does not want to or cannot believe.... Since you asked me, I have answered as a man of faith. The atheist's point of view is different. I cannot choose the ways to freedom for him. However, his human condition is the same as mine. We are both wounded, and one day we shall both find ourselves face to face with God.

WOLTON: *Certain theological currents have insisted on a conception of salvation that is, shall we say, more sociopolitical.*

LUSTIGER: Understanding God's salvation strictly in terms of human history is a part of a perpetual temptation that the Jewish and Christian tradition has always combatted. This sociopolitical reduction of salvation is of the same nature as the *césarismes*[3] that confuse Christianity with a temporal power. Whether one replaces the Emperor Constantine with Marx or the proletariat, the illusion is the same: that of earthly messianisms.

MISSIKA: *Then there is no fundamental difference between a revolution of the masses and a power incarnated by one man?*

LUSTIGER: Frankly, for me it is six of one and half a dozen of the other, because the perversion is the same. Christian action must assume the ethical demands of the human condition; it must take its risks without pretending to realize the Kingdom of God here below. Christ says in the apocalyptic discourse, "Then if anyone says to you, 'Lo, here is the Christ!' or 'There he is!', do not believe it. For false Christs and false prophets will arise" (Mt 24:23). In advance, Christ shows us that he does not regard history as sacred: he makes us responsible for it, whereas temporal messianisms treat history as sacred by making constraints and hopes absolute and discharging us of our moral and political responsibility. Pretending to localize the Kingdom here or there is simultaneously putting the good people on one side and the wicked on the other. The wicked can be killed, but "we" are the good who must survive. That is the Manichaeism or dialectic in which some people would like to enclose us. A Christian cannot accept such a deviation. It is just not possible!

WOLTON: *But sometimes it is the Christians themselves who deviate and who are responsible for what you call anti-Christian action.*

LUSTIGER: Then they are either sinners or in error. But it is true that it is one of the great ideological temptations of our contemporary world.

Vatican II: A Doctrinal or a Pastoral Council?

WOLTON: *It has sometimes been said that one of the weaknesses of the Second Vatican Council was that it was more pastoral than doctrinal.*

LUSTIGER: Vatican II occupies an original position in the Church's series of councils. It pronounced no anathemas—that is, no negative formulations that would exclude from full Catholic communion anyone who denies or affirms such and such a position—one touching on the Christian faith, obviously.

[3] *Césarisme* refers to the theory that contends that the prince of a Christian state or empire, co-extensive to "Christendom", has the inherent authority or competence to make theological and dogmatic decisions. The Popes, from the time of Constantine to the late Middle Ages, struggled against this claim.—TRANS.

A negative definition has the merit of leaving open a vast field for research and interpretation. It is content simply to limit the impugned area as being unfaithful to Tradition. However, there is obviously a crisis in modern thought, and it remains useful to redefine a philosophical and theological equilibrium for the major questions. The Council attempted to express itself affirmatively on a number of these questions instead of denouncing the errors. This desire for a positive contribution has been defined as "pastoral".

What does the word *pastoral* signify? It refers to a very precise symbol: the image of the shepherd, of God the Shepherd of his people. Jesus presents himself as the true Shepherd, the one who leads the people in God's name, according to God's will, on the path of truth and life. The Apostles and the bishops, their successors, have been given a pastoral responsibility in the name of Christ the Shepherd. But Christians are not the flock of their priests; they are Christ's flock. And Christ says to Peter when he gives him this pastoral charge, "Simon, son of John, do you love me?" "Yes, Lord; you know that I love you", and Jesus adds, "Feed my sheep" (Jn 21:16). Notice that he says "*my* sheep". I would say that the Council was pastoral in that it wanted to define orientations and choices—including those on the doctrinal terrain—positively, for the good of God's flock. On certain very controversial subjects like the theology of history and the relation of the singular to the universal in the economy of salvation, the Council preferred not to pronounce itself. It spoke in the name of faith. In doing so, it chose balanced expressions on this side of or beyond these controversies. Without resolving them, it gave to the faithful, for their good, certain markers taken from the Church's Tradition. This is the way that the Council wanted to be pastoral, and being pastoral, it teaches truth, dogma and morality.

WOLTON: *The comparison between Vatican II and Vatican I shows that the latter was focused rather more on a theology of God, on faith, while the former, with its "pastoral" approach, gave more attention to the Church herself—hence, to ecclesiology. But, conversely, Father de Lubac wrote, "Vatican II is an operation of christological concentration."*

LUSTIGER: The centers of interest for the contemporaries of Vatican II were, on the one hand, problems concerned with the functioning of the ecclesiastical society in modern society. They dealt with the problems of power, the relations of the various parties within the Church to each other and to the whole, to the different strata of her hierarchy, her interaction with civil societies and states. There was in all this a dominant theme reflecting our century's tremendous interest in social life, which has become a prime object of commentary, research and surveys. Many contemporaries of Vatican I and, subsequently, of Vatican II were fascinated by these problems. But although

Vatican I studied the problem of faith and the knowledge of God, the only thing that many people have retained from it is the definition of pontifical primacy and infallibility. Similarly for Vatican II, some authors and many of the commentators retained only the teachings on the social—indeed, functional—dimensions of the Church: its internal operation, the authority of the college made up of the Pope and the bishops, the responsibility and organization of laymen, etc. Many of them also echoed concern with the Church's condition in our present world, of her moral standards in social and political matters, notably for the civil respect of consciences and of their freedom in regard to God's truth. In fact, if you look at the published texts, you will see that the Council did many things in addition to what interested public opinion. It unveiled the true mystery of the Church in showing how she receives what she is and conceives of herself only in the figure of Christ, Light of the nations, *Lumen gentium.*

Following the wishes of Paul VI, the prominence given to the Church's mystery consisted of a meditation and was like an unfolding of the Church's living relationship with Christ. Besides, you have to go all the way: there is a true "christological concentration"—to use Father de Lubac's expressive words—only in the elucidation of the relationship to God, Father of his people. It is here that the connection with Vatican I and its doctrine of the divine revelation remains important. In other respects, the Vatican II texts discreetly evoked the role of the Holy Spirit and his charisms, and, in recent decades, this has appeared to be one of the major spiritual fruits of the Council.

WOLTON: *You have said that Vatican II wanted to insist on the notion of pastor. But there have been conflicting interpretations. In particular, the Council emphasized the definition of the Church as "God's people", which is more like an Old Testament definition. But, classically, doesn't one speak of the Church as Body of Christ? What is the difference between these two appellations?*

LUSTIGER: The exclusive use of the expression "God's people" would be quite amazing! It is not used more than seven times, as far as I can recall, in the New Testament, and each time it almost certainly designates the people of Israel. Because the notion of God's people is defined, in the first place, by divine election: God's people are those whom he has gathered together, who have become a people only because God has chosen them to be obedient to him.

Besides, the chapter on God's people begins with a reminder of Israel's vocation. But the Council used a whole range of images to describe the Church; it compiled an anthology of all the figures and symbols that have designated the Church in Scripture and tradition. Among them, three indicate the Church's relationship to each of the divine Persons. Father Congar, who was one of the instigators of this text, accentuated them: "God's people", "Christ's Body", and "the Spirit's temple".

General opinion perhaps understood "God's people" as meaning "sovereign people", as in the statement "in the name of the French people". But the term refers rather to the Father who calls and assembles, across history and cultures, his dispersed children. Moreover, the Church can call herself "God's people" —that is, "children of the Father"—only if she is the "Body of Christ" by participating through faith in his Passion and Resurrection and by entering into his grace; she is to become, in him, "temple of the Holy Spirit", called to be the place where God dwells.

WOLTON: *Why is the expression "temple of the Holy Spirit" used so infrequently?*

LUSTIGER: I do not know.

MISSIKA: *There seems to be an overuse of "God's people"....*

LUSTIGER: The notion of the Body of Christ is as old as the Church. It is one of the centers of gravity of Saint Paul's thought. The promotion of the biblical expression, God's people, is something new.

WOLTON: *I insist: Why has the dimension of the Holy Spirit been so little talked about during the past twenty years?*

LUSTIGER: The conception of the Church as the temple of the Holy Spirit is obviously found in the texts of the Second Vatican Council, but perhaps it was not emphasized enough, even by the Council Fathers. It may well reflect one of the West's deficiencies in contrast to the Eastern churches, which have always been extremely sensitive to the presence of the Holy Spirit. But we are currently witnessing a revitalizing movement that is reminding us of the active presence and unexpected gifts of the Holy Spirit, who is "the Lord, the giver of life".

IV

PRIESTS AND LAITY

Taking Stock of the Spiritual Crisis

DOMINIQUE WOLTON: *Since the end of the war, the number of people entering religious vocations has drastically decreased, and a good deal of research in religious sociology has tried to analyze the causes. Do they stem from society's evolution or from strictly religious sources linked to the Church's internal evolution?*

JEAN-MARIE LUSTIGER: This is a phenomenon that spreads over a very long time. If the curves are to be significant, they have to be extended into the past, even—if possible—as far back as the French Revolution. That leads to considerations of the priest's role in society and of his place in French history. As the priest's social role disintegrated, the capacity for recruitment gradually dwindled. But is that explanation sufficient? No, because the priesthood in the Catholic Church is not uniquely a social function but depends on the spiritual health of a Christian people.

Suppose we look at things from another angle—at the root—not focusing on the priest's social function but on the generosity that the priesthood mobilizes. The decline in vocations is an unmistakable symptom that there is a crisis within the entire Christian body. Thus, it is not the drop in numbers that has to be examined but the spiritual health of Catholics within French society. Having arrived at this point, people often protest that it is not the Church but society that is in crisis. I accept the objection on the condition that it is understood in its strongest sense: if there is a spiritual crisis among Catholics, it is a reflection of the waning spiritual vitality of society as a whole.

JEAN-LOUIS MISSIKA: *I find your explanation inadequate. You have a tendency to label as a "crisis" what we would call an "evolution" or perhaps—even as concerns the Church's place in society—a "decline". Why do you insist on considering secularization or the rise of atheism as a tragic or calamitous element in Western societies?*

WOLTON: *If I may add something to the objection. . . . You have spoken of the technological and imperialistic crisis of the nineteenth and twentieth centuries as being connected with the progress of rationalism. But if you look at sixteenth-century Europe, certainly just as imperialistic—with Spain and Portugal—you will note that it was made up of Christian nations par excellence.*

LUSTIGER: I am saying that Western society is at a crucial turning point; it is rocking on its foundations and challenging all of its value systems. Even so, what happened earlier was not necessarily better or worse. One spiritual observation suffices: we are living in a period of deadly serious choices. Modern society is being tempted in the exercise of all its new powers. The temptations are reinforced by the mass media, which subject an increasing number of people to increasingly greater trials.

MISSIKA: *But hasn't that always been the case? Has* crisis *not become something of an all-purpose word?*

LUSTIGER: Its use should be more precise; I understand your objection. I am saying that, because of technological innovations and intervening mutations, there is a spiritual testing of choices and values, a testing that is much more explicit and consequential than in former times when the world was compartmentalized, when people who lived along the Seine did not communicate with those living along the Loire or still less with those in the valley of the Garonne. In those days, the repercussions of choices made by the inhabitants of the Ile de France did not have the same impact. Today we live in a new system of human interaction, of communication of thoughts and choices. It is not only a technical problem to be treated by electronic engineers; it is freedoms and their values that are being challenged, profoundly challenged. For the Faith, before God, this is called a spiritual "crisis".

WOLTON: *What are the characteristics of this crisis?*

LUSTIGER: It sets into motion, much more imposingly and brutally, the consequences of the fundamental choices man makes in exercising his freedom! These options were already set forth in the typology of Exodus. They reappear in the temptation of Christ: the control of one's own life, the appropriation of the world, the will for power, the defiance of God. The stakes are always the same, in every generation, and no one escapes such choices. In this respect, we are not any more or less tempted than people were three centuries ago. All human freedoms are constantly being tested spiritually, on that fundamental level where human existence unfolds.

But our era has its special characteristics. There is no doubt that a certain world collapsed in the sixteenth and seventeenth centuries. Perhaps it died from inevitable obsolescence, because it is an illusion to think that an empire or civilization can endure forever. There have been more or less static, archaic civilizations, but they too are mortal. Our Western European civilizations, as far back as human memory goes, have never ceased to evolve. They are constantly being reborn, through incessant changes and confrontations, invasions and mutual fertilizations. In the sixteenth century there was a dreadful ordeal. That period is fascinating because it is truly the dawn of modern times, with both the worst and the best. After all, it was characterized by the greed for gold, by the *conquistadores* who operated by fire and blood, by the rebirth of slavery. . . . But at the same time the mystical experience was ablaze.

WOLTON: *Is it the contrast between this mystical fervor and the confusion existing in the world that characterizes a "crisis" as you understand it?*

LUSTIGER: Yes. The sixteenth century was the age of the Catholic renaissance, of the French "mystical springtime" and of the great Spanish and Italian spiritualities. But the same period witnessed, with the Reformation, the internal religious schism of Western Europe. There was obviously a need for an evangelical and spiritual reform of the Church; everybody was calling for it. But how did the best intentions bring about such great calamities? Spiritual divisions were created that, later, were re-inforced by national ones and have been the source of many subsequent conflicts and wars.

WOLTON: *You are saying that the religious divisions that came about in the sixteenth and seventeenth centuries, at the dawn of modern times, had a considerable influence that went well beyond the spiritual realm. But the same question can be asked today about the much more secularized societies of the twentieth century. Is the religious crisis not likely to have more effects on civil society than ever before, even though our society is much more "secularized"?*

LUSTIGER: It seems that human history is reaching a turning point. It presents a searing trial for Western man, for the gifts he has received—the gifts of understanding, knowledge and control of his environment. Simultaneously, we are also seeing a conversion, a renewal taking place in some people. Will these people be recognized, heeded and understood as they were in the sixteenth century? That was already the debate Abraham had with God, in the case of Sodom and Gomorrah. Everything depends on knowing if there will be ten righteous men, on believing that the righteous can save the city from destruction.

The Crisis of Vocations in France

WOLTON: *The decrease in numbers of young men entering the priesthood is often linked to a triple demand: the right to have a profession, the right to marry and the right to a political commitment.*

LUSTIGER: First of all, it is public opinion—and not priests—that is making the demand.

WOLTON: *But priests themselves have often insisted on these changes....*

LUSTIGER: Yes, and that stems from an explanation given earlier: the particular case of priests reflects the serious crisis of conscience for Catholics—and society as a whole—in those three domains: economic, sexual and political. On these three subjects Christians find themselves confronting a complete contradiction between the fundamental values that their faith gives them—with concrete implications—and the dominant opinion of society with which, unconsciously, many align themselves. These are the three spheres where the absolute of the faith in the Christ-Messiah, crucified and resurrected, presupposes a conversion of man's desire. It is perfectly understandable that a society in the throes of a spiritual crisis questions first those who are the carriers of the highest symbolic system in each of these domains, because there is definitely an economic crisis, a sexual crisis and a political crisis in contemporary society. And on these matters, Catholics are not exempt from a fundamental wavering. They share the misgivings of present-day society, whose interrogation aims first at those who support its symbolic weight most explicitly by having agreed to relinquish desires in these domains as a result of their call and mission: economic renunciation to show in our consumer culture that man is not fulfilled by the goods he produces and consumes; renunciation of marriage to show the eschatological fulfillment of sexuality; renunciation of the will for power to demonstrate that politics is not responsible for the totality of man's vision. And so the criticism of a people avid for possessions, for sexual pleasure and the control of sexuality and for the exercise of power falls on the figure of the man who, poor and chaste, is the servant of God.

WOLTON: *You are shifting the burden of proof! You are saying that priests' confusion in these matters is only a reflection of society's disarray. But what is bothersome in your response is that it skips over what is strictly interior to the Church.*

LUSTIGER: To perceive the internal causes, you must first understand just how much France is an exceptional case in comparison to world statistics.

MISSIKA: *Do you mean that the decline in vocations is less dramatic elsewhere?*

LUSTIGER: There are countries, like Poland, where the numbers have never decreased and, in fact, have only increased. In Africa, there is a definite growth in the number of vocations, even though they no longer lead to government or political influence. South America, which until recent years was in a colonial position as to vocations, has now reversed the trend thanks to the greater numbers of the intellectual elite from the universities who are entering the priesthood. Today in France, we have about a hundred sacerdotal ordinations each year for the dioceses—there are probably considerably fewer for the religious orders. But thirty years ago there were more than a thousand ordinations of secular priests each year. Not since the French Revolution has there been a drop as significant in numbers and duration. In the Fifties, the number of clergy in proportion to the number of practicing Catholics was numerically much higher than in virtually any other country. A simple calculation will serve to illustrate this. The figures for the periods preceding the present situation can be found in a book by Boulard, *Essor et déclin du clergé français* [*The Rise and Fall of the French Clergy*], published in 1950. If the religious are included, there was one priest for 823 inhabitants, of whom 686 were Catholic. So, with a national average of about 20 percent of those Catholics who were practicing, that meant one priest for 140 of the faithful. Or one priest for seventy practicing adults. And, finally, one priest for thirty-five practicing adult men! Moreover, this number did not include the many religious who went to all parts of the world as missionaries.

At the same time, Poland had one priest for 2,194 inhabitants, of whom 2,134 were Catholics, most of them practicing. Proportions were similar for all the other European countries. The French situation was unique in the world, at least if one looked, as was done here, at a national average, without taking into account the wide differences in numbers of practicing Catholics in the various regions. How can this superabundance of vocations in one of the richest countries of Europe, and one of the earliest to be secularized, be explained? There is no truly satisfying response. In any case, a consequence should be noted: just after the war, half of the missionaries—priests and religious—in the world were French.

WOLTON: *France was, as has been said so nicely, "the eldest daughter of the Church".*

LUSTIGER: Such a thing can happen only in periods of extreme fervor, in relatively circumscribed populations, and it represents an absolutely phenomenal gift of grace. Sometimes there are periods in human history when, in certain sectors of a society, there is a great flowering of rich personalities, or literary geniuses or geniuses in art or holiness. There is no mistaking the sign, and it has been pointed out ever so often by foreigners: "You are the country of saints." There was, in fact, in the two centuries following the seventeenth century, an amazing period of French mysticism. And the question I ask myself, as a Frenchman and a spiritual inheritor of that situation, is: "What have we done with these extraordinary gifts?" I was saying a while ago that people are always tempted to misuse the gifts they receive from God. This is true for spiritual as well as material gifts. According to some statistics, the turning point came with the separation of church and state at the beginning of this century, when the priest's social role was threatened. It did serve as a kind of purging—whether good or bad, I do not know.

A second shock occurred when the priest's ministry lost some of its sacramental and mystical significance in the eyes even of many Christians. As long as he was supported by a Christian "compost", mystical and rich, the priest stood fast. But he very often found himself cast off and stranded. Bernanos' *Journal d'un curé de campagne*[1] is a remarkable account of this situation.

WOLTON: *Would you say that the priest's temptation by secularization is all the greater when the country's spiritual compost is depleted? Would priests' temptations to become involved in politics not be a consequence of this?*

LUSTIGER: The priest is made for a people to whom he is sent and whom he serves. Reciprocally, those people mark "their" priest, as they say. But what do people really want? The priest who, like Saint Paul, wants to make himself "all things to all men" cannot escape this question.

WOLTON: *Then it was after the separation of church and state that priests were drawn into sociopolitical affairs to which they were all the more receptive since their spiritual roots had been weakened?*

LUSTIGER: They were all the more receptive since they were filled with the passionate desire to transmit the love of Christ to men and women who were the poorest and the most removed from the Church. They had the feeling that they ought to leave the familiar shore to go toward non-Christian lands. This was expressed by the immediately acclaimed book by Godin and Daniel, *France, pays de mission* [*Does France Need Missionaries?*], which was published in 1941.

When Paul of Tarsus says, "I must go to Macedonia, I see a Macedonian who is calling", he loses nothing of his communion with the Church as a whole; he simply carries it with him. Saint Francis Xavier pushed on as far as

[1] This book was published in English under the title *The Diary of a Country Priest*.—TRANS.

the shores of China and cast off nothing of what had made him. He was alone, but he was supported by the prayer of those who had given birth to him, and he never ceased to nourish that prayer within himself. When he is uprooted, when he has become a foreigner, he is most himself, as Christian and priest. He and Father de Foucauld were completely isolated, cut off from the familiar context that customarily allows a man to survive. But these two remarkable individuals were capable of living in personal solitude after having made an almost total break with the social links that normally reinforce personal convictions. Just imagine: a trip to the other side of the world in the sixteenth century, arriving in unknown lands, hearing unknown languages. And imagine Father de Foucauld in Islamic countries, surrounded by the Tuaregs, in the vast and empty desert.... However, the farther away these men are, deprived of their usual social connections, the closer they come to the native peoples by identifying with them, the more they are spiritually faithful to themselves and to what has made them who they are; they construct rather than destroy themselves. Their identification with the indigenous populations, their transculturation makes their self-realization greater than it was perhaps at their departures, to the point that, at the end of their journeys, they appear more like Christ, including the Christ who suffered his Passion and death.

The experience of cultural mutation, of the cultural passage from a Catholic milieu to one that is not, has weighed on a generation of our priests. This experience has produced saints, but it has also sometimes had the opposite effect. Perhaps you remember the title of a celebrated novel by Cesbron called *Les saints vont en enfer.*[2] They became "naturalized", as we used to say. They felt that they had to adapt to a modern world, or to the working class or to what was supposed to be the pagan environment, just as if they were adopting another nationality, making themselves "citizens" of that "other" world.

MISSIKA: *Then you think the crisis was more mystical than social?*

LUSTIGER: The social crisis only catalyzed and accentuated the mystical crisis. Another index concerns the sixteenth century, a very good period for comparison. It was the time when the greatest mystics developed negative theology. Saint John of the Cross and Saint Teresa of Avila, in approaching the mystery of God, describe it as a "dark cloud", beyond all knowledge and experience. These categories and this language have been used in identifying the mystery with atheism, which is its exact opposite. Negative theology is not atheism; the two brush against each other perhaps, since they are both mysteries, but they are definitely opposed. It is true that the greatest mystic

[2] Gilbert Cesbron (1913–79) became famous as a Catholic novelist with *Even Saints Go to Hell* (1952), a story about Catholic militants in a working-class suburb of Paris.—TRANS.

can have a better understanding of the atheist and that the most convinced atheist can always become a mystic. But, at the same time, it must not be said that the mystic who loves God is an atheist or that the man deprived of God is initiated into his mystery.

If, as I have just said, the social crisis only catalyzes and emphasizes the mystical crisis, the only positive in-depth changes to be hoped for in the status, ministry and life of priests will be the fruits of a new mystical flowering among Christians.

Where do vocations appear today in France? It is tempting to define their origin socially. But, precisely, social background can no longer be reasonably interpreted as a determining factor. Formerly, the high number of vocations was attributed to the desire for upward mobility among Christian peasants. But what promotion can young men—most of whom have excellent professional qualifications—hope for today? Because this is the new profile of those who are currently entering the priesthood. We are seeing something quite new in France, something that cannot be detected by numbers: it is the extraordinary spiritual vigor, moral health and Christian fidelity of the novitiates and their families, and also the fervor and faith that these young men have been able to find and share in the Church, which are the basis for their vocation.

WOLTON: *Of the three demands for change—political, professional and marital commitments—it would seem that it is marriage, or rather the question of procreation, that is the most difficult to accept, especially in a religion where actually the question of filiation, of father and son, is a central concept.*

LUSTIGER: This is not the determining factor, not the decisive problem. Experience has produced the counter-proof: in Anglicanism, priests can be either unmarried or married; moreover, they all have quite a comfortable salary, like the German Lutherans. And in the Eastern churches, whether Orthodox or united with Rome, you also find a married clergy. So here we have three denominations—one in the tradition that calls itself Catholic, another from the Reformation, and the third from the Eastern tradition—where married men are ordained. In each case, there is no correlation between vocations and marriage. Yet the decrease in vocations in the Anglican church is greater than it is in the Catholic Church. And in Germany, the drop in numbers of married Lutheran pastors is as striking, if not more so, as that of celibate Catholic priests. Simultaneously, the number of unmarried priests is growing in all the Eastern churches. Therefore, the argument so widely used in France is contradicted by the facts. In that case, the clamor for a married clergy has to be explained by something else. It is here that we have to return to an overall spiritual explanation. Our society is sorely tempted by sexuality, and those who are called by vocation to celibacy, to chastity for the Kingdom, have not escaped the temptation. Since it is from among them that the Church chooses her priests, it is normal that attention focuses on the most visible difference between them and others, just as it is normal that these men are subjected to the shock of the ordeal more than others, because they occupy the most vulnerable, the most advanced position.

Now, as far as canon law is concerned, everybody knows that the ordination of married men and the marriage of priests are two completely separate issues. The latter poses the problem of a man who has chosen to dedicate his celibate life to serving the Kingdom of God. He has already committed all his life, with full knowledge of the facts; he has done it freely, in response to a call from God. If there has been an error in this choice of vocation, on his part or on the part of the Church, the Church can release him from his vows by saying, "There was a mistake, we must be honest, and you should return to secular life. Certainly, you have received the sacrament of ordination—forever. But may God forgive both of us for this mistake. Go in peace." If there was no mistake, then things must be called by their name; that is, if a man is unable to withstand his trial or temptation, then he is lacking in what has been given to him. God will be his judge. Judging him ourselves is another matter. But priests' getting married is something that has happened at each revolutionary crisis in France! And sometimes they have been forced into it! Remember the French Revolution. Why was that?

MISSIKA: *And why not ordain married men?*

LUSTIGER: The Catholic Church in the West, as you know, made the spiritual choice of taking its priests from among men who have received the charisma of celibacy. It is more than a canonical discipline: it is an option inspired by the love of Christ. Nevertheless, the Catholic Church maintains and recalls also the possibility and her right to ordain married men. It is in the tradition of the Eastern churches to do so. Moreover, we see the appearance, in a persistent and significant way, of vocations of celibate priests in churches that accept the ordination of married men as being canonically legitimate. For more than a century, this tendency has been obvious in Anglicanism, German Lutheranism and among certain French Protestants. But nobody ever mentions this fact, only the contrary one. The spotlight of publicity is trained on the opposite face of things.

WOLTON: *But is the renunciation of paternity not more difficult than the renunciation of conjugal life?*

LUSTIGER: A quote from the Gospel is appropriate here. When Peter said,

"Lo, we have left everything and followed you", Christ himself responded—because the invitation to leave everything behind and follow the Messiah on his path is not the Church's invention—"Truly, I say to you, there is no one who has left house or brothers or sisters or mother or father or children or lands, for my sake and for the Gospel, who will not receive a hundredfold now in this time houses and brothers and sisters and mothers and children and lands" ("with persecutions", Saint Mark points out in 10:30) "and in the age to come eternal life." The exercise of the sacerdotal ministry, whether by a religious or a diocesan priest, introduces one to the mystery of divine paternity; the priest has been granted, as a bonus of fecundity and love, the power to give spiritual birth to children of God. That implies a great selflessness, sometimes greater, more immediate and more radical than that of biological parents; but all parents also know that their children will one day leave home.

MISSIKA: *Yes, but, in the meantime, there are twenty years or so that bring a certain number of pleasures and difficulties.*

LUSTIGER: Yes, pleasures or illusions, conflicts and suffering. Spiritual fathering can be the promised hundredfold. It is true; I can vouch for it. These notions are difficult to handle because they can be abused. Freud has made us suspicious of these kinds of stories. We do not like to go too far, without precautions, into terrains where the symbolic system can also be misleading. But the fact remains, I am giving you my personal witness as a priest, that spiritual paternity is a reality. For a great many people, the priest is an instrument of God's spiritual paternity. Without trying to, and perhaps even without realizing it, he can restore to those people the impaired image of their human fathers. It is a very great joy on the condition that its limits are accepted. From the moment that the priest might want to appropriate a human paternity, he destroys the spiritual one and loses the grace whose witness he is. But if he accepts the distance and frustration, he receives the joy. It is not imaginary and makes all that viable. Really, you cannot conceive of the extent to which this is true! A fundamental part of my experience as a priest is to realize how much I have loved people to whom I have been sent, even if they have disappeared over the horizon. I will always love them. And I know that they also love me. Even when they attack me, I know that they are counting on my love.

WOLTON: *What you are saying leads us to something that we have not talked about very much: your emotional attachments during your childhood and adolescence, especially since you decided very early to become a priest.*

LUSTIGER: As it is for every human being, it is a matter of choice, discipline and the reason for choices. I was an assiduous reader of Stendhal. Perhaps you remember his theory on the crystalization of affections in the description of amorous feelings. A person falls in love only if he wants to, if he consents to it. From the moment that someone believes that he has been called to give himself to God, his asceticism consists of avoiding this chain of circumstances. That does not mean becoming insensitive, but you know very well that there is always a succession of incidents, of desire and emotional attachment, which leads, if one is not careful, to this "crystalization". And one day the hero suddenly falls in love with his heroine. As a student chaplain, I had fifteen years to observe the emotional and relational life of young people from eighteen to twenty-five years old, and I saw how they fell in love. I could virtually predict the particular conditions in which it would happen.

The French Clergy: More to the Left and Community-Oriented?

WOLTON: *In the evolution of the French clergy since the end of the war, one notes a gradual movement toward the left, among priests as well as the hierarchy. How can this phenomenon be explained?*

LUSTIGER: It is related to the misadventures of French society. There was the enormous shock of the war. . . . Remember: most of France was Pétainist; all of France's traditional memory found itself—at least at the beginning of the occupation—as if coagulated in this feeling. It was a painful time in French history, a time of bad consciences. After the liberation, there was a change of direction to try to restore, to heal, the French conscience. It was, in appearance at least, a balancing act, and the Church was caught up in it. But there are also older historical causes. We can point to, for example, the existence of *l'Action française* between the two wars and the way in which it influenced a certain number of Catholics. A period of time had to elapse before its condemnation in 1926 took effect—it was a condemnation that also included, by the way, the opposite deviation. There is nothing very surprising about this. The explanation is tied to the historical circumstances of France's evolution.

WOLTON: *We also witnessed the rise of the word* communautaire, *sometimes, in fact, in opposition to the hierarchy. Priests progressively refused an elite status in order to act more as pastors—indeed, as organizers.*

LUSTIGER: The *mouvement communautaire* is a typical outgrowth of the intense urbanization that we have been undergoing for the past fifty years. Because before, when communities existed, nobody talked about them. Nobody bothered to make theories about them, because they corresponded to normal modes of integration into social life, whether it was a matter of village communities or urban parishes. Forty years ago, urbanists adopted the term *parish* as an element of the urban structure. It designated a grouping together of about two hundred to two hundred fifty families. The *mouvement communautaire* was born when there were no communities left. It became an ideal charged with nostalgia and hope. When the villages began to disappear, the kibbutzim, the kolkhozes or the sovkhozes were invented. The personalist and community movement, originating in France with Mounier in particular, expanded rapidly after the war with the hyper-urbanization of the Fifties. The word *parish* was replaced by *community,* which was loaded with a powerful emotional potential, whereas formerly the specific usage of the word designated monastic communities—that is, communities that were much more *"communautaires"* and at the same time more structured and hierarchical.

MISSIKA: *Yes, people tend to forget that those communities were structured and hierarchical!*

LUSTIGER: They were very structured and hierarchical, and yet they lived under a democratic regime. I call a democratic regime one in which the authority is regularly elected, which is the case in all monastic life. According to the statutes, all members of the community have definite rights concerning these elections. In ecclesiastical language, the word *community* was reserved for religious communities. Not so long ago, if somebody asked, "Where is the community?", the immediate thought was of nuns or monks, whereas today one hears young people everywhere talking about "community life". What social functions are filled by this ideology, and what role can it play? The priest's role has simply followed this evolution and has been affected by all these factors—if the ultimate meaning of your question revolves around the refusal of the differentiation of roles, which is not excluded from your mind, I suspect.

WOLTON: *This refusal of differentiation is an implicit aspect of my question. . . .*

LUSTIGER: One can take note of it and place this "given" among observations already made. It comes back to the regressive and fusional facets of contemporary society; they also affect the religious domain. Perhaps they are linked to the decrease in vocations, because if there is no longer any difference between the clergy and the laity, how do you expect there to be an identification of a call to a function that does not stand out more distinctly? The same is true for the falling birthrate: when paternal images have been destroyed, perhaps the sons have no desire to have children.

The Laity, the Churches, the Parish

MISSIKA: *Do you think that there is a connection between the growing role of laymen and the decrease in vocations, or are there other causes?*

LUSTIGER: Take the example that is most familiar to us: France in the early twentieth century. The revival of sacerdotal vocations, the increased numbers of ordinations seemed, in fact, to be the consequence of the revival of Christian life among laymen. It came at a period when the apostolic initiatives of the laity were most numerous, most varied and innovative for the service of the Gospel (from the revival of the parish "patronage" to the multiple groups of all types: the university parish, *Semaines sociales,* Christian labor unions, *Équipes sociales,* etc.), at the period when the lay movements were developing with spiritual fervor and enthusiasm (Scouts, *Coeurs vaillants,* JOC, JAC and all the other groups of *l'Action catholique, Équipes Notre-Dame,*[3] etc., and I am not including the innumerable organizations that, although not as well known, have nevertheless had just as much influence), at the period of a powerful intellectual revival of Christianity whose eminent names belonged to laymen (from Blondel to Maritain and Gilson, from Léon Bloy to Péguy, Bernanos, Mauriac, Claudel and so many others). It was precisely at that time that the call for sacerdotal vocations was most heeded in the Church. And do not think that the generation of laymen I have just mentioned could not take complete initiative in their domain.

It was often in the same families that the vocations of priests, monks and nuns and the vocations of a lay apostolic life were seen. It was from lay movements that future priests came. Just as military recruits are found among civilians . . . When there is a falling off of sacerdotal and religious vocations, a good method for detecting the causes would be to examine the religious vitality of the baptized as a whole. In order to live the Faith and announce it, Christ's disciples, whether they be priests or laymen, must draw from the same source of God's love. And I would be able to make a similar demonstration with facts from the seventeenth or nineteenth centuries in France, not to mention the modern period. Therefore, it is preposterous to attribute the responsibility for the "seesaw effect"—according to which the priests' roles diminish as the laymen's roles expand—to Vatican II.

[3] These are allusions to various Catholic organizations: the "patronage" was a parish club for the young; Scouts and *Coeurs vaillants* (brave hearts). During this period, there was also a great deal of social work and concern, leading to the growth of such *l'Action catholique* movements as the JOC (*Jeunesse ouvrière chrétienne*) and the JAC (*Jeunesse agricole chretiénne*), which were for young Catholic workers and farmhands, respectively. Finally, the *Équipes Notre-Dame* (Notre-Dame teams) bring together married couples so that they can help each other in their spiritual lives.—TRANS.

WOLTON: *But that is the way things are perceived. Vatican II is considered a council of progress, of change, which has reasserted the status of the laity, perhaps in part as a reaction against priests and the hierarchy. You know this argument....*

LUSTIGER: In a nutshell: just like the night of August 4, 1789?[4] I see it all very clearly: you assimilate the laity to the Third Estate, and the priests and hierarchy to the clergy and aristocracy of the *Ancien Régime.* Let us follow it through to the end: "What is the laity?" "Nothing." "What must it become?" "Everything."[5] But in our modern version, where is the nobility that renounces its privileges? Unless it happens to be made up of scholars, commentators and shapers of public opinion? You have surely heard about the numerous and voluminous commentaries on the constitution *Lumen gentium* that reduce it to an inversion of the "pyramidal" structure of the Church: until and including Vatican I, one departed from the summit, the Pope. Since Vatican II, one departs from the base, the people. But it is still a pyramid, unless one succeeds with one hard blow in flattening the summit to the center of the base.... Such commentaries are only a bad joke.

In religious history, the Christian faith presents an absolutely original character that is described in an expression from the book of Exodus used by Saint Peter: "You are", he writes to Christians, "a chosen race, a royal priesthood, a holy nation, God's own people, that you may declare the wonderful deeds of him who called you out of darkness into his marvelous light" (1 Pet 2:9). He also calls them a "holy priesthood" destined "to offer spiritual sacrifices acceptable to God through Jesus Christ" (1 Pet 2:5). The pagan religions reserve the perfection of their ideal for a limited number of paragons. The Christian faith places the source of perfection for every man in the union with Christ given at baptism. Thus, from the beginning of faith, holiness is the personal vocation of each Christian and their common good that makes them into a holy people. The priest's ministry, its irreducible originality and authority, is in the service of this vocation common to all. He serves the holy and priestly people—*laos* in Greek, from which the word *laïc* was formed, as Father Congar rightly reminds us.

At the time of the Reformation, the Council of Trent defined the sacramental character of the priest's mission and his authority. Vatican II completed this long meditation of the Church on her own nature by pointing out the

[4] On this date, the National Assembly, which included a majority of laymen but also numerous priests and even aristocrats, abolished the privileges that the nobility and the clergy had enjoyed under the *Ancien Régime*—TRANS.

[5] This is a parody of a well-known pamphlet by Sieyès, one of the priests who made the French Revolution possible. In the name of democratic rationality, he advocated a greater role for the Third Estate (that is, those who were neither clerical nor noble) in the nation's political life.—TRANS.

singular correspondence of the sacraments: on the one hand, baptism and confirmation, which creates God's people, permitting them to understand and celebrate the sacerdotal eucharistic mission of all the Church; on the other, the sacrament of ordination (the college of bishops of which the Pope is the head, and those whom they ordain for the presbyterial and diaconal ministry) is, in and for these baptized people, the effective and personal sign of the presence of Christ, priest and head of his Body: "And lo, I am with you always, to the close of the age" (Mt 28:20). Vatican II carried the work begun by the Council of Trent to its conclusion by defining the sacramental originality of Christian life and of the Church and by taking a distance in regard to certain social and political modes in order to affirm the specificity of the Catholic communion and its functioning. The Church has forged the principal concepts that permit her to confront the major upheavals of modern society. Consequently, giving prominence to the conflicts over status and competition for power, to which we are accustomed by social analysis, does not provide the right key for understanding the relationship of the laity to the priests and the hierarchy.

WOLTON: *In spite of your analysis of continuity, most of the texts that we have read present Vatican II as a "democratic" breakthrough, upgrading the place of laymen, who were in any case playing a more and more important role in the Church, notably through the movements of* l'Action catholique.

LUSTIGER: The problems must be classified: first, there is the model or models for the functioning of the ecclesiastical institution; then there is the part that laymen can and must take in a certain number of tasks that recent practice had placed in the hands of the clergy or nuns (preparation of the sacraments, catechism, adult education, aid for the sick and dying, the organization of means for sharing with the poorest members of society, management of the Church's property, etc.); and, finally, there are the Christian commitments connected with the "secular" condition—that is, characterized by professional, social and political activity and that do not necessarily exclude marriage. Each of these three areas elicits concrete and variable responses, depending on the countries or times. Although interconnected, they have to be treated separately. All three trace the contours of the Church's mission in the world, without defining or getting to its heart, however.

The mission is described in the last chapters of the constitution *Lumen gentium* of Vatican II. They define the historic vocation of the entire Church, and hence of each of its members, as the call to holiness that must labor without respite for the transformation of our world, according to God's plan for salvation, for men's happiness and his glory. These chapters place this vocation in its true context—not that of a specific culture, civilization or homeland, all just as mortal as man—which is the long duration, set forth as a hope for all of humanity and whose plenitude will be realized at the end of time.

MISSIKA: *Do you think that there is a need for churches to be built in France?*

LUSTIGER: Yes, definitely, because in the last ten years or so there has been an enormous movement of the French population into urban areas. The villages, where churches were constructed in the past, are empty. However, the new churches should be constructed on a modest scale—not with eight hundred seats. We have to build them like the Germans, English and Americans do, for a congregation of two hundred or so. They are less costly and more flexible, lighter. They are absolutely necessary!

In the Paris region, there is a glaring inequality in religious facilities—perhaps we have not known how to look ahead and organize ourselves in time. Future generations will accuse us of negligence or lack of foresight. We have inherited the disproportionate facilities of the nineteenth century, and in some places there was a presumptuous overexpansion, while we allowed others to lie fallow. . . .

The church is a place of sacramental nature. It is the place where all the functions and dimensions of Christian life, which are organized around the Eucharist, are integrated. A church, a parish, is first of all a site, in both the geographical and symbolic sense. It is an *ekklēsia,* a bringing together of God's people for the Eucharist, from which ensues the totality of tasks and missions with which priests and laymen are associated in parish life. The church, the parish, is first of all a place of charity—that is, of love, taken in the strongest sense—because the Eucharist implies fraternal love among those who are called together in a particular place, even if they have not chosen each other, and especially if they have not done so: "For if you love those who love you, what reward have you? Do not even the tax collectors do the same?" (Mt 5:46). "Love your enemies" (Mt 5:44), Jesus says. The church and parish are places where those who have come together show love to each other; they are also places of solidarity, of charity in regard to any brother who presents himself. We must not forget the commandment referring to the immigrant, as it is expressed in the Bible—it is God's commandment, not a sociological theory: the foreigner, the one who is passing through, the one without hearth or home, the exiled, the poor, the prisoner must be welcomed as brothers. And it is essential that this commandment be put into practice somewhere!

Reflection on the parish involves taking a firm stand against the functionalism of modern society. It is normal and necessary that important services and social functions exist. But the parish should be the place where a vital "despecialization" of society and its social relations can be experienced. Generations are linked with one another in sacramental life. Birth and death, these two extremes, are borne by a community that receives grace through the sacraments. The parish church is the place where children are baptized and the place where the community prays for the living and the dead. God's forgiveness is granted there; through the priest's ministry, reconciliation is made in the form of the sacrament of penitence, as is the mutual forgiveness of Christians, exercised in the Spirit as a force of communion within the social fabric they inhabit. The parish is also the place where faith in the celebrated mysteries is transmitted and proclaimed, because faith is not presented as an ideology or subjective conviction but in the concrete and carnal reality of an assembled people who live what it announces and what is announced to it. It is a place where the Word, the Bible, ceases to be an abstract word given over to the scalpel of exegetes or archaeologists. Rather it is to be given mouth to mouth, as a nourishment and Word of life, shared as a living Word. The parish is the place where the eucharistic community, nourished by the Body of Christ, becomes his Body, which is the Church. In the Eucharist, the particular community represents and actualizes the Church's universality, because no congregation or parish can exist without the ministry of the priest, thanks to whom a community of baptized persons receives its dimension and assumes its Catholic responsibility. Priests, in fact, are sent by bishops who exist only in communion with all the bishops of the entire world. And together they are the concrete, earthly, historical and personal sign of the Church's catholicity.

PART FIVE

THE UNIVERSAL CHURCH

I

WHAT IS A PASTOR?

Bishop of Orléans, Archbishop of Paris

JEAN-LOUIS MISSIKA: *You were appointed bishop of Orléans in December 1979. What did this nomination mean for you? You were, after all, returning to the scene of your conversion.*

JEAN-MARIE LUSTIGER: I felt that, by giving me an apostolic and sacerdotal mission in one of the places that had been most decisive in my life, God had put a seal on my personal history. When I was told that the Pope had named me bishop of Orléans, I literally did not understand what was being said. It had to be repeated two or three times before it registered. And then, it seemed that God was asking this of me. My sense of propriety makes it hard to talk about such personal matters, but I swear to you that to find myself in the cathedral in Orléans, at the exact spot where, for the first time, I had had the intuition of the mystery of the suffering Messiah—his body given and his blood shed, his presence in his brothers and the Eucharist—to find myself in the places where I had been shaped and my life had taken its direction, gave an extraordinary intensity to each detail, but really to *each detail* of my existence in Orléans. I forbade myself from thinking about it too much for fear that my head would burst—because the past was rushing back upon me with such a flood of memories, personal *souvenirs* and symbolic riches. The bishop of Orléans' office, where Monsignor Courcoux had instructed me, became my office. I celebrated Mass in the same chapel in which I had been baptized. I found priests or laymen who had been classmates, and there I was, so unexpectedly serving as their pastor, as an apostle. God was asking me to give them what I had received from them.

Something in this situation remained strangely disconcerting. I felt at home, and yet I knew very well that I had come from somewhere else, because I had first arrived there in flight from persecution, living clandestinely, almost a foreigner, expelled from the national community by Vichy's laws. Moreover, when I became a bishop, I immediately came under the fire of the press, which lost no time in revealing to everybody what I had kept private, through discretion and respect. Up to that time, I had been free to say what I wanted, to whomever I had wanted to say it. I had never hidden, but neither had I exposed myself. But, at that time, I was forced to take the initiative. . . . The media did not let me off lightly . . . not through malevolence—quite the contrary. I am not reproaching them; that is just the way things work. What I had kept as a personal story to be confided to a friend had to be told to everybody. So, being bishop of Orléans was all that—and so many other things of such incredible richness that I can hardly explain my feelings. Chance circumstances that can hardly be communicated—the fleeting view of a street corner, a patch of sky, a landscape, a tree, a boulder—sent me hurtling back to my earlier life, to my family's history, to French history and to my place in it, the mission that I had to fulfill. My memory was nourished by the emotional and symbolic responsibility that the mission represented, and I was carried well beyond myself. It was not I who had chosen such a destiny; I would never have been able to invent such a situation. I had in no way sought it, and I found myself exactly like a piece of wood inserted in the corner of a framework. This ordinary piece of wood—so similar to the other wood and which had asked for nothing special—found itself placed at the spot where the framework joined and was obliged to be there to prevent the structure's collapse. According to legend, the Cathédrale Sainte-Croix d'Orléans was consecrated not by men but by the hand of God. This hand, then, had to come to take me back there. So that was where I was meant to be, and I went there with all the more inner strength because I was relying on what appeared to me as a providential plan, on God's will.

I was filled with both the indescribable pain of remembering and by an intense elation at being able to repay, to serve and to give. It was as though God had taken me at my word. "Taken me at my word"? For more than ten years, I had continuously meditated, reflected on the Church's problems, on her relationship to modern society and her fidelity to the Gospel, and I had concluded that an additional faithfulness and freedom were being required of the contemporary Church. Suddenly, with the apostolic mission entrusted to me, I became responsible for what I had been allowed to see. Providence was saying to me, "What you have been given the power to perceive so keenly, you must now act upon." If a light had been granted, it was so that I could more steadfastly respond to this mission.

I was ordained bishop on December 8, 1979, at the cathedral in Orléans. December 8 is the feast of the Immaculate Conception, whose profuse symbolism struck me on that day with incredible force, if only because of the liturgical texts. It is a feast of the Virgin, anticipatory figure of the Church; she receives beforehand the gift of salvation from the one who will be given as Son. The Church celebrates Mary's conception in prayer and veneration. In fact, just as Israel's election precedes in time the Messiah who is given to it, Mary, daughter of Zion (Is 62) and prefiguration of the Church, receives in advance the salvation that allows her to give birth to her Savior. In Mary, the Church precedes the One who constitutes her. This is why the liturgy has a historic and cosmic scope, at the limits of history. It begins with the account from Genesis of our beginnings. The next reading is taken from the Epistle to the Ephesians, which sets forth the mutual relations between Jews and pagans in the Church of God: they are both reconciled with God by the Cross of his Son; the former have been chosen in him for all eternity to be the first among those whom God loves and calls to serve him, and henceforth the latter, those who were far away, are called in their turn to come close and enter into the same communion. In this "convocation", this Church, the Marian figure is the figure of the people, composed of both Jews and pagans. Finally, the Annunciation from the Gospel contains and condenses, with an extraordinarily prophetic and symbolic force, the entire history of salvation.

MISSIKA: *What did you choose as your motto?*

LUSTIGER: I had not planned to have one. I refused to have a coat of arms, a heraldic blazon, and I had not really thought about a motto, but as it turned out, one was chosen for me. In the Gospel's account of the Annunciation, Mary—after having been told about the birth of the Messiah—says to God's envoy, "How shall this be, since I have no husband?" And the angel replies, "For God nothing is impossible." These are also the words that the angel had used much earlier when announcing Isaac's birth to Abraham, and they are repeated by Jesus himself when he reminds his Disciples of the stringencies of salvation (Mt 19:26). In my parish in Paris, I had been in the habit of preparing weekly liturgical bulletins, and I always chose a central phrase from the scriptural reading as a title. On the day of my ordination in Orléans, I had chosen *"Tout est possible à Dieu."*[1] For me, these words summed up the liturgy of December 8. I was filled with the sentiment that my nomination represented a tremendous challenge. I did not know how the Pope could have reached such a decision, but I knew that, however difficult the challenge, I could not turn away from it.

MISSIKA: *Are you referring to your nomination as bishop of Orléans or as archbishop of Paris?*

LUSTIGER: Well, I suppose you can say both, since my feelings about Orléans can apply to Paris as well. As I was saying, I had chosen *"Tout est possible à Dieu"* as a heading for the liturgical booklet for the celebration. The Orléans journalists, who were paying a lot of attention to me at the time, said,

[1] "Everything is possible for God."—TRANS.

"Here is your motto! '*Tout est possible à Dieu.*' " And that is how it happened that it was journalists who came up with a motto for me.

MISSIKA: *You did not stay in Orléans very long?*

LUSTIGER: For less than two years. One year and three months, to be exact. I was convinced that I would remain in Orléans, that I had reached my home port. And yet, from the first day, I was seized by a sense of urgency. I do not know why, but I felt that I had to act quickly. I wanted to do everything as rapidly as possible. Is that simply my temperament? Happily, I did not know that my days there were numbered, much more so than those of Monsignor Riobé,[2] my predecessor, whose spiritual depth I was discovering little by little.

As for my appointment in Paris, several persons had spoken to me about it before the Pope's decision. The rumor had circulated. I refuted it with undaunted serenity, basing myself on the argument that the Pope is a pastor, that he knows what a diocese is; therefore, why would he want me to abandon the one in Orléans for another one when I had just begun to work? It seemed inconceivable to me. And then, I need not tell you that when I was informed that I had been named archbishop of Paris, I was initially overcome by sadness at having to leave Orléans again. Furthermore, I weighed the difficulties that were awaiting me in Paris! Really, I came here . . . I do not dare to say as on an impossible mission, but almost. I did not think that I was the most capable person for the job. I felt that there were men who were much more suited to the situation here, more prepared for it, from the inside. And since there were such obvious and well-known problems, it seemed to be something of a defiance to ask me to go virtually in the opposite direction from my temperament and experience.

My nomination to Paris on February 2 coincided with another feast, the Presentation of Jesus at the Temple, and here again, it was a feast of both the Virgin and Christ. Its spiritual significance is also extremely rich. The Virgin, previously sanctified, exempted from sin and therefore the hope of a transfigured humanity for the nations as well as for Israel, carries into the Father's house the child Messiah, the living Word who has not yet begun to speak. There in the temple, all of Israel's prophets are represented by the figures of Simeon and Anna, day and night giving thanks to God. And the elderly Simeon says to Mary, "Behold, this child is set for the fall and rising of many in Israel, and for a sign that is spoken against (and a sword will pierce through your own soul

[2] Monsignor Guy-Marie Riobé (1911–78) had died in an accident after gaining a national reputation as a staunch supporter of nonviolence in particular and of a certain evangelical radicalism in general.—TRANS.

also), and thoughts out of many hearts may be revealed" (Lk 2:34–35). And so the figure of the suffering Messiah is proclaimed in the temple, the place where God dwells.

I saw it all clearly: what was being asked of me in becoming archbishop of Paris touched my deepest personal commitment. I felt a great love for those people whom I was being asked to serve, the love that Christ has for them; and many of them had shown me friendship. But I knew that it was going to be a way for me to share Christ's Passion. I had no illusions on that point. When I had been appointed to Orléans, my first thought had been that the cathedral there is dedicated to the holy Cross. That, too, seemed to be a part of the most personal logic, and I was acutely aware of it.

DOMINIQUE WOLTON: *Do you still have the feeling that you are participating in the Passion?*

LUSTIGER: Yes, definitely. In one way or another, that participation is asked of all disciples and in particular of those who receive the apostolic mission. When I arrived in Paris as archbishop, someone who had been close to Cardinal Veuillot said to me, "It is because of him that you are here." The memory of the time when the Cardinal was dying and called me to his bedside did not leave me. What he had said to me then, the sense of having received a confidence from him, became a transmitted mission.

One last thing, and I will have finished with this subject. In 1946, when I entered seminary, I was very sensitive to the often-encountered objection that the Church was "a social system for advancement, a power structure". I had drawn my own conclusions from that objection and was determined to live strictly outside the channels of influence, doing what I had to do. Never, in any way whatsoever, would I put myself in positions that would favor what, in the eyes of social or administrative systems, is called "promotion". Never would I enter those circuits. Never would I make any concessions in any of these domains.... And that resolution had prevented all equivocation or interior complicity. Of course, you can say to me that I could have refused this nomination. But everything appeared so much to have come from God that refusing it never crossed my mind for an instant. Nevertheless, I later asked myself questions: Had others not judged me too favorably? On what human assessments, what system of consultation had the choice been made? People are mistaken, I said, they do not know who you are, they are overestimating your strengths or underestimating your weaknesses.... A person can always be invaded by such doubts.... But later a close associate of the Pope confided something to me that was a deliverance: "Listen, your nomination is the fruit of the Pope's prayer. He hesitated a long time, and he prayed at length to know whom he ought to appoint." Then I understood: the way the decision had been reached by the one responsible for it had obeyed the logic of prayer and receptivity to God. That does not mean that it was an infallible decision, but at least it was soundly taken. And I repeated to myself: What is being asked of you is to remain yourself. You are not to be anyone other than who you are. Cardinal Marty[3] had given us an example of this in a delicate period. I had in my turn to accept what he had had to accept: going somewhere I did not wish to go.

WOLTON: *Here you are speaking about Paris?*

LUSTIGER: Yes. But implicitly I had also said this to myself before going to Orléans. This understanding and the increased responsibility gave me, on the whole, a greater inner serenity, a greater security, in that I felt supported by the Church's prayer and by a decision taken under God's eyes. Consequently, I also felt that, in spite of my personal weaknesses, I would be protected in the vulnerable positions that God would have me take. Just as a reasonable and responsible officer does not send someone to the battlefront without giving him the arms to survive, I knew that I would receive what was necessary for fulfilling the mission asked of me, with the least harm possible. But what most struck public opinion at the time was one unusual aspect of my biography: for three years afterward, I was known as *"le Polonais".* And from that identification to imagining that I had had a previous connection with the Pope, there was only one step, which was blithely taken.

MISSIKA: *But it was not just that you were "the Pole", but "the Polish Jew".*

LUSTIGER: I had immediately and publicly declared that I was a "Jew and the son of Polish immigrants". It was for me and no one else to say. But many people retained only "Polish". Some of them, when speaking about Poland, still say to me sympathetically, "your homeland", "your compatriots". . . . It is amazing!

WOLTON: *But even so, the other part, the Jewish origin, must irritate some Catholics. . . .*

LUSTIGER: Yes, I know. I am a living provocation that obliges people to question themselves on the historic figure of the Messiah. My own story is partly linked to this historic figure. It is a provocation that remains salutary for the Church, regardless of my "case" or my person.

[3] François Marty (1904–) was Archbishop of Paris from 1968 to 1981.—TRANS.

WOLTON: *Do you think that the Pope wanted this to happen?*

LUSTIGER: Who knows?

WOLTON: *And since then? Have you ever spoken about this with him?*

LUSTIGER: Yes, insofar as it regards the good of the Church and mankind. But be that as it may, the Pope already knew everything about me. Nothing had been concealed. And he did not act inadvertently.

MISSIKA: *Do you feel that you are controversial in the French Church because of your Jewish origin?*

LUSTIGER: Because of that? I have no idea.

WOLTON: *Perhaps it does not matter to you?*

LUSTIGER: I do not know. I meet with contrasting attitudes. Some of them touch me deeply because they show that among certain Catholics there is an understanding of Israel's mystery, and it surges forth like a spring. I consider that a sign of the Catholic Faith's vitality. This awareness is often linked to the deep, keen and authentic spiritual sense of Christians who know or discover the love of Christ in his human condition, who pray with the Virgin and have a fervent love of the Church. They are grateful to God for the graces given to the Jewish people, and at the same time sensitive, as though anticipating the wound of anti-Semitism. There is also the inverse attitude, often of a baseness and coarseness that astonish me—because, up until that time, I had benefited from a providential blindness. I had scarcely ever been exposed to such remarks.

WOLTON: *Anti-Semitic remarks?*

LUSTIGER: Yes, I had heard them, of course, but elsewhere.

WOLTON: *And not directed at you?*

MISSIKA: *Not from within the Church?*

LUSTIGER: Directed at me, yes, but not from the Church, not from the

Church I knew. I had read Drumont; he was a Catholic. I knew about Dreyfus and what *La Croix*[4] had written.

MISSIKA: *And since then?*

LUSTIGER: Since then, I detect it in satirical tracts, in certain newspaper articles. . . .

MISSIKA: *When Jean-Marie Le Pen cites your name along with four Jewish journalists, do you think he is making an anti-Semitic allusion?*

LUSTIGER: If he is, I am very much honored. It is aimed at the archbishop of Paris in communion with the Pope and the college of bishops. I have said that my nomination was a provocation; it twisted the knife in the wound; it forced people to reflect and know the truth. My presence alone as archbishop of Paris reveals in an obvious, very striking way, the true nature of anti-Semitism; it is a way of being anti-Christian and a blasphemy against God. Anti-Semitism is not simply a variant of xenophobia; it is the refusal of something that belongs to Christ and comes from Christ. It is a test, an indicator, like litmus paper.

WOLTON: *Yes, but not all anti-Semites are Christians. What does it mean when Christians hold such views?*

LUSTIGER: I repeat, it is a test. The Nazi or Communist anti-Semitism reveals its true nature. The tactic consists of asking populations belonging to the Christian tradition to disassociate themselves from Jews; without people's realizing it, this is a way of attacking the Christian faith by cutting off its root. It is perverse. So it is not surprising that totalitarian atheisms of the Nazi or Communist type always have an anti-Semitic component. This is clear. Take the present case of Poland: it is simpler to strike out at the Jews who are active in Solidarity than to make a frontal attack on Solidarity itself. But it would be naïve not to understand that when these Jews are slandered, it is really Christianity as a source of Solidarity that is the target.

[4] *La Croix* was a Catholic daily newspaper founded in 1883. Until the beginning of the century, it spoke out against secularization and participated in nationalist and anti-Semitic campaigns, especially during the Dreyfus affair. It later changed its position altogether.—TRANS.

The Powers of an Archbishop

MISSIKA: *What is the nature of your power as archbishop?*

LUSTIGER: I am a successor to the Apostles and, to begin with, responsible before God, the Church and my brother bishops for a people's fidelity to the Gospel of Jesus Christ and for the constitution of his Body that is the Church.

WOLTON: *To us, that does not seem very concrete.*

LUSTIGER: But your question about my "power" threw me off. Have a look at the Code of Canon Law, if that is what interests you.

MISSIKA: *Fine. But, after all, there is a hierarchy in the Church, and that means that some people are placed in command of others.*

LUSTIGER: Here is the reason I react as I do to such questions. In the Gospel, when the sons of Zebedee ask to be seated at his right hand and left in his glory, Jesus replies, "You know that those who are supposed to rule over the Gentiles lord it over them, and their great men exercise authority over them. But it shall not be so among you; but whoever would be great among you must be your servant, and whoever would be first among you must be slave to all" (Mk 10:42–44). Christ deals with the question explicitly in speaking to the Apostles. He approaches it head on to show that the exercise of power is an identification with Christ-Servant. I am well aware that the Emperor Napoléon identified the bishop with the *préfet*[5] or the general, integrating the functions of the episcopal body with those of the other institutions of the state. And I admit that they are similar in one respect. But, as a successor to the Apostles, every bishop is bound to reject a belittling identification. I have answered your question in terms of duty rather than in terms of power.

MISSIKA: *Yes, but sometimes you have to make authoritative decisions.*

LUSTIGER: The authority is given by Christ. It is the power to forgive sins, to administer the sacraments of salvation and, thus, to constitute the Church. It is the power and the duty to proclaim the Word of God, the power to give the sacraments of resurrection and to call together the scattered children of God. These are spiritual powers coming from Christ, from the

[5] The *préfet* is the highest civil administrator in each of France's ninety-five main administrative divisions, called *départements*. —TRANS.

One who is Pastor. The specific authority of the bishop is situated in this sacramental domain of the service of divine charity.

WOLTON: *Could you be a bit more explicit? Do you have, for example, the authority to appoint priests, to assign them to particular parishes? How does that work?*

LUSTIGER: A bishop takes on the apostolic responsibility for a certain diocese. He must ensure that the Church in his diocese receives what Christ wants to give to his people. And he has the authority to do this. However, he is assisted in this task by different committees whose makeup and powers are defined by canon law. Thus, the bishop freely appoints those responsible for pastoral duty—priests, deacons or laymen. Depending on the duties, diverse conditions are set forth in the law. In France, for example, a curé is appointed for six years during which he cannot be recalled except for serious and clear-cut reasons presented in a juridical procedure.

The bishop must see to it that the Church in his charge receives the Word of God. Faithfully. He has the authority to be the guarantor of the Faith. Is it sufficient for a bishop to open his mouth for Catholic truth to come forth? No. Rules of obedience determine the authority of his word. A bishop speaks the Catholic truth infallibly when, associated with the totality of the apostolic college united with the Pope, he speaks as a witness to the Faith. The Faith's truth coincides with its universality in space and time, with the communion of all. Men are always tempted to particularize their opinions, and what is called tolerance or pluralism is all too often only an attitude: *"Pense ce que tu peux, je pense ce que je veux"*;[6] hence: *"À chacun sa vérité"*.[7] But the Church is not performing Pirandello! The truth is communion with the Truth that surpasses everyone, respecting each person and his individualities. The bishop is charged—and has the authority to carry out his responsibility—with being the normal witness of the normative communion of all the faithful in the Church's Faith.

WOLTON: *Then the bishop can call certain priests to order if he feels that they are moving away from the common Word.*

LUSTIGER: Not especially or exclusively "certain priests". Public opinion is presently very fickle, since it suffices for a poll to be taken to have some idea or other accepted as the new truth. Amid this flood of opinion, I have the duty to recall the primary and inalienable truths of faith—not by "telling off" anybody who might have "gotten out of line", but most often by taking it on

[6] Literally, this means: "Think what you can; I think what I want to think."—TRANS.

[7] Literally, this translates: "To each his truth", which is the French title of a well-known play by the Italian playwright Luigi Pirandello.—TRANS.

myself to declare publicly that truth which I have received and have the obligation to transmit.

WOLTON: *But when somebody speaks out in a society that is as much swayed by public opinion as ours, he has no power other than his convictions and influence! Is there no other means the Church can use? Are you able to sanction someone, for example?*

LUSTIGER: I do have that prerogative, determined and limited by law. If you wanted me to specify the circumstances and the very precise forms of its exercise, then I would have to recite at least thirty pages of the Code of Canonic Law. Because, contrary to what some people think and the picture sometimes given, the Church is not a society subjected to the arbitrary. At the risk of a sometimes frustrating slowness, she sees to it that the rights of persons are respected.

It is up to the Church to verify whether a particular thought or research or expression of the Faith belongs to the Catholic communion or not. The procedures used are more respectful and temporizing than academic or judiciary procedures. A certain facile tendency in public opinion has made some priests and theologians into martyrs, victims of the denial of justice. It is all a part of the situation created by the current means of shaping opinion.

WOLTON: *But the image that predominates is that of a rigid system sanctioning deviation and neglecting the complexity and open character of the discussion.*

MISSIKA: *It is the question of legitimate speech, authorized speech, that causes the difficulty. In societies like ours, where all opinions are legitimate, it is hard for some people to understand that certain declarations, certain arguments can be "condemned" because hierarchical authority judges them to be inadequate or contrary to dogma, to the rule of faith.*

LUSTIGER: The model to which we refer today is the political model of an ideology that maintains its "party line" in an iron-handed and restrictive manner.

MISSIKA: *Exactly. The Communist model.*

LUSTIGER: I have met two types of persons who intuitively understand the difference between obedience to the Faith and ideological conformity. The first have a historical culture that is sufficient to acquaint them with the proliferation of Western and Christian thought: even if they are not believers, they can appreciate how a source—unvarying—serves as a reference for a living thought and how the Church—through her authority, hierarchy and Magisterium—is basically the guarantor and expression of this unique source. Those whose perception is fine enough can observe how this Magisterium is exercised, sometimes narrowly, sometimes broadly. At certain times, admittedly, the authority has been abusively confining and has committed the faults of inflexibility or undiscerning judgment. History shows, however, that this is far from being the most frequent case.

The others who understand are the pure-hearted and the mystics. They spontaneously detect the voice of the living Tradition and the signs of the Spirit—and always with a great deal of liberty. They have the intuition of fidelity. It is amazing—and it is a phenomenon particular to Christianity and the biblical tradition—to see simple people go straight to the heart of things, often with more depth than scholars. And the work of these artless souls quite unexpectedly becomes a source of progress and knowledge. Typical modern examples of these types are Saint Thérèse of Lisieux, the Curé d'Ars, Saint Bernadette, etc.

WOLTON: *Have you had any difficult or painful decisions to make since you became archbishop?*

LUSTIGER: No, not juridically. But in an era when public opinion has such weight, the faithful, just like priests, have the right to know what the Church believes, and it is my duty to articulate it. In doing so, I have never been led to sanction by name such and such a person for such and such an idea. On the other hand, I have testified positively, proclaiming—sometimes loudly—the Church's Faith. If a critical reflection is to do any good, the person to whom it is being made has to be living the Faith in a healthy spiritual equilibrium. If this person cannot imagine what the truth coming from God is like, then you can spend all your time "correcting his homework" without its changing anything. But it could happen that I may find myself facing more flagrant or serious cases that would oblige me to follow the procedure foreseen by Church law.

WOLTON: *Would you say that there have been more or fewer enforcements of dogmatic truth in the past thirty years as compared to previous centuries?*

LUSTIGER: The past thirty years have been a time of considerable fluctuation. The Church is sensitive to the fact that she has repeatedly been put on trial by public opinion, and a confusion has sometimes arisen between what is called the *sensus fidelium*—a Latin expression designating the sense or intuition of faith, shared by believers as a whole—and what public opinion holds to be true. Why favor this common understanding of the Faith? Because the Church believes that, as the Body of Christ, she is the dwelling place for God's Spirit who allows her faithful to discover and understand the Word, given to her in communion. Consequently, the shared meaning is one of the criteria by which the living fidelity to the Faith is verified. But since the *sensus fidelium* is often equated with public opinion, and public opinion is formed by pronouncements of the mass media, it suffices to have four articles written in respected newspapers for some people to conclude that the "popular understanding of the Faith" is demanding such and such a change. Thus, we find ourselves in the strange situation where we are thrown off balance by the pressure tactics of public opinion, which cannot be confused with the traditional procedures for verification in the Church. The rule of Saint Vincent of Lérins,[8] which dates from the sixth century, says that what is held to be Catholic truth is what has been upheld by everyone, always and everywhere. It is the principle of consensus and communication in the Faith.

MISSIKA: *There is a traditional objection to your argument. Your definition, in a way, boils down to what Jean-Jacques Rousseau calls the general will. And there can be a conflict between public opinion—which presupposes a majority and a minority—and the general will, which presupposes unanimity.*

LUSTIGER: Basically, you are posing the question of freedom. Faith designates the personal relationship of man with God. It leads to freedom. The various expressions of faith, received and transmitted by the Church, set forth the conditions for experiencing this freedom. To anyone looking on from the outside, these conditions can seem like constraints, whereas, for the believer, they define a field of liberty. Look at the fascination that the supreme spiritual liberty of Saint John of the Cross, doctor of the Church, holds for so many unbelievers. Note how the same fidelity to these components of the Faith is found in temperaments as different as Saint Teresa and Saint Ignatius of Loyola, if we limit ourselves to sixteenth-century Spain. The truth, received and imparted by the Church according to the authority belonging to her, establishes the Church's communion and the believer's freedom.

The bishops' apostolic mission is to guarantee fidelity to God and to his Word and to ensure the Catholic authenticity of the understanding that the faithful must have of that Word. The men who carry out these missions can abuse them, but their sins and errors cannot prevail over the Church's Faith, which is stronger than the failings and limitations of men, even those invested with authority. They are sinners just like everybody else. But that does not

[8] Saint Vincent of Lérins († 445), a monk, was known for his *Commonitorium* against heresies, a work written for the Council of Ephesus, in which, for the first time, it is affirmed that, for a dogma to be accepted, one must be able to show that it is universally recognized.—TRANS.

cause God to withdraw his steadfast support of his Church. This is why we believe the Church to be faithful to God's truth and guarded from error in the predication and definition of faith.

MISSIKA: *When one observes, as we have been doing lately, your activities as archbishop of Paris, they bear a close resemblance to those of a political leader. You have meetings, you have to see and entertain all sorts of people, you are often interviewed by journalists.... What makes you fundamentally different from that category of public figures who are in government or industry?*

LUSTIGER: Actually, I spend almost a third of my time—it represents at least two full days per week when the hours are added up—in celebrating the Eucharist, in preaching God's Word, in sacramental meetings with the Christian people. I am not including in this time my personal prayer when I am alone, only the public acts of my mission as bishop. This is the most important part of my responsibility. Everything else is done in its service. Of the time remaining, a third is spent in meeting other bishops or priests or in getting their help in the accomplishment of my ministry.

When a bishop preaches the Word of God, he is not like a professor who lectures or a teacher who instructs, nor is he like a politician who harangues the crowds. He is participating in the act by which God himself shares the bread of his Word with those whom he has called to know him. The most appropriate image for classifying this predication is that of the good steward: he gives in his turn the desired nourishment to those who have been entrusted to him, and he must account for the way he has carried out the distribution. The Word judges both the bishop who preaches it and the faithful who receive it. It is an active Word, which calls people to repentance and prompts their turning back toward God. Similarly, when the bishop celebrates the Eucharist and the sacraments, he is himself inscribed in the work of Christ, who sanctifies his people. This is how I spend most of my time, and the rest of my job, the administrative side, is done for the benefit of the liturgy of the Word and the sacraments.

MISSIKA: *How about the administration or management? What is the financial situation of the French Church, for example?*

LUSTIGER: First of all, it owns some real estate. At the beginning of the century, the law separating church and state turned over to the state and the *communes*[9] most of the Church's property—that is, all the churches built before

[9] A *commune* is a territorial division administered by a mayor and a municipal councillor.—TRANS.

that date. Since then, it is the public authority that is entirely responsible for their upkeep; however, a part of the cost is most often paid by the Church—i.e., by the generosity of the faithful. In fact, contrary to what was felt at the time by the mass of Catholics to be a despoilment, these churches were from the beginning assigned by law, irrevocably, for Catholic worship. Since that time a considerable number of unanimous judicial precedents have specified that the *affectataire*[10] of each church is the Catholic curé at the head of the faithful. The courts have determined what is meant by "Catholic": the curé named according to the Church's code, by the bishop in communion with the Pope. The curé's right to use the premises is exclusive and unrestricted as long as he uses the building for worship. Furthermore, out of respect for the state's secularism, the law of separation forbids civil authority to allocate public funds to any religion whatsoever.

Hence, there exists a very subtle equilibrium with which the Church and state have learned to live in the past eighty years. It would be extremely dangerous for civil peace, if the status quo, so patiently elaborated, were to be tampered with—all the more so since it maintains the life and significance of these historic buildings in the national heritage, instead of reducing them to mere *monuments-musées* open to international tourism.

WOLTON: *Are all religious buildings presently maintained by the state?*

LUSTIGER: Only those that date from before the law of separation. However, the upheaval in housing, the beginning of urban growth before the war and, for forty years, the enormous concentration of a formerly rural French population in new urban constructions have obliged Catholics to undertake, at their expense, the building of new churches. Too few, really, because within one generation we had to complete an undertaking that would have required from earlier churches the raising of funds over a few centuries.

In addition, since the beginning of the century, the Church has received, most often in the form of bequests, a certain amount of property whose extent has frequently been exaggerated. The religious orders, which from this point of view are totally independent from the bishops, have also been willed properties destined for multiple services (hospitals, schools, dispensaries, orphanages, youth fellowships, etc.). It should be noted that this patrimony, as important as it is, is not a significant source of income. At best, it pays for its upkeep. Its value comes from the fact that it is being used for worthy activities that justify its existence.

As for her operating budget, the French Church has no resources other than gifts from the faithful. It is on their generosity that the financing of all

[10] The *affectataire* is the person to whom a building is legally assigned.—TRANS.

the Church's action, including new initiatives, rests. In comparison with the church in Germany, where the state collects a tax destined for churches or social work—depending on the taxpayer's choice—our situation seems precarious and miserable.

The French clergy arouses a keen admiration throughout the world because it is so poor. In fact, it has often been quite wretched. For a few decades now, a national system of dividing up our resources has been gradually set up, not without a great many rather formidable problems.

MISSIKA: *How much does a priest earn, for example?*

LUSTIGER: The *Smic.*[11] But it often integrates the advantages being paid in kind and the living expenses entailed in a particular parish position, and it is difficult to calculate exactly and uniformly how much this represents.

WOLTON: *And a bishop?*

LUSTIGER: The *Smic*—the personal resources are the same, except that most often he lives in a building where he would not be able to pay the rent and so his expense allowance is greater.

The Church and Political Power

WOLTON: *You have just told us that you challenge the notion of political categories for describing the intervention and role of the Church. Then what kind of authority does the Church use when she contests decisions by political power?*

LUSTIGER: She expresses an ethical or moral criterion in a loud and clear voice. It is the criterion in whose name she can speak to everybody. She has the duty to do it. Not that she presents herself as a court or universal censor, but she receives from God a light on man and on God from which, in her eyes, man's rights and obligations ensue.

MISSIKA: *Then the Church intervenes in political affairs in the name of a specific morality that she upholds?*

LUSTIGER: Yes, because she considers herself responsible not only for her own good but for the good of all. For example, imagine a country where the

[11] The *Smic* is the *salaire minimum interprofessionnel de croissance,* which means the minimal pay guaranteed by government regulation for a full-time job.—TRANS.

Church is protected, while a religious minority is being persecuted. In the name of her convictions, the Church must demand respect for the rights of every citizen. In particular, the civil right to religious freedom must be recognized by all and for all.

WOLTON: *I do not understand how the particularism of the Catholic Faith permits it to approach a universal morality.*

LUSTIGER: Take the speeches of Paul VI or John Paul II at the United Nations. The Pope says that he is going to speak in the name of what he is, a disciple and apostle of Christ. And it is from this particularity that he feels himself able to state a universal truth about man. In other words, the Pope does not confuse the source of truth with the statement he is making.

WOLTON: *If the source is particular, how can the Word be universal?*

LUSTIGER: But the Pope pays the price for the claim of universality in identifying himself as a disciple of Christ. By rerooting the universal truth about man in the Christian experience and in the singularity of the Messianic condition, the one who states it shows that he is not satisfied with a general and abstract statement. He first accepts being identified with the Son of Man in order to receive from him the truth belonging to every man. In the classical age, the Church's predication was able to give itself references in a rational and religious order that was taken for granted. In the name of faith, the Church still thinks that there is a universal order of reason, of law accessible to every man. But in a period when humanism is contesting its own foundations, this affirmation is made more modestly and is paid for by a higher price: you have to confess the salvation of Christ in order to restore man to his original and common truth.

MISSIKA: *Do you agree with the idea, quite widespread today, that in the political domain the Church functions like a pressure group?*

LUSTIGER: I can very well conceive that some governments think that. . . .

WOLTON: *And some sociologists, too.*

LUSTIGER: Is this really the way the Church manages her action? She does not see herself as some kind of pressure group; she knows, through faith, that she disposes of a "resource" of humanity that is necessary to all men and that she has the duty to mobilize it in situations where humanity is wounded. What is happening in Poland is an example of this—very special, it is true.

What does the Church do there? She seems now to be the only possible recourse.

MISSIKA: *Does the Church in France play a similar role?*

LUSTIGER: In both countries, the Church can bring to light specifically human factors. Of course, in Poland, she appears to be the refuge for the only opposition possible, which is completely different from the French case. But look at what Pope John Paul II has unceasingly and resolutely hammered out in Poland—as did Cardinal Wyszynski before him and as Cardinal Glemp is doing how: each of them has played the music according to his instrument. What has been done in the name of the Church, is to make the stakes known, to make people aware of a force that does not emerge in the ordinary analysis of the social conflict. And what is that force? It is man's humanity in his spiritual dignity. The strength that the Church points out and brings into play cannot be reduced to slavery, unless a political power succeeds in making citizens founder in sin, despair and infidelity—in short, unless it succeeds in debasing man. It can try to make people lose their souls by starving them, because then they are going to become more rapacious, or by surreptitiously encouraging drunkenness, or abortions or lying—in short, by encouraging perversions. This is what the Nazis tried to do in their concentration camps and among occupied peoples. They wanted to erode people's spiritual resistance. But as long as a people have not become the accomplice of the power that wants to abase it, it is not conquered. Its resistance can go on for centuries and is a force that no tyrant can overcome. In Poland the economic collapse is deliberate, because the countries of Eastern Europe were economically developed before the war, almost as much so as those in the West. To what have they been reduced? But the Church has fostered the reappearance of a spiritual stamina that the government has been unable to suppress.

WOLTON: *But it is a spiritual force of which she is neither the guardian nor owner.*

LUSTIGER: No, the force belongs to God, who gives it to all the Church. Not just to the hierarchy, who have to be its spokesmen—more or less faithful, more or less inspired. There can be times when the hierarchy is weak. And, in that case, it is as though a people's strength is waterlogged, imprisoned: it no longer has the signposts it needs.

Take the other extreme, the case of France and the *affaire scolaire* in 1983–84. Our history is very far removed from Poland's. Here there is another kind of coincidence among the nation, religious values, civil society and political life. In France, the Church was formerly compromised or enclosed in certain political stands, either willingly or because of her adversaries. The situation was all the more difficult to manage since the debate over Catholic schools had been at the heart of this dispute for more than a century. In 1983–84, a certain relationship between civil society and the state became strained. Paradoxically, in these circumstances the Church could appear to be the credible voice for civil society's claim in regard to the education of its youth, whereas the political parties either went too far or simply wanted to take over the movement. This kind of gap or disagreement of political leaders with civil society is always dangerous, and perhaps people should be grateful to the Church for having known how to act wisely, thus preventing one of the most serious problems of civil society from being reduced to a political tug of war.

WOLTON: *I understand your argument, but the school question can also be interpreted as an antagonism between the right and the left.*

LUSTIGER: You are giving the classical analysis of the political power struggle in France. But both the left and the right had it in for the Church, sometimes even for the same reasons.

WOLTON: *Shall we say that the left was entrenched in its traditional positions and felt that the Church's position consisted, as always, of simply defending the private school?*

LUSTIGER: But it was more complex than that.

WOLTON: *What original stand did the Church take that went beyond the political cleavages or the divisions in public opinion?*

LUSTIGER: The object was to increase the understanding of the Church's relationship not just to political powers but to civil society in specific circumstances. It was more than a question of juridical or statutory relations, because you must not forget either that, regardless of the stands and interplay of the political parties, 63 percent of the French were in favor of freedom of choice in education, and that figure did not match up with any electoral divisions.

MISSIKA: *What did the Pope say to you about all this?*

LUSTIGER: I can reveal, without betraying a confidence, that I did not submit the French *problème scolaire* to the Pope. In fact, the entire matter was very competently managed by the people in charge. Everybody remembers the role played by Monsignor Honoré, Canon Guiberteau and Monsieur

Pierre Daniel. As for me, I was looking beyond, worrying about the effects that this quarrel would have on the relations between the Church and the nation. It was about this that I consulted the Pope. He asked the right questions and, thus, helped us to make progress in this regard.

After the turbulent periods that the French Church had lived through since the end of the nineteenth century, it seemed to me that in a time of relative peace it would be possible to reclaim the normal place—historically justified—of Catholicism in the constitution of French culture and the nation. Not in clerical or partisan terms but as a fact of our society. I felt that this could be accomplished today without undermining the laity, the state's sovereignty or the Church's freedom, and that the part of the patrimony of the French consciousness that is made up of the mystical, spiritual and religious experience of French Catholicism could be restored. And the same could be true for Judaism and Protestantism—just as much as for the secular tradition. This mutual acknowledgment could signify that the "Franco-française" war had ended. As a "product of state education", I know just how lucky I was to have had as professors free men, some of whom did not hesitate—I realized this over time—to contravene official instructions in claiming their part of the Catholic heritage. That is a part of a positive definition of secularism and the freedom of consciences.

WOLTON: *Are you saying that you felt it was time to reintegrate the Catholic Tradition into the French tradition, to contribute to a form of syncretism?*

LUSTIGER: No, not syncretism, but simply an acknowledgment of the facts.

MISSIKA: *A time to get rid of the disputes of the past!*

LUSTIGER: Not to close a debate that is a part of the French tradition, but to have it continue with mutual respect and recognition of rights. In a word, to have the two sides talk, rather than rail against each other.

When I was made a cardinal by the Pope, two years after having been named archbishop, I held a reception at the archdiocesan chancery to which I invited the president of the republic and representatives from legislative, administrative and judicial branches of government. For the first time since the separation of church and state, the French president came to the Church's headquarters in Paris. From now on, whoever the Cardinal-Archbishop of Paris may be and whoever is president of the Republic, they will fulfill their duties by holding and attending, respectively, a similar reception, when and if the archbishop is made a cardinal. It was time for a page to be turned. Since then, if I want to see the president or the prime minister, or if any political leader—whether appointed or elected—or a labor union official, etc., wants to see me, I find that normal. It is legitimate that Church leaders, too, should have their freedom of speech and action. Even so, they do not become *notables*.[12]

WOLTON: *Although they were for a very long time!*

LUSTIGER: We have to seek conditions for a forthright exchange of ideas. A word can be all the more candid if the one who speaks it is recognized for what he is, neither more nor less. Those people who converse with the archbishop of Paris should understand that he has no self-interested aims and that if he asks for something, it will be within the strict limits of what he deems to be the Church's right. Second, they must know that he will not make concessions, through fear or external pressure, on what is essential to the Church's fidelity. Third, they should realize that he can be a useful interlocutor precisely because he is impartial. And as far as the public good is concerned, perhaps it is no small matter that men who have responsibility in the religious domain can at a given moment dialogue with those who shoulder the major responsibility for the country.

It ought to be the same for all those who have roles of moral or intellectual leadership. I would be delighted if the university were once again to play a comparable role. Citizens are justified in looking to personalities who serve the life of the mind to be valuable partners in a dialogue with political power. That relationship has existed in our country, but the social function of the university is no longer understood in the same way. Similarly, I would like to see a greater appreciation of the magistracy as a judicial arm of government. It seems to me that we must restore the role of social institutions as a source of thoughtful and constructively critical authority. But if the role is to be restored, then the various functions must merit it.

WOLTON: *The room for maneuvering is small; in proposing that the Church, just like any other important social body, should be reintroduced into the field of communication, you are reinforcing the Church's institutional dimension, which is precisely what has been contested for the past fifty years. From what you are saying, it is not very easy to see the difference between the internal dimension of the Church and that of a secular organization.*

LUSTIGER: I am convinced that in certain sociopolitical situations the Church can be a source of original proposals that cannot be provided by others. She has the duty to do it, after all. That is a part of her mission.

[12] Notables are citizens who occupy an important rank in a state or city.—TRANS.

WOLTON: *Don't you think that you would risk reintroducing the Church into the political arena and on to a course of action that she would not be able to control?*

LUSTIGER: It is a risk, but there is the inverse risk: that of leaving aside the real stakes of social and human life. Take the case of Latin America with the reminder that the Pope has just given us about "liberation theologies". What has been remembered is the condemnation of a Marxist orientation. What has not been retained—and I am positive that the silence is not innocent—is that he takes an extremely vigorous stand for the defense of the rights of the poor, but his principles are entirely different from those of Marxism-Leninism. Westerners focus on the ideological struggle against Marxism, but what the Pope was saying was something else. The Church's proposal in the political realm consists of passing a moral judgment on a given situation and the forces that are at work there, of calling evil by its name, of bringing the good to light and encouraging Christians to invent solutions positively.

Even so, the bishops are not about to seize power. That would be an appalling error. At the very moment when the Pope was speaking out against an ideological deviation, he was reinforcing the ban against the exercise of political functions by priests or other clergy. What is said to the priests-ministers in the Sandinista government in Nicaragua applies just as much to the bishops.

MISSIKA: *It has been quite some time since there was a bishop in a ministerial position.*

LUSTIGER: Has there been one in France since Talleyrand?

The Intervention of the Church in Society

MISSIKA: *You have said that the Church ought to be a source of original proposals. But when you look at the declarations of the French bishops or the episcopal conference on social and economic questions, you are struck, well... shall we say, by their banality. They always contain the high principles, excellent sentiments, noble words. Whether they are talking about immigrants, poverty or unemployment, they are always for good and against evil. But they stop there. What good do they do?*

LUSTIGER: *"Travaillez, prenez de la peine, c'est le fonds qui manque le moins"*,[13] the plowman said to his children.

[13] "You must work and spare no effort. It is not capital that is most lacking." This is a quotation from one of La Fontaine's fables.—TRANS.

WOLTON: *Can you be more specific? For the school issue, you succeeded in having a well-defined position, whereas for the economic and social questions . . .*

MISSIKA: *Take the example of immigration. It is obvious that there is a need for imaginative and concrete proposals because none exist. But, in fact, the Church intervenes—and this is much to her credit—to say that one must not be a racist. Certainly, nothing less is expected of her, but beyond that, there is nothing.*

LUSTIGER: You are being slightly unfair. Because of her catholic structure, the Church is one of the very rare transnational organizations capable of arousing a feeling of mutual responsibility among all the world's peoples. For all Catholic "parishes" throughout the world, welcoming immigrants can be a step toward getting to know the parishes from which those immigrants have come. It can be the basis for a sharing between "here" and "there", from population to population, which is quite unusual in the domain of international aid. It is clear that French Catholics have played and still play an important role, and not just verbally. This is as true for all of Europe as for the other developed countries.

In regard to immigration, we are not satisfied with words. In France, those who volunteer (teachers, social workers, nurses, etc.) to serve in the new ghettos, as in those deprived areas that have been called the *quart monde* [Fourth World], are numerous. Among them there is an important proportion of Catholics—both lay and religious. As for an overall solution, nobody is inspired on command. It is a difficult problem for society, and it has to be posed before we can begin to solve it. For the time being, if the Church did nothing more than state the problem and announce her rejection of a simplistic solution—which would neglect those who are the victims of racism—she would be in the right to do so. If you look back on the social ills of the past, there is too little known about the side of French social history that illustrates the inventiveness of many Catholics. It was they who originated the *Allocations familiales* and *Sécurité sociale*.[14] The development of a large part of the social legislation that we now have owes as much to social Catholicism's efforts as to the cooperative movement and pressure from labor unions, Marxist or not. And that was spread over a century.

WOLTON: *It began a little later than socialist unionism, but it is true that the movement was very influential, although in the minority after* 1880.

[14] *Allocations familiales* are state benefits such as maternity leave, income supplements, rent rebates, etc., paid to the family. *Sécurité sociale* is legislation that insures citizens against certain social risks (illnesses, accidents, etc.).—TRANS.

LUSTIGER: That point is contested by contemporary historians who date the rise in influence of Catholic social work from 1830, under the impulse of numerous laymen. This great effort for justice and charity produced fruits that have not yet been brought to light.

WOLTON: *But what is striking about the issue of the Church's intervention in economic and social matters—or in others—is the impression that she is using a double language. In most cases, she intervenes with a relatively complicated argument and vocabulary, a kind of* langue de bois.[15] *On the other hand, when her vital interests are involved, she speaks more directly, the most recent example of this being the school affair.*

LUSTIGER: This overall impression stems from several factors, among which mass communication occupies a central place. When a pontifical document appears, it is first released to the press agencies, and an opinion is produced and diffused even before the people to whom it is addressed have received it. It is a press agency's almost instantaneous dispatch of thirty lines, rather than a careful reading and study of thirty pages, that forms public opinion! When French bishops release a painstakingly worked-out document, there are ten lines from an agency reporter to sum up their position.

WOLTON: *This is a general problem that is not limited to the Church. By definition, the job of informing people consists of selecting and reducing, sometimes to the point of caricature, it is true. But I am not talking about that, but about the* langue de bois.

LUSTIGER: No, it is not always *langue de bois.* It does not shock me in these years, 1985–90—economic theory being what it is, the disagreements among the most eminent economists being what they are—that a bishop, even if he had a doctorate in economics, would not suddenly have the inspiration of the century and come up with a new economic theory unknown to the experts in the field. But the inability to develop a systematic and functional theory does not dispense him from the duty of recalling moral requirements, even if they are expressed clumsily and repetitively. Economics is a subject in which everybody founders, and, admittedly, our exhortations can appear to be very much upstream from the problem.

WOLTON: *On the subject of the family, the Church does not say very much that is original in comparison with what the demographers are saying, for example.*

[15] The *langue de bois* (literally, "wooden language") is obscure, shallow and virtually meaningless talk prompted by ideological prejudice.—TRANS.

LUSTIGER: I do not know if she is saying anything original, but she is definitely saying something that runs counter to the dominant opinion. Even so, it is impressive to hear demographers say today just the opposite of what they were saying thirty years ago about the worldwide demographic explosion and its dangers. The Church's discourse—judged to be archaic at the time—is justified a posteriori. Not because Churchmen had a superior scientific competence, but because they were considering human behaviors according to humane principles. And happily, every now and then, it happens that the soundness of conclusions that have been drawn from the conscience can be verified by experience.

I am ready to concede, not that Catholic doctrine on the family has been insufficient, but that the weight of history and the pressure of public opinion have been so strong that, involuntarily, a large number of Frenchmen, including those in the Church, have exercised a kind of self-censorship.

WOLTON: *There is a third area where the Church makes her stand very plain: that of morals. Here she seems to have no doubts. The acceptance of contraception remains relative, the condemnation of abortion is unequivocal and the trend toward greater sexual freedom has met with little favor. For twenty years, the Church has been denouncing a "freedom" that she considers to be an illusion, and now that sexual emancipation has been pushed to the limit, she is saying, "I told you so."*

LUSTIGER: Another remark about the economy: the encyclical released by John Paul II on the dignity of human labor is a very important text that lays the foundations of the economics of man's work. Of course, the Pope recalls basic truths and, like all basic truths, they are relatively simple, even though their technical implications must not be underestimated. His position is in marked contrast to that of both liberalism and Marxism. It redevelops the anthropological problem of labor and proposes various elements for reflection. Certainly it is not an economic theory on the production of riches or the functioning of international currencies, of investment, etc., but economic theories, whether Marxist or liberal—indeed, even uniquely monetary ones—all have implicit anthropological presuppositions. It is that implicit part of economic theories that the Pope deals with explicitly and on his own terrain. He would be delighted if a few economists would agree to come out of their "sacristies" and listen to the Church's language.

But to come back to the problem of sexuality and morals, the Church takes a very vigorous stand that, in relation to the desires or constant deviations of societies and human beings, can appear conservative. But she is motivated by a keen sense of her responsibility: there is something sacred to be saved in man and the human species. The subject of sexuality, however, taps such a guilty conscience! When the Church says, "You must help feed the poor", everybody listens with only one ear and nobody feels guilty. Why is it that when, in talking about abortion, she reminds people of the respect for life, everybody starts to cry thief? Why? Somewhere there is a feeling of guilt, linked perhaps to the specific domain of the contemporary conscience. Why are the same words perceived differently by listeners in different eras and different countries? The discourse on sexuality is not understood in the same way in some underdeveloped countries; they see things from quite another angle. I have heard Africans reject those dramatic calls, coming from the rich nations, to limit their birthrate—by compulsion, if necessary—as reflecting a colonialist point of view.

WOLTON: *But here we are speaking exclusively about the West.*

LUSTIGER: But it is impossible to reduce the Church to the West! By definition, her language is universal; it is meant for everybody. Even if we accept the criticism that we lack clarity or timeliness, we know that we shall be judged over the long term.

MISSIKA: *I would like to make an objection. You have said that there is a difference in the public's reactions that depends on whether you are intervening in sexual and moral matters or in matters of poverty and unemployment. But perhaps citizens react negatively to the former intervention not for the reason you cite—namely, guilt—but simply because they think that this domain is none of the Church's business, that it belongs to their private life, to the sphere of individual liberty.*

At the present juncture, there are three general areas where the Church intervenes politically. First, human rights, collective and political freedoms, and the public heartily approves: John Paul II is seen as the champion of human rights. There is a similar approval for the maintenance of the private school in France. There is a second area, morals, where people are generally opposed to the Church's stand. Of course, it depends on the milieu, but even in Catholic Poland, it is very well known that the number of abortions is very high and that many people go to church and do not disapprove of abortions any less or have them any less. Perhaps this is because—in the Western world, where individualism exists—this intervention is seen as an intrusion into private life. And then there is the third domain, that of social and economic questions—the right to work, immigration, etc.—and here the reactions provoked depend on each person's political and ethical choices, but it is considered normal that the Church should speak out on such issues, as long as she sticks to generalities. These three areas are, after all, relatively distinct. There is one having to do with social and economic questions, on which there is a kind of neutrality; one concerning human rights, on which there is complete agreement; and one, involving morals, on which there is sharp disagreement.

LUSTIGER: An anecdote: in 1985, a weekly magazine had the idea of asking some *lycéens* from public schools to interview three personalities who were supposedly representative of public life: Giresse, Laurent Fabius[16] and myself. I do not know the reasons for our having been chosen, but, in any case, one day I found myself with some students from a *lycée* in the fourteenth *arrondissement.* There were three delegates, a girl and two boys, about whom nothing would have led me to conclude that they were believers. There was definitely no identifiable religious connection. In one hour they asked me twenty questions collected from their classmates, and among them there was one that almost struck me dumb: "You, the Church, you, adults, you, the older generation: have you not lacked courage in failing to warn us, to tell us what we ought to be doing in moral and sexual matters?" The same question came up again several times. I was amazed by the maturity of these young people who were querying whether we had acted responsibly toward them. They were without standards because we had not known how to give them, and hence they were obliged to situate themselves in the void. They were a striking demonstration—they had not yet read Freud—of a generation suffering from a neurosis because they were without law. They were reproaching adults, including those in the Church, for not having been able to explain, especially in sexual matters, that good and evil exist.

WOLTON: *How can the effectiveness of the Church's public statements be judged?*

LUSTIGER: By her fidelity to the received truth. I take the example of those first Germans who dared to oppose Hitler and who died, with heads severed, in prisons. As far as the Nazi regime was concerned, the effectiveness of their action was probably judged to be nil at the time. But it was invaluable for the future of the German nation. Those few men and women went as far as martyrdom in order to witness to the truth.

The Church, Public Opinion and the Mass Media

WOLTON: *The Catholic Church has always shown expertise in the field of communications; she was one of the first to use the written press, then radio and, indeed, television. However, she gives the impression, just like any other social force, that she is simply trying to reach public opinion without giving any particular reflection to the way she does it.*

LUSTIGER: If we allow the media to shape the message and reduce its

[16] Alain Giresse (1952–) was a popular French soccer star. Laurent Fabius (1946–) served as the Socialist government's prime minister from 1984–86.—TRANS.

contents, there will not be any message left, or rather it will be diminished to what can be communicated by the procedure.

There is really something tragic in present society; it risks atomizing individuals to the point that there will be no more human relations other than through the media. Paradoxically, that provokes an impoverishment of possibilities for communication, first of the Gospel, then perhaps among men, which is in great contrast to the enrichment that the media can bring from other sources. The experience of faith does not take place in the way a spectacle or the feigned naturalness of a talk show does: it happens in a symbolic, concrete way. It is born from an act addressed directly to each person. You may protest that the media do precisely that. But no. Being a part of a congregation at a Mass results in genuine participation. Looking at a Mass on television is just not the same thing. Invalids know very well what the televised Mass can and cannot bring them.

WOLTON: *I agree, but then why does the Church use the media so widely?*

LUSTIGER: Because the media are a part of our society. We have to use this means, too.

WOLTON: *But, after all, you do use it quite a lot! You ask for time on television channels, you go on the radio. Your approach is no different from that of any other social group that wants to have access to the techniques of mass communication.*

LUSTIGER: Perhaps we do use the media like everybody else. Maybe we even use them very badly, I would be willing to concede it, although I am not entirely convinced that you are right. But we have to be present in the media, because they are a part of our civilization, even if they pose a basic problem for it and for our Faith. We have no choice. The only question is how to use them discriminately.

WOLTON: *I am going to take another example regarding public attitudes: opinion polls. Over the years there have been an incalculable number of surveys on religious practices, priests' views, etc. The French Church, just like any other social organization, multiplies these surveys so as to know what Monsieur Dupont—Paul or Jacques—is thinking.... Between 1944 and 1976, three hundred opinion polls having to do with the country's religious climate were made public in France.*

LUSTIGER: Can you answer this question for me: Who commissioned them and who paid?

WOLTON: *The Catholic press and the episcopate?*

LUSTIGER: I dare you to find me ten that were financed by the episcopate. It was the press that paid for those polls. One of the particularities of the French press—whether Catholic or not—is to have used polls to such an extent for promotional purposes.

WOLTON: *Do you mean to say that the episcopate itself is not such a user or commissioner of this kind of survey?*

LUSTIGER: There is a great deal of uncertainty about these means; we have no mastery of them, especially since we have no critical authority that would allow us to interpret them. I do not think that such polls are very significant for the study of the religious phenomenon, especially the Catholic one. They can be helpful for sketching a profile of contemporary France. But, given the nature of the survey procedure, the conditions in which they are carried out and the working hypotheses that underlie them, such surveys point to nothing truly symptomatic or beneficial for religious action.

WOLTON: *But, all the same, one has the impression that the Church is seeking this kind of information.*

LUSTIGER: That is not my impression. Apparently, some people do a great many surveys, but it is because they have specific objectives.

MISSIKA: *Apropos of the mise-en-scène, the public performance, the Pope's trips are currently quite controversial. While some people may approve of his leaving the Vatican and going out into the world, others complain about the spectacular and televised dimension, the "one-man show" aspect of these trips. Is this a matter of communications strategy, or does it just happen?*

LUSTIGER: When the big television networks transmit images of the Pope's journeys in as many directions as there are countries in the world, they send out exactly the same reportage, because for most countries—other than the one the Pope is visiting—a few minutes will suffice. The journalists on the spot will scarcely have time for anything more. The difficulty is to succeed in translating a singular emotion when, from the outside, all the trips seem to be alike. I experienced this when the Pope came to Paris in 1980 and France-Inter[17] asked me to do a three-minute commentary every morning. Journalists are sometimes blasé, and they do not always see what is happening between the Pope and the people he meets. If you really want to inform people—and at

[17] France-Inter is a popular, government-run radio station based in Paris and broadcasting to the whole country.—TRANS.

least the reporters from the written press could do this—you have to examine the interaction produced by the Pope's visit.

I have been present at a few segments of the pontifical travels. Each of them struck me by its originality, not only as to the situation of the local Church but that of the country and its relationship to Catholicism and to other nations. For example, in Vienna in 1983, there was a large gathering of Austrian Catholics on the Heldenplatz, Heroes' Square, where Hitler had come to proclaim the *Anschluss.* It was there that that formidable challenge to Christianity had been launched, and it was there, forty-five years later, that Cardinal Koenig had assembled the crowd to celebrate the Pope's coming. The ceremony included a theatrical presentation, a big popular liturgy that explored the themes of Good Friday—that is, of the Cross. There we were, exactly at the heart of the Austro-Hungarian Empire, at the heart of the old crossroads of Europe, at the heart of Nazism's first victory; and what was symbolically presented—in the very spot where the Nietzschean will for power had been affirmed most brutally and cynically—was the mystery of the Crucified.

There were five speakers. Cardinal Koenig had asked four bishops to comment on a few words from the Beatitudes, which formed the framework for the liturgy. Cardinal Meisner, Bishop of Berlin, represented the North; Cardinal Kuharic, Archbishop of Zagreb, the South; Cardinal Macharski, Archbishop of Cracow, the East; and I, as Archbishop of Paris, the West. We spoke without having consulted each other, but the convergence of thoughts was extraordinary because, at that moment, we were all Europeans. Rare were the journalists who pointed this out. And Cardinal Macharski had the audacity to say to that crowd, "I am leaving you, as a relic, a little earth from Auschwitz; I want you to remember it." Nobody reported that. Then the Pope delivered a very surprising discourse. He recalled Europe's history, its failings and its glories, citing among other things the victory of the Polish King Sobieski who stopped the Turkish invasion of Vienna just outside the city's walls in 1683. For hundreds of thousands of Austrians there on the Heldenplatz, for Europeans who were conscious of their history, this moment was fantastic. The impression that the moderately informed Frenchman would have received of that trip would have been simply that the Pope had celebrated a Mass, still another one, and that the Austrians still loved Mozart and their folkloric costumes....

WOLTON: *But, in general, have the written press, radio and television given good coverage to events concerning the Church in the past thirty years?*

LUSTIGER: Quantitatively, they have done their job well, and there have been some excellent moments, but the sometimes questionable quality of the coverage shows how complicated it is to make the religious field understood. It is the sensational that piques curiosity: the processions of the Council, the final days of John XXIII, the prognostications surrounding the pontifical elections, the Pope's first trips. . . .

WOLTON: *But it is the Church herself who creates the spectacle.*

LUSTIGER: No, she is not creating a spectacle, she is merely being herself. She is only continuing her customs and traditions without worrying about whether they are considered a spectacle or not. Inserted as she is among all the planet's current events, the Church offers an interesting, provocative object for the media whose professionals have applied to her the only categories of which they dispose—dramatization, putting the limelight on a person or a polemic, and calculating the balance of power insofar as they are able to conceive of it. It is true that the reporter sometimes adopts the perspective of a filmmaker and allows himself to be drawn toward the beauty of the gestures and visual images. There are also some priests among journalists. . . . But, I repeat, to convey the religious event itself is extremely difficult. The essential is never said. Thus, in the end, the truly important happenings are not covered. And the repetition of the same images wears thin and becomes boring if the information is reduced to showing John Paul II in the popemobile or giving the benediction. . . . A media "star" does not last very long. Media information consumes what it spotlights and then throws away the "packaging". Having treated the religious event in a folkloric or political way, they discard it, forgetting that religion is a major phenomenon that touches people over a long period and that it is no small challenge to give a true understanding of it to the public. The political or bellicose demonstrations of the Iranian Shiites, the acts of Rabbi Kahane in Israel, the occupation of the Golden Temple by the Sikhs and the Pope's travels are all lumped together. Just from the simple point of view of ethnological rationality or the observation of society, such treatment is inadequate.

WOLTON: *You are saying that religious ceremonies have always taken place. Granted. But the Pope's travels are a relatively new phenomenon. John Paul II is the Pope who has made the greatest number of trips. In the era of satellite television, it looks as if the Church has recognized the potential of the spectacle and has begun to organize it.*

LUSTIGER: When the Pope travels, he is "covered" in the same way as is a president of the United States, to take a point of comparison. For the latter, whose mandate is for four years, a favorable rating by public opinion is essential. But the distinct reason for the Pope's travel has not been detected.

Only the ceremonial aspect is retained, although it is much less extravagant than the queen of England's annual opening of parliament, or even a parade down the Champs Élysées on Bastille Day. But the most important aspect is perceived poorly, if at all, and is rarely mentioned. The Pope is fulfilling his function, which is not to be a part of a public pageant but to bring together in a given country the Church, its members and hierarchy in such a way that she can become more fully aware of her mission, her originality, her specificity. Where can you find, for example, reports on the Pope's speeches in the various countries that are relatively astute and probing, although his trips are often centered on an explicitly oriented message? Certainly the press is not about to publish dozens of pages of papal discourses, but even if not every sentence contains something new, with each trip there is a definite angle of approach, something to rally the people, something revealing about particular conditions as he meets a particular population. All that is seldom analyzed. At best, the commentators situate the Pope in the context of their political interpretation of the local scene. They hardly ever allow one to see the religious context that the Pope is using to evaluate the overall situation, including its political dimension.

WOLTON: *Does the Catholic press give better coverage to religious affairs than the general press?*

LUSTIGER: Sometimes it covers them better quantitatively, but it is aiming at another audience, one made up of the "clerics"—that is, people who are well informed on these matters. They have their own jargon and explicit concerns. Their point of view is not that of the ordinary citizen, believer or unbeliever. Of course, it can be interesting to underline, for the better informed, the more "pointed" questions that can be understood only by those who have a certain acquaintance with biblical language and the Church's sacramental life. It is both normal and necessary that specialists report on religious affairs. But here again, there have to be criteria for judgment, underlying principles according to which words and acts are selected or emphasized. That entails honesty and rigor. A reporter can describe the Pope's trips in the same way that he describes the internal debates of a political party, but the average citizen would like to have a better understanding of the religious stakes involved in these disputes or rivalries, either real or alleged. The general public should be told about the purely religious aspects of an issue. Take liberation theology as an example: most often it is treated in terms of European ideologies and not in the concrete terms of a grass-roots pastoral strategy.

WOLTON: *But, as for liberation theology, the public did not get the impression that there was a debate going on, but rather it saw a condemnation accompanied by a convocation before a kind of court.*

LUSTIGER: What was said and done in the Pope's name was very moderate and restrained. In the first place, there was no condemnation falling like a thunderbolt. After a long discussion, developed over decades, there was a sorting out of the diverse liberation theologies. It was perhaps twenty, thirty or forty years ago that people began to examine the various links between the announcement of the Gospel and "temporal commitments" in the service of justice and human rights. Several of these interlocutors explained themselves at length before their peers—academics and theologians. An open and public debate—to which many books and journal articles bear witness—took place. But, at a certain juncture, it is the authority's duty to assume its responsibilities and make a judgment. As to the convocation of those involved, that also was done in a regular way, with known, codified and respected procedures. In reaction to this, some dissident groups tried to mobilize public opinion. And, admittedly, the Church authorities did not defend themselves very well in face of what turned out to be a partial manipulation of the channels of information. The Church has no particular hold over the media, as governments or special-interest lobbies sometimes do. I wish to point out to you that the Pope has incessantly commended the Christian commitment to greater social justice. He calls on the conscience, he denounces injustice and violence and he preaches the preferential love of the poor. And on several occasions, he has paid special tribute to the dedicated pastors in Latin America.

MISSIKA: *You have remarked that when journalists deal with religious events they show a certain lack of perspicacity and a tendency to liken them to political questions. But when one looks at the general press and television, many of the commentators on religious issues are priests. How can they fail to comprehend the religious phenomenon?*

LUSTIGER: Your generalization is very much exaggerated. Presently, on the world scale, information is "prefabricated" by large news agencies or networks that are staffed by numerous correspondents. There is not—and far from it—a preponderance of priests among those who cover religious affairs . . . when that specialization exists, which, alas, is all too seldom.

The difficulty that the specialist faces is to identify what is interesting for the nonspecialist. You have to have competent people who know what is going on, but you also need those who have the necessary distance and vision for making the true stakes understandable. The best information on religious events often comes from the most unexpected quarters. All of a sudden, one can discover a reporter who casts a fresh perspective on issues; he is not necessarily ignorant of the internal quarrels, conflicts and other systems of interpretation, but he spots what the true dangers are and makes them known to a broad public. Talent and integrity always end up by piercing to the heart of the matter.

II

THE NEW CENTERS OF GRAVITY

The Pope

JEAN-LOUIS MISSIKA: *The existence of the Pope, the unique head with important powers, distinguishes the Catholic Church from all others. Ever since Vatican I, the Pope's authority has been constantly reinforced, and the techniques of modern communication, by stressing personalization, have contributed to increasing it even more. Isn't there a risk that the Pope's personality and his individual choices will have too much influence on the Church's life?*

JEAN-MARIE LUSTIGER: The Pope, unique head of the Church? You are presenting the Church as though she were an imperial world order. But that is not at all the way the Church functions and defines herself. The authority in the Church belongs to Christ, who gives the Apostles and their successors, the bishops, a share in his authority. If you examine Church law as it is formulated in the juridical codes as well—the last code of canon law was published in 1983—you will notice that the legislation concerns first of all the rights and duties of the people of God. The law is meant to serve the faithful and establish the provisions that pastors need to transmit the Faith to them, to communicate to them the sacraments and means of sanctification and guide them in the communion with God. There are three levels on which the hierarchy's powers have been codified by canon law, and they define the exercise of the pastoral ministry. These powers are concentrated in the person of the bishops, and the primacy of the Pope is in the service of the communion and cohesions of the bishops' college. Each bishop legitimately exercises his authority with considerable power. But his power has a limit that is determined by his communion with the totality of the episcopal college to which the Pope belongs as its head. The mission of the Pope, successor to Peter, is to ensure the regulation of this pastoral power. His authority and primacy consist in carrying out this regulation and creating this coherence.

The theological argument for the Pope's primacy, at the heart of the collegiality of the bishops, is based on the interdependence of the Apostles with Peter and his authority among them. The two notions of primacy and collegiality were highlighted at both the First and Second Vatican Councils.

They are truly correlatives as early tradition expresses it. But, as for the government of the Church, there have been times of more or less centralization, depending on the periods and places of evangelization. The early Church saw the installation of the patriarchates. This is still the status of the Eastern churches, whose original law is respected by the Roman Church. The feudal periods had an organization internal to the Church where the functioning of civil and political society gave its form to the hierarchical system of bishops, to their mutual subordination—indeed, to their relations with the Pope. On the other hand, in the Church of Gregory VII, Roman centralization was a way of struggling against the feudal system and of allowing the Church to reconquer her independence vis-à-vis the empire. Just as in other epochs—like the ones ruled over by Frederick Barbarossa and the Roman-Germanic emperors and also by Napoléon—the Roman predominance made it possible for the Church to resist political pressure. There exists here a twofold relationship, mimetic and antagonistic, of the Church to the state and vice versa.

General theological principles are conditioned by time and history, by the historical circumstances in which the Church finds herself. But, in any case, and here I am finally responding to your first question, the Pope does not have an exclusive power but a unique one. History teaches us that his primacy has been infinitely valuable to the Church because there have always been nations and kings who wanted to take control of her: I am thinking of Gallicanism in France and Josephism in Austria. A good part of the Reformation can be explained by the determination of German princes to be in command of the Church. And Anglicanism was an outright seizure of the Church—look at Saint Thomas More—just as the czars took over the Holy Orthodox Church.

DOMINIQUE WOLTON: *Are you saying that the Catholic Church is the most independent of all the churches?*

LUSTIGER: In a sense, yes. To that end, it was necessary to reinforce papal power. The Roman communion and the Pope's power, even if there were excesses at some periods, still remain a criterion of the Church's independence from political power.

MISSIKA: *The nominations of bishops in Eastern Europe, for example?*

LUSTIGER: There and elsewhere. It is not so certain that French ministers of the interior, in all the republics, have not dreamed of being able to appoint bishops.

WOLTON: *Many people in France believe that a bishop is appointed by the Pope but that political authorities have to approve the choice.*

LUSTIGER: Not since the separation of church and state. That is one of the gains of the separation.

WOLTON: *And in other countries?*

LUSTIGER: Since Vatican II, the Church's independence from political powers has been strengthened even more. For example, in the sixteenth century, a law of patronage had been accorded to the Spanish and Portuguese sovereigns; it allowed them to give their opinion—often determining—on the nomination of bishops. The Second Vatican Council asked for the modification of these clauses. On this point, there are currently major conflicts with some of the East European countries because they want to appoint, or have appointed, priests who are in the hands of—or at least at the mercy of—the government. Since the Church does not accept being totally subjected to civil or political rule, she is presented as a foreign organization in the service of a foreign power. To that end, the governments play on nationalism and cultural identity. Of course, bishops in these countries can only identify with the culture of people whose pastors they are; they are "patriots", but they can never be high priests of their homelands.

MISSIKA: *I insist: Isn't there a risk in giving too much influence to an individual—the Pope—the risk that the personality might become more important than the function?*

LUSTIGER: There are always risks. If you take the preceding phase of history, the veneration shown to bishops in general and to the Pope in particular was copied exactly from the social hierarchical system. Thus, the temptation was strong for those in charge of the Church's highest functions to identify themselves with the sovereigns of this world.

MISSIKA: *As Catholicism becomes "worldwide", how can one man be attentive to and competent to deal with the problems posed on a global scale?*

LUSTIGER: The Pope does not replace the bishops in governing the Church: he presents himself as Bishop of Rome. He is the one who, in the name of his primacy—that is the technical term for designating the function of the Pope, successor to Peter, the first Pope—is in the service of others, of all the others, pastors and faithful. Although the First and Second Vatican Councils have recalled his universal and direct spiritual authority over all believers, this authority is exercised to the benefit of the other bishops' authority. The necessity of personalizing the execution of his universal mission stems from the profound nature of the Church, communion of human persons with God tri-personal. Besides, it is very valuable in our cultural universe. Just suppose that the Pope's function, ensuring the Church's unity and desired by Christ himself, were to be exercised in complete anonymity. Imagine that the Pope, to avoid personalization, hid himself from view, never allowed himself to be photographed, remained in the background more like a Big Brother, never spoke publicly, communicated by written word, etc. That would be absurd, tyrannical. The Pope acts and speaks openly, with his character fully visible. I do not see how he can be blamed for that.

In our times, with the advent of the "global village", the primacy of Peter seems to be more necessary than ever for safeguarding the freedom of each of the churches and their faithful. We are living in a society that has spread over the entire world, but as the world comes closer together, it divides itself into opposing cultures. Formerly, cultures differed because they were ignorant of one another; now they are in danger of clashing precisely because they have become acquainted and share the same backyard, so to speak. For centuries, there were scarcely any conflicts between the cultures of China and the West for the simple reason that slow caravans were the only means of transporting silk and manufactured goods over the long and treacherous route connecting the two worlds. Now that all cultures communicate so easily, the differences are exacerbated by the temptation of uniformity. The Pope's ministry of unity is the only one that crosses all cultures and all frontiers to put all Catholics in communication. The task of his ministry is to ensure this communication and to aid the college of bishops to consolidate the historic communion of the Church, as the witness of the unity of all humanity, of its salvation and hope.

Episcopal Conferences

MISSIKA: *The episcopal conferences, which bring together the bishops of each country, are now presented as a "democratic reform" growing out of the Second Vatican Council, and the question arises as to the distribution of powers between the episcopal conferences and the bishops. Who, in the end, holds the legitimacy? The bishops or the conferences? And who predominates in relations with Rome?*

LUSTIGER: The idea of coordinating the ordinary functioning of a nation's churches by grouping them into an episcopal conference is more or less contemporary with Vatican II. The present Pope was among the Fathers of the Council who decided to develop this type of organization. Thus, it is not a demand that came up from the grass roots against the central authority of the universal Church; it was within the context of Vatican II that it was felt to be desirable. The realization of a symbiosis of the churches or the dioceses of a nation is not new, since there have always been national realities. But the

Fathers of Vatican II vigorously advocated a practice going back to the beginning of the twentieth century when "indigenous" hierarchies were created in countries that were still colonies. The first black bishop of Africa was named in the 1920s, a time when colonialism was in full flower. The churches, including those in colonized countries, were always meant to have their own life and hierarchy. From the beginning of their evangelization, missionaries worked toward this end. It is the age-old and immemorial practice of the Church. There had already been national churches in previous periods. But the creation of episcopal conferences grew out of the wish to recognize the national and cultural diversity of churches while encouraging them in a communion without frontiers. Such a system is a way of acknowledging a new political fact in the contemporary epoch: the appearance of political states coinciding more or less with cultural nations. It was a way of bringing distinct churches into a system of communication and responsibility that would respect differences while ensuring the Catholic communion. Without this communion, churches bound to a culture, a specific ethnicity—indeed, to a specific political system—would be prisoners of their particularities and would therefore cease to be Catholic.

So that is why the episcopal conferences, whose rights and limits are clearly defined, were organized. But the sovereign elements in the Church are the dioceses and, also, the totality of the episcopal body under the Pope's authority; and the Pope's relationship with each bishop guarantees the solidarity of all the bishops and the communion of the whole Church. There is no equivalent to this system in the political world.

WOLTON: *Then why has the system been likened to a political structure?*

LUSTIGER: That is a re-interpretation. There is a constant temptation for everyone, Church leaders as well as members, to view it on the political level. Just look at the fluctuations in feelings about the Ultramontanes and the Gallicans in French history. The relationship of Catholics to Rome was sometimes seen as an abuse and resented by a majority of citizens as subservience to a foreign power; sometimes, on the contrary, it was a condition of freedom. But to come back to the episcopal conferences, if they spark controversy, perhaps it is because we live in democratic systems that are often ruled by technocracies or bureaucracies. There is a strong tendency to see in groups like these conferences a confirmation that the Church has switched to a democratic system.

In fact, majority rule dates from the Church's early days. She is presented as a hierarchical power with several levels, hence, as "monarchical", but her organization is based on constant co-opting and elective systems. The Pope has always been elected; the Church has used the elective system across the centuries. Moreover, the elections within monasteries and chapters inspired urban rights in the free cities of the Middle Ages. The Church has always united election by the people ("democracy") and obedience to a personal authority ("monarchy"). Actually, the foundation of power in the Church is the sacrament, and the sacrament of Christ's authority is presented as a service to God's people. It is never the property either of those who receive it or of the one who gives it.

MISSIKA: *On the whole, you challenge the idea that the episcopal conference should increase its power in order to make the internal functioning of the Church more democratic?*

LUSTIGER: The episcopal conferences have a defined purpose, to be of service to the bishops' exercise of responsibility; their powers are regulated by law; the implementing of most of their decisions in matters determined by law is conditioned by the rule of unanimity. Except for Roman intervention, a decision of an episcopal conference can be imposed only if every bishop agrees to subscribe to it, whereas a bishop, on the contrary, cannot renounce the use of his received authority, which does not belong to him. This right is not the claim of a privilege; it is a duty based on God's will. When a bishop has a specific right, he has an obligation to exercise it. Thus, he has the right to call Christians to communion in the Faith, because he has the duty to instruct them. The bishops' conferences are rather a means of bringing people together, of confrontation, of coordination of action on the cultural level, but there could be and there exist, in fact—for example, in Brazil—several episcopal conferences in the same country.

WOLTON: *Why is there talk about a potential conflict between the episcopal conferences, which are relatively democratic in character, and papal power, which is directly connected with the bishops?*

LUSTIGER: Some episcopal conferences can be criticized for giving greater importance to the internal administrative apparatus, just as parliamentary democracies do. Given the multiplicity of subjects broached and their technical nature, the exercise of episcopal authority with the personal responsibility it involves risks depending on research organizations or other systems intended to reinforce it. The relationship to pontifical authority, on the other hand, is a guarantee of the bishops' personal freedom.

WOLTON: *In democratic societies, it is rarely accepted that the relationship to an individual on whom you depend and who has appointed you is a source of freedom.*

LUSTIGER: The Church is the institution where the steps between the levels of hierarchy are the fewest and shortest. In principle, a believer or a priest can see his bishop without an intermediary, and his bishop is in communion with all the other bishops and the Pope. So, after just two steps, you can reach the summit. The criticism of the episcopal conference reflects the fear that an anonymous organization blurs the individual pastoral responsibility connected with a sacrament. In other words, who governs the Church? Organization men or pastors? Should authority be conferred by the sacraments or by other qualifications and procedures? Should research groups share the responsibility for the Church, or, on the contrary, should she be led by those who have received the sacrament and the apostolic charge?

MISSIKA: *Would you be in favor of greater democracy in the designation of priests and bishops?*

LUSTIGER: I do not know quite what you mean by that. . . .

MISSIKA: *Having an elective system, for example?*

LUSTIGER: It had a role in the early Church, at least in certain cases. There are striking and celebrated examples, such as when Saint Ambrose, a provincial governor, was chosen to be bishop of Milan by the people's acclamation. At the present time, there are preliminary investigations of individuals and a diocese's needs. In fact, the systems for selection are far from rigid; they have varied over time, the nominating procedures having evolved like all human procedures. But the invariant that is always considered is that selections are a matter of vocations—that is, calls from God. This criterion operates in two directions: first, in the choice of the one who is called and, second, in the way of co-option of those who call or ordain. The precautions taken by the Church are not only those used for the "selection" of personnel or executives in other areas of human activity. They also entail respecting the distinct character of a divine vocation. Appointing someone as a priest or a bishop presupposes a choice based not only on aptitude or a person's potential for adapting to a specific job but on something more: the will of God. God has to have called this particular man to make a gift of his existence and to have sent him to serve his brothers. Without this criterion, which is not one of mere suitability, the essential disappears and is wanting.

In this regard, the Church has an original way of functioning that merits being scrutinized by sociologists: for choosing bishops, as in the Latin Church for choosing priests, the institution makes herself dependent on a charism—since the Church considers the spiritual vocation of permanent celibacy as a charism, the vocation of the free gift of one's life through love of God, when

God calls. And, as to this charisma, she has no authority other than that of recognizing and authenticating it. I can think of no other example of a functioning institution, statutorily subjecting itself to charismatic decisions, that has been tested for so long and to such an extent.

WOLTON: *Then what standards of effectiveness can be used to judge the Church, since political or economic ones are not applicable?*

LUSTIGER: Certain criteria—such as those in parables drawn from economic realities—are given by the Gospel. Christ speaks of stewards to whom the master has entrusted his property, the property being the gifts that God makes to his people. What are the criteria used in these parables? First of all, there is the fidelity with which the stewards will have carried out the master's intentions. However, the master's thoughts often oblige the steward to reason in just the opposite direction from his own thoughts. In the parable of talents—often badly interpreted today because, to understand it, you have to refer to the Jewish law of the time—there is one man to whom five "talents" (they are pieces of money) are given and from them he earns five more. Another man is given two talents, and he earns two more. And then the last man, who has received only one talent, says, "Master, I knew you to be a hard man, reaping where you did not sow and gathering where you did not winnow; so I was afraid and I went and hid your talent in the ground. Here you have what is yours." Only the last man acted within the Jewish law, because the conditions for accepting a deposit stipulated that no risks could be taken with entrusted property, that it had to be guarded scrupulously in order to be given back intact to its owner. But the master—and the parable is deliberately paradoxical—praises the two other stewards who have broken the law. Why? Because they have dealt with the master's property according to the master's own logic, taking the same risks that he would have taken—that is, they have followed the logic of fecundity. According to Saint Matthew (25:14–30), the parable of the talents describes how the Church will be judged.

The Church must not aim for more effective seduction or conquest. That is not her mission.

Her mission is to bear witness before all men to God's love, to the infinite love with which they are loved. Her means are the same as those Christ used: giving one's life for those one loves—which obliges the disciples of Christ to accept the paradox that "whoever loses wins". Christ repeats this truth to his Disciples: "For whoever would save his life will lose it, and whoever loses his life for my sake will find it" (Mt 16:24–25).

The Ecumenical Movement and Relations with Other Religions

WOLTON: *Although the ecumenical movement has a relative importance today and in any case stimulates interest, it seems that the Popes were hostile to it for a long time. Leo XIII staunchly maintained his opposition to the Reformation and reaffirmed the invalidity of the Anglican ordinations. There was even an encyclical in 1928 in which Pius XI rejected the movement, and in 1948 Pius XII forbade Catholics from participating in the first meeting of the Ecumenical Council of Churches. How do you explain the change in the Church's attitude in such a short time, and what are the reasons for her previous antagonism?*

LUSTIGER: The problem of the Church's unity is coextensive with her birth and life. Again, we need to take a step backward. In the prophecy of sacred history—that is, in the existence of the people of Israel—division lasts longer than unity. One of the eschatological signs is the reunion of the two kingdoms of Israel and Judea. In the apostolic writings, in Saint Paul's letters, division is repeatedly presented both as a menace and a reason for hope. This internal threat has always been understood in relation to sins against unity, against mutual love, against fidelity to the truth, because it is a division of the unique Body of Christ. It is like an ordeal being perpetually reborn. The question of unity is still that of a reunion. As long as history endures, unity is never achieved, it is always given; only an imperial vision of things can lead us to believe in an effortless integration. Only dictators imagine that they have created "an empire to last for a thousand years". There always remains a formidable source of separation: its name is death. A static vision of unity is unrealistic because unity is an act of gathering together by God in the course of history, and the unity given in Christ remains a hope here below.

That being so, the history of Christianity over twenty centuries shows how the divisions of Christian churches have conformed to—I think that I have mentioned this already—cultural divisions: the Greek East from the Latin West, for example. Even before, there were separations among the cultures who wanted to escape Byzantium (Armenians, Copts, Chaldeans, Syriacs . . .), and then came the detachments among the Germanic and Anglo-Saxon peoples, etc. There would have been many other national separations had it not been for the Pope's role in the Catholic Church. But, at the same time, there are the stakes for the Faith, of unequal gravity in the diverse situations. Thus, Pius XII recognized that the Christology of the Copts (the early Egyptian church), preceding the dogma of Chalcedonia and criticized for a long time, was expressive, in different terms, of the unique Christian faith. Some early churches, far from the Latins' horizon, broke away from Byzantium, and Rome has often been attentive to these churches, some of whom are in communion with Rome. The Maronite church, for example, is a Semite church that originated in Antioch. It refused the Greek of Byzantium and kept its original liturgical language. Later the liturgical language became Arabic, but it remains directly united with Rome.

The really great schism of the Church occurred when she was cut into two empires, two cultures—East and West—and it has always been deeply troubling to the Christian conscience. Beginning in the thirteenth century in Lyon, two ecumenical councils searched for solutions; doctrinally, they seemed possible. In the fifteenth century, a few years before the fall of Constantinople, the Council of Florence (1438–45) celebrated the reunion, the communion of the Eastern and Western churches. A remarkable intellectual effort had been made to assess the cultural and dogmatic differences between the Greek and Latin traditions and to show the doctrinal equivalences that existed beneath the differences of expression. Hence, there was a labor of understanding and of mutual recognition of the same faith in its divergent assertions. Pope John Paul II sees the ecumenical effort as a major objective of his pontificate; it is as though he has taken the torch from the Council of Florence.

WOLTON: *Do you think that reunification is possible, after so many centuries of schism between the Eastern and Western churches?*

LUSTIGER: The foundations of the Council of Florence certainly furnish sufficiently solid elements for such a step.

The Catholic Church has unilaterally admitted that the Catholic faithful, isolated in Orthodox countries, can have recourse to the sacraments and ministry of Orthodox priests with a completely clear conscience, because they are the sacraments and priests of the Church.

WOLTON: *And is the converse true?*

LUSTIGER: The converse is not equally true. A dogmatic question is pending; it is relatively likely to be resolved—the Patriarch Athénagoras has virtually said so—but there are still three other kinds of difficulties. First, there is the wide gulf of cultural incomprehension between traditions and peoples who have become strangers to each other. Second, there are theological and disciplinary obstacles that have to be overcome. The two most sensitive points are the Pope's ministry and the definition of new dogmas, but there are other minor points in regard to common patrimony. Paradoxically, the Eastern churches probably consider us as more heretical than we consider them. Undoubtedly, they view us more severely than the Roman Church views them! But, third, the political factor plays a much greater role today. Even if the hierarchies of the Eastern churches were ready to re-establish communion between the churches of East and West, they would certainly clash with the political powers, because these churches are in part national and depend on those powers.

MISSIKA: *Some of these churches are in Eastern Europe and the Soviet Union.*

LUSTIGER: That is the problem. It is the schism of European culture.

WOLTON: *But, in your opinion, if that were to happen . . .*

LUSTIGER: The Pope wants it to happen and has said so.

WOLTON: *If ever the two churches decided to be reconciled, there would be political interference, but could the political powers in various countries prevent it?*

LUSTIGER: Alas, it is more likely that they would oppose it and would succeed in stopping it!

The internal schism in the West, creating the churches of the Reformation, came later. It involves various realities, connected with national histories and the misadventures of modern culture since the fourteenth century. Here the dogmatic difficulties are much greater. Protestantism touches the sensitive issue of the reformation of the Church. Both before and afterward, many saints have labored incessantly to bring it about; they have worked tirelessly for the conversion of those who have already been called to the Faith. It is a permanent problem for the Church. The equivalent situation existed in the Eastern churches, but it is less well known, and the more or less dissident reform movements did not have the same scope. In the West, the phenomenon is tied to three factors. First, the call for internal reform of the Church: how can it be brought about—that is, in the communion of faith and charity, in sacramental unity—without a breaking off. Next, there is a Western crisis: how to give rights to particularisms in a universal religion, because the Reformation was concomitant with the appearance of European nationalities and favored them. And, finally, there is a divergence on the conception of man and his relationship to God. This difference, to say the very least, is very perceptible in Lutheranism and Calvinism and corresponds to the major turning point of the Christianized West. It is an outgrowth of the crisis of modern man, where the philosophical and critical emancipation of the West and the question of its fidelity and infidelity are joined together in a conflictive way. But who can say that fidelity would have left everything exactly as it was!

The desire for communion and ecumenism with the Reformation churches reappeared forcefully at the end of the nineteenth century. Among the instigators of the movement were Lord Halifax and Cardinal Mercier. In this century, the Abbé Couturier, Jean Guitton[1] and so many others, from here and there, have initiated efforts for the healing of this division, which remains an open sore in the Church's conscience. But the problem is far more difficult to solve than with the Eastern churches. It would require everybody to take a new direction, to reinterpret history, and that is no small matter. After all, Hegel comes from Luther, and so does Marx, as Jaurès used to say. Hegel's association with Christianity is tied just as much to the development of Lutheranism as it is to Kant's pietism. The West's awakening to reason and critical freedom constituted a religious experience. It is at the heart of our culture's crisis. I continue to affirm that we are not looking at a religiously neutral evolution exterior to Christianity; in the end, it is a matter of an interior movement within the confines of faith.

So the problem of the Reformation poses much more serious and complex questions for the reunion of the Church than Orthodoxy does. In the latter case, we are brothers who quarreled, but nevertheless we ought to be able to recognize ourselves as brothers who have inherited the same patrimony. With the Reformation churches, we are dealing with the crisis that pervades all of Western civilization, and its contradictions have to be resolved before a reconciliation can be reached. Consequently, for the reuniting of Catholics and the churches born of the Reformation, a very thorough, deliberate study has to be done; otherwise, all the old disputes could re-emerge overnight. But ecumenism is an urgent task, all the more so since it concerns the destiny of Western humanity and its responsibility to other countries and cultures.

MISSIKA: *With Judaism, there is still another problem.*

LUSTIGER: With Judaism, the tragedy is still more "radical"; it is the problem of origins, in the sense of the Pauline image of the root and the graft. Israel is the root. Mutual gratitude is one of the basic conditions for the reconciliation of humanity. Two aspects have to be considered in discussing the Church's relationship to Judaism: what can be said about it as of today, and what will always remain our hope. A symptomatic fact: many people were surprised by Rome's decision to attach Jewish relations to the secretariat for Christian unity and not to the one dealing with non-Christian religions. But that was a recognition, at least implicitly, of a unique bond of filiation. In an original and historical way, the relationship with Israel poses the problem of the spiritual unity of God's plan for the world's salvation.

[1] Lord Halifax (1839–1934), a British Catholic, and Désiré Mercier (1851–1926), a Belgian prelate and professor of philosophy at Louvain, were pioneers in ecumenism. Later, Abbé Couturier († 1953) in Lyon and the French philosopher Jean Guitton (1901–) were among the main Catholic contributors to interdenominational meetings and dialogue. —TRANS.

MISSIKA: *But here there is a major obstacle. Can it be overcome simply by earnest and thorough discussion?*

LUSTIGER: What would happen to Judaism, which does not now regard Christ as the Messiah, if one day all of Israel recognized him as such? That question falls within the realm of hope—powerful, but inexpressible, unimaginable. On the other hand, the Church's acknowledgment—even if it is made in a strained atmosphere—of God's gift to Israel appears to be an accessible goal. That would already be a real step forward, even if it remained limited by the understanding that each group has of the other and also of itself. Because the Christian is more Christian when he concedes the promise and gift made to Israel, and I think that the Jew would be more himself if he conceded the Gift made to all nations. This is in the order of recognizable progress.

WOLTON: *Can that mutual gratitude between Jews and Christians be envisaged as happening within a generation?*

LUSTIGER: Who knows?

MISSIKA: *On a different level, how do you see relations between the Catholic Church and Islam? In particular, how have they been influenced by the revival of fundamentalism?*

LUSTIGER: I remind you first of all of a point of view that, I know, is not accepted by the Muslims themselves. Scholars in religious history have suggested that Islam seems to have had its origins in both the marginal Jewish milieus of the Arabian peninsula and certain Christian heretics, or perhaps in Judeo-Christian sects. If one makes a comparison of the Koran and the Bible, even while keeping in mind the singular personality of Mohammed and his reinterpretation, the influence of his Jewish and Christian sources is unmistakable.

A second point has to be made about Islam: you cannot ignore the way its history came about. It is fascinating! Islam was spread by people coming from the Arabian peninsula, and we must take this basic fact into account when considering Islam as a religion. We French of the twentieth century are inclined to consider religions as modalities of existence, belonging more or less to private life—distinct if not separate from civil and political life, which is a part of the secular world. But the contact of the Arab world with Islam and the Islamic world with other countries took place in the form of invasions and powerful acculturations. For the West, the experience of this history was traumatic. The countries that were the sources and major centers of Hellenic-Christian civilization toppled into another cultural zone. This happened first with Asia Minor and North Africa, which were areas of Greek and Roman civilization and colonization that had become Christian. And, with the Muslim conquest, they even changed their language.

All of Asia Minor had spoken Greek, and under the rule of Islam they began to speak Arabic! Also, Egyptians spoke Greek as much as Copt—Alexandria is a Greek city—and they too began to speak Arabic. And, with Islam's spread to the West, with Tunisia, the countries that had spoken Latin and Punic also started to speak Arabic. Thus, there was obviously a radical mutation with wars and the defensive reactions of people coping with a substitution of culture imposed by force. The West has kept the memory of a formidable threat from the Turks in the sixteenth and seventeenth centuries, nine hundred years after Poitiers and Charles Martel. The battles of Lépante (1571)[2] and of Kahlenberg, just outside Vienna's walls (1683), were extreme points of this threat. For twelve centuries, the Christian West felt menaced, and conversely the Muslim world suffered—with an unquenchable passion—the Crusades, colonialism and the carving up of Egypt, the Near East and the Turkish Empire by England and France—when there were attempts to settle accounts going back to the Turkish oppression of the Balkan countries.

All this made for a truly turbulent history. And there is a final element that must not be overlooked: the survival of the Eastern churches in the Levant. They were traditionally the focus of a harsh confrontation between Islam and the Christian West. The colonial period in Africa was not so simple either, since the French administration favored the Islamization of populations because they felt that they would be easier to control than Christian populations.

WOLTON: *I do not understand. Do you mean to say that the eldest daughter of the Church preferred Islam to Christianity?*

LUSTIGER: As freethinkers, numerous colonial administrators were hostile to evangelization. So, in the midnineteenth century, one sees the blessed Libermann and his *Spiritains*[3] meeting with the resistance of French colonial officers when they wanted to implant the first churches in West Africa. I remember the point made by the "Great Muslim" of Dakar[4] (that is one of his familiar titles); he recalled that the Catholics and the disciples of Libermann, the fathers of the Congregation of the Holy Spirit, had been able to land and install themselves in Dakar only because his predecessors had given them a

[2] Lépante is a formerly important Greek port near which Don Juan of Austria defeated the Turks in a great naval battle.—TRANS.

[3] François Marie-Paul Libermann (1802–52), the son of a rabbi, converted to Christianity in 1826 and was later the superior-general of the Congregation of the Holy Spirit (*Spiritains*). He played an important role in the evangelization of blacks in Africa and America.—TRANS.

[4] This is the Muslim leader in Dakar (Senegal), where Christians remain a minority. —TRANS.

little plot of land, contrary to the wishes of the French governor. It was the French government that forbade Lavigerie[5] to baptize the Kabyles.

WOLTON: *But how do you explain the extraordinarily fervent dynamism of Islam today?*

LUSTIGER: It can be understood as resulting from the clash of cultures and civilizations. Could it not be the equivalent, making due allowances, of a *jacquerie?*[6] The triumphant West has been exporting its overabundance of material objects and industrial technology, its liberalization of moral standards to Muslim countries and, in general, stimulating their desire for consumption. Is fundamentalism not a defensive reaction of traditional civilizations that have kept the memory of their former supremacy?

WOLTON: *Then the present ardor of Islam can be explained by the reaction to the evils they feel the West has brought to their countries?*

LUSTIGER: I do not know. But just analyze the content of what so many Muslims say. Consider the theme of the "great Satan" and the argument that the Iranian Shiites or other fundamentalists are developing: it is precisely what I am telling you. I am noting their own interpretation. And if this interpretation is listened to by the common people, it means that vast numbers of Muslims have considered Western civilization to be an unacceptable aggression, as well as a seduction. The collision of cultures produced by the West's encounter with countries of the Islamic tradition could have been lessened if the West had been more Christian. And this, in fact, was true for a while in the past, in a micro-climate such as the one in Lebanon prior to its explosion. Certainly Lebanon had experienced stormy relations between the communities, with violent persecutions of Christians by the Muslims and sometimes cruel acts of vengeance by Christians; but the best of Christianity appeared in the positive relations between Christian and Muslim. That kind of harmony has existed in other micro-climates—at one time it reigned in Spain between Islam and the Jews. The paradise of Córdoba was built on it, in those amazing centuries before the *Reconquista.* That proves, then, that there are other ways of living together.

WOLTON: *What can the Catholic Church do in response to the rising tide of Islam?*

[5] Lavigerie (see p. 155 n. 2) founded the *Pères blancs d'Afrique* and worked for the abolition of slavery.—TRANS.

[6] This is a peasant revolt, especially a bloody one.—TRANS.

LUSTIGER: She must work unflaggingly to tell the truth, to bring to the fore, as the Pope did in his speech at Casablanca, the best of Islam. At the same time, she must affirm unequivocally but tranquilly the right to civil liberty in religious matters and, hence, the need for a clear distinction between the religious and political realms of society. And, to this end, we can call on the part of Islam that is nourished by biblical sources. Perhaps human rights would not be so bad as a theme, so long as the common theological and anthropological foundation is brought out, permitting Islam to shoulder the consequences of its own obedience to the omnipotent and merciful God.

WOLTON: *I gather that the Catholic Church is presently more favorable to the ecumenical movement than are the other religions.*

LUSTIGER: Strictly speaking, the ecumenical movement concerns only the Christian churches. The term does not apply to relations with Islam, and it can be applied to Christian-Jewish relations only very circumspectly.

WOLTON: *Aren't the Catholics alone in their pursuit of unity?*

LUSTIGER: I do not know if that is true. But, by their very structure, the Eastern churches, inasmuch as they are autocephalous—that is, independent of an archiepiscopal or patriarchal jurisdiction—have for a long time now accepted the broad identification of a church with a nation and cultural zone. And the Protestant churches born of the Reformation have accepted the multiplicity of Christian confessions as inevitable. Whereas an Orthodox member of an autocephalous church can live in harmony alongside other self-governing churches and perhaps the shattered vision of the Protestant Reformation can live with these religious splinterings without too much discomfort, Catholicism, with its principle of unity represented by Peter's ministry, has a more exacting idea of ecumenism and its internal logic.

There are two types of unity, however. One is much more political: it can take on an imperial or national face, to which the autocephalous churches of the East conform, or else it is subject to the liberal breaking up of Anglo-Saxon democracies, which adapt quite well to Protestant disparities. The other type is the model of Catholic unity, which is of a sacramental nature; it takes on the diversity of cultural particularities in a universal communion without frontiers. The Catholic understanding of unity embraces the totality of nations in the singular unity of one people.

Opening onto the World

WOLTON: *We have been witnessing, especially since Vatican II, the Catholic Church's openness toward the rest of the world and the growth of what are called "the young Churches". Can the development of these young Churches, in Africa, for example, contribute to the formation of nations? How can the success of the Catholics in Asia be explained? And how do you explain the distance progressively taken by the Church in Latin America from the political regimes of the right to which she was linked for such a long time?*

LUSTIGER: First a point to rectify the formulation of your question, or to add a precision that is often overlooked. The Catholic Church—from her origins and not just in the past forty years—has never endorsed colonial systems, even if sometimes she has been politically and physically carried by the vehicle of colonialism. From the moment that there is an evangelization, contact between Christianity and an exterior culture—called "pagan" by convention—there is an explicit will to establish a local hierarchy so that a growing Church becomes identified or identifiable with a people or nation. This has been a constant of Christian history.

An example of this policy has been brought to light recently by the millennial celebration of Saints Cyril and Methodius, who evangelized the Slavs. These two brothers were monks from a Greek culture in communion with both the patriarchate of Constantinople and the Roman Pope; they launched an extraordinary adventure of bringing the Gospel to the Slavs, and to do so, they were obliged to invent the cyrillic alphabet. It is their evangelization that brought into history and literature peoples who until then "were nothing" and risked sinking into oblivion just like all the non-literate civilizations of antiquity who were engulfed by other cultures and forgotten.

The success of evangelization in Latin America can be attributed in one sense to the coincidence between the culture and the people. South America, in a very indigenous way, is a Catholic, profoundly Catholic, continent.

MISSIKA: *Well, that may be, but they have had a little encouragement!*

LUSTIGER: It is much to the Church's credit that one can cite a certain number of individuals, notably from religious orders, who fought—sometimes to their death—against the Spanish and Portuguese princes to defend the Indians.

MISSIKA: *But that has not passed into the collective memory. It is more likely the saber and aspergillum*[7] *that are remembered in Latin America and Africa.*

LUSTIGER: Yes, that is said, but it is a terribly biased assessment. The official history touching on the Church's past remains impregnated by the anticlericalism of the nineteenth century. Even the history that Catholics themselves receive from the collective memory is partially infiltrated by prejudices.

As far as the Church is concerned, there has always been the goal of establishing a local hierarchy. Seminaries were founded in Latin America, Asia and Africa while evangelization was still in progress. Only it takes a long time before the fruits are ready to be gathered. The educative and evangelizing efforts of the Church have furnished the economic, political and cultural framework for young nations and have given body and substance to cultures that had previously been outside of history and literature.

MISSIKA: *On this point, what do you say to the frequently heard criticism—which falls within the context of colonization in general—namely, that for the local populations, evangelization resulted in a brutal cultural uprooting and produced a submission to Western culture?*

LUSTIGER: The reproach is in part well founded, in part unjustifiable. It must be weighed and nuanced. To imagine that, in a world as unified as ours is, there can be reserves of populations whose archaic cultures survive intact is a chimera. In fact, contact was inevitable. And contact means change.

WOLTON: *It is true that cultural exchange is inevitable, but it has been disproportionate.*

LUSTIGER: I wish to remark, however, that the simple vision of an autonomy of cultures and their peaceful coexistence as equals presupposes the absence of exchange.

WOLTON: *Yes, but in this case, there was more than exchange; there was proselytism.*

LUSTIGER: A comparative study of the imperial, colonizing and evangelizing strategies is really imperative—as far as I know, it has not yet been done. It

[7] In French, the saber and the aspergillum are frequently paired as symbols of the collusion between church and state or, more specifically, between the military and the clergy. The "alliance of the throne and the altar" has also often been denounced.—TRANS.

should consist of a meticulous examination of documents and rely on various points of reference. Most of the time, historians have started from the hypothesis that, essentially, the Church behaved just like the colonizing empires. The reality is far more complex.

The Christian announcement changes the vision that men have of each other because it immediately implies that all men are brothers, since they have been born of the same Father. They are created by God, and the physical representation of humanity's unity—thus, of human fraternity—stems from filiation and fathering. That truth is found in the first pages of the Bible. From the beginning, there is a universal fraternity, despite physical differences and cultural divisions, skin colors and other particularities. And the object of Messianic hope is not that men be subjected to an elected nation but that all of them, in their ethnic, cultural and linguistic distinctions, come together to acknowledge and sing the glory of the unique God. This is foretold by the prophets and by Saint John in Revelation (7:9): "After this I looked, and behold, a great multitude which no man could number, from every nation, from all tribes and peoples and tongues", and at the time of Pentecost, each person hears the announcement of the unique Word of God in his own language. The universalism of the Bible and the Gospel, the Good News of the same salvation proclaimed to all nations, signifies the recognition of the diversity of cultures and languages in the adoration of the unique God. That conception does not come from a speech made at the United Nations but from a page in the Acts of the Apostles and from the mouths of the biblical prophets. You have to discern the singular content of these words and their formidable difference from all the imperial ideas of antiquity or the modern era. Because the Roman Empire inevitably imposed Latin, just as the French Empire imposed French, and the British Empire imposed English . . . and five o'clock tea.

WOLTON: *It could be objected that Catholic universalism is itself marked by a cultural model: Jesus is white and belongs to the history of the Mediterranean basin.*

LUSTIGER: That particularity—and it cannot be denied without denying history—obliges us to admit that Jesus is forever white and Mediterranean—even if men are tempted to make a Jesus in their own image: the infant Jesus as an African or Asian or with blond hair. Each century has rewritten or repainted the Gospel scenes with the subjects often being given the features of people known to the artist and wearing the dress of the times. Besides, in the end, how should they be depicted, since we know so little about how people dressed and lived two thousand years ago?

But, in this case, the particularity is not the source of imperialism. John Paul II repeated this forcefully in commenting on the rebirth of non-European cultures: "Christ becomes black or yellow in his brothers." It was on being identified with a pronounced word in an explicit human language—Hebrew or Aramaic—that the Word was spoken. It is through the singularity of history that the mediation of the universal takes place. Otherwise, the universal becomes abstract and without substance. Through the announcement of the Gospel, men are going to discover that they are not alone in the world, that God is God of all and that all men are brothers, even when circumstances and violence have created strikingly unequal relations among peoples and when cultural clashes have become destructive. But experience shows—and it is here that I would like to see a detailed and scrupulous comparative study done—that Christianity has played a role that consists in giving substance to particularities, precisely by integrating them into the universal entente. Christianity makes it possible for these differences among men to enter into history, because it unveils history's mystery. This fact struck me forcefully in Yugoslavia in 1985 when I read the account of the lives of Cyril and Methodius. It contained a memorable accolade of a Slavic prince who writes to the Pope about them: "We, who were ignored by everyone, were nothing. They came and gave us existence." Until then, these people were not in the community of nations, and it is on entering universal history that they exist according to their own characteristics. It has to be admitted that the missionaries, who were of the same generations as the military, the *compradores,* the merchants and the captains, behaved very differently! The contrast between the behavior of a Saint Francis Xavier and the Portuguese governors is especially impressive. The former was concerned about learning languages. He dressed in Japanese style, and not just for the sake of efficacy. Similarly, in Africa and Latin America, whose civilizations were based on oral traditions, it was missionaries who collected the first ethnological documents. If you want to know about historical ethnology, you have to turn to the missionaries. The merchants could not have cared less about their traditions, and neither could the military.

WOLTON: *Today the Catholic Church seems to be counting more on Asia, Africa and Latin America than on the traditionally Catholic European countries.*

LUSTIGER: The Church does not use a strategy; she takes note of the facts. The Catholic continent is Latin America! The Catholic peoples who are most numerous, most endowed with the human and spiritual vitality of the Faith, are found in Latin America, Africa and certain Asian countries.

MISSIKA: *But it is especially since John Paul II that she has begun to observe all this....*

LUSTIGER: That is inexact! John Paul II has brought this situation to light because his trips have uncovered certain facts that we had ignored, that we had not wanted to see. Do not imagine, however, that such changes could have occurred since the last papal election! We were simply not aware of what was going on in the world and in the Church. To understand what is happening now in South America, you have to go back to the origins of colonization and evangelization and look at what has evolved in less than five centuries. The initiators of this reversal of perspectives in the Church did not foresee it, but it is the fruit of their efforts. For example, if you had said to Saint Augustine or Saint Cyril of Jerusalem, "France is the eldest daughter of the Church", they would have laughed in your face: Who were these Gaulois engulfed by barbarous tribes? What did they represent for the Church at that time?

MISSIKA: *For the time being, the European cardinals are still in the majority.*

LUSTIGER: No, and it seems that their proportion should be still lower. The Popes of this century have wanted to increase the number of cardinals in order to deal with the spread of Christianity throughout the world. The number of cardinals from the old European countries is diminishing in relative importance. In the synods, the young Churches have practically as much weight, if not more, than the European Churches, if only because of the existence of the episcopal conferences whose representation is proportional to national populations—and the Church is now established in every country. The composition of this world assembly is entirely different from one based on political considerations. The Church functions in a completely singular way. She is altogether different from the United Nations, because the U.N. is a place of confrontation and exchange marked by the relations of political forces. But the Church, with her apostolic assembly, is a place of communion and consensus. Henceforth, the recently born nations will have exactly the same rights, the same apostolic authority as the old nations.

MISSIKA: *Do you get the feeling, when you attend these assemblies, that you come from a continent on the decline?*

LUSTIGER: It is one of the questions that I incessantly ask myself. Are we really about to die? I know that such words spoken to Europeans generally elicit indignant reactions: "What a pessimist you are! What a defeatist!" But the risk is real. In 1981, I had the opportunity to converse at length with the leaders of the African episcopate. It was very impressive. These men of the Church are not holding the old anticolonialist discourse. They claim us as their Fathers in the Faith. They have no complexes. They love us because we have brought to them, transmitted to them, a certain number of material and spiritual riches. But, at the same time, they judge us and conclude, "Are we not more Christian than you? Our social, political and economic difficulties may be much greater than yours, but where is the spiritual strength to be found? We do not understand what is happening to you. Where are you heading?" Furthermore, the question of whether the West is dying raises another one: What does the West really want and believe?

MISSIKA: *The election of a non-Italian Pope was deemed to be an event of considerable significance. Is the election of a non-European Pope conceivable, and if so, how soon could it happen?*

LUSTIGER: From now on, anything is possible, but when is absolutely unpredictable. There were non-Italian Popes in earlier times, but it is the first time that we have had a Slavic Pope. It was none too soon! Almost ten centuries went by between the evangelization of the Slavic peoples and the election of one of them as Pope. His election signifies that the Church has at long last become independent of Western powers: the kings of France, Spain, Portugal or England, the Germanic emperors no longer play a determining role. The election of John Paul II is a kind of belated victory for Gregory VII. But how many centuries were needed? Nine centuries for the unmistakable appearance of the consequences of the Church's will for independence. But, for the future, we can envisage a lot less time before the election of a non-European Pope. Just imagine if tomorrow we were to see a black president of the United States—it could happen within the next twenty years—a Muslim secretary-general of the Soviet Communist Party, and a Chinese Pope!

III

PROFANE FUTURE, SACRED FUTURE

The Just War?

JEAN-LOUIS MISSIKA: *Speaking of war and peace, the positions taken by Christian churches—both Protestant and Catholic—are often put in the pacifist category. Peace movements, notably in Northern Europe, are supported by the churches, especially by the Protestant denominations. However, there are much more nuanced positions in Catholic doctrine. I would like to ask you to explain the doctrine of the "just war".*

JEAN-MARIE LUSTIGER: Violence for violence's sake is never justifiable. The use of force is legitimate only when it serves a just cause. What is a just cause? The defense and protection of the essential goods of a people and a nation, its physical survival, its freedom, the real characteristics of its independence and existence. Wars of aggression, conquest or reprisal are never just wars. On the other hand, the defensive war can be acceptable as long as all lawful means of settling a dispute have been exhausted and as long as the damages done remain commensurate with the goods threatened. In taking possible negotiations into account, the destruction that a war would bring about must not be superior to the advantage, albeit warranted, that a state or nation can gain from it. Actually, it boils down to the right to self-defense—understood on the level of nations and peoples: if somebody wants to take your life, you have the right to defend yourself. But this right, like all rights, has several limits. Nobody has the right to defend himself by any means whatsoever: the end does not justify the means. Even though every war is itself a great evil, this does not exonerate every transgression of morality: there are war crimes!

Thus, the Church, in her reflection and her action, aims to "moralize" man's bellicose behavior as much as she can. In the face of conflicts, throughout her history, the Church has constantly tried to substitute a negotiated order or negotiating procedures for settlement by warfare. That presupposes the existence of a juridical order, arbitration and its recognition. But, in any case, war remains an evil, one that is more and more fearsome as the dangers of total extermination of human life increase. Because, in our modern period of nuclear weapons, there has been a dramatic qualitative change in the way war is viewed by mankind.

When the positions of the Christian churches—including those of the Catholic Church—are labeled as pacifist, the justification for the category depends on what is meant by the word *pacifist.* Was Paul VI being a "pacifist" when he said at the United Nations, "No more war"? A person can advocate "no more war" because wanting war is a crime and a sin: war is the worst of ways to settle disputes between nations. But that does not mean that, in an ultimate and extreme case, you do not have to muster the courage to lose your life to save the reasons for living. This is the drastic and paradoxical situation in which Christian reflection finds itself in face of war: war is an evil for which we must try to find a remedy; to desire it is outrageous and insane, but it can be morally acceptable to tolerate it and to participate in it when the preservation of essential and fundamental rights is at stake.

One last reflection on pacifism in regard to the figure of Christ: the Gospel expressly urges a person to give his life sooner than take that of another. I am thinking of Christ's saying to Peter, "Put your sword back into its place" when, wanting to defend him, Peter has drawn his weapon and cut off the ear of one of those who had come to arrest Christ. "Put your sword back into its place." Other precepts with the same significance are often invoked in a Christian perspective: "Do not resist one who is evil", "If anyone strikes you on the right cheek, turn to him the other also. . . . If anyone would sue you and take your coat, let him have your cloak as well", etc. These words spoken by Christ are clear. They are addressed to the Disciples of whom it is being asked in advance to accept the fate of the unjustly condemned righteous man. The logic of this attitude consists of not responding to evil with evil or to violence with violence, but in calling on the logic and the strength of love and forgiveness that come from God. It is the logic of Christ's sacrifice in face of human powers whose iniquity culminates in the cruel act inflicted upon him, the Innocent, whom Roman justice has condemned. Should I find myself in a similar situation, I should have to behave in the same way if I am to be faithful to Christ. With God's grace, I could do it. But I do not wish—and morally nobody can—to impose a policy of resignation and abandon on a people by saying, "This is what you must do to obey Christ." That would not be true. It would be gravely derelict to prevent a people from using armed resistance to protect itself from aggression. It is certainly morally legitimate for a nation to insist on being defended. The spiritual response to violence, the offering of one's life, is at the heart of the Christian theme of peace. But that spiritual attitude corresponds to a vocation. It cannot be imposed by political constraint. It can be chosen, responsibly, by free subjects exercising their freedom to react to violence with nonviolence—indeed, with forgiveness. But depriving citizens of the protection of the state's strength and leaving them vulnerable in the face of an arbitrary and unjust attack would be an act of political irresponsibility. Mysticism degenerates into bad politics when it does not give moral consideration to the juridical mediations and constraints of violence. Mystical abandon risks becoming a political dupery and cowardly surrender to violence. The fact remains that, using all available political means, men must work to substitute peaceful and reasonable negotiation for armed struggle.

DOMINIQUE WOLTON: *But how do you explain that, contrary to what you have just been saying, certain churches confuse the mystical personal level with the political collective one?*

MISSIKA: *We are thinking in particular of the demands for unilateral disarmament.*

LUSTIGER: Unilateral disarmament is the transposition of the martyr's attitude to the collective plane of nations. The believer can and must sometimes assume this vocation after having recognized and chosen it spiritually: this has been done by many men and women across the centuries. But it is morally indefensible to propose to an entire people—to the detriment of its identity and present life—an ideal that politically is utopian. Obtaining such a political suicide through public pressure is unacceptable; the object of a spiritual choice cannot be imposed on a nation. Thinking that the spiritual laws of the Kingdom of God can be transformed into a mode of political management of human history is dangerously idealistic. That would imply believing and letting it be understood that the eschatological reconciliation had been realized everywhere, that the Kingdom of God and its justice had become terrestrial realities on a human and historical scale. The same is true for the notion of ownership, for the appropriation of possessions. Christ's disciples are urged to renounce their riches, but a society cannot be juridically constructed on a vow of poverty. That Christians in a society should endeavor to live in holiness and follow the evangelical counsel by renouncing worldly belongings is well and good, but morally they cannot make this a political requirement for their fellow citizens at the price of everyone's dignity and freedom. Disregard for material goods cannot be made obligatory: that would be a tyranny.

MISSIKA: *You have just alluded to the fact that nuclear weapons have radically changed the nature of the problem of war, since they make possible the destruction of all humanity. So the Church is confronted by an ethical question of overwhelming dimensions that, as you know, has already been treated differently by different episcopates. The French episcopate published a declaration on the subject of nuclear war but did not resolve the problem confronting it: how to construct an ethical position in regard to nuclear arms and the potential annihilation of mankind.*

LUSTIGER: It should be noted that in France—until recent years—opinion was never fundamentally hostile to nuclear weapons, in contrast to what has been going on in Germany for some time. Perhaps the French are still remembering that they were victims of invasions and humiliated by defeat three times within a century. They do not think of themselves as having been an aggressive and warlike nation—perhaps wrongly because some European peoples have quite another impression based on their memories of earlier wars, most recently the Napoleonic invasions. In the national consciousness, our wars have always been just, linked with the freedom of peoples and individuals. Consequently, nuclear arms as a means of defense have appeared to be legitimate, convinced as we are that France would never give in to a belligerent will. I think that this is the way the French see themselves, even if there also exists a nonnegligible part of French tradition that is antimilitaristic and was outraged and disgusted by the slaughter brought about by the two world wars.

Is this kind of reasoning sufficient for arbitrating the debates? Can Church and government leaders be satisfied with memories and strategic calculations of this type? The qualitative change you mentioned—nuclear armaments—forces us to reflect more profoundly on civilization. My preceding remarks would have sufficed in earlier times for justifying the bombardment of a city's walls with stones or cannonballs or for the use of crossbows or for raising a militia in Switzerland for the independence of its cantons. But we have entered another age of humanity where the danger comes not only from the possibility of war but also from the technology that is being spread by the manufacture of nuclear weapons and other instruments for military use. This calls for an overall deliberation on civilization's values, the finalities of political life and totalitarianism, because the risks of war are linked to the correlation of several factors: the determination to be in a position of ideological hegemony, to practice political totalitarianism, to maintain technological supremacy and vital economic interests—and, of course, the elements of nationalism or racism that can be mixed into all this.

MISSIKA: *In the bishops' statement, there was an extremely subtle distinction between the threat and the actual use of nuclear weapons that resembled a "provisional morality" more than anything else. Can a position like that be upheld for any length of time?*

LUSTIGER: It is a moral judgment, made at a given time, and I hope that it is provisional in the sense that the balance of terror we now live with is provisional.

MISSIKA: *On the issue of nuclear armaments or other new weapons, there is an interweaving of strategic questions and moral reflection.*

LUSTIGER: Yes, on one side, strategic reasoning rests largely on the theory of games, and the theory of games deals with only one kind of quantifiable probabilities. However sophisticated the instruments of calculation and prediction may be, the present analysis must include other factors that cannot be reduced or quantified in the same way: these are human freedoms and value judgments on good and evil. Do war and peace arise out of a strategy, like a game of chess whose rules, albeit complex, can be entirely integrated into the calculation? Or do many other kinds of parameters intervene, other values that cannot be reduced to calculable data? Civilization is precisely that: the capability of bringing into the political context elements other than those used merely to estimate the balance of power—symbolic, moral and spiritual elements that attest to the dignity and destiny of man.

Relations between Human and Sacred Histories

WOLTON: *This question can be enlarged to include the relationship between the sacred and profane futures—that is, between human history and divine history. How can the tragedies of human history over the past two thousand years be explained if the Messiah has already come?*

LUSTIGER: The Messiah is hidden now, but we believe that he will come again. I believe that redemption and the hidden presence of the Messiah in humanity are a mystery of compassion. To represent the coming of the Messiah as the end of history—because that is the sense of your question—can be completely legitimate, and that also corresponds to Christian hope. But this end of history is not just a past event; in God, it is our present, and it remains our future as well. History will be completed and all sin will be forgiven, all tears will be dried, death will be conquered, swords will be beaten into plowshares, the desert will reflower and man's heart will be completely transformed. Only then will the work of redemption have borne its fruit.

This time, our time, the time of the Messiah, is a period of watching and waiting: we Christians know whom we are waiting for, since he has come already. But the waiting period is not endless, not like the hours spent in a station when, because of a strike, only an occasional train is running, and nobody knows when it will arrive or where it will be heading. We are not waiting for Godot! The time of the Messiah is an interval of labor, and the scriptural image for it is the labor of childbirth. The saving power has already been given; it is already at hand. And what is this power that dwells in the Messiah and that he gives to his brothers? It is the power of the Holy Spirit who bestows life on God's children. It makes it possible for them to live according to divine holiness by conquering the evil that crushes man. What brings man down, what defeats him, is his own blindness, his lying, hate and cupidity—in a word, everything that takes him farther away from God and lessens his similarity to God. It is the powers of death that man is subjected to, because all sin is a stigma of death. But God's strength is at work in the world; it is a force of life that is greater than all the divisions, heartbreaks and derision that stigmatize humanity. The Spirit gathers together the brothers and sisters of the Messiah, Christians, those who accomplish the Messiah's work in this world. From the world, through the throes of labor, the Church of God's children is slowly being born and eventually the work will be completed. This is the enigma of history. "All of creation is now groaning with the pains of childbirth", and we do not know when this labor will end. We have no way of measuring it, because we are neither the Father nor the one giving birth. We know neither the day nor the hour when the new creation will be born. We are obliged to keep watch throughout the night. And Isaiah's (12:11) question: "Watchman, what of the night? Watchman, what of the night?" never ceases to echo in the Christian conscience.

WOLTON: *When you look at all the insanities of human history, particularly those of the twentieth century, it is hard to understand how anybody can say, "History is already saved, and the end will be positive."*

LUSTIGER: The Bible presents various visions that are in stark contrast to the tranquil assurance that the best of all possible worlds is to come. Reread the apocalyptic discourses: they are often "political" revelations. Following a literary genre present in Jewish literature and in Christ's words, they reveal the secret of the ages. The language is symbolic and must not be taken literally. But it depicts an insurpassable tragedy, which gives us a foreboding of tragedies to come; hence it is in complete disagreement with the passage you have just quoted. Humanity has always imagined its future and culmination in either dark or brilliant colors, without God's having wished or any man's having been able to make a decision one way or another. Christ said to his Disciples, "You will be hated by all because of me", and "Charity may dissolve itself on earth". He asks, "When he comes, will the Son of Man find faith on earth?" The apocalypse describes humanity's future and the Messiah's reign as an increasingly fierce combat between the forces of freedom and the forces of enslavement, between the forces of death and the forces of life. How can one derive a linear vision of history from Scripture and the revelation? Those who have meditated on this, in the light of revelation or simply in the light of human experience, cannot doubt that there is salvation, but they have had to dismiss all naïveté.

In a word, does history have a meaning? That was the question that obsessed me when I was in my twenties, and I posed it to Marrou,[1] Aron and several others. At the time, my contemporaries and I had in mind the horizon of a "brighter future" here below—that is, the Marxist horizon. Those whom we questioned led us back to greater modesty, to the learned ignorance of those who observe human history and know that there is really very little that one can say about it. Mounier spoke about "the hope of the desperate", echoing the Scripture in urging us to "hope against all hope". I am speaking of my generation; I do not know how you felt about it or how your children will feel. But we had the impression of having seen the worst (which was undoubtedly an illusion, alas! I fear that the worst has not yet been imagined and lies ahead). In brief, we thought that the most dreadful calamities were behind us. Nevertheless, Christian hope assures us that the salvation already given is always active, even in the most distressing of times, including those that man can still bring about, whose abysses we have been led to discover by the revelation of God's love. After all, the worst abyss for humanity is sin. When humanity dreams of its own destruction, it does not realize what it is saying. It is like a drunkard or a suicide who no longer knows what he is doing. Only someone who has recognized life and love can understand this suicidal penchant of humanity, this sin, this blasphemy, this destruction, because when you come right down to it, it is hell. . . .

WOLTON: *What do you mean when you say that it is "hell"?*

LUSTIGER: I mean that this destruction caused by sin is the temporal and terrestrial face of hell and the eternal ruin of humanity. But when one has understood the revelation of God's love, then the hope we have overcomes all despair, not naïvely but realistically. It is the after-Auschwitz theme, if you wish, the theme of after-totalitarianism, beyond hell. . . . To hope is to attest to a possible redemption of man, to announce that the Messiah is here but hidden and that the world is giving birth to salvation, to be convinced that we should never despair of man since God has never despaired of him.

The Bible clearly states: The world was lost; it should have been obliterated. This is conveyed by the powerful symbolism of the flood, of Sodom and Gomorrah: "Are there ten righteous men? Five?" "No, there are not." The world is lost, and it may seem that God has abandoned it to its fate. But, no, God swears that he will never abandon men. This is the way the indestructible Covenant between God and his creation is formed. It is on this Covenant that the hope of salvation is based.

[1] Henri-Irenée Marrou (1904–77), French historian and archaeologist who was a specialist in the history of thought and education.—TRANS.

WOLTON: *But there are two histories, and what is the relationship of human history to supernatural history?*

LUSTIGER: There is really only one history, but there are several ways of viewing and living it. What is called human history is history as men see it; sacred history is history as God sees it, as he makes it with men. As long as God has not given us his light, we can have nothing more than a "feeling" for history. It would be presumptuous in the extreme to imagine that we can perceive it completely, as God perceives it, and appropriate the place that he alone can occupy, the place of judge.

Sacred history is both the history of man's redemption and that of the judgment carried out during this history. Factual history that men record is one in which we accumulate memories—without ever being capable of mastering them, however—memories that erase themselves as they accumulate. We cannot recall all of history, and it is poignantly regrettable to think that we lose the memory of those who precede us. Ancient civilizations thought that they were remembering their ancestors, but that was not true! Men forget. We forget because it is impossible to channel the vast stream of life into human memory. And even if we were to stock the computer's memory with the totality of names gathered from all the birth certificates in the world, it would still not be a living memory. There is really a kind of overflow back into the abyss of nothingness. Human memory is inadequate for recollecting all of mankind. This is something that fascinates me: although I am a man, belonging to the human species, I am powerless to know and recognize the totality of individuals who exist in this world. How is it possible to accept being limited to the point of knowing only a few human beings and knowing them so imperfectly, when they are brothers? Humanity is forgetful of its own, inevitably so. This is no reproach, but a simple observation. But this regret can be assuaged by the hope of eternal salvation, when the innumerable crowd will be recognized and known. Only God can have this view of all humanity.

WOLTON: *But what is there of human history in all this? God makes history, knows history, sees men's personal histories. . . .*

LUSTIGER: It is a difficult problem to explain in a few words because the relationship of the divine will to men's freedom is involved. It is far too simplistic to picture men as marionettes whose strings are pulled by God. And the contrasting vision of a principle so transcendent that it is absent from history—that is, does nothing at all—is no less simplistic. Discard these two caricatures of the contingency of human liberties and the absolute of divine liberty, of time and eternity, and you will find the intuitive position of the believer. The believer "knows" that he has received his freedom from God and that the arena of human experience is a place of freedom; he "knows" that his freedom develops with all the more strength as it submits itself to God. It is a paradoxical affirmation: God acts all the more as he gives man a greater and more independent freedom to act. Far from being two antinomical and contradictory entities exclusive of each other, man's freedom is received from God's freedom. Then, "God knows" and "God sees"? Yes, these are the words from Scripture that must be kept in mind—they are a powerful consolation, a great strength! "God knows." Yes, he even knows what men do not know; he sees what escapes their eyes. Remembering the Covenant is a fantastic source of freedom.

WOLTON: *What you call freedom is not generally experienced like that.*

LUSTIGER: I am reminded of Victor Hugo's words: *"L'oeil était dans la tombe et regardait Caïn."*[2] It is a beautifully written sentence, but it has the fault of shifting God's paternal regard to the level of guilt. Hence, it is a gross misinterpretation, because guilt expresses precisely the absence of freedom for sinful man.

WOLTON: *Are you saying that freedom is knowing that one is a sinner?*

LUSTIGER: It is knowing that one is a forgiven sinner, whereas guilt is, in the end, the refusal to recognize both the sin and the forgiveness; it makes God the image of its own torment. When Hugo writes "the eye" was in the tomb, looking at Cain, he is saying that Cain's crime, his guilt—not his forgiveness—was looking at him. And, furthermore, he specifies that the eye was "in the tomb". The literary style may be admirable, but the words are misleading because God is not the God of the dead but of the living.

The End of Time

WOLTON: *Shall we come back to the subject of the end of time: How do you situate it in regard to human history, and what meaning can be given to the word* reprieve *—the delay until Christ's final return?*

LUSTIGER: Honestly, I cannot possibly conceive of the end of time—I do not think that anybody can. Even in the apocalyptic description of the world's end, Christ himself warns us, "And they will say to you, 'Lo, there!' or 'Lo, here!' Do not go, do not follow them." He continues, "Take heed that you are

[2] Literally, this means: "The eye was in the tomb and was looking at Cain."—TRANS.

not led astray, for many will come in my name saying, 'I am he!' . . . For as the lightning comes from the east and shines as far as the west, so will the coming of the Son of Man. . . . " Even though the Gospel presents us with imaginary descriptions, it dissuades us from trying to picture and predict the time of this judgment. "But of that day and hour no one knows, not even the angels of heaven, nor the Son, but the Father only." These are absolutely prodigious words. They refuse to speculate on the millennium and thus cut short any conjecturing on the end of humanity. We simply know nothing about it.

It is very impressive to see how, in the space of one or two centuries, scientific theories have changed and given such inconsistent images. I have retained nothing from them except their proof that man's imagination is always being stimulated by thoughts about the end of time. The truth is that we find it hard to accept our ignorance of both the origin and completion of the universe. Human reason has a normal curiosity about its history and future, and science is certainly justified in attempting to respond. But it is striking to see how much fantasy takes hold of these attempts.

MISSIKA: *Certain physicists are now saying that the expansion of the universe can be historically dated and that one can make a hypothesis of an inverse phenomenon of contraction. . . .*

LUSTIGER: Others, not so long ago, were thinking of the universe as an indefinite length of time. . . . I am no astrophysicist.

MISSIKA: *But, as to the question about the end of time, a religious problem is raised. If ever, from the point of view of physics, one is able to foresee . . .*

LUSTIGER: What seems obvious today risks being taken for foolishness the day after tomorrow or in two centuries. Because we remain basically ignorant! We do not know how a theory will be redeveloped in five or six years. The image connected with it can appear naïvely anthropomorphic, as the desire for individual survival projected on the scale of all the universe.

WOLTON: *Then you think that these theories could disappear in a few years, and thus we should not give too much weight to them. But you are circumventing the question we asked: What is the connection between a scientific knowledge of humanity's history and the role of an exterior intervention. . . .*

LUSTIGER: Whatever the scientific discoveries, the question of the "this side" of point zero and the unimaginable, beyond which one cannot go, will always be raised. . . . Saint Thomas Aquinas was already posing it. The response is to say: Yes, before the first imaginable instant, there is the unimaginable,

God. A beginning and an end imply a closed and created universe, and the Creator is—outside of the universe—what explains it and gives it its raison d'être. The spatiotemporal image illustrates the principle of causality that rationally establishes the affirmation of the existence of the Principle transcending humanity and the universe. But such reasoning does not let us know who God is. The knowledge of God, such as it is given to us, comes from a transformation of our intelligence and our heart, of our conduct and our learning, by the light that God himself gives us. In revealing himself to us, in speaking to us, God tells infinitely more about himself, in the "now" of our history, than we can conceive of when we affirm him—and perhaps project him rather imaginatively—as cause of causes, first cause or ultimate end. These notions have their own rationality that must not be underestimated, but it is at their level, which is abstract and metaphysical. Metaphysics should not be transformed into a "pre-physics" or a "post-physics"; it would be a shocking error to pretend to make these two distinct levels of reflection coincide unduly. The philosophical affirmation does not claim to be a verifiable scientific understanding of the world; it opens up to reason the space that is indispensable for the mind's recognition of its ends and its creation. But abstract reason is human and finite; it does not give access to the absolute mystery of God. Nevertheless, the revelation of God and the understanding of the world are both inscribed in the relationship of the human intellect to the world and to its God. I have always been fascinated by the phrase from Psalm 19: "The heavens are telling the glory of God." How is it that the human mind can be co-extensive to the world and that man can discover in it a rationality and beauty through which God lets himself be perceived? It is here that I recognize the coherence of creation, much more so than in such and such a scientific theory, which may be appealing but which the history of modern thought has taught me to look at as a limited and temporary state of reflection.

WOLTON: *I do not understand in what way the phrase from the Bible is for you the best proof...*

LUSTIGER: "The heavens are telling the glory of God." The world is a language, because it is a creation. The world tells more than just about itself; it tells us about the Creator. Similarly, man tells about his Creator since he is made in the image and resemblance of God.

MISSIKA: *That makes me think of Einstein's remark that is no doubt familiar to you: "The most incomprehensible thing about the world is that it is comprehensible."*

LUSTIGER: Yes, it is that fact which is totally incomprehensible and marvelous. Moreover, the Bible, in Psalm 19, directly correlates the language of creation with God's language given in the law. It would be an error to separate the Psalm into two parts. The verses, "The law of the Lord is perfect, reviving the soul . . . " and "The precepts of the Lord are right, rejoicing the heart . . . ", in the second part correspond to the opening lines: "The heavens are telling the glory of God; and the firmament proclaims his handiwork. Day to day pours forth speech, and night to night declares knowledge. There is no speech, nor are there words; their voice is not heard; yet their voice goes out through all the earth, and their words to the end of the world." The language of creation and the language of revelation are together the key to the historical perception that man has of his relationship to the cosmos.

Salvation

WOLTON: *Coming back to human history, do you find that as the third millennium approaches, there is a growing interest in everything concerning salvation?*

LUSTIGER: The more man sees himself as capable of being his own healer and liberator, the more he discovers the true extent of his ruin. The doctor cures more, the psychologist sometimes helps people to cope better, the engineer has greater control over the environment and certain natural hazards have been minimized; man is convinced that he is no longer afraid of fire, at least not as an obscure power, or of lightning as an unpredictable power. But the more man is alone with himself, the more he becomes aware of his ruin: he is like a forsaken child. And this is the setting for redemption. What the Savior wants to say is that man has gone astray and that to be saved is to be found and shown the way. Having chased away numerous cosmic fears, man is now faced with his solitude, and in his solitude, he is faced with sin.

WOLTON: *In regard to the question of salvation, what would you say specifically characterizes our generation?*

LUSTIGER: We are more wary for fear of being duped. Such a fear can paralyze us, send us shuddering back into ourselves, prevent us from advancing and truly saving ourselves. We can even be so skeptical that we race ahead blindly, straight to our destruction, just like some of the very civilized and refined people in antiquity. But, on the other hand, we can also be more willing to get down to the essential. But, for that to occur, the coming generations must keep the memory of what has happened in recent times: it is terrifying to think that they might forget. We have already evoked this theme several times: to have worn out in the space of a few centuries so many simplistic theories of salvation, to have anticipated this salvation by mobilizing so many resources, to have worked so much for man's emancipation and then to have realized that all this has not brought it about can result in so much cynicism and forgetfulness! Perhaps, as Camus thought, man's nobility is revealed in his confrontation of this deception, which perpetually repeats itself.

If we refuse to let ourselves be paralyzed by our failures and intoxicated by our successes, we can go—albeit perhaps more painfully and rapidly—to the center, to the very heart of the human condition. The interesting difference of our era is that lost illusions have shown up our condition in a stark light; it has been laid bare for us to see. Things have been named and the drive for power has been grimly exposed. From the time of Caesar Augustus—indeed, of Charles V or Louis XIV—the royal figure, in his thrust for political domination, enjoyed an immense prestige and appeal. . . . A kind of spiritual courage was necessary to demystify that figure and say: No, all that amounts to nothing. Today, even the youngest schoolchildren ought to know that. And the same is true for all of man's illusions about his condition and the way societies work. Losing them can leave a people exhausted, but it can also give rise to new fantasies; or sometimes, when people see something too clearly, they want to blind themselves. All disillusionment entails great risks. But it can also provide an opportunity: maybe this generation will be able to reach holiness more directly.

MISSIKA: *At the end of his* Mémoires, *Raymond Aron uses a curious expression. He says that, in his youth, he and his classmates at the École Normale used to talk about achieving their "secular salvation". And he asks himself whether he has done it. Does that expression have meaning for you? And do you think that believers and unbelievers pose the question of salvation in the same way?*

LUSTIGER: It is a very human question. Everyone asks it in one way or another. The terms are never exactly the same, because each person is facing his own life, but everyone weighs up his "losses and gains". *Loss and Gain,* by the way, is the title of Cardinal Newman's autobiographical novel that was published under a pseudonym. Nobody can escape this reckoning, especially somebody like Raymond Aron. He was too familiar with history and its stakes, I believe, for the notion of "salvation" to be naïve on his lips—and the word had more than one meaning in his mind, I am sure. I imagine that he was remembering that because he was growing old and thus approaching death. A person faces death in the best way that he can, with more or less courage or more or less stoicism. But what is involved here is, after all, much more than death as a brutal termination: it is the ultimate ordeal of freedom and the human condition; it is the fact that man can never take full control of his life, he can never grasp it. Life is like a hemorrhage. It flows away from us. Toward what? Toward the void? Toward nothingness? Or does salvation consist in believing that somewhere our lives are gathered up, that our freedom is not just an open wound or that life is more than a hemorrhaging of ourselves, that it is a positive achievement and fruitful joy? How can what is being lost be saved? The question of salvation is universal, and every human being has to confront it. That seems inescapable. Then, is it secular salvation or Christian salvation? I understand that Aron could speak like that and that such things were discussed in the twenties on the Rue d'Ulm: it was the epoch of *Jean Barois,*[3] a time of secular triumph. That proves, precisely, that the question of salvation is universal.

WOLTON: *How is this expectation of the Kingdom of God connected with human history?*

LUSTIGER: The Kingdom of God is an object of hope. Its anticipation is a light present in history whose meaning, in any case, eludes us. I can know nothing about history, my memory is compartmentalized, the vision I have of humanity is constantly being fragmented, my understanding is obscure. Although God's plan appears to me as a sovereign act of love for all mankind, it remains a mystery beyond my grasp, and yet it does not strike me as absurd or unreasonable. It is a wisdom introduced into a world that escapes my comprehension.

I cannot dream of bringing about the Kingdom of God on earth without sinking into the worst of insanities and tyrannies. But if I keep my hope in the reign of God as a source of wisdom and blessing for humanity, then history is no longer the nightmare "full of sound and fury" evoked by Shakespeare. Expecting the Kingdom of God means committing oneself to something greater than oneself. It is, in the end, the assurance that God's steadfast love is at work in history.

[3] *Jean Barois* (1913) is the title of a novel by Roger Martin du Gard (1881–1958) that illustrates the illusions of the late secular positivism.—TRANS.

INDEX